The Art and Science of Marketing

The Art and Science of Marketing

Marketing for Marketing Managers

GRAHAME R. DOWLING

OXFORD
UNIVERSITY PRESS

OXFORD

UNIVERSITY PRESS

Great Clarendon Street, Oxford OX2 6DP

Oxford University Press is a department of the University of Oxford.
It furthers the University's objective of excellence in research, scholarship,
and education by publishing worldwide in

Oxford New York

Auckland Bangkok Buenos Aires Cape Town Chennai
Dar es Salaam Delhi Hong Kong Istanbul Karachi Kolkata
Kuala Lumpur Madrid Melbourne Mexico City Mumbai Nairobi
São Paulo Shanghai Taipei Tokyo Toronto

Oxford is a registered trade mark of Oxford University Press
in the UK and in certain other countries

Published in the United States
by Oxford University Press Inc., New York

British Library Cataloguing in Publication Data
Data available

Library of Congress Cataloging in Publication Data
Data available

ISBN 0-19-926961-0

1 3 5 7 9 10 8 6 4 2

Typeset by Newgen Imaging Systems (P) Ltd., Chennai, India
Printed in Great Britain
on acid-free paper by
Biddles Ltd., King's Lynn, Norfolk

PREFACE

This book is written for marketing managers. It recognizes that marketing is largely an applied discipline and that good marketing practice requires a subtle blend of art and science. The artful side of marketing involves understanding marketing problems and selecting the appropriate tools to solve these. Experience and practice are the best teachers here. The scientific side of marketing involves using the accumulated knowledge of others to help structure and solve marketing problems. This knowledge base is codified as concepts, generalizations, frameworks, and principles. These are discussed in Chapter 1.

Robert Joss, the former Managing Director of Westpac bank in Australia and then Dean of Stanford Business School, suggests that the role of a book like this is to help managers understand the behaviour of their organization, the markets in which it competes, and the behaviour of consumers who evaluate its products and services. Then, this knowledge, together with your experience, can be used to help solve situation-specific problems.[1]

This book takes a different approach to the many others on marketing. Its content is based on discussions with hundreds of marketing managers and the general managers to whom they report. These discussions have taken place during twenty years of executive teaching and consulting. What these managers say they need to do their job in an increasingly competitive business environment, is:

- an overarching conceptual framework that identifies the basic tenets of marketing—that is supported by
- a set of specific frameworks that guide analysis of the current business situation that can be used to design marketing strategy and programmes,
- links to other business functions such as accounting, corporate strategy, and production,

- a recognition of the personal constraints under which marketing managers work, such as the key performance indicators used to appraise one's work,
- examples of good and bad practices to highlight the use and abuse of marketing, and
- the identification of traps and pitfalls to avoid.

Another feature of this book is that it introduces a number of research-based 'strategic principles'. These are based on empirical generalizations and theoretical research. Their aim is to help managers identify what is unique about their local situation and what is common with their competitors. Thus, they suggest what a manager should do in some commonly encountered situations—especially when the marketing budget is limited! However, the risk with stating strategic principles is that they may change as new marketing knowledge accumulates.

The book makes no particular distinction between business-to-business (B2B) and business-to-consumer (B2C) marketing, nor between product and services marketing. Examples from each domain are interspersed throughout each chapter. The reason for this approach is that what we learn in one environment is often transferable, with minor modification, to another environment. For example, the current fascination with relationship marketing in B2C marketing had its origins in B2B marketing.

Throughout the book I use the term 'organization' rather than 'company' to refer to the entity initiating the marketing activity. The reason for this is to signal that corporations, professional service firms, not-for-profit organizations, and government departments all conduct marketing activities. In fact, any organization that deals with customers needs to understand marketing.

[1] R. Joss, 'Management', *Australian Journal of Management*, 26, Special Issue (August 2001), 89–103.

CONTENTS

Part IV   Administration

LIST OF EXHIBITS

LIST OF FIGURES

LIST OF TABLES

LIST OF ABBREVIATIONS

ABC	audience, benefit, and compelling reason
AIDA	awareness, interest, desire, action
ARPU	average revenue per user
ATM	automatic teller machine
B2B	business-to-business
B2C	business-to-consumer
B2E	business-to-enterprise
C2B	consumer-to-business
C2C	consumer-to-consumer
CB	consumer behaviour
CEO	Chief Executive Officer
CFO	Chief Financial Officer
CLV	customer lifetime value
CRM	customer relationship management
CVP	customer value proposition
DIY	do-it-yourself
EV	expected value
EVC	economic value to the customer
FMCG	fast moving consumer good
IDU	importance, delivery, and uniqueness
IMC	integrated marketing communication
ISO	International Standards Organization
IT	information technology
KPI	key performance indicator
MBA	Master of Business Administration
NPD	new product development
OEM	original equipment manufacturer
PC	personal computer
PDA	personal digital assistant

QFD	quality function deployment
RFM	recency, frequency, and monetary value
SBU	strategic business unit
SOM	share of market
SOV	share of voice
STP	segmentation, targeting, and positioning
SWOT	strengths, weaknesses, opportunities, threats
TCO	total cost of ownership
TQM	total quality management
USP	unique selling proposition
VIU	value in use
VMS	vertical marketing system
WOM	word of mouth

1

The Nature of Marketing Management

> There is only one valid definition of business purpose: to create a customer.
>
> (To achieve this purpose:)
>
> Any business enterprise has two, and only two, basic functions—marketing and innovation.
>
> Peter Drucker
> (The founder of modern management)

Marketing is the business discipline most responsible for developing programmes to attain and retain customers. Thus, one of its primary functions is to understand customers and their patterns of consumption. It is often said that today's consumer landscape is being shaped by two powerful forces—technology and globalization. Statements such as these often lead to claims about how the rate of change is accelerating and how technology is changing our lives. In the 1960s, Marshall McLuhan captured this sentiment in his sayings that 'the medium is the message' and the world is becoming a 'global village'.[1]

The counterpoint to these sentiments is that most consumers are agnostic to particular forms of technology. What they really want and value are the benefits and the solutions to problems that the technology can provide them with. Also, many people are very uncomfortable with the idea of globalization and the implications it has on their daily lives. What they like to do is to pick and choose options from around the world to use at their discretion. What they dislike are global forces that cause structural changes to the economic conditions that shape the evolution and culture of their country.[2]

This book tries to strike a balance between the recommendation to 'hang on tight because the only constant is change' and the opposite recommendation to 'stick to your knitting and ignore change'. The recommendation is to 'look forward, but do not forget the past'. In other words, become a true learning organization. Hence, the book will build on the tried and tested ideas before introducing more recent, and less tested ideas about marketing. If you believe that disruptive change is the way of the future and, thus, constant reinvention is the only viable strategy, this is not the book for you. Put it back on the shelf and pick up something with a title like *The New Marketing*.

Marketing

Marketing, as the root word in the term implies, is the function of a business or a not-for-profit organization that focuses on the marketplace. This begs the question of what is a market. The discipline of economics comes to the rescue here. It suggests that a market can be defined both from supply and demand perspectives. When we talk about the needs and wants of customers or the benefits and/or solutions to problems that products and services provide, we are using a *demand* perspective. The traditional measures of marketing success here are linked to customer satisfaction and loyalty.

The demand perspective can lead to some novel descriptions of markets. For example, a market research study done by the Polaroid company in 1995 in Europe suggested that their instant picture camera, when bought by 18-to 30-year olds, competed in the entertainment market. It was taken to parties and used in conjunction with alcohol, party games, and karaoke to have some fun. In Australia, a 'Live for the Moment' television advertising campaign was targeted to this customer segment, and it resulted in a doubling of sales.[3] As this example shows, the definition of a market is not always obvious, namely Polaroid was competing in the entertainment market and not in the camera market. Thus, how customers perceive their market should drive how companies respond to their needs.

For practical reasons associated with the way that firms manage their transactions with customers, many firms adopt a *supply*-side view of their market. This perspective traditionally focuses on all the competitors that supply physically similar products and services. It is often described in terms of the type of industry, the number and nature of competitors, and the dominant type of business model used, namely, the type of manufacturing process, cost structure, technology, logistics, distribution channels, etc. A market in this context is a competitive arena. As such, it is amenable to quite a rigorous analysis—a service often provided by the world's major management consulting firms.

Adopting a supply perspective, however, can result in losing sight of the needs of customers. For example, an Australian bank client expressed this view as:

> They treat me as a source of profit, not as a person.

This customer's sentiment was driven by his bank's market segmentation strategy. It ranked all its customers by their profitability and then assigned each customer to a group such as 'private banking', 'premier banking', and 'mass banking'. Share of the customer's wallet and market share are two key indicators of successful supply-side marketing.

The demand- and supply-side views of marketing highlight a fundamental dilemma facing many marketing managers, namely, how to achieve a balance between (a) the value offered to customers; and (b) the value (or profitability) of customers to the organization. When these 'values' get out of balance, the outcome is either dissatisfied customers or a disgruntled Chief Executive Officer (CEO) because the customer mix is not sufficiently profitable.

Because the success of a business depends on how efficiently and effectively it matches supply and demand, both perspectives are used in this book. With this in mind, a good description of one of the key tasks of marketing is to provide customers with the level of value they require at a cost that is profitable for the organization and in a way that maintains the organization's desired position in the marketplace.

Customers

Marketing takes a broad view of customers. Sometimes, the focus is on individuals who are seeking products and services to satisfy their own personal needs. At other times, the focus is on individuals buying for other people— such as a gift, or provisions for a household. Marketers also consider public and private sector organizations as customers. This is the world of business-to-business (B2B) marketing. Here, a group of managers called a 'buying group' makes purchase decisions on behalf of their organization.

Another group of people to whom the ideas of marketing can be applied is employees. Here, the task is for managers to 'sell' the vision, culture, control systems, operating procedures, etc. of the organization to employees and agents (such as distributors and retailers). This is buisness-to-enterprise

(B2E) or 'internal marketing'. It manifests itself in three main forms. First, how does the organization achieve the compliance of employees (such as its salespeople) with its directives? Second, how can managers 'sell' their ideas for change to others within the organization? Third, how do internal service functions like legal, management accounting, and internal audit 'sell' their services to other colleagues?

Figure 1.1 shows these three domains of marketing. The emphasis placed on each one will depend on one's role in the organization. For example, the marketing group in a major law firm will focus on B2E and business-to-consumer (B2C) marketing. Their B2E tasks are to convince the partners of the firm to use their services to help prepare tenders, win new clients, and design client relationship management practices. Their B2C tasks include market research, brand positioning, new service development, and the monitoring of client satisfaction.

While much of marketing in the visible spectrum to us is B2C, there is actually much more money spent on B2B marketing. The reason for this is simply that business organizations not only sell their products and services to their customers, but they are also the customers for many of the components used to produce their products and services.

Products and Services

A pure product is composed of a set of features designed to perform (a set of) functions and, thus, satisfy a specific customer need(s). Another way to define a product is to say that it is a service delivery system. Thus, the features

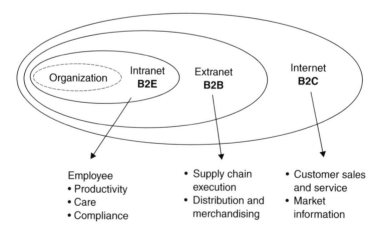

Figure 1.1. Domains of marketing

of a 'product' can be tangible, intangible, or service in nature. For example, when you buy a BMW, you get a car or a motorbike with all its physical features, a service warranty, plus the image of 'the ultimate driving machine' or 'the ultimate riding machine'. (These were two of BMW's old corporate advertising slogans.)

A pure service is a need-satisfying activity performed for a buyer. Sometimes this will be performed by a person (e.g. the waiter in a restaurant), sometimes by the customer (e.g. shopping in a supermarket), and sometimes by a machine (e.g. an automatic teller machine, ATM). The latter two are examples of 'self-service'—which to many old-fashioned customers is an oxymoron.[i] What distinguishes a pure service from a pure product is that services are:

- intangible in the sense that *you* cannot experience the service before it is delivered to you;
- perishable because a potential service not used is lost forever;
- inseparable because the producer and consumer interact to deliver the service; and
- variable because the customer plays a role in the service delivery and resulting experience, and in the case of personal service, so does another person.

As discussed in Part III of this book, the relevance of these attributes of a service is that they can create some unique management problems.

This book takes a broad view of products and services because many pure services are provided with a tangible component, for example, the visit to a doctor may be accompanied by setting one's broken arm in plaster. Also, many pure products come with a service component, such as how a BMW buyer is served before, during, and after the sale. Hence, there is a blending of product and service in many situations.

To summarize, marketing is the function of a business that manages the product–service exchange relationships between the organization and its intermediate and end customers. To do this effectively, marketing managers need to help the organization design its offer to appeal to target customers. To do this, they must have a good understanding of customer needs and the way in which they buy. Hence, two of the key roles of marketing are to act as:

- the 'match-making' function of the organization; and
- the market-sensing part of the organization.

Sometimes, these two functions are being called 'market focused'.

---

[i] An oxymoron is a figure of speech that produces a seeming self-contradiction, such as cruel kindness; to make haste slowly; a safe bet.

Over the past few years, marketing has seen some significant changes. The one receiving the most current publicity involves the Internet. The newspapers tell us that the Internet and its manifestations, namely, dotcoms, e-business, and m-business, will revolutionize business in general and marketing in particular. Here, a more circumspect view is taken. By looking through the rhetoric of the 'new economy', it is possible to see the Internet, Intranet, and Extranet (Figure 1.1) for what they are, namely, enabling technologies. Michael Porter suggests that they are a potentially powerful set of tools that can be used—wisely or unwisely, in many industries and as a part of many strategies.[4] The Internet may produce revolutionary changes or it may be evolutionary—it is too early to tell. One way to get this change and others in perspective is to review the various styles of marketing that have emerged over the last 100 years.

A Review of Marketing Practice

Many people argue that the discipline of marketing is going through another major transformation. To see where the discipline might be headed, let us briefly review how it becomes established in a new area. The first three phases (or styles) of marketing can be described as:

1. *The production concept.* When demand for a product (or service) exceeds supply, marketing is practised under the assumption that customers favour those products that are widely available (and low in cost). Managers focus their efforts on lowering production costs and increasing distribution coverage. In a country like Russia, which is moving from a planned economy to a more free-market economy, this form of marketing can be seen in action. McDonald's, Pepsi Cola, and others are mass-producing and distributing their products to eager customers.

2. *The product concept.* Here, the assumption is that consumers want, and will pay for, the best quality, performance, reliability, or the most innovative features. The total quality management (TQM) movement is a manifestation of this approach. Sometimes, this approach to marketing results in products that are difficult for many people to operate. For example, my VCR, TV remote control, and the personal computer (PC) software used to write this book are so complicated that they require a considerable amount of learning in order to get all the functionality that I had to pay for.

3. *The selling concept.* When supply exceeds demand, the focus of marketing at many organizations shifts to hard selling. Many car manufacturers and their dealers practice this version of marketing. Companies like Avon, Amway, Mary Kay, and Tupperware practice what is known as mass-selling. They use an army of self-employed people to sell their products door-to-door. This is a well-established practice in the United States and is growing in popularity in countries like China and Indonesia.

In essence, these three styles of marketing have the factory as their primary focus, namely, producing the product, making it better, and selling what is produced.

In countries like Australia, Japan, Western Europe, the United Kingdom, and the United States, a fourth generation of marketing set out to replace these three in leading marketing organizations. Its focus was the customer—what were the target customers' needs and wants, and how could an organization get these customers to exchange their money for products and services designed to meet these needs. The two key concepts here are understanding customers and consummating profitable (to the organization) exchanges. This concept of marketing was implemented by what became known as the 4Ps approach to marketing. Each 'P' became the focus of a marketing programme, namely:

- Product,
- Price,
- Place (of distribution),
- Promotion (advertising).

See Exhibit 1.1 for how this approach to marketing can be applied inside the organization.

Exhibit 1.1. B2E: the forgotten domain of marketing

One of the forgotten areas of marketing is B2E. In this situation, selling something—an idea, the need for change, a (marketing) plan, a new strategy, etc.—is the focus.[5] To make these sales, managers often use the techniques of marketing outlined in this book. For example:

- What is generally termed a 'product' or 'service' is the idea, project, or plan you want to sell to other managers.
- The 'price' of your product is the time, effort, and budget allocation you want other managers to give in exchange for your new idea.
- You will 'promote' your new idea to get acceptance for it.

cont.

Exhibit 1.1. *cont.*

- The 'place' where your project or idea is implemented in the organization will determine how much 'value' it contributes to both the organization and your internal 'customers'.

These are six of the major concepts of external marketing translated into internal marketing—product, price, promotion, place, customers, and value. Some other external marketing tactics used inside the organization are:

- Managers use brand names like 'Chief Financial Officer' (CFO), 'Sales Director', and 'Business Development Manager' to signal their status and function to other employees and customers.
- The internal company newsletter and website are really forms of advertising.
- Managers use different sales messages and different selling approaches with different groups of employees—or 'customer segments' as these are called in this book.
- The vision statement is really an internal advertisement.
- A planning document is like a long-copy advertisement.

While B2E and personal marketing are not the main focus of this book, most of the basic ideas of B2C and B2B marketing can be applied to these situations. (For example, the discussion of branding in Chapter 7 can be applied to creating the 'brand you'.)

If the organization sold a service, three additional Ps were added, namely:

- People,
- Physical evidence,
- Process.[6]

If it sold products and services to other organizations (i.e. it is involved in B2B marketing), an eighth P was particularly important:

- Personal selling.

Figure 1.2 illustrates this overall approach to marketing.

During the early 1980s, two advertising consultants, Al Ries and Jack Trout, introduced a ninth P:

- Positioning

and summarized their ideas in a terrific little book titled *Positioning: The Battle for Your Mind.*[7] Position here is a noun, and refers to an attribute associated with a company or a product/service. For example, what car

Figure 1.2. The expanded offer

holds the safety position in most people's mind? (Volvo.) What car was (advertised as) the best to drive? (BMW—the ultimate driving machine.) The mid-1980s to the mid-1990s is often referred to as the Positioning Era of marketing. Positioning is one of the more interesting elements of modern marketing. As such, it deserves a little more discussion than the others.

The Positioning Era was really the rerun of an idea introduced and formalized by the legendary advertising guru David Ogilvy, namely, the 'brand image'. Ogilvy stated his thesis thus:

> The greater the similarity between brands, the less the part reason plays in brand selection. The manufacturer who dedicates his advertising to building the most sharply defined personality for his brand will get the largest share of the market at the highest profit. By the same token, the manufacturers who will find themselves up the creek are those short-sighted opportunists who siphon off their advertising funds for promotions.[8]

This passage, published in 1964, reflects two of the key issues facing marketing managers today—how to differentiate their almost parity products (airline seats, plastic pipes, instant coffee, bottles of vodka), and the effects of putting a brand on promotion—which are usually positive in the short run and negative in the long run. David Ogilvy and his contemporaries established many of the foundations of modern marketing and advertising. For example, William Bernbach advocated that the way an advertisement is executed can be just as important as what is said. The power of this approach is demonstrated when you like an advertisement but you cannot remember the brand name. Another advertising legend, Rosser Reeves, proposed that the key to advertising effectiveness is for each product to communicate its unique selling proposition (USP)—such as 'M&M candies melt in your mouth instead of your hand'.

Today, brand image positioning has become a fine art. Companies like Benetton, Nike, Reebok, and Virgin have integrated the idea of branding into the fabric of their companies. Richard Branson sums up this idea as building brands not around products but around a reputation—in the case of Virgin, it is the reputation of Branson himself and his set of companies that position themselves as challengers to the well-established incumbents, in airlines, cola, financial services, music, radio stations, and others.

For a marketing manager, the crucial question is what the role of the brand is. Is the product or service central to your success, or is it the brand image? This question can be reformulated along a four-part continuum, namely:

- The product is everything—diamonds.
- The product comes with a logo attached—Argyle (coloured) diamonds. (See the Argyle story at the end of this chapter.)
- The logo/brand is more important than the product—Nike shoes that are made in the Export Processing Zones of various Asian countries.
- The logo/brand is everything—Tommy Hilfiger's business is signing his name on clothes or anything else he thinks will sell.

When brand is important, marketing managers focus much of their attention on building and maintaining 'brand equity'.[9] We will talk more about this concept in Chapter 7.

In the mid-1990s, the focus of marketing shifted again. This time, marketing drew some of its insight from the theory and practice of negotiation, namely, how to create and capture customer value. Figure 1.3 illustrates this approach. This is an integrated approach to marketing management and is grounded in the operational aspects of marketing. (Part III of the book focuses on the elements shown in the arrow of Figure 1.3).

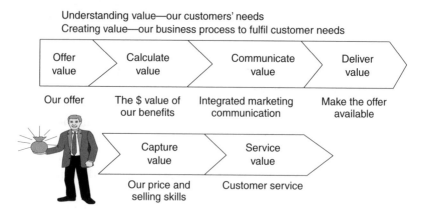

Figure 1.3. Creating and capturing customer value

As we enter the twenty-first century, yet another style of marketing is fighting for prominence. This time it is Relationship Marketing. Here, the idea is to build 'relationships' with the firm's suppliers and customers in order to increase the 'loyalty' of these two groups. In B2B markets, this approach has a long and distinguished history. In B2C markets—where an organization may have tens of thousands of customers—it has been more problematic. Why this is so is discussed in Chapter 12.

The relevance of each of these styles of marketing is that they help you think about the culture of marketing in your organization. Is marketing:

- A strong or weak force in the organization?
- Outsourced to the advertising agency, a headquarters function, or a business unit function?
- Primarily focused on selling products and services, or sensing and responding to customer needs?
- Able to capture the inherent value in what is offered to customers?

Marketing Challenges

As an applied discipline, marketing faces many challenges. So do marketing managers. What is interesting is that these can be quite different. For example, some of the biggest challenges for the discipline are to:

- codify the core elements of marketing and show how these should guide the practice of marketing;
- design techniques to link marketing expenditures to financial outcomes;
- get the chief marketing officer of the firm a seat at the boardroom table;
- better understand the factors that influence the adoption and diffusion of new products and services and, thus, reduce the current high failure rates;
- understand the role of the Internet across the functions of Figure 1.3;
- respond to the sometimes stinging criticisms of marketing made by social commentators such as Naomi Klein in her best-selling book *No Logo*.[10]

Some of the biggest challenges for managers are how to:

- help their organizations avoid what Professor Ted Levitt of the Harvard Business School labelled as 'marketing myopia', namely, the failure to define the organization's purpose around customer needs not products and services;[11]

- meet the often conflicting objectives set by general managers—such as increase sales and reduce marketing costs; be first to market with high-quality and reliable products; establish direct links with customers (e.g. via the Internet) and maintain good relations with the retailers who also sell to these customers; regularly sell the brand on special but do not dilute the brand image;
- link the objectives of the organization and the marketing function with one's personal key performance indicators (KPIs);
- get the advertising agency to spend less money while producing break-through advertising;
- design insightful customer and market research;
- consistently delight customers without creating escalating customer expectations;
- be an aggressive competitor but do not start a price war;
- acquire new customers without upsetting existing customers;
- replace the old-fashioned interruption marketing that is often organized around mainstream advertising with a more customer sympathetic form of marketing.

There are no easy solutions to these challenges—otherwise they would not be challenges. However, what can be said is that once one is aware of the dilemmas inherent in these situations, it is possible to design pro-grammes that get a balance between the opposing forces. For example, take the case of a health insurance company that wants more new cus-tomers or that wants to win back previous customers. One dangerous strat-egy is to appoint a 'customer acquisitions' manager whose KPIs are tied mainly to increasing the size of the customer base. He or she is tempted to offer a lower 'introductory' price than that currently charged to existing customers. Once existing customers see this new or 'win-back' price, they make the 'customer retention' manager's job that much harder. Whenever customer churn is an issue (as for airlines, financial services, insurance, and telecommunications), there is often a tension between customer acquisition and customer retention.

What Marketing Managers Do

As marketing managers typically approach their task in a systematic way, this can be used to introduce the key aspects of marketing management.

Step One is to articulate one's understanding of the current situation. There are various aspects to this, namely, the overall:

- objectives and strategy of the organization;
- resources and capabilities of the organization;
- state of the industry in which the organization operates; and
- state of the market in which it competes.

These four factors set the broad context in which marketing takes place. Here, this context is called the organization's go-to-market business model. Chapters 2 and 3 provide the frameworks that many organizations use to develop an understanding of their current situation.

Step Two involves the development of a marketing strategy. This is the process of linking the organization's business model to the needs of specific target groups of customers. Chapters 4 and 5 focus on understanding customers and the market opportunities revealed through this understanding. Chapters 6 and 7 use the segmentation, targeting, and positioning (STP) approach as the foundation on which to build marketing strategy.

Step Three involves developing marketing programmes (sometimes called tactical marketing)—Chapters 8–11. These are the specific actions intended to implement the strategy for a specific group of customers. For example, a consulting firm has to design a customer value proposition (CVP) (the resulting experience of employing the firm) for its target group of clients as well as developing programmes for acquiring new work (such as competitive tendering for new projects), pricing (such as a blend of hourly charges and a performance bonus), maintaining existing customers (such as a process for account management), and delivering the work. Consultants and professional service firms often describe these programmes as 'finding', 'minding', and 'grinding'. Some people are typically better at finding clients, same at minding them, and others at grinding through the work.

Step Four involves tracking the efficiency and effectiveness of the strategy and programmes. Audits, budgets, plans, organizational design (lines of control and reporting), and individual control mechanisms (such as the performance-appraisal scheme) are the tools used here. Chapter 12 discusses these issues.

In summary, marketing management is the process of planning, implementing, and controlling the activities necessary to achieve the organization's objectives, as these relate to the exchange relationships with its target customers. Figure 1.4 illustrates the recursive nature of this process.

At the centre of Figure 1.4 resides the repository of what the organization knows about its market and customers. The quality of customer data, the way that it is organized in a database, and the techniques used to analyse

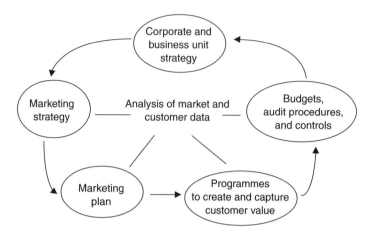

Figure 1.4. The process of marketing management

these data are instrumental to good marketing—both planning and the modelling of how customers respond to the actions of the organization. In the last decade, there have been significant advances in (*a*) database technology offered by companies such as Oracle, (*b*) software to analyse customer purchasing and design marketing programmes (Epiphany, Siebel, Oracle), and (*c*) PC-based tools to analyse customer data. This is the area where much of the science of marketing has been developed. It is becoming known as the 'marketing engineering' approach to marketing.[12]

Marketing Roadmap

Marketing managers are required to make a number of decisions that will impact on the marketing effectiveness of their organization. For example, should they launch a new product/service at a low price or a high price? Should they rush the new product to market or wait until all the bugs are out of it? Should they allocate $5 million to developing a customer loyalty programme or spend it on advertising? How should they respond to a competitor's new advertising campaign? How should they measure customer satisfaction? Should they invest in upgrading the website? How can they use the Internet to increase the efficiency and effectiveness of marketing?

These are tactical questions that cannot be answered out of context. As noted earlier, this context is defined by the organization's go-to-market model, the broad characteristics of the market in which it operates, and the marketing strategy outlined in the corporate and business unit planning documents. Thus, while the heart of much marketing management is tactical in nature, it is useful to approach the task of marketing by breaking it into the four modules shown in Table 1.1.

The first module deals with the context in which marketing takes place. The organization's overall goals, business unit strategy, and the industry conditions in which it operates are the structural foundations of its marketing programmes. Also, the market(s) chosen in which to compete (consumer, business), defined in broad terms the type of customers the organization seeks to attract. The combination of these factors presents a set of opportunities that the organization will seek to exploit. The second module focuses on marketing strategy, that is, designing options to exploit the opportunities identified earlier. It is in this area that we find one of the central frameworks of marketing, namely, market segmentation. The third module deals with marketing programmes—the tools of the trade of the modern marketing manager. This is also the realm of many consultants and advertising agencies. Here, the focus is on creating and capturing customer value (Figure 1.3). The final module deals with administering the marketing function—planning and control systems and working with outside service suppliers like research firms and advertising agencies.

The *art of marketing* is usually practised in the design and implementation of marketing strategy and programmes—Parts II and III of this book. Art in

Table 1.1. The architecture of marketing management

I—*Foundations*
2—The organization
3—Industry and market analysis
4—Analysing buyer behaviour
5—Market opportunities

II—*Strategy*
6—Market segmentation and targeting
7—Positioning and branding

III—*Programmes*
8—Attaining customers by creating customer value
9—Capturing customer value
10—Retaining customers—service quality
11—Retaining customers—CRM

IV—*Administration*
12—Planning and control
13—Working with external service providers

this context involves the skilful creation of strategy and its execution in marketing programmes. As Aristotle once observed:

> What we have to learn to do, we learn by doing.

While experience and practice are the best teachers of the art of marketing, the role of theory is to ensure that practice is built on sound foundations.

The *science of marketing* has involved:

- Building simplified models of selected aspects of marketing such as pricing, advertising spending, promotion activity, new product adoption, salesforce allocation, etc. These models are tested with data and often provide useful insights about how to optimize the allocation of a marketing budget.
- Modelling the patterns of buyer behaviour for frequently purchased brands—how many customers buy a particular brand, how often they buy it, and how much they also buy other brands in the same product category. Some well-established patterns of buyer behaviour have been validated—as outlined in Chapter 4. These can be used as a benchmark against which to compare a particular brand—what type of brand it is and, thus, what broad marketing programmes will be cost-effective.

Both the art and the science of marketing offer managers insight into how to do their jobs better. This book combines evidence from both sources.

The Evidence Used in this Book

Over the last two decades, a debate has occurred about what types of marketing knowledge actually advance the practice of marketing management.[13] This debate was stimulated in part by a large-scale study that found that neither the short-run nor the long-run success of marketing managers (as measured by their income and job title achieved) was dependent on having acquired a degree in marketing! Shelby Hunt and his colleagues who conducted the study observed that this did not bode well for the usefulness of marketing knowledge as taught in academia.[14] Many practising managers endorse this comment. The counter argument, as articulated by Robert Joss, formerly the Managing Director of Westpac bank and then the Dean of the Stanford Business School, is that managers need knowledge (conceptual understanding) and experience (on-the-job practice) to do their jobs well.[15]

The thesis of this book is that marketing managers need both declarative ('know what') and procedural ('know how') types of knowledge. Raw declarative knowledge can be found in the discipline's major research journals, such as the *Journal of Consumer Research*, the *Journal of Marketing*, and the *Journal of Marketing Research*. Piecemeal procedural knowledge can be found in the more applied journals such as the *Harvard Business Review*; business magazines such as *Business Week* and *Fortune*; and consultant/ practitioner books such as Al Ries and Jack Trout's *The 22 Immutable Laws of Marketing*.[16] It is noteworthy that the sources of procedural knowledge have a far greater readership, and thus potential influence on marketing practice, than the top twenty sources of marketing declarative knowledge.

The approach of this book is to introduce five types of marketing knowledge, namely,

- *Marketing concepts*—terms like 'product', 'service', and 'marketing' as defined earlier.
- *Generalizations*—descriptive statements based on the analysis of many sets of data or from the quasi-experiments conducted by practitioners as they see what works in the marketplace. They are 'if, then' statements, such as 'if the market looks like X, then Y is likely to happen'.
- *Structural frameworks*—static, descriptive lists of concepts that organize or 'frame' a marketing problem.
- *Strategic principles*—dynamic conditional, prescriptive 'if, do' statements of the recommended course of action to take given a particular situation. Academic-based principles are usually derived from empirical generalizations and theoretical models. Practitioner-based principles are usually derived from experience.
- *Market-sensing principles*—conditional, prescriptive 'if, use' statements of the best research techniques given the need for a particular type of knowledge.[17]

The marketing concepts provide much of the language of the discipline. The other types of knowledge provide what can loosely be termed part of the science of the discipline.

Because all authors speak authoritatively and convincingly from their particular point of view, the role of these five types of marketing knowledge is to help you to evaluate the evidence presented in the following chapters and in articles about marketing in the business and popular press.

Also, because marketing knowledge is evolutionary, I offer the following warning:

'Beware of False Prophesies'

All current marketing knowledge should be subject to the legal warning caveat emptor—let the buyer (user) beware. This occurs because:

- all knowledge consists of our 'best beliefs' rather than any absolute truths;
- physical scientists are much more concerned about issues of replicability than their social science counterparts—especially marketing researchers.[18]

Thus, while scanning both the academic and business press to discover new findings it is important to determine if these findings are generalizable. Table 1.2 lists the tests you can apply to calibrate each piece of new information you encounter.

To illustrate this notion of replication and generalizability, consider the classic finding about subliminal advertising. In 1957, Vance Packard published his classic book about the advertising industry titled *The Hidden Persuaders*.[19] In 1958, Jim Vicary, a market researcher whose business was not doing very well, revealed a test he had made in a New Jersey movie theatre that projected the (subliminal) messages 'Hungry? Eat Popcorn'

Table 1.2. Generalizability tests

Level		The new information
1	Worst	Seems interesting
2		Matches your experience
3		Other people say they believe it (e.g. a journalist)
4	Better	Other people say they are successfully using it (e.g. consultants in their in-house magazines)
5		Another scientific, peer-reviewed research study has replicated the finding
6	Best	A review suggests a common pattern of findings
7		A meta-analysis[a] supports the finding

[a] Meta-analysis is a statistical technique for combining the results from a large number of studies on the same topic.

and 'Drink Coca-Cola' for 1/3000 of a second on the screen during a movie. This caused sales of popcorn to jump 57 per cent and Coke to jump 18 per cent over the six-week term of the experiment. Soon after the results were reported in *Advertising Age*, Henry Link, president of Psychological Corporation, challenged Mr Vicary to replicate the results. He accepted the challenge but could not reproduce his claimed effect. Vicary then admitted he had fabricated the results of his test in the hope of reviving his business. This was again published in *Advertising Age*.[20] However, this was not the end of subliminal 'advertising'. In 1974, this issue was still running hot when Wilson Bryan Key published a book making sensational claims about subliminal sexual and death imagery in advertisements.[21] The big problem here is that scientists have been unable to find reliable empirical support for the persuasive effectiveness of subliminal advertising.[22]

Also, when reading research, be mindful that:

- most academic research makes only a token effort to draw out managerial implications;
- much practitioner research is based on shaky scientific foundations.

To illustrate the second point, consider the research methodology used by Tom Peters and Robert Waterman to compile the data used in one of the best-selling management guidebooks of all time: *In Search of Excellence: Lessons from America's Best-Run Companies* (1982). Through their consulting experience at McKinsey & Company, the two consultants identified many outstanding companies, such as IBM, Digital Equipment, Hewlett-Packard, Intel, Procter & Gamble, Johnson & Johnson, Eastman Kodak, 3M, and Boeing. They then studied these companies to discover what made them more successful than their peers. They discovered that these companies had the following eight characteristics:

- a bias for action;
- close to the customer;
- autonomy and entrepreneurship;
- productivity through people;
- hands on, value driven;
- stick to the knitting;
- simple form, lean staff;
- simultaneous loose–tight properties.

Each of these characteristics has what scientists call 'face validity', that is, it seems plausible. However, within a decade after the book was published, some of these excellent companies had lost much of their lustre. (For example, between 1990 and 1993, IBM suffered some of the biggest losses in commercial history—nearly US$18 billion.) How could this have happened? It turned out that Peters and Waterman did not compare their sample of companies with either a matched group of less well performing companies or a randomly selected control group. Thus, they had no way of knowing whether the characteristics they observed actually discriminated between high-performing and low-performing companies.[23] They didn't—whoops!

This example is a powerful reminder that all new knowledge needs to be read with care. (When I first read *In Search of Excellence* and listened to Tom Peters address a big audience of academics and businesspeople, I accepted what was said without question—duh!) In a world drowning in information, it also alerts us to be selective in where we source our new knowledge. Most journalists have little formal training in economics or psychology—the foundation disciplines of marketing—nor marketing itself. Hence, the structural frameworks they use to understand and present information in their publications are often not based on those used in the marketing discipline. In a similar vein, most academics have little or no practical business experience. Thus, their managerial insights sometimes fail the test of day-to-day practical reality.

Marketing Skills

The art and science of marketing can be practised with varying degrees of skill. This is the ability that comes from knowledge, practice, and aptitude. This book focuses on knowledge. Practice is gained through studying cases and working in a marketing role. I am often asked where is the best place to start to learn the practice of marketing. Advertising agencies are good because they service a variety of clients and they often act as marketing consultants for their clients. Another good place to learn the trade is with a direct marketing company. Why? Because you get instant sales feedback about what actually works.

Aptitude is the natural tendency or acquired inclination to learn the science and practice the art of marketing. My experience suggests that two key talents of the very good marketers are their ability to (*a*) tolerate uncertainty (you never have all the information you want) and (*b*) to frame a problem. To illustrate this framing ability, consider the various customer loyalty schemes that have been introduced around the world—the airline frequent-flyer programmes, the multi-retailer FlyBuys programme in Australia, etc. A key question that faces the managers of the companies that support such programmes is 'Are they cost effective, or would the considerable funds employed have been better spent somewhere else?' Another topical issue is 'How will the Internet change the way that customers buy products and services?'

It is questions such as these that trouble marketing managers and their direct reports. The best way to answer them is to start by reviewing what we currently know about customer behaviour. For example, from the customer point of view, the Internet and a customer loyalty programme are really just a new product/service. Hence, the place to start thinking about their likely success or failure in the market starts with an understanding of customer segments (namely, which types of customers see value in these new services) and the adoption of innovations (who will be the first to adopt and how will others follow). To these two perspectives, we can add some thinking about competitors, such as, if the new product looks as though it will be successful, then competitors are likely to launch a similar product (e.g. nearly every airline has its own frequent-flyer programme).

Framing the Internet issue as a new product adoption problem immediately suggests that its adoption will be selective (not everybody sees a need to be e-enabled) and quite slow (significant change and investment is often required to be able to use the Internet). This has been the pattern for such new products over the last 200 years—from the printing press, to the telegraph, to the PC. Just because journalists and stockmarket analysts got very excited about the Internet (as they do with many new technology breakthroughs) it does not mean that this time history will not repeat itself.

It is this style of 'back-to-basics' thinking that pervades the following chapters.

RECAP

Marketing is the management of the exchanges between an organization and its stakeholders—customers, employees, community groups, and others. In this book the focus is on customers. The skill in managing the marketing function is to take a broader view than simply designing products and services for sale to target consumers. This broader view is shown in Figure 1.5.[24] It suggests that marketing success is achieved by assessing:

- *Market opportunities*—which are customer needs that can be profitably served by the organization.

And in exploiting these to ensure that there is

- *Internal fit*—where the capabilities of the strategic business unit (SBU) are sufficient to meet the stated objectives.

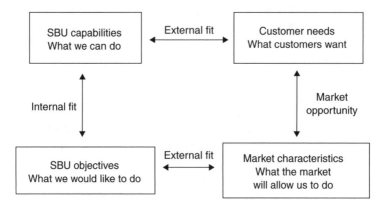

Figure 1.5. Achieving fit

- *External fit*—where there is a latent or expressed need for what is offered to target consumers.

Marketing also has prime responsibility in an organization for attaining and retaining target consumers. Many marketers consider that 'growing' consumers is also a key task of marketing. When growing means increasing the number of customers or enhancing the advocacy of customers for one's products and services, this is an admirable objective. However, when growing customers means either gaining a greater share of the customer's requirements of a product category (such as McDonald's seeking to move from 20 to 40 per cent of a person's eating-out meals) or increasing the volume purchased (such as Coca-Cola trying to get people around the world to drink as much Coke as Americans), this is a questionable objective. It is questionable because it can be manipulative and it may not be in the best interests of the buyer. (For example, more than one million Americans drink Coke with breakfast every day!) It also makes the implicit assumption that most consumers do not really know what is best for them and that companies driven by a profit imperative offer the best guidance.

KEY IDEAS

- Marketing is the function that is primarily responsible for the design and management of the exchanges between the organization and its customers.
- Marketing concepts can be used to facilitate exchanges in B2E, B2B, and B2C situations.
- The two primary roles of marketing are to attain and retain target customers.
- Markets can be defined from both supply and demand perspectives. Supply reflects the mechanics of the business while demand reflects the desires of customers.

- Marketing managers must engineer a balance between the value of the benefits and solutions to problems offered to customers and the value (profitability) of customers to the organization.

- As products and services share more common features, the distinction between product and service marketing becomes more artificial.

- Organizations have their own unique culture that can help or hinder the marketing function.

- Marketing management is a four-stage process: (*a*) understand the current situation; (*b*) design a marketing strategy to meet the organization's objectives and to exploit market opportunities; (*c*) develop programmes to implement the strategy; and (*d*) track the efficiency and effectiveness of the programmes.

ARGYLE DIAMONDS: CREATING A MARKET FOR COLOURED ICE

In the world of diamonds, the dominant player is the South African controlled company De Beers. In the 1970s, they controlled almost 90 per cent of the market. De Beers' ability to drive the world diamond market has been engineered through a rigid control of the supply of diamonds onto the market and through some astute marketing. However, as more diamond fields were discovered in Australia, Russia, and North America, this control weakened.

De Beers is the miner and buyer of most of the world's diamonds. As such, it is the arbiter of price. It has manipulated supply through its network of 125 'trading partners' (cutters, polishers, and dealers), by stockpiling gemstones (in 2000 it had approximately US$4 billion worth), and by controlling the Central Selling Organization—the cartel that controls about 75 per cent of the world's rough diamond distribution and marketing. In 2000, De Beers exercised direct control over about 60 per cent of the world trade in uncut diamonds.

Demand has been manipulated by some clever marketing and a big marketing budget—about $170 million in 1999. For example, for years De Beers has run advertising proclaiming that 'A diamond is forever' (www.adiamondisforever.com). This campaign is aimed at minimizing the second-hand market for gem-quality stones. A very clever move when one considers that diamonds are not rare gemstones—millions of carats are mined each year and hundreds of millions of diamonds are owned by people around the world. A more recent marketing initiative is to start branding diamonds. For example, in 2000, De Beers proposed that its diamonds would carry the name Diamond Trading Company to guarantee to retailers, and those customers who were interested, that these stones were mined under humane working conditions and were not used to finance any wars. (Diamonds from war-torn areas in the Africa continent are known as 'blood' diamonds.)

Argyle Diamonds

The Argyle mine in the West Australian Kimberley region is the world's largest diamond mine. Production commenced in the early 1980s, and in 1993 the mine produced over 40 million carats—about one-third of the world's natural supply. (40 million carats of diamonds would fill the load trays of eight suburban utility vehicles.) Alluvial river extraction and then open-cut mining of the AK1 diamond pipe produced mostly industrial quality product (used for grinding, cutting wheels, and other abrasive uses) and a small number of gem-quality stones—whites, pinks, yellows, and browns. See the table below. Initially, all the diamonds were sold through the Central Selling Organization.

Argyle and the World Supply of Diamonds

In the early 1990s, this table illustrated one of Argyle's problems, namely, that the volume of diamonds mined was more than the value captured.

In 1993, Argyle Diamonds was awarded the title of Australia's best resource company by the business magazine *BRW*. The award was based on Argyle's 'Marketing expertise … Operating a world-class mine … Innovative product development …' . In large part, it recognized the company's emerging success in reinvigorating the retail market for coloured diamonds, and in the process capturing more of the value of its production. The story behind this initiative is worth the telling.

| | % Argyle's production | Argyle's % of world supply | |
		Volume	Value
Gem	5	8	3
Near gem	45	25	10
Industrial	50	40	35
Total	100	33	5

How Do You Sell Coloured Diamonds?

In 1991, Argyle renegotiated its contract with the Central Selling Organization such that it gained greater control over the marketing of its coloured diamonds. This was an extremely important concession from the cartel because it provided Argyle with the opportunity to create and then to capture the value of its rare coloured diamonds. While pink diamonds are very rare and highly priced in the jewellery market, yellow and brown diamonds were not as highly valued. Hence, one of the tasks facing the marketing team at Argyle was how to add some extra intrinsic value to its yellow and brown diamonds.

When most jewellery buyers expect a diamond to be white (i.e. colourless), it is quite difficult to persuade them that a brown diamond is not only worth considering, but that it should command a price premium—especially if it is presented as a 'brown' diamond. In order to reposition Argyle's coloured stones, the marketing team used three tactics. First, they renamed the yellows as 'champagne' and the browns as 'cognac'. (The cachet of the pinks meant that these diamonds did not need a new name.) In effect, the new names 'rented' the image of up-market beverages. (Yes, the French wine and brandy producers did object to the use of these names.) Second, Argyle used advertising, direct marketing, and promotions such as the International Coloured Diamond Awards to enhance the prestige of jewellery featuring coloured diamonds. This marketing was designed to increase awareness about coloured diamonds and to overcome the resistance of retailers to stock these diamonds. The third tactic was to work closely with Indian cutting centres and jewellery makers where most of the coloured stones are processed. The quality of the settings in which the stones were presented—especially for the growing United States market—was not good enough to command a premium price.

As these marketing initiatives took hold, the value of Argyle diamonds rose as did the stock-market value of the company.

NOTES

1. M. McLuhan, *Understanding Media: The Extensions of Man* (London: Routledge, 1964).
2. T. Friedman, *The Lexus and the Olive Tree* (London: HarperCollins, 1999).
3. N. Shoebridge, 'Polaroid Stumbles on a Hip New Market', *Business Review Weekly* (February 17, 1997), 62–3.

4. M. Porter, 'Strategy After the Net', *Harvard Business Review* (March 2001). For the contrary view, see L. Downes and C. Mui, *Unleashing the Killer App* (Boston: Harvard Business School Press, 2000).

5. J. Carlopio, *Implementation: Making Workplace Innovation and Technical Change Happen* (Sydney: McGraw-Hill, 1998).

6. R. T. Rust, A. J. Zahorik, and T. L. Keiningham, *Service Marketing* (New York: HarperCollins, 1996).

7. A. Ries and J. Trout, *Positioning: The Battle for Your Mind* (New York: McGraw-Hill, 1986). This book was updated twice: J. Trout with S. Rivkin, *The New Positioning* (New York: McGraw-Hill, 1996); J. Trout with S. Rivkin, *Differentiate or Die* (New York: Wiley, 2000). I think that the original book is better than the updates.

8. D. Ogilvy, *Confessions of an Advertising Man* (New York: Atheneum, 1964).

9. K. Keller, *Strategic Brand Management* (Upper Saddle River, NJ: Prentice Hall, 1998).

10. N. Klein, *No Logo* (London: Flamingo, 2000).

11. This paper is considered by many scholars and practitioners to be one of the most influential papers in the discipline of marketing: T. Levitt, 'Marketing Myopia', *Harvard Business Review* (July–August 1960), 45–56.

12. See, for example, G. Lilien and A. Rangaswamy, *Marketing Engineering* (Upper Saddle River, NJ: Prentice Hall, 2002).

13. See J. Rossiter, 'What is Marketing Knowledge? Stage 1: Forms of Marketing Knowledge', *Journal of Marketing Education* Vol. 1 (September) 9–26.

14. S. D. Hunt, L. B. Chonko, and V. R. Wood, 'Marketing Education and Marketing Success: Are They Related?' *Journal of Marketing Education*, 6, 1 (1986), 2–13.

15. R. Joss, 'Management', *Australian Journal of Management*, 26, Special Edition (2001), 89–103.

16. A. Ries and J. Trout, *The 22 Immutable Laws of Marketing* (London: HarperCollins, 1993).

17. This framework for classifying marketing knowledge was proposed by Professor John Rossiter in the reference in Note 13.

18. R. Hubbard and J. S. Armstrong, 'Replications and Extensions in Marketing: Rarely Published But Quite Contrary', *International Journal of Research in Marketing*, 11, 3 (1994), 233–48.

19. V. Packard, *The Hidden Persuaders* (New York: David McKay, 1957).

20. W. Weir, 'Another Look at Subliminal "Facts" ', *Advertising Age* (15 October 1984), p. 46.

21. W. B. Key, *Subliminal Seduction* (Englewood Cliffs, NJ: Prentice Hall, 1974).

22. For a good discussion of this, see M. Sutherland, *Advertising and the Mind of the Consumer* (Sydney: Allen and Unwin, 1993), chapter 3.

23. T. Peters and R. Waterman, *In Search of Excellence* (New York: Random House, 1982); D. T. Carroll, 'A Disappointing Search for Excellence', *Harvard Business Review*, 83, 6 (1983), 78–88; 'Who's Excellent Now', *Business Week* (5 November 1984), pp. 76–88. For a more contemporary study that uses matched-pair companies, see J. Collins and J. Porras, *Built to Last* (London: Random House, 1994).

24. This framework was proposed by John Roberts of the Australian Graduate School of Management.

FOUNDATIONS

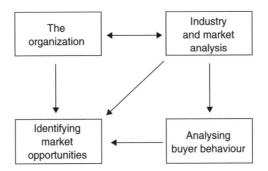

2

The Organization

There are three types of organizations: those that make things happen; those that watch things happen; and those that wonder what's happening.

As noted in Chapter 1, one of the first tasks of a marketing manager is to understand his or her organization's broad strategic objectives and the business model through which these are achieved. This sets the broad context in which marketing strategy is designed and programmes implemented.

This chapter explores the business context in which marketing decisions get made. Although many of the concepts and structural frameworks presented have their origins in the discipline of corporate strategy, the discussion is framed from a marketing point of view, that is, the emphasis will be on products and services, customers, innovation, and sources of competitive advantage.[1] The perspective taken is that of a marketing manager who must work within the constraints imposed by the organization's current business model, and who is motivated by the personal objectives agreed to, or imposed by, senior management.

To set the stage for the following discussion, consider two direct competitors, IBM and Oracle. Both are major competitors in the US$50 billion corporate software market. However, in 2001, their competitive philosophies were very different. While both have product lines in the database, applications, and e-business foundation software markets, Oracle's strategy is to offer customers a complete and tightly integrated package of software—everything a company needs to manage its e-commerce, financials, logistics, manufacturing, salesforce, and suppliers. In contrast, IBM adopted a 'best-of-breed' strategy in which it stitched together a quilt of business software from various companies, including itself. The Oracle–IBM example illustrates how two companies can compete for the same customers in quite different ways. In the next section, this idea is called the Strategic Intent of the organization.

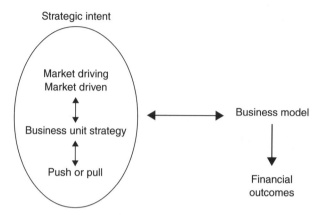

Figure 2.1. Understanding the organization

Figure 2.1 provides an overview of this chapter. The place to start the process of analysing an organization, or in many cases one of its SBUs, is with the notion of strategic intent. This can be examined through three lenses—first, whether the organization sees itself as driving its markets or being driven by them; second, the generic strategy adopted by the organization; and third, whether the organization has a 'push' or 'pull' system of production and marketing. The first lens looks at the innovation profile of the organization, while the second looks at the sources of competitive advantage and competitive scope of the organization. The third lens reminds the marketing team how established production procedures constrain new approaches to marketing. After this, the focus turns to describing how an organization's business process is configured to create products and services that customers will value. Finally, a framework is presented that shows how marketers can link their decisions to financial outcomes. Recall that in Chapter 1 this issue was identified as one of the key challenges facing marketing managers.

Strategic Intent

For the marketing team, it is extremely important to understand the overall strategic intent of their organization as this is the guiding philosophy of marketing strategy. Sometimes, journalists will state a company's strategic intent as follows:

- Aldi (a retailer)   pile it high and sell it cheap
- Amazon.com   get big fast, and hope that the winner takes all

- BHP Billiton
  (resource company)   dig and deliver
- Komatsu   beat Caterpillar
- 3M   innovation
- IBM   e-business infrastructure from IBM and partners
- Oracle   the one-stop shop
- Many early dotcoms grab the money and run

While these statements are a succinct way to communicate the *raison d'être* of an organization, we need to look behind them to more fully understand the strategic logic and the sources of competitive advantage used.

Market Driving or Market Driven

The founding father of modern management, Peter Drucker, and many other writers on corporate strategy suggest that innovation is a primary source of competitive advantage. Hence, senior managers invariably see this as one of the big issues facing their company—how much should be done and what type of innovation can be sustained given the capabilities of the organization. This topic often lands at the feet of the marketing team in the form of a directive to develop and launch more new products. (Chapter 5 outlines how various organizations do this.) For 3M, this aspect of their strategic intent has been stated as the goal of achieving 30 per cent of sales from products introduced in the last five years. In 1992, for Sony, it resulted in the launch of 1000 new products—800 were improvements and extensions of previously successful products, while 200 were radically new. For Nokia, it resulted in launching a new model of mobile phone every 35 days.

If a company has a poor record of NPD—as most do—then a directive to become significantly more innovative can be daunting. The marketing team cannot walk away from the innovation challenge, but it can reframe it to increase the odds of success. To do this, it must help shape the type of innovation that is within the current capabilities of their organization.

Figure 2.2 presents a useful way of classifying the approach organizations use to innovate.[2] Strategic leaps are infrequent innovations that have a substantial commercial impact for the organization. They are often driven by the development or acquisition of new technology. Often, these result in the creation of a new company or a new business unit. The role of marketing here is to help other managers understand the commercial potential of these new technologies—something they did not do very well for many of the Internet initiatives launched in the late 1990s and early 2000s.

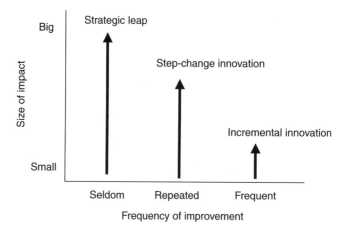

Figure 2.2. Types of innovation

As we saw with Sony, most innovation involves the continuous improvement of products and services. Mostly this results in minor improvements to the product or its packaging—such as the sale of beer in big bottles, small bottles, cans, six-packs, home kegs, etc. Over time, it often results in product proliferation—too many varieties of the brand chasing too few different usage situations.

Sometimes, innovation will result in a step-change improvement that still fits closely with the organization's core processes and target customers. For example, Austal Ships is a world leader in aluminium, small (less than 150 m), fast ships. They started life building crayfish boats in Western Australia where speed to get to the crayfish pots was very important for the fishermen. (They got to empty all their own pots and any 'unmarked' pots.) Over time, Austal developed the capability to build small luxury cruise ships, fast (people, car, and cargo) ferries, and fast, stable naval craft (e.g. some can outrun the fastest US torpedoes). Successful step-change improvements in engine and hull design came from accumulated learning.

In general, the role of the marketing team with step-change and incremental innovation is to enhance the organization's ability to *create* and successfully *market* new products and services. Chapter 5 elaborates on this task.

Through both product and business process innovations, some organizations have the ability to (re)shape the current market. I call these firms 'market-drivers'. Argyle Diamonds and Amazon.com are good examples of such firms. Argyle had to create a new market for coloured 'ice' (as discussed in Chapter 1) in order to capture the value of these gemstones. Amazon.com opened up the Internet book-buying market.

There is another type of organization that innovates in response to pressures in the existing market. I call these 'market-driven' firms. They often present as one of two types. One group is driven by the desire to beat their competitors (e.g. Coke versus Pepsi in the cola wars, Reebok versus Nike in the sneaker wars, Airbus versus Boeing in the airline wars, and Anheuser-Busch versus everybody in the US beer wars are typical competitor-focused companies).[3] Sometimes, these firms lose sight of their customers as illustrated when Coca-Cola withdrew the original version of Coke from the market and replaced it with New Coke. (It was only when their distributors and loyal customers made a considerable fuss that management relaunched the original brand as Coke Classic.)

The second type of market-driven organization is one that sets out to delight customers. A good example was the airline SAS when it came under the control of Jan Carlzon. His book titled *Moments of Truth* documents how he transformed a staid European airline into a pre-eminent customer-focused competitor.[4] The trick here is to be customer-focused, though not necessarily customer-compelled.[5] (It is easy to have cost blowouts when the customer really is the King or Queen and the organization tries to respond to their every desire.) Customer-focused organizations employ customer relationship management (CRM) systems, they routinely measure customer satisfaction and respond quickly to customer complaints, they strive to improve the current product/service offerings to current clients, and they grow by finding new groups of similar customers.

Figure 2.3 contrasts the innovation strategies of market-driving and market-driven organizations. Innovation is a critical activity for both

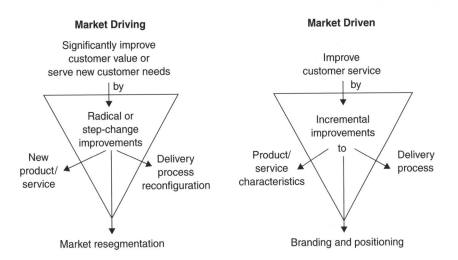

Figure 2.3. Styles of innovation

types of organizations—however, it has a different origin and character in each. Core capabilities and new technologies often drive the innovations of market-driving organizations, while the current perceived needs of a target segment of customers, and/or the actions of a competitor, drive market-driven organizations. Some big companies like Sony have the resources and capabilities to practice both types of innovation at the same time.

As a marketing manager, it is crucial to be clear about what type of organization you are, and what types of innovations to pursue. The reasons for this are to influence the debate inside the organization about the types of innovation and the role of marketing in their success. For example, for Intel, their innovation is based on a combination of technology (pushing the price–performance equation of chip design) and marketing (making the Intel brand salient and valuable to consumers). For Austal Ships, the innovations were a combination of technology and manufacturing process. The role of marketing here is to find new buyers for the new and improved ships. For Argyle, the innovation was mostly strategic marketing—create a market for coloured diamonds.

Marketplace and/or Marketspace

One aspect of innovation that is currently bedevilling strategic planners and marketing managers is e-business. Peter Weill and Michael Vitale define e-business as:

Marketing, buying, selling, delivering, servicing, and paying for products, services, and information across (nonproprietary) networks linking an enterprise and its prospects, customers, agents, suppliers, competitors, allies, and complementors.[6]

This definition places e-business squarely in the domain of marketing.

The current problem with e-business is that it is getting a bad name. Media commentators are referring to the dotcom companies as 'the tech wreck', 'the dot-comedy', 'dot-bombs', and 'dot-come, dot-go'. At the heart of this criticism is the claim that the people who created many of the early dotcom companies did not understand the revenue streams and cost structures associated with digital technology. Marketers were also blamed because they did not advise, or their advice was not heeded, about how quickly customers would respond, and how bricks-and-mortar distributors would react to these new companies.

The question is not so much whether the Internet and other digital technologies will change business, but how, and how fast this will occur. From a marketing perspective, e-business can be examined at strategic and tactical levels. Here, the focus is strategic and in Chapter 8 it will be tactical.

For marketing strategy, two key issues are (*a*) how will e-business change the relationship between the organization and its customers, and (*b*) how will existing distributors and retailers react to the organization establishing a direct relationship with customers. Organizations that already serve the customer directly (such as banks and hotels) generally see the Internet as another channel to communicate with their customers—sometimes with a better service and sometimes at a lower cost. (For example, Hilton hotels via Hilton.com has one of the fastest reservation systems in the hotel industry.) In this situation, a marketing problem is how to 'nudge', as opposed to 'force', more customers to use the new, cheaper channel without causing their resentment. Many banks have had trouble enticing their low-value customers out of their branches to use ATMs, telephone banking, and Internet banking. Another e-business problem is how to avoid conflict with existing channel members when the organization's Internet service (marketspace) competes with the service provided by these intermediaries (marketplace). For example, in 1998, Levi Strauss offered jeans buyers the opportunity to order their jeans online and have them delivered to their homes. In 1999, under pressure from their retailers they abandoned this service. Channel conflict is a persistent problem in marketing. It is discussed in more detail in Chapter 8.

The challenge for most organizations that have an Internet presence is to make this strategy profitable. This requires generating enough revenue to cover the full costs of the e-business (information technology, IT infrastructure, databases, management time, advertising and promotion, cannibalizing sales from other channels, etc.). Profit opportunities in the marketspace can arise from:[7]

- Direct sales—sometimes called e-tailing (for electronic retailing). Amazon.com, CDNow, Cisco Systems, Dell Computer, Egghead, Gap, and many others make money this way.
- Advertising sales from banner ads on a website—these are often priced on a per exposure basis and appear on Netscape and most search engines.
- Content sponsorship by another company—for example, ACO, an Icelandic computer retailer, sponsored the Dilbert cartoon written in Icelandic on the website of Iceland's dominant newspaper.

- Retail alliances—preferred vendors are charged fees to have a clickable button located in a prominent spot on the website. For example, CDNow has such an arrangement with Lycos.
- Prospect fees—these are click-through fees for visitors to a website that complete some action. For example, someone who clicks-through on a banner ad.
- Subscription fees for access to information (such as the *Wall Street Journal Interactive*—www.wsj.com) or the use of services (such as those offered by share-broking firms).
- Becoming an intermediary to bring buyers and sellers together—a market maker such as eBay's 'person-to-person online trading community'. The original eBay model was consumer-to-consumer. It later evolved into B2C and B2B. The company Priceline (www.priceline.com) established itself to become a consumer-to-business intermediary. Consumers name their own price for items like airline tickets and hotel rooms and Priceline communicates this demand to participating sellers.
- Cost elimination—when an organization has hundreds of thousands of customers, getting them to serve themselves via the Internet can result in small savings per enquiry and transaction that accumulate into huge reductions in the costs of customer service.
- Disintermediation—where the job done by a current independent distribution channel member is brought back into the selling organization at a lower cost. For example, when Dell stopped using independent retailers in 1994 (CompUSA, and PC World in the United Kingdom) it took over some of the functions performed by the retailers (such as helping the customer choose the most appropriate PC) and outsourced other functions to another organization (such as delivery of the PCs).

Some organizations have been successful, although in many cases not yet profitable, by developing a pure 'Internet strategy'. Amazon.com is well known, and AccWeather less well known. AccWeather (www.accu weather.com) is the world's largest weather service.[8] It employs meteorologists and computer graphic artists to create accurate and easy to use weather information that is fed to thousands of websites, radio and television stations, and newspapers. AccWeather's core competencies include a critical mass of world-class professionals who can tailor the presentation of weather information to the people who need it. The value added by the Internet is that of time—the continual updating of weather forecasts. Being able to identify clearly the value added by the new digital technologies is a key to their commercial success. Another critical success factor is the realistic pricing of this added value. The discussion in Chapter 9 of economic value to the customer (EVC) pricing looks at this issue.

Strategy: Competitive Advantage and the Scope of Competition

The key issue here is to understand how and where an organization seeks to compete. This is at the heart of the organization's strategy. One classification of 'pure' strategies is: cost leadership, segmentation, playing the spread, or the focused niche. The reason for choosing this classification is that it highlights the types of innovation (product, and/or marketing, and/or business process) that support the scope of competition. It also draws attention to four other key drivers of competitive advantage, namely, economies of scale, scope, and focus, and customer segmentation.

Having a low-cost position relative to rivals is a favoured strategy by many organizations because it opens up the greatest market potential. Low cost comes about because the organization has a scale of operations that allows a more efficient utilization of its resources than its rivals. *Economies of scale* are typically driven by efficient production or through accumulated knowledge not otherwise embodied in the economics of production. Toyota is an often-cited example of a company that has achieved lower production costs through the design of its operations.

A second type of cost advantage arises from what are called *economies of scope*. These arise because of the ability to spread the organization's production, service, and business technologies across different products. For example, Canon shares its expertise in fine optics, precision mechanics, and microelectronics across its cameras, photocopiers, video cameras, and fax machines. The giant pharmaceutical companies Pfizer and Glaxo SmithKline were formed through mergers to achieve economies of scope in research and development of new drugs. The big consumer goods companies like Procter & Gamble and Unilever share their expertise in marketing and market research across their vast product range. So do the big automotive companies like Ford, General Motors, and Toyota. Sony and 3M share their expertise in NPD across their numerous development teams.

If the actions taken by the marketing and production managers are to be coordinated, then they need a shared vision of the intended scale and scope of operations. They also need to be aware of how they can cooperate with other parts of the organization to capture the benefits of scale (e.g. by minimizing the number of special orders) and scope (e.g. by sharing technology to develop new products or learning from market research done for other parts of the business).

Sometimes, a firm develops an expertise that allows it to remain small yet produce specialist products and services at low cost. This phenomenon is known as *economies of focus*. A good example is the academic-consultant who develops a knowledge-based expertise that is sold to various companies, for example, as an expert witness in legal disputes.

The furniture company IKEA is a good example of an organization that has achieved a low-cost position through both economies of scale and focus. IKEA's strategic intent is to be the 'lowest delivered cost furniture company'. By this, they mean getting furniture into the customer's home at the lowest cost relative to their rivals. To do this, they have been clear about the selection of their target customers—the DIYs or 'do-it-yourself' type of customer. They have invested heavily in designing furniture that can be packaged flat so that it can be taken home by the buyer and is easy to assemble. To further keep the total cost down, they have a minimal retailing format in the sense that the customer is asked to be their own salesperson. IKEA calls their target customers 'pro-sumers'—producer-consumers.

A fifth primary source of competitive advantage arises from market segmentation (which is discussed in Chapter 6). As we saw in the previous section, market-driving companies seek to create new products for new segments, and market-driven companies seek new insights into the market by deeper analysis of their current customers.

Table 2.1 identifies the sources of competitive advantage that drive each of these strategies. As a marketing manager, it is important to understand which of these particular strategies the organization is trying to implement and the role of marketing in its implementation. It is also important to understand that these generic approaches to strategy are rarely implemented in their pure form. For example, Intel has aspects of both cost leadership (through its experience and scale of operations) and segmentation (through its product innovation) in its strategic intent.

There is one other primary source of competitive advantage that is important to marketers and that is often the joint responsibility of the Chief Marketing Officer, the head of Corporate Affairs, and CEO of the organization. Can you guess what it is? *The Corporate Brand*. This goes under a number of names such as corporate brand, image, or reputation that all refer to the global evaluation of the company. This global evaluation is a source of competitive advantage because people use it to form their opinions about the organization's credibility, honesty, responsibility, and integrity. There is now a significant body of research that suggests that organizations with a good reputation are more attractive to more customers.[9] This in turn

Table 2.1. Generic approaches to strategy

Drivers	Strategies	Examples
Scale Process innovation Experience Control over the value chain	Cost leadership (low cost/few segments)	Ikea
Product innovation Capture synergies across product lines	Segmentation (moderate cost/multiple segments)	Procter & Gamble
Product and process innovation Economies of scale and scope	Playing the spread (low cost/multiple segments)	Toyota
Customer insight Marketing innovation Economics of focus	Focused niche (high cost/one segment)	Argyle

enhances the credibility of their advertising, new products, pricing, service, and people. For companies in industries like airlines, banking, education, healthcare, and insurance where customers 'buy' (i.e. have to trust) the company as well as a particular product or service, a good reputation is doubly important. As we will see throughout this book, corporate and product brands are key marketing assets for every organization.

Strategic Push or Pull

In the last decade, the idea of mass customization was thought to be the future of manufacturing and marketing. The idea was that consumers would get a reasonably priced, tailor-made product. Producers, for their part, would have more satisfied customers and would be able to reduce manufacturing costs, inventories, and waste in the supply chain. The order process would also provide them with more timely and accurate information about demand.

Mass customization involves selling highly individual products and services to a large number of consumers. It is like craft production on a large scale. The success enjoyed by Dell Computer is the most published example. (See the case at the end of this chapter.) Dell, and other companies that build products to order, implement what can be called a pull model of manufacturing and marketing. Here, the customer initiates the order and specifies the allowed (by the manufacturer) combination of product features. The manufacturer then builds to order. The key success factors for mass customization to succeed are:

- Elicitation—getting the correct information from the customer.
- Process flexibility—to produce variety at an acceptable cost to the customer.
- Logistics—getting the product to the customer in a timely manner and without too much added cost.

Achieving all three of these conditions has proved difficult for most organizations.

The alternative is a mass-manufacturing or 'push' system of production—much favoured by automobile companies and many producers of consumer products and industrial supplies. Here, products are designed for mass production and broad appeal. They are packaged in various sizes to cater for different levels of demand. Price discounting is often required to move excess inventory. The role of distributors is to stock and display the products for sale. If they are very good at this, as many big retailers are, they can exert considerable influence on the manufacturers to give them special trading terms and conditions (such as product slotting fees in supermarkets

Table 2.2. Push and pull manufacturing and marketing

	Push	*Pull*
Design	Wide range of vehicles with mass appeal; limited customer input	Suppliers and car manufacturer co-design and develop parts; high level of customer input
Sourcing	Adversarial relationship with suppliers; high inventory levels used as supply buffer; component sourcing	More collaboration with suppliers—some located at plant; module sourcing; JIT inventory
Manufacturing	Volume through maximum production; manufacturing as core competence; downtime unacceptable	More profit through less inventory and lower overheads; build to order; downtime acceptable
Marketing	Pricing based on budgets and targets; high incentives to move cars	Market-driven pricing on order-by-order basis; fewer customer and dealer incentives and discounts
Distribution	Cars allocated to dealers; 60-day order-to-delivery; price discounts at dealers	Customer-originated order; 30-day order-to-delivery; low inventory

and cooperative advertising money). Table 2.2 compares the push and pull approach to selling automobiles.[10]

The current production model of many organizations restricts how much they can convert to a pull model of manufacturing and marketing. For example, for a major automotive company to implement this system would require changing the way they absorb fluctuations in demand and production, which would in turn involve changing the work practices of a highly unionized and often adversarial workforce—not an easy task. It would also necessitate changing the business of the (independent) dealerships—from sales push to consultative customer order taker, and making less money from selling high-priced accessories.

The critical issue for marketers with the idea of mass customization/build-to-order is whether consumers will buy it and, thus, should they recommend that their organization move in this direction. In many markets, the answer seems to be a qualified yes. Some consumers are prepared to pay (a little) more and wait longer, while others value the convenience of 'drive in and take away'. Chapter 6 (Figure 6.1) revisits this issue in the context of market segmentation.

The Organization's Business Model

This section introduces the concept of, and a framework to analyse, an organization's business model.[11] In simple terms, a business model is a more extensive story of the organization's strategic intent. The story is in two parts—a description of the major activities associated with (*a*) making something (designing it, manufacturing, and so on), and (*b*) selling it (finding customers, distribution, pricing, and so on). The plot of the story turns on either designing a new product or service for an unmet need, or creating a better way to make, distribute, or sell an already proven product or service.

Business models often reside on a senior business planning manager's spreadsheet. What-if questions about the drivers of costs and revenues help to model how the business 'works'. By continually updating the model, it allows managers to tie the 'story' of the business to the profit and loss (P&L) statement. Of course, the spreadsheet model is only as good as the assumptions and the numbers that go into it. When a business model fails, it is because the story does not make sense, or the P&L does not produce a profit. At any particular time, this business model is something that cannot be changed and that must be worked with by the marketing team.

The Dell case at the end of this chapter is a good example of a new business model that passes both the 'story' and 'numbers' tests. Another such success is that of the traveller's cheque. In exchange for a small fee, a traveller buys a widely accepted, safe (they are insured against loss and theft), easily negotiable cheque for local currency. For American Express, the original provider of these cheques, they were a virtual money machine. Because travellers always paid cash for the cheques they gave American Express an interest-free loan. And because some of the cheques were never cashed, the company got an extra windfall. Traveller's cheques were the preferred method for taking money overseas until the ATM provided travellers with even more convenience. (They are still widely used when travelling in less-developed countries.)

The business model for many online grocers is another interesting example. Groceries is an industry with very thin margins. While a small group of consumers were prepared to pay a little more for home-delivered groceries, there were not enough of them, and the price premium was not high enough to cover the extra costs associated with this service. Because this new venture failed the story test for most shoppers, it also failed the numbers test for most online grocers.

The design of a business model is built around the two frameworks illustrated below—value chains (developed by Michael Porter[12]) and the business process map (developed by Timothy Devinney[13]).

Consider the case of a company whose strategy is to provide more efficient earth moving machines than any other producer. This statement defines a global value that most customers for these machines would welcome—a demand-side perspective as noted in Chapter 1. And it says that the company will be in the earth moving machine business—a supply-side view of the market. To better understand how this business 'works', we need to decompose this statement of strategic intent into more operational customer values such as low machine downtime, low servicing costs, and the appropriate machine for the job at hand. Because we are modelling the business at a strategic level, the key is to identify the handful of critical operational factors that deliver value to the target customers.

We can think of a business as a four-tiered customer value creation process. On top (because we are marketers) sits the core customer value that the organization has decided it will deliver. Under this is the set of operational customer values that provide this core value. Under these values are the key business processes that create this value, and under these are the capabilities, resources, and assets necessary to support these processes. Figure 2.4 shows the structure of a generic business model.[14]

What is missing from this picture of a business is a logic that reflects the operations of the organization. For example, the production of a product or

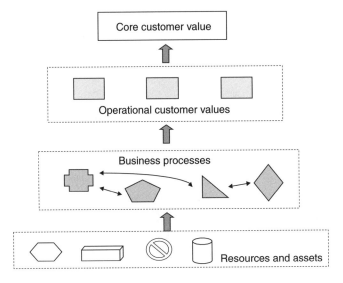

Figure 2.4. A generic business model

Support activities	Control systems				
	Business and information technology				
	Human resources				
	Knowledge systems				
Primary activities	Inbound logistics	Operations	Outbound logistics	Marketing and sales	Service

Figure 2.5. A generic value chain

the delivery of a service can be broken down into a series of direct and supporting activities. The value chain framework made popular by Michael Porter is as good as any other to reflect this logic. A generic value chain is shown in Figure 2.5. In practice, some companies will control all aspects of a value chain, while in other cases more than one company may combine to deliver the global customer value discussed above. For example, the big petrochemical companies often undertake exploration, extraction, refining, and marketing. At the other extreme, the Tommy Hilfiger clothing brand is just that—a brand. The company is run entirely through licensing agreements—different organizations handle the design, production, and retailing of the clothes.

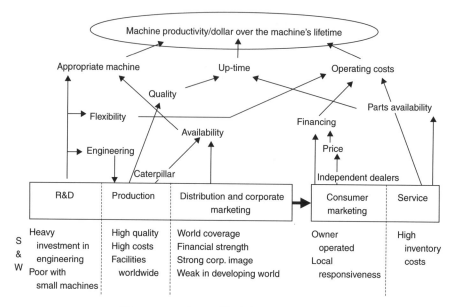

Figure 2.6. Caterpillar's business model

When we take the generic business model in Figure 2.4 and organize it according to the logic of the value chain, what emerges is a very insightful picture of a business. Figure 2.6 shows a simplified picture of the Caterpillar company—makers of heavy-duty construction equipment. Caterpillar chooses to serve those customers who value the lifetime value of a machine, expressed in Figure 2.6 as 'machine productivity per dollar spent over the lifetime of the machine'. To do this, it has chosen to concentrate on the design and production of equipment and to outsource the sales and service to a small number of high-quality, independent dealers around the world. This arrangement allows Caterpillar to 'think global and act local'. The Caterpillar brand stands for product quality and back-up technical support, while the local dealers are often long-established and respected members of their communities who deliver personalized service.[15]

The bottom of Figure 2.6 shows a partial strengths, weaknesses, opportunity, threats (SWOT) analysis of each value creation activity. Here, we see that Caterpillar has strong R&D for big machines but not small ones. Also, it is heavily dependent on the quality of its dealers for its market success. SWOT analysis used like this can be very insightful and it stands in sharp contrast to many of the SWOT analyses found in (marketing) planning documents. If you see a strategic plan that has a page of strengths, then a page of weaknesses, a page of opportunities, and a page of threats, there is a good chance that this could be relabelled as a *Substantial Waste Of Time*.

The usefulness of this business model framework is that it forces the organization to articulate the customer values that a segment of customers desire. It then helps to identify the key parts of the business that deliver this customer value—to which all managers need to pay attention. Also, because organizations start out with different endowments, they compete by placing different emphases on the different parts of the map. Thus, a map like Figure 2.6 can be a powerful analytic tool and a useful summary statement of an organization's strategic intent.

Timothy Devinney and I used this type of analysis when we were asked to help a company decide if it should expand its operations into Asia. We were asked to facilitate the resolution of an argument between two groups of managers about whether the company could and should open for business in various Asian countries. What we did was to get the 'Go to Asia' group and the 'Stay at Home' group to draw a business model map of the company. The Stay-at-Homes drew a map of the current very successful operations while the Go-to-Asia group drew a map of the type of company they thought would be needed to succeed offshore. What resulted from this process was two quite different business model maps. That is, to go to Asia, the company would need to significantly re-engineer itself, or at least its offshore operations in order to succeed. What these maps did was to highlight the nature of the task the company faced if it decided to go to Asia.

For big organizations that seek to serve multiple types of customers a Strategic business Unit (SBU) is often created to serve a particular market segment.[16] This pairing of SBUs and markets defines the organization's competitive scope. For example, Australia's four biggest banks each have a broad market coverage strategy. They have decided to serve millions of customers—personal, business, institutional, and government. Because each group has different needs and exists in a different environment as defined by its social trends, economic conditions, politics, regulations, etc., the banks create an SBU to serve each strategic market. While each of these SBUs is tied to the 'bank' by human resource policies, operating controls, the corporate mission, and the corporate brand, each has a distinct modus operandi for the way that it goes-to-market.

While the business model map is a useful strategic framework because it 'unpacks' each SBU to show how it is organized to create customer value, marketing managers also need to look at the organization from a more tactical perspective. The next two frameworks are presented do this by focusing on the elements of marketing that are typically the responsibility of a marketing manager. The first framework looks at measures of operational customer values and internal measures of performance. The second framework focuses on the 4Ps of marketing described in Chapter 1 in the section titled 'A Review of Marketing Practice'.

Linking Internal Processes to Product/Service Quality

Customers are the ultimate arbiters of the quality of a product or service. When they judge quality to be high (i.e. at or above their expectations), the following effects may materialize:

- a satisfied customer is more likely to be retained as a customer;
- a satisfied customer is also more likely to engage in positive word-of-mouth (WOM) communication about the product or service.

The combination of these two effects helps the organization to both defend (by retaining customers) and grow (by attaining new customers) its market share. Thus, customer perceived quality is a key success factor for many organizations.

Quality management for an organization means managing and controlling internal business processes to deliver quality to target customers. From a customer perspective, overall quality will be perceived as a combination of one or more of the following things that the organization can offer:

- the physical product,
- the service, and
- the environment in which the product or service is delivered,

relative to the price paid—as this is compared to the prices of other similar products/services. For example, consider buying a new car. The physical product is the car itself. The service is how the sales staff interact with the customer. The service environment is the showroom.

The critical issue for managers is to improve those internal business processes that have a statistically significant relationship to quality—as perceived by the target customer. In many cases, these linkages are obvious—such as how well the new car conforms to specifications. However, in some cases, perceived quality can only be determined through some insightful research—such as the robustness of a car may be judged by the sound of its doors closing.

Figure 2.7 shows an example of how measures of internal business processes can be linked to operational customer values (as per Figure 2.4) for the General Business Systems Division of AT&T.[17] The percentages were determined from customer research. They represent the relative importance of each factor's influence on overall perceived quality.

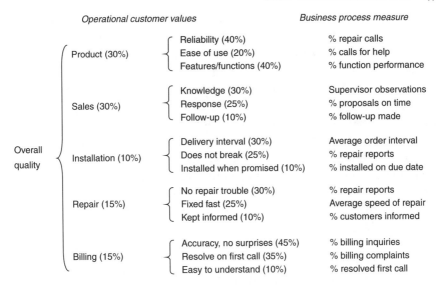

Figure 2.7. Linking internal processes to customer perceived quality

A map such as Figure 2.7 is useful for any organization to compile. The processes selected will vary according to the focal product/service, and each should be the responsibility of a particular manager. In this way, internal business processes will be linked to management KPIs, which in turn will drive creating customer value through perceived product/service quality.

4Ps and 3Cs

One of the most popular and enduring models of marketing (both in textbooks and practice) is called the 4Ps or the marketing mix.[18] These are typically product, price, place (i.e. distribution), and promotion. Recall that Chapter 1 added five others, namely, people, physical evidence, process, personal selling, and position. The issue is not how many Ps we use, but to select the ones that are critical to creating a desirable offer to target customers.

The offer to target customers at the top of the business model in Figure 2.6 will generally be created through a combination of three or more of these Ps. For example, Honda and Harley-Davidson are both very successful motorbike manufacturers. However, because they serve quite different customer segments, they blend the various Ps in a different way in order to be successful in the marketplace. As we will see later in the book, Harley-Davidson's target customers are people who want to participate in part of an American dream—as expressed in the company motto 'live to ride, ride to live'.[19] Thus, the distinctive product, the company people who are visible advocates for the product, and the Harley-Davidson position Ps are key elements for their success. Alternatively, Honda sells a wide range of bikes to all the major segments of bike riders—from racers to urban commuters. Thus, product range to suit different needs, price points to suit different budgets, promotion through their advertising and bike racing, and wide distribution (place) are the key elements of their mix.

The first step to using the 4Ps and 3Cs framework is to be clear about the mix of Ps used to configure your offer to target customers and the relative importance of each one of these. For the sake of illustration, this section uses the traditional 4Ps as the generic mix. Part III of the book, which discusses developing marketing programmes and tactics, elaborates each element of the marketing mix. However, for now, a rudimentary under-standing of each P is all that is necessary to illustrate this framework.

The 3Cs of the framework stand for:

- Customers,
- Competitors,
- Company.[20]

The business model in the previous section described the company and linked it to a customer segment via some broad-based customer values. What was missing from this analysis was any mention of Competitors. This was a critical omission and one that I start to rectify here. (Chapter 3 has much more to say about competitors.) One of the things that annoys and worries very senior managers in a company is that often their marketing managers either ignore competitors or they implicitly assume that they will not respond to the organization's marketing initiatives. This is seldom the case.

Figure 2.8 shows a generic 4Ps and 3Cs framework. When a manager looks at the columns, the challenges are to:

- create relevant and distinctive products and services;
- set prices to reflect and capture the value that customers see in the product;
- make the products available when and where customers want to buy them;
- use an integrated set of communication vehicles to promote and position the product.

When looking across the rows of Figure 2.8, the issues are for the company to:

- develop the capabilities and organizational structure to create and deliver what customers really want;

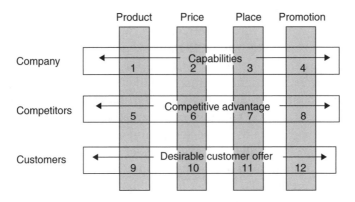

Figure 2.8. 4Ps and 3Cs framework

- build a competitive advantage on some dimension;
- create an offer to fit the needs of target customers.

Notice that there are twelve intersections between the Ps and Cs. Each one of these represents an area of specific concern for a marketing manager. For example, questions such as the following illustrate these concerns:

1. Does the organization have the capabilities to design and manufacture products to the quality desired by target customers?
2. Are costs low enough to provide sufficient margins?
3. Is there sufficient distribution coverage?
4. Do promotion activities achieve awareness and support the brand positioning?
5. How does the product compare to that offered by competitors?
6. Are prices competitive?
7. Do competitors have better distribution?
8. Do we have enough share of voice in the market?
9. How close is our product to the ideal product desired by target customers?
10. Is the product affordable and is it priced at a price point acceptable to customers?
11. Is the product available within 'an arm's reach of need'?
12. Does the promotion and position add value to the brand?

The 4Ps and 3Cs framework can be used to guide a marketing audit and as the backbone of a marketing plan. In both these roles, it will need to be expanded beyond the simple structure in Figure 2.8. For example, Honda would need a separate analysis for each of their tactical customer segments (racers, commuters, pleasure riders, etc.) because they will have a different offer, different capabilities, and different competitors in each segment.

Using a framework like the 4Ps and 3Cs is quite different to the list-oriented suggestions found in many marketing auditing and planning guides. For example, Philip Kotler's popular marketing management text lists thirty broad areas to consider in a marketing audit—everything from social and economic trends to salesforce compensation.[21] At the conclusion of such an extensive review, one is typically left with a large report containing an overall evaluation of marketing competency (often used to 'evaluate' the marketing group), and another list of things requiring attention. What lists fail to capture are the various interactions that are at the heart of strategic marketing.

The recommendation embodied in this chapter is to avoid, as much as possible, presenting list-based audits and plans to senior managers. Rather, use a few broad frameworks such as those illustrated here to focus on the key drivers of success for your organization. Lists of strengths and weaknesses of the various elements of marketing can be valuable input into planning, but they are not sufficient to provide the insight necessary to create effective strategy and tactics. Also, they really annoy many senior managers.

I now turn to the vexing issue of how to link marketing strategy and programmes to the accounting measures of SBU performance that are the key concerns of financial managers and top management. When marketing actions are not linked through to accounting outcomes, the marketing function often loses credibility within the organization.[22]

From Marketing Actions to Accounting Measures of Performance

The approach outlined in this section has its roots in the discipline of cost accounting and dates back to the 1960s.[23] A key issue then, as now, is the measurement and thus control of the performance of the business units of an organization. What has changed since this time is that there are more ways of measuring business unit performance, and consequently there are disagreements about the best approach to adopt. Hence, this section starts with the following recommendation. Before using the generic framework outlined here, co-opt a friendly accountant to help modify it to fit the internal accounting protocols used in your organization. Thus, what follows is best described as a guide to marketing financial management.

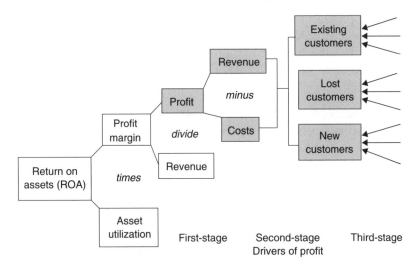

Figure 2.9. Du Pont analysis: linking marketing to accounting

On balance, a dominant financial perspective is that the share market value created by a strategic initiative is best reflected by the net present value of the future cash flows expected to accrue to the organization. Marketing can add directly to creating shareholder value by:[24]

- increasing net cash flow by increasing total revenues, prices, and average revenue per user (ARPU), and reducing costs;
- accelerating cash flows by getting products to market faster and by speeding up their adoption and diffusion;
- reducing the risks associated with cash flows by increasing the loyalty of customers;
- reducing the volatility of cash flows by developing relationships with distribution channel members that smooth out the peaks and troughs of sales.

Although measurement difficulties abound, the challenge for marketing is to link its activities to net cash flow (i.e. revenues minus costs).

With this task in mind, Figure 2.9 shows the key elements of a technique to link the key marketing tasks of customer acquisition and retention to net cash flow and thus the creation of shareholder value. (This technique was originally developed by Du Pont and has been modified here to fit the needs of a marketing manager.)

The shaded areas of Figure 2.9 are classified as first-, second-, and third-stage drivers of profit. This chapter restricts attention to the first- and second-stage drivers. Part III of the book focuses on third-stage drivers, that is, the programmes under the control of marketing managers that directly effect customer acquisition and retention.

To illustrate the usefulness of Figure 2.9, consider the following hypothetical case of a seller of a business service to small business customers:

- For the full reporting period, the organization has 1.2 million customers.
- During this period, 352,000 customers ceased to use the company's services.
- During this period, 648,000 new customers were acquired.
- Assume that the ARPU is $800 per customer for a full period.[25]
- Assume that the time pattern of customer arrivals (new) and departures (loss) is similar and that each of these types of customer generates 50 per cent of the ARPU of a full-period customer.
- Assume that based on the pattern of service mix, the costs that varied with the services provided (VC) were allocated as follows:
  —Full period, existing customer $350 per customer;
  —Lost customers $175 per customer;
  —New customers $175 per customer.
- Assume that total new customer acquisition costs were $263 million and, thus, $202 per customer.

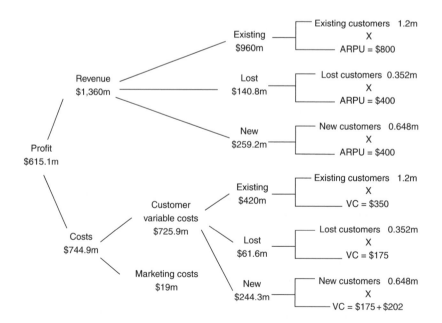

Figure 2.10. Revenue drivers for a service company

- Assume that other costs associated with marketing and customer relationship management were $19 million.

Figure 2.10 shows the first- and second-stage drivers of profit for this organization.

Consider Figure 2.10 as the base case for a 'what-if' analysis. What if lost customers could be reduced by 10 per cent? What if the ARPU could be increased by 5 per cent by introducing a customer loyalty programme that would cost $2 million to establish and $1 million annually to run? What if service costs could be reduced by 3 per cent? What if the advertising agency was offered an incentive contract for their next campaign that would reward them by $5 for each additional customer they attracted? Would it be worth paying $200,000 for a detailed customer satisfaction survey that would enable the loss rate of customers to be reduced by 5 per cent? These and other questions that focus on the ways that marketing can increase net cash flow discussed earlier are well suited to analysis using the Du Pont framework.

It is important to finish this section with a reminder that much of the information used in this analysis relies on understanding and accepting the allocations of costs made by the organization's accountants. Also, the example described here is for a single period. When the returns to marketing actions like advertising accrue over more than one period, this should be factored into the third-stage drivers of profit.

RECAP

Marketing scholars agree that a good business strategy makes marketing much easier and its productivity more achievable.[26] Even the most enlightened marketing efforts cannot compensate for a flawed strategy in the long run. For example, over the years, South West Airlines has spent far less on marketing than its major rivals, yet has outperformed them on every index of marketing productivity in its chosen markets. This is simply because Southwest does not have to market heavily to push a message that is intrinsically attractive to a large and growing market, namely, cheap, on-time, fun air travel.

While marketing managers typically have little direct influence over their organization's strategic intent and business model, their actions can affect the efficiency and effectiveness with which it implements strategy. They do this through their understanding of target consumers' buying behaviour and making sure that the voice of the customer is not lost in the process of strategic planning. In this process, they will gain more credibility in the organization by linking marketing actions to accounting outcomes.

KEY CONCEPTS

- *Strategic intent*—a short statement of the organization's overall strategy. This is often stated in a few words to communicate with employees, company analysts, and journalists.
- *Market-driving organizations*—those that try to create new markets.
- *Market-driven organizations*—those that try to better accommodate the stated needs of current customers and/or follow the actions of competitors.
- *Generic strategy*—how the organization competes through its use of economies of scale, scope, focus, and innovation.
- *Push marketing*—using quotas and sales incentives to push products through the distribution channel to customers.
- *Pull marketing*—sensing and responding to customers' needs for product and service variety.
- *Value chain*—the collection of activities that are performed to design, manufacture, deliver, and support the organization's products and services.
- *Marketing mix*—the set of marketing tools used to implement the organization's marketing strategy.
- *Customer perceived (high) quality*—perceptions of quality that meet or exceed the customer's expectations.

KEY FRAMEWORKS

- *Styles of innovation*—Figure 2.3
- *Business model*—Figures 2.4 and 2.6
- *Quality management map*—Figure 2.7
- *4Ps and 3Cs*—Figure 2.8
- *Du Pont analysis*—Figures 2.9 and 2.10

KEY QUESTIONS

- Can you state your organization's strategic intent in fewer than ten words? If not, it is probably unclear to many people, most notably employees and target customers.
- Is it clear what type of organization you are (driving or driven) and the role of marketing to support innovation?
- What is the prime source of your competitive advantage (cost leadership or some form of segmentation)?

- Does the organization have the three key capabilities (elicitation, process flexibility, logistics) to provide mass-customized products?
- Is the organization's business model compelling and widely understood?
- Are there accounting procedures in place to link marketing actions to internal processes and financial performance?

DELL COMPUTER:DRIVING ITS MARKETS

History

Since its foundation in 1984, when Michael Dell started selling PCs from his college dorm, the DELL Computer company has grown into one of the top PC sellers in most of the 170 markets in which it competes. DELL has achieved this market position through its unique business strategy—it was the first major PC company to sell custom-built PCs directly to end-users. Since its inception, the company has refined its internal business processes and its direct marketing approach so that it has a lower cost structure and a sharper customer focus than most of its competitors.

Innovation—both inside the company and in its relationship with customers—has been the defining characteristic of this company.

Corporate Strategy: Direct Mass Customization

DELL has carved out a long-term, defensible position in arguably one of the world's most competitive markets. It has achieved this through an innovative combination of products, after-sales service, and marketing.

The bulk of DELL's sales are PCs and servers made from industry standard components available to any competitor. Hence, it has effectively no superior technical design, reliability, quality, or intellectual property.[26] Like the other PC manufacturers, the (branded) hardware (e.g. the Intel processor) and the operating system (Windows from Microsoft) are almost commodities. Service is also not an area where DELL is a clear leader. All the major manufacturers offer customer support—although some better than others. As a marketer, DELL is no better than the other big brands. It does have the high-profile Michael Dell, but he does not actually 'sell' computers.

What DELL has done is create a mass-customization production process and a direct selling process that has enabled it to form a special type of relationship with a special type of customer. It has also effectively 'branded' this strategy in the minds of consumers—people know that DELL stands for both 'direct sales' and 'build your own computer,' two of its marketing slogans.

Most computer manufacturers design, produce, distribute, and sell their products in a fairly standard sequence. This process involves forecasting demand (which is difficult to do in a fast-changing market) and holding inventory—of components for production and finished goods for sale (both of which are expensive). Not DELL. It takes an order for a desktop PC directly from a customer (increasingly over the Internet) and *then* it builds the CPU to these specifications. When the CPU is finished and tested and the software installed (in less than 5 hours from order), a courier will pick it up from DELL and the monitor and keyboard from a supplier's warehouse for delivery to the customer. This process has a number of advantages:

- Component suppliers are electronically linked into DELL's order-processing system (Valuechain.dell.com) and are located near DELL's factory. This allows DELL to achieve faster component inventory turnover than a typical competitor and thus have lower inventory carrying costs.

- There is no inventory of finished goods that can become obsolete when demand wanes or technology changes.

- Once installed, the Internet is a low-cost way to receive orders and provide after-sales service for most customers.

- DELL's total costs of production are less than most of its competitors. Add to this no dealer mark-ups, and there is considerable scope for the company to offer its products at a lower price.

- Customer orders represent a continual 'reading' of the desires of the marketplace.

Target Customers

For innovation inside the company to pay off, a segment of customers must be willing and able to buy direct. A look at DELL's website indicates that the company segments its market into four broad groups: business, education, government, and home and home office. Further analysis reveals that business customers are segmented according to their revenue and number of employees. For example, there are the Enterprises (Fortune 500 companies), large corporates (Fortune 501 to 2,000 companies), accounts (400–2,000 employees), and small businesses (<400 employees). However, such demographic and firmographic segmentation provides only a very limited understanding of DELL's target customers.

Typically, the type of customer that warms to the 'design your own PC offer' is one that is experienced and confident—either through extensive prior use of computers and/or previous purchases. When they first entered the market, they tended to be price conscious. Now they tend to have a broader view of value, namely, customized hardware and software for a competitive price. Customization gives these customers a clear value add and a feeling of being in control. It also means that they get exactly what they want and can afford. Hence, DELL appeals to a special type of customer that is willing to invest the time and effort to think about exactly what they want a computer to do for them, and what hardware and software is needed to achieve these goals. DELL describes the overall benefit they seek as achieving a lower total cost of ownership (TCO). (This is similar to the IKEA customer value proposition described earlier.)

DELL's customer value proposition can be described as a customer-designed (i.e. better) product at a very competitive price, targeted to a DIY-type of customer. To use an old Apple Computer advertising slogan—DELL provided its customers with 'the power to be your best'. This value proposition was delivered through direct contact between DELL and the customer—at the time of purchase, and post-sale via the company's customer support services. This often led to a stronger relationship being developed between company and customer. To date, this has been a very successful formula.

However, periodically DELL seems to lose its focus. For example, it pioneered direct selling, but in 1990 it entered the retail market—only to withdraw in 1994. Recently, the company has decided to try to sell office equipment—a questionable extension of the DELL brand.

NOTES

1. See, for example, J. G. Davis and T. M. Devinney, *The Essence of Corporate Strategy* (Sydney: Allen & Unwin, 1997) for a discussion of the core concepts of strategy.
2. R. Carnegie and M. Butlin, *Managing the Innovating Enterprise* (Melbourne: Business Council of Australia, 1993), p. 57.
3. See R. F. Hartley, *Marketing Mistakes* (New York: John Wiley, 2001), chapters 2–5.
4. J. Carlzon, *Moments of Truth* (New York: HarperCollins, 1987).
5. M. Lanning, *Delivering Profitable Value* (Oxford: Capstone, 1998).
6. P. Weill and M. R. Vitale, *Place to Space* (Boston: Harvard Business School Press, 2001), p. 5.
7. R. A. Kerin and R. A. Peterson, *Strategic Marketing Problems* (Upper Saddle River, NJ: Prentice Hall International, 2001), pp. 460–2; W. Hansen, *Principles of Internet Marketing* (Cincinnati, OH: South-Western College Publishing, 2000), chapter 5.
8. From Weill and Vitale (2001), chapter 2.
9. G. Dowling, *Creating Corporate Reputations* (Oxford: Oxford University Press, 2001).
10. This example comes from M. Agrawl, T. V. Kumaresh, and G. A. Mercer, 'The False Promise of Mass Customisation', *McKinsey Quarterly*, 3 (2001), 62–71.
11. J. Magretta, 'Why Business Models Matter', *Harvard Business Review* (May 2002), 86–92.
12. M. Porter, *Competitive Advantage* (New York: Free Press, 1985), pp. 33–61.

13. From Davis and Devinney (1997), pp. 61–70.
14. From Davis and Devinney (1997), p. 62.
15. D. Fites, 'Make Your Dealers Your Partners', *Harvard Business Review* (March–April 1996), 84–95.
16. SBUs are organizational units that compete in well-defined markets serving distinct groups of customers with well-defined families of products and services.
17. R. E. Kordupleski, R. T. Rust, and A. J. Zahorik, 'Why Improving Quality Doesn't Improve Quality (Or Whatever Happened to Marketing?)', *California Management Review*, 35, 3 (1993), 82–95.
18. The 4Ps/marketing mix framework is one of the most enduring in marketing: N. H. Borden, 'The Concept of the Marketing Mix', *Journal of Advertising Research* (June 1964), 197–208; E. J. McCarthy, *Basic Marketing: A Managerial Approach* (Homewood, IL: Richard D. Irwin, 1960).
19. For a good insight into the world of Harley-Davidson, read J. Schouten and J. McAlexander, 'Subcultures of Consumption: an Ethnography of the New Bikers', *Journal of Consumer Research*, 22, 1 (June 1995), 43–61.
20. K. Ohmae, 'The Strategic Triangle and Business Strategy', *McKinsey Quarterly* (Winter 1983), 9–24.
21. P. Kotler, *Marketing Management* (Upper Saddle River, NJ: Prentice Hall, 1997).
22. R. Srivastava, T. Shervani, and L. Fahey, 'Marketing, Business Processes and Shareholder Value: An Organisationally Embedded View of Marketing Activities and the Discipline of Marketing', *Journal of Marketing*, 63, Special Issue (1999), 168–179.
23. D. Solomons, *Divisional Performance: Measurement and Control* (Homewood, IL: Richard D. Irwin, 1965).
24. R. Srivastava, T. Shervani, and L. Fahey, 'Market-Based Assets and Shareholder Value: A Framework for Analysis', *Journal of Marketing*, 62, 1 (1998), 2–18.
25. ARPU is used here as one of the primary drivers of an organization's net cash flow from customers because it has been shown that this is the primary driver of the lifetime value of a customer to a company. See, for example, W. Reinartz and V. Kumar, 'On the Profitability of Long-Life Customers in a Noncontractrual Setting: An Empirical Investigation and Implications for Marketing', *Journal of Marketing*, 64, 4 (2000), 17–35.
26. J. N. Sheth and R. S. Sisodia, 'Feeling the Heat', *Marketing Management*, 4, 2 (1995), 8–23.

3

Industry and Market Analysis

Over the last fifty years the disciplines of economics, strategy, and marketing have gathered many insights into how markets 'work'. This chapter introduces some of this knowledge, or to use the terminology of Chapter 1, some structural frameworks and market-sensing principles. This knowledge defines the terrain on which companies compete—the opportunities and threats in a SWOT analysis—and is a crucial element in marketing planning. And, as one of the world's great strategists has attested:

> Know your enemy, know yourself, and your victory will not be threatened.
> Know the terrain, know the weather, and your victory will be complete
>
> Sun Tsu, *The Art of War.*

This chapter complements Chapter 2 by drawing attention to the environment in which organizations operate and compete. This environment is analysed from two complementary perspectives. In Part A of the chapter industry dynamics are considered. Here the focus is on understanding the nature of competition and cooperation in markets. The problem of price wars is used to illustrate some of the triggers that initiate competition and the dynamics involved. As noted in Chapter 2, one of the criticisms of marketing strategy formulation and programme development is that marketing managers often do not consider how competitors will react to their initiatives.

Part B of this chapter examines market evolution. There are two complementary reasons for examining the broad patterns of change in a market. One is that successful organizations take an outside–inside view of their business. Change detected in its early stages often represents an opportunity or threat to which the organization can respond. The second reason is that many customer needs emerge from changes in the social environment. For example, the ageing populations and increasing life expectancy of people in many countries signal the growing need for government programmes, and products and services, to cater for this group. Studying the evolution of markets and particular products also sets the context for Chapter 4, which focuses directly on understanding consumer behaviour.

PART A

Industry Analysis and Competitive Rivalry

Framework 1—The Five Forces Model

One of the more popular frameworks managers use to describe an industry and its competitive structure is the Five Forces Model introduced by Michael Porter.[1] This framework is a good way to describe the economics of competition. It helps to identify the constraints under which a company operates and the nature of the rivalry that will exist within the industry. The generic framework is shown in Figure 3.1. Some investment banks use the Five Forces Model as a qualitative tool to better understand the relative growth opportunities between industry sectors. The rationale here is that industries with a less competitive structure will have higher rates of return that will stimulate the inflow of capital.[2] A detailed example is provided at the end of this chapter—'Worldwide Wine—Australia'.

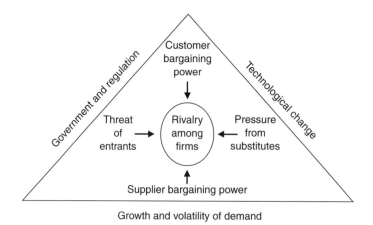

Figure 3.1. The Five Forces Model

The usefulness of the Five Forces Model to a marketing manager derives from the guidance it provides for gathering information about the industry participants competing in a market (segment). As noted in Chapter 1, this is a supply-side view of the market. Use of this framework has also revealed some basic insights about the attractiveness and the level of rivalry in a market. For example:[3]

- Strong customer buying power tends to force prices down, create demands for increased quality and free services, and set competitors against each other—at the expense of seller profitability.
- The availability of substitute products and services places a limit on prices.
- Suppliers tend to be powerful when they are concentrated or organized, when the supplied product is important to the buyer, and when customer switching costs are high.
- Easy-to-enter markets soon become crowded and often resort to price wars as the dominant form of competition.
- Rivalry is most intense when competitors are equally powerful. When one competitor clearly dominates (having a market share 50 per cent larger than the second biggest organization), rivalry is more subdued.

A key issue that troubles marketing managers is the dynamics of competition or rivalry. This is the ultimate game of marketing strategy for many managers. Some of the concepts of marketing suggest that rivalry is really war. For example, there are price wars to capture market share, advertising campaigns, companies introduce price-fighting brands to damage competitors' brands, competitive positioning strategies are created, competitive intelligence is collected, customer loyalty programmes are launched, product/ market battlefields are mapped out, etc. Translations of old books about warfare are popular—such as Sun Tsu's *The Art of War*, Alexander the Great's *Art of Strategy*, and von Clausewitz's *On War*. New books about marketing warfare are even more popular—such as Al Ries and Jack Trout's, *Marketing Warfare* (New York: McGraw-Hill, 1986). The ultimate expression of marketing-as-war can be summed up with a quote from the US author Gore Vidal:

It is not enough to succeed. Others must fail.

There are two problems with the marketing as warfare approach. One is the damage done to the antagonists and the bystanders. For example, a commonly quoted statistic about the US airline price wars of 1990–3 was that the airline industry lost more money during this period than it had previously made in its entire commercial history.[4] As profits tumbled, so did levels of customer service. The second problem with the marketing as warfare approach is that in many markets you do not need to beat a competitor to win—there is enough pie for everyone to share. In fact, in some new markets, it is actually better to have more rather than fewer competitors. More suppliers provide added legitimacy to what is being sold in a new market, and thus help it become established and grow—such as with Internet services, mobile phones, personal digital assistants, and MBA degrees.

Framework 2—Co-opetition

If marketing strategy should not be war-like competition, and a look outside the office suggests that it is not about peaceful cooperation, then what should it be? A new perspective suggests that 'co-opetition' might be the answer.[5] (See also http://mayet.som.yale.edu/co-opetition.) Here, the idea is for companies that cooperate when creating new markets and compete in mature markets. Or in other words, they practice 'enlightened self-interest'. Co-opetition is a new mindset for many marketing managers.

In the world of co-opetition, there are four crucial parties:

- customers
- suppliers
- competitors
- complementors.

Each party has a role to play and there are interdependencies among them. But first, two important definitions.

If customers value your organization's product or service alone *less* when they have another organization's product, then this organization/product is a *competitor*. For example, just after you buy a Lexus, you value the equivalent BMW and Mercedes Benz a lot less. Nothing surprising here as the competitors are in the same industry making the same type of product. However, remember the example of the Polaroid camera in Chapter 1. In this example, when the young people bought the instant camera, they then valued going to a movie a lot less. Here, Polaroid and the local movie theatre are competitors because they both satisfy the same need, namely, tonight's entertainment. The first example defines competitors from a supply perspective, while the second one is based on customer demand. Both perspectives should be used.

If customers value your organization's product alone *more* when they have another organization's product, then this organization/product is a *complementor*. Examples of complementary products are: cars and auto insurance, television sets and video-cassette recorders, pies and tomato sauce, wine and cheese, personal computers (PCs) and printers, etc. Examples of complementary companies are: Intel and Microsoft, Netscape and www.everything, banks and real-estate agents, commercial law firms and merchant banks, airlines and travel agents, etc.

Sometimes, companies will be competitors and complementors at the same time—Air Canada, Air New Zealand, All Nippon Airways, Austrian Airways, British Midland (BMI), Lufthansa, Mexicana Airlines, SAS, Singapore Airlines, Thai Airways, and United Airlines are all members of the Star Alliance. All those car dealerships lined up beside each other on the same road complement each other by making it easier for buyers to 'shop', and compete because they are after your business. The crucial issues in situations such as these are which effect dominates—competition or cooperation—and how to manage these effects?

Figure 3.2 shows the interdependencies among the four parties as a market map. This is called a 'Value Net' by the creators of this framework because each arrow offers opportunities to create and/or capture value in the marketplace. In this sense, Figure 3.2 is a more expansive version of Figure 1.3, which focused on the Organization–Customer link.

To operationalize the Value Net framework is quite simple. First, identify all the parties, namely, major competitors, complementors, suppliers, and segments of customers. Second, describe the current relationships (the eight arrows in Figure 3.2) between the parties. For example, in relationship #1, who are the organization's target customers and how are they served (Figure 1.3)? In relationship #8, as we will see in Chapter 4 and other parts of this book, a key issue is whether or not your customers are also the customers of your competitors. (The answer turns out to be yes most of the time.) Finally, describe the type of relationship you want to develop

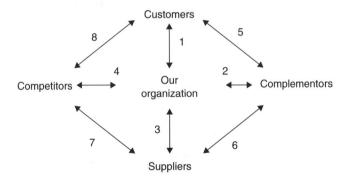

Figure 3.2. The co-opetition value net

with each set of parties (i.e. arrows 1–4). This step is the key to implementing relationship marketing. As mentioned in Chapter 1, managers are struggling to implement this style of marketing in B2C situations because they do not articulate, to both customers and employees, what type of 'relationship' they seek to foster. (More on this in Chapter 11.)

The Value Net framework is useful because it provides a complete map of the organization's relationships, and thus helps avoid limited strategic thinking (such as 'let's outsmart the competition'). It is also useful to reinforce an outside–inside view of the organization.

Framework 3—Competitor Profiling

Before any type of competitor analysis can be practised, managers need to identify who are their competitors. Obvious, I hear you say. Research, however, indicates that for many companies this is not the case.[6] First, managers tend to name too few competitors—three major ones and another three or four minor ones. Second, there is a strong tendency to identify competitors using supply-side as opposed to demand-side variables. This is not very insightful if satisfying customer needs is the key to success. Third, many managers all but ignore identifying potential competitors. Not every organization is as bold as General Electric, which in 1999 ran an exercise called 'destroyyourbusiness.com' to force managers to consider how the Internet might make them vulnerable to unexpected competition. Hence, as market conditions change, marketers need to continually reassess who their competitors are, and how they compete.

Table 3.1 lists some of the more common supply and demand factors that are used to profile an organization's competitors. (Many of these could also be used to profile complementors.) A key insight here is that when it is difficult to determine a competitor's objectives and strategy, one should look for leading indicators of future commitments, such as investments in plant and equipment, an increase in employee training, the appointment of new senior managers, etc.

Two supply-side factors are particularly important not to ignore. One is the dependence of the competitor on the market in which you are competing—the greater the importance, the more likely a swift and savage competitive reaction. A second is the key manager's level of accountability for meeting targets in the market. Often this is specified in the manager's key performance indicators (KPIs). When KPIs include specific target outcomes, managers become very motivated to achieve them.

Table 3.1. Competitor profiling

Supply-side factors	*Demand-side factors*
Corporate Objectives (e.g. % growth)	Customer segments—needs/wants, size, profitability, etc.
Capabilities and weaknesses	Customer decision-making
Financials (e.g. debt, costs, revenues)	Brands considered by customers
Competitive strategy (Figure 2.4)	Relative brand preferences
Marketing strategy and tactics— pricing, advertising, etc.	Brand loyalty—single-brand versus polygamous
	Demands for quality
Organizational culture	Price sensitivity
Suppliers and distributors	Customer switching costs
Key managers—their KPIs and competitive mentality	Past purchase history—heavy or light user
Competitive reaction pattern (e.g. fast or slow; broad or selective)	How, when, where, and why the purchase occurs

The key demand-side issue is to understand, from the target customer's point of view, what products and services actually can fulfil the expressed or latent need you are trying to satisfy. As we will see in Chapter 4, consumers in a broad range of markets—from high-level legal services to ready-to-eat breakfast cereals—typically buy a number of competing brands during the course of a year. Thus it is crucial to use the demand-side factors in Table 3.1 to profile the brands used and the relative strength of preference for each one. Internal customer databases seldom contain this crucial information because most simply record sales from your organization.

In essence, what Table 3.1 shows is that competitors should be profiled on exactly the same characteristics that are used to describe your organization and its markets. From this perspective, it is possible to identify two broad types of competitors, namely, those like you and those who are different in some important way(s). For example, some of the forces that lead to similarity are:

- imitating a particular competitor
- following the lead of a dominant firm
- serving the same markets
- having a similar business model
- managers in the industry migrating among competitors and/or having similar education, training, or career profile
- a strong industry tradition—vocabulary, norms, customs, and inertia.

In markets where competitors are similar, some organizations ask a small group of their managers to role-play particular competitors to help forecast how they will act in a market.

Price Wars

> A dangerous tool from the toolbox of limited strategic thinkers
>
> Anonymous.

Arguably one of the best illustrations of the above quote is known as 'Marlboro Friday'. Here's the story in a nutshell.[7] In the early 1990s the major cigarette companies were finding that their premium cigarettes were losing share to discount brands. To counter this trend, on 2 April 1993 Philip Morris announced a 15 per cent price reduction on its premium brands, including the leading brand Marlboro. Immediately following the announcement, RJR Nabisco and BAT industries reduced the price of their flagship brands. From a market share perspective, Philip Morris' action had the desired effect—market share started to climb. However, from a profit perspective, the effect was disastrous. At the end of 1993, Philip Morris profits were down by 46 per cent and those of RJR Nabisco were down by 43 per cent. (BAT's profits did not fall as much because they were less reliant on cigarettes.) What was even worse, when the stock-market opened for trading on the Monday following the price cut, the Philip Morris stock price fell from US$64 per share to US$49 per share—effectively wiping 23 per cent off the market value of the company. Not bad for a 15 per cent price cut! The anti-smoking lobby also generated plenty of negative publicity about how lower prices would entice more new smokers into the market.

This section uses a five-part approach to analysing price wars. First, it reviews the general industry factors that make price wars likely to happen. Second, it identifies the events that trigger this warfare. Third, reasons why they continue are outlined. Fourth, some common-sense strategies for avoiding price wars are noted. Finally, some strategies and tactics to fight a price war are suggested. Following this, the discussion broadens to look at defensive strategies in a more general context.

Industry Risk Factors

Research by economists, game theorists, strategists, and marketers has uncovered a number of conditions that facilitate the ignition of a price war.

Table 3.2. Risk factors for price wars

	Risk of a price war	
Characteristics	*Lower*	*Higher*
Industry		
Capacity utilization	High	Low
A financially weak competitor	No	Yes
Ratio of fixed to variable costs	Low	High
A recognized price leader exists	Yes	No
Barriers to exiting the market	Low	High
New entrants to the market	No	Yes
Market		
Stage of product life cycle	Growth	Stable/decline
Customers	Dispersed	Concentrated
Market share	Stable	Falling
Economic downturn	Early warning	Unexpected
Product		
Type	Differentiated	Commodity
Price visibility to customers	Low	High
Customers		
Brand loyalty	High	Low
Price sensitivity	Low	High
Switching costs	High	Low

Table 3.2 lists the most important of these factors. Some of these are inter-related, such as the ratio of fixed to variable costs and barriers to exiting the market, while others are largely free-standing, such as whether or not a new company has entered the market. These factors should be considered with some care because it is their profile that increases or decreases the risk of a price war igniting. Also, while there is empirical and theoretical support for each factor individually, we know less about how they work in combination.

Starting Price Wars

In the Marlboro Friday example it was falling market share that triggered the price war. In many consumer-goods companies these figures are collected on a routine basis and they enjoy strong credibility at all levels of management—hence, they tend to be acted on rather than argued with. Also, there is a tendency to attribute changes in market share to changes in the relative marketing activities of the competitors. This notion of linking a brand's marketing activities and spending to that of its competitors is quite common. For example, prices are often set after considering the prices of other brands at the same quality level in the category. Also, advertising budgets are often set with reference to the amount spent by the dominant brand in the market. (The idea here is to maintain a certain 'share of voice' in the market.)

Another market-share based reason that price wars start is that there is a belief that increased share provides greater market power and thus pricing discretion. This strategy often plays out as a price cut, or the introduction of a new brand at a low price, in the hope of driving one or more competitors from the market. The problem with this strategy is that it may only succeed in wounding the competitor. And when such a competitor has less profit, they have less to lose, and thus may become more aggressive.

One organizational culture issue that contributes to starting a price war is that brand managers can face severe consequences if they do not react to a competitor, when with hindsight they should have. On the other hand, there is less consequence for reactions that, with hindsight, would seem to have been unnecessary. Thus, there is an asymmetry in the consequences for reacting—especially for such a visible aspect of the marketing mix as price. This effect, when coupled with short time horizons (quarterly versus annual results), and objectives such as 'grow sales' rather than maximize profits, can foster quick-fire responses to competitors.[8]

Sometimes the organizational culture of a company and the measures it uses to reward and control its managers encourages competition—either starting a fight or responding quickly at the first hint of aggression from a competitor. For example, August Busch III, the fourth generation of his family to head the world's biggest beer company, Anheuser-Busch, is a classic case in point.[9] His philosophy is total market dominance backed up by a 'get 'em before they get you' attitude. Anheuser-Busch is a very competitor-focused company and would not think twice about defending its territory. This style of company often uses market share as a key metric of success. One of the side-effects of this measure is that it encourages managers to think of business as a zero-sum game—what I win, you lose.

Price wars have also been known to occur when one industry participant misreads the actions of a competitor. For example, what is thought to be a long-term price cut may be nothing more than a clearance price to get rid of unwanted stock. In the automotive industry, 'end-of-model clearance sales' are promoted to entice customers and to signal to competitors the true reason for the sale. The broader issue involved here is that many organizations lack good information about their competitors. Thus they can be surprised by new information and they may respond in a way that is unnecessary. For example, one price war in an industrial electronics market started when an industry trade journal misreported the total market volume as 15 per cent higher than it actually was. Each of the four major competitors responded by dropping their prices to recover market share that was never lost.[10]

The final reason that price wars start can be labelled as management stupidity. This occurs in two instances. First, some wars have started because a price reduction was made on the assumption that the big, well-established incumbents would either not notice, or if they did, they would not respond. The Australian domestic airline industry has seen this scenario played out twice by Compass Airlines in the early 1990s and then again by Impulse Airlines in 2001. The problem here was a new entrant competing head-to-head on price with two bigger, better capitalized, well-entrenched, and nasty competitors. Both the new airlines ran out of money before the incumbents. The second instance occurs when one organization attacks another organization's favourite product—or to use the vernacular, they attack the 'family jewels'. For example, in the market for professional services such as auditing, when a prize client puts its work out to tender, a low-price competitor may win the work, but the incumbent may retaliate with a similar low-ball quote for one of the attacker's prize clients.

Why Price Wars Continue

There are five common reasons why, once started, price wars continue:

- The psychology of entrapment—the more a manager or his or her organization invests in a series of price cutting decisions, the harder it is to walk away from this strategy. This is especially true when the manager's career is on the line.
- Previous price cuts train customers to ask for more price cuts. This in turn puts pressure on all competitors to keep lowering prices.
- The price of many (technology-based) products declines in real terms over time. Hence, customers expect new versions of these products to be cheaper. If one competitor can meet this expectation, then others are forced to follow.
- Poor marketing—the product has no strong customer value proposition or it has not been differentiated from other brands. When pressure builds to maintain or increase sales, price is the easiest and quickest thing to change.

- Barriers to exit—to protect investments too big to write off, organizations will try to maintain their sales volume at any price above marginal cost. This is often the case in continuous-production industries like aluminium, chemicals, and steel.

Avoiding Price Wars

The following are some tactics different organizations have used to avoid a price war:

- Do not attack a big competitor with an identical product or service at a lower price.
- Keep customers focused on value (benefits relative to price), not price. (All those retail advertisements that shout 'low, low price this weekend' train people to focus on price.)
- Understand competitors' strategies—do not misread their reasons for changing their price.
- Establish a reputation for retaliation as outlined in the next section.
- Sell at various price points—if a customer can not afford the high-priced version, then sell them the lower-priced version—do not discount.
- Pre-announce price moves and the reasons why. (The banks often do this as follows: 'We are lowering our interest rate because the cost of funds on the market is now lower.')
- Become the recognized industry price leader.
- Talk publicly at industry gatherings about the horrors of a price war.
- Use a research company or a consultant to gather and publicize industry information about prices and sales levels.
- Have the industry association publish a recommended price list— a practice followed by some health professions.

Fighting Price Wars

There is not much reliable advice about how to fight a price war. The reason for this is because so many different factors can cause them to start and continue. Hence, the advice that follows should be considered as advisory. It is also restricted to an organization's first few moves. The underlying logic, however, is a tried and tested approach from game theory, namely, a strategy called 'tit-for-tat'.

Tit-for-tat is a simple strategy—I do to you tomorrow what you did to me today. And I do not escalate my response above yours. It has proven to be a very robust strategy for eliciting cooperation in a wide range of situations. The reasons for this are that it is:

- *Clear*—both parties know what is coming.
- *Nice*—it never initiates an attack.
- *Provokable*—it retaliates instantly—like for like.
- *Forgiving*—if the transgressor returns to cooperative behaviour the other party will follow.

Tit-for-tat is not designed to beat a rival; it is a strategy to wear them down. It is also a strategy that works best with rivals that have similar payoffs in a game. For example, if one big company has decided to drive a smaller rival out of the market, then the strategy would be unlikely to keep the big predator at bay. Tit-for-tat is also a strategy that is premised on the fact that both parties have good information about the other. When it is difficult to interpret the (cooperative or cheating) actions of the other party, any mistake will echo back and forth. Also, this strategy by itself lacks a way of saying that 'enough is enough'. (Someone has to signal that they would like to stop.)

When fighting a price war in a fog, that is, in an environment where it is difficult to read the other party's signals, a variation of tit-for-tat may be worth considering. Here, the strategy is to begin cooperating and to continue with this position until the other party defects a number of times. At this point, initiate a tit-for-tat strategy—sometimes with your 'tat' bigger than their 'tit'.

Defence

Defence against competitors is one of the most important areas of strategic marketing. For example, for every new product or service launched there are a number of existing ones that need to defend their customer base. One of the early attempts to articulate how managers should respond to a competitor was captured in the decision-making model called Defender.[11] The question addressed by this model was: 'When faced with the entry of a new competitor in a mature market, how should an incumbent adapt its marketing mix in order to maximise its profits?' Subsequent research has shown that the prescriptions of this model were quite generalizable.[12] For example, two general prescriptions from the model are that the brand most similar to the new entrant should (*a*) reduce its price, and (*b*) reduce its general (or 'awareness') advertising. Another prescription is that after the entry of a new brand, a dominant brand with a market share over 50 per cent should increase marketing spending (e.g. on its distribution and 'positioning' advertising).

During the 1970s and 1980s a number of mathematical decision-making models like Defender were formulated and tested. Many were made available commercially and were popular with some of the big consumer-goods companies. While they focused on a range of topics, at their heart was the issue of how to compete more effectively. These models capture much of the scientific approach to marketing. Thankfully, Gary Lilien has reviewed many of these models and produced PC-based versions of some of them.[13]

What is somewhat surprising about this stream of research is the relatively few robust generalizations about competition and defence that are forthcoming. There are three interrelated reasons for this. One concerns the assumptions and/or data sets used by the modellers. These are often so specific that generalization becomes meaningless. The second reason is that the arena in which competition takes place is so complex, that what seems to work in one case may not work in another. The third reason can be called the *paradox of the strategic principle*. When something becomes ingrained as an industry-wide 'if, do' principle, it will stimulate others to think about how they can compete differently. This has been the way that many a military battle has been won.

In an attempt to overcome the first two problems noted above, market researchers are starting to watch how managers actually compete and draw insights from their behaviour. Two interesting results are:

- Consistently high levels of marketing activity relative to competitors helps a company gain a reputation as a credible defender.[14]
- When faced with a new product entry, managers should (*a*) respond quickly, (*b*) use as few marketing mix elements as possible, and (*c*) use the instrument with the highest elasticity—that is, the one with the biggest impact on consumer preferences.[15]

Recently John Roberts has suggested that a defender can use three broad strategies to (*a*) try to reduce the appeal of the attacker, and/or (*b*) retard the rate at which the attacker gains share.[16] The strategies are:

- enhance, and communicate the defendant's strengths—a positive strategy
- increase customer switching costs—a negative strategy, and/or
- expose and exploit the entrant's weaknesses—a negative strategy.

To use a strategy of communicating strengths presupposes that the defendant has some strengths that customers perceive as unique and valuable to them. Southwest Airlines used this strategy when, soon after its entry into the US market, it was attacked by the major incumbent, Braniff International Airways, in an attempt to drive it out of the market. (When they entered the market they attacked with lower prices and a fun-loving attitude to service. However, soon after their entry they became a defendant.) Southwest's strengths were that it had brought competition to the market, more flight schedules, and better service to the commuters of Houston, Dallas-Fort Worth, and San Antonio. Also, by flying point-to-point rather than through a major airline hub, its reliability was higher than that of Braniff and the other major airline serving the region at that time—Texas International Airlines. (Southwest survived and went on to become one of the world's most successful airlines.) This example also highlights the fact that consumers often use different criteria to evaluate attackers and defenders.

A good example of a negative strategy targeted at slowing down the rate at which customers defect was AT&T's 'Get it in writing' advertising campaign. When it was defending its customer base against other telephone companies that were offering a lower price, AT&T suggested that before switching, customers should ask the attacker for a written statement of their potential savings. This had intuitive appeal to customers, and slowed down their defection. It also made the attacker's job that much harder by doubling the paperwork and increasing the time it took to convert a prospect.

One strategy that is not advisable is to try to convince customers that the weaknesses they may attribute to the defendant are unfounded. All this will do is to get them to focus on the defendant's weaknesses. Another dangerous strategy is for an incumbent, especially if they are the market leader, to expose and exploit the weakness of a new entrant. To many customers this appears to be a bullying tactic.

RECAP

One criticism of marketing managers made by their senior managers is that they do not focus enough attention on understanding competitors. This criticism can be expressed in some quite colourful language. For example: 'They (the marketing managers) either think that competitors are stupid or brain-dead!' As the examples described in this chapter testify, competitors are seldom asleep.

Knowing one's competitors is critical to designing an effective marketing strategy and the programmes to support this strategy. It is also an important aspect of developing an outside–inside view of the organization. However, some organizations take this perspective too far and in the process they lose sight of their customers. A competitor-focused organization is one whose actions are dictated by trying to beat or match those of competitors and whose KPIs are calibrated too heavily against competitors. In contrast, a customer-focused organization concentrates on creating and claiming customer value (Figure 1.3). For these organizations, competitors are important, but only to the extent that they inhibit the organization achieving its goals.

KEY CONCEPTS

- *Competitor*—customers value your product (or service) less when they have someone else's product than when they have your product alone.
- *Complementor*—customers value your product (or service) more when they have someone else's product than when they have your product alone.
- *Competition*—the damaging actions used by organizations when competing for sales within a market.
- *Co-opetition*—the cooperative actions used by organizations when creating new markets.
- *Tit-for-tat*—a variation of the 'eye-for-an-eye' rule of behaviour.

KEY FRAMEWORKS

- *Five Forces Model*—Figure 3.1
- *Value Net*—Figure 3.2
- *Competitor–Complementor Profile*—Table 3.1
- *Price War Risk Factors*—Table 3.2.

KEY QUESTIONS

- Is there a concise summary of the characteristics of the competitive rivalry in your market available?
- Is there an accurate profile of your key competitors and complementators (e.g. in the marketing plan)?
- Have the competitors who are most likely to start a price war been identified? And are the factors that will trigger a price war being monitored? And is there a plan to respond to a price war?
- Is there a plan in place for defending your key markets?

Having looked closely at industry factors and competitive rivalry, attention now turns to examining how markets evolve. Here, the focus shifts away from supply-side issues to the demand-side of the equation, namely, customers and the forces that shape their needs and wants.

WORLDWIDE WINE.AUSTRALIA (WWW.AU)

Wine is one of the world's most fragmented industries, a business with an annual turnover of $150 billion, thin profits, approximately one million individual producers, and no dominant companies or global brands. This situation has inspired the following industry joke:

> The first miracle from Jesus was to turn water into wine.
> The industry is still waiting for another miracle, to turn wine into profit.

The betting is that the Australian wine industry has a good chance of showing him how to do this.

Wine is a uniquely nationalistic business, especially in the Old World wine producing countries like France, Italy, Spain, and Germany. Here, it is predominantly an agricultural business subject to climatic variables and held captive by its history and traditions. While this scenario adorns wines from these regions with uniqueness and allure, it focuses the industry more on being supply driven than demand driven.

In the last decade, as wine consumption has spread around the world, there is more attention being given to customer demand. One catalyst for this new focus is the big retail chains like Sainsbury's in Great Britain. The buying power and product requirements (e.g. for screw-top closures rather than cork) of a big retail chain can have a significant impact on demand for various styles of wine and the price points at which they will be offered. This in turn can affect a wine producer's economies of scale and scope.

From a more general trade perspective, there is an unhealthy proliferation of brands. In a liquor shop wine brands can take up to 60 per cent of the retail space, but only produce 35 per cent of the profits. This diverse selection of wine labels has stock management implications for retailers and can create confusion among the majority of customers—which of the twenty different brands of chardonnay should one choose? One forecast is that many retailers will eventually be forced to carry just 15–20 core wine brands.[i] Complementing this set of wine brands will be a revolving set of new brands for those people who want to try something different. These brands will be priced and selected to suit the retailer's customer profile.

---

[i] For example, in June 2003 the *Penfolds* name was used to brand eleven varieties of white wine, twenty-one red wines, and six fortified wines.

Why Australia?

Industry forecasters suggest that in the next decade the worldwide wine industry will start to rationalize. Figure 3.3 summarizes many of the important forces shaping competition in this industry. The key question arising from this analysis is whether any Australian company can play a leading role in reshaping the worldwide wine industry.

Australia lacks the history and hang-ups of European producers. It also lacks a vast domestic market such as exists in the United States. It has a number of different geographically separate major wine growing regions (Hunter Valley, Margaret River, Clare Valley, Coonawarra, and Barossa Valley) that enable it to produce a variety of wines and to mitigate any climatic catastrophes. The Australian companies have also developed world-class wine-making technology. These factors combine to enable the country to produce a range of good quality wines in a quantity far exceeding the requirements of the domestic market. Hence, the need to export.

In recent years three 'catalyst companies' have emerged in the Australian wine industry—BRL Hardy, Mildara Blass, and Southcorp. These companies are among the top twenty in the world and in the top ten premium wine producers. They are also leading the push to consolidate the world wine industry by expanding their international operations, acquiring foreign production, establishing international distribution networks, and creating companies that appeal to the international capital markets. Most importantly, they are focusing on the needs of the retail market, for example, by building brands in new markets—particularly those countries without a domestic industry like Great Britain.

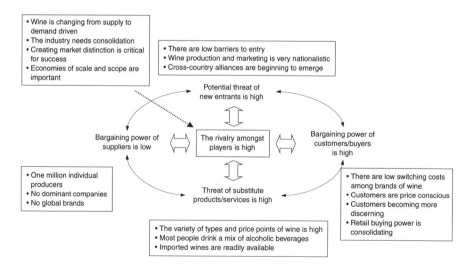

Figure 3.3. The world wine industry

Analysts suggest that over the next decade two or three big multinational wine companies will emerge to reshape the volume side of the industry. They will be dominant in their domestic market, professionally managed (as opposed to run by wine-makers), have access to capital, and adopt a more customer-marketing focus. The two most likely Australian contenders to help drive the worldwide wine market are BRL Hardy and Southcorp.

PART B

Market Analysis

> It is useless to tell a river to stop running. The best thing is to learn how to swim in the direction it is flowing.
>
> The future won't be what it used to be.

These two witticisms capture the challenge of analysing the evolution of markets.

Many years ago the Shell oil company studied thirty long-surviving companies.[17] What they discovered was the importance of market analysis and learning. The managers of these companies were able to change their 'shared mental models' of the marketplace faster than their competitors. This gave them more time to innovate, imitate, and avoid crisis management.

In present-day parlance, what the Shell study uncovered was that organizations could gain a competitive advantage by adopting a market orientation. In Chapter 2 this was labelled as being either market driving or market driven. The premise of this chapter is that market-oriented organizations avoid marketing myopia (referred to in Chapter 1) by better understanding customers' expressed and latent needs, and creating superior solutions to these needs. This generally entails developing good market sensing skills, sharing this information throughout the organization, and making sure that information about customers and competitors is taken into account during planning. While the marketing function often takes prime responsibility for developing a market orientation, it is not necessary that this be so. In some organizations this responsibility lies with cross-functional market segment teams. In small organizations, and many professional service firms, the responsibility lies with senior managers or the partners of the firm. In recognition of the importance of a market orientation, a periodical entitled the *Journal of Market-Focused Management* was launched in 1996.[18]

A market orientation suggests that the organization develop formal systems to regularly:

- analyse broad market trends
- analyse customer product usage and attitudes, decision-making processes, satisfaction, etc.
- update the customer database
- predict changes in customer preferences and how these are distributed throughout the market
- monitor competitors—strategy, capabilities, organizational culture, product/service offerings, new product development, marketing programmes, etc.

This section looks at the first of these issues. The previous section looked at the last issue and the next chapter deals with the remaining issues.

Market Trend Tracking

> Forecasting is difficult, especially about the future.
>
> Victor Borge

The market in which a company competes is influenced by both evolutionary and revolutionary forces. In many cases it is easy to classify something as either evolutionary or disruptive. For example, the changing demographic profile of a country evolves slowly, while the change in a specific piece of legislation that deregulates an industry as has happened for airlines, banking, and electricity in some countries changed the competitive landscape quite quickly. Sometimes, however, it is difficult to tell whether a change will be evolutionary or revolutionary. Consider the Internet. In the latter part of the twentieth century, all bets were that this was a disruptive technology— something that would threaten the existing way of doing business and create new opportunities for new firms. However, at the beginning of the twenty-first century, the picture is less clear. The crash of many Internet-based businesses forced businesspeople, and even some futurologists, to reconsider the potential impact of this technology and the speed with which it would impact on our lives.

There are many other examples of futurologists and business leaders making wild under- or overestimates of the market for specific new products and services. Here are a couple from the IT industry.

- 'I think that there is a world market for maybe five computers'. Thomas J. Watson, Chairman of IBM, 1943.

- 'There is no reason for any individual to want a computer in their home.' Ken Olson, President of Digital Equipment Corporation, 1977.
- '640K ought to be enough for anybody.' Bill Gates, 1981.
- 'One-to-one (consumer) auctions will become the most pervasive form of online commerce.' Stuart Feldman of IBM's T J Watson Research Laboratories, 1999.

While there are many big-trend futurologists, they often come to prominence via the publication of an interesting book. Some of the classics are: Alvin Toffler's *Future Shock* and *The Third Wave*, John Naisbett's *Megatrends, Global Paradox*, and *High Tech-High Touch*, and Faith Popcorn's *The Popcorn Report* and *Clicking*.[19] In Australia, Hugh McKay has written a series of books profiling changes in the socio-demographic landscape (*Reinventing Australia, Generations, Turning Point*) and the economic consultants IBIS World track changes in the economic landscape. In the United Kingdom and United States research companies like MORI (www.mori.com) and Opinion Research Corporation (www.opinionresearch.com) track market trends, as do many major advertising agencies. Exhibit 3.1 provides a sample of what to expect from these gurus.

What is clear from Exhibit 3.1 is that many, if not most, market trends are culture and country dependent. For example, most of the population of countries like Algeria, China, Indonesia, India, North Korea, and South Africa

---

Exhibit 3.1. Trends from Faith Popcorn's *Clicking*

A. *Cashing out*: the impulse to change one's life to a slower but more rewarding pace.

B. *Cocooning*: the impulse to stay inside the house when the outside gets too tough.

C. *Down-aging*: the tendency to act and feel younger than one's age.

D. *Egonomics*: a person's desire to develop an individual profile so that they are seen and treated as different to others.

E. *Fantasy adventure*: people have a growing need for an emotional escape to offset their daily routine.

F. *99 Lives*: this is the desperate state of people who are trying to juggle too many roles and responsibilities.

G. *SOS—Save our society*: the drive to make society more socially responsible.

H. *Small indulgences*: stressed-out people need the occasional emotional indulgence.

I. *Staying alive*: people's drive to live longer and better lives.

J. *The Vigilante Consumer*: the trend against accepting poor quality products and inadequate service.

would not consider many of the trends in Exhibit 3.1 to be realistic options. Also, in countries where religion plays a big part in people's daily lives, this influence would need to be considered. This observation leads naturally to the questions of:

- What factors should managers monitor?
- How should they go about doing this?

The next section introduces two frameworks and the process used to implement each one. The first is simply a list of things to monitor. The second is one of the most enduring frameworks in marketing—the product life cycle.[20] Together they can be used to monitor the evolution of a market.

Market sensing principles and frameworks

#1—The Macro Environment

At a broad level, managers can monitor their markets by scanning six generic forces:

A. *Natural resources.* In countries like Australia, Canada, Chile, Russia, Saudi Arabia, and South Africa that are endowed with vast deposits of minerals and energy, it is important to understand how changes in resource stocks and worldwide prices can affect the general economic and business environment. For example, to a large extent Australia's economic well-being is heavily dependent on its 'dig and deliver' companies that supply coal, iron ore, and natural gas around the world. (Two of the biggest commodity trade flows in the world are black coal and iron ore from Australia to Japan.[21]) The South African company De Beers is the most powerful player in the world diamond trade and has been instrumental in manipulating the supply of industrial and gemstone diamonds. The 1991 Gulf War was fought about oil. Sometimes, the side-effects from the use of various types of natural resources can open up new market opportunities, as we see with the effects of global warming and the development of non-polluting sources of power and products (such as electric cars).

B. *Population.* Changes in the size, composition, distribution, and location of populations are important to monitor especially as they affect social and economic conditions. These patterns can influence the structure of markets and the distribution of consumer preferences. For example, the ageing of many Western populations is putting a strain on the healthcare systems of those countries and at the same time it is opening up opportunities for companies to offer managed care services to older people. The changing structure of the 'family' is another far-reaching population trend. For example, in the city of Sydney in Australia, a significant proportion of adults go home each evening to a place where there is no other adult to talk to. Many radio stations have responded to this trend by including talk-back programmes in their format.

C. *Cultural and religious values*. Religious beliefs and cultural values shape the attitudes and behaviours of populations. In multicultural countries like Australia, Israel, and the United States, some companies are using these variables to segment their markets and target specific ethnic groups. A key concern in many countries is the culture-dampening force of globalization—both its groundswell and its backlash.[22]

D. *Technology*. It comes in many forms—biotechnology, materials technology, medical technology, information technology, etc. It is a fundamental driver of innovation—new ways to work, new products and services, and new companies. It can introduce new competitors—fax machines and e-mail instead of snail-mail. It is becoming more and more pervasive in our lives—from ATM machines to mobile phones. Its effects on consumers can be subtle, complex, and situational. For many people, technology comes with mixed approach-avoidance motivations. Thus for marketers, a key issue is to understand how technology can serve expressed and latent customer needs. Too often in the past technology has been pushed at consumers with the expectation that they will enthusiastically adopt it.

E. *Economic conditions*. Economic systems are characterized by their enormous complexity and if there is one area where the quote that introduced this section seems to be true it is here. In fact, over the years economists have so struggled to model and predict economic conditions that economics has been labelled 'the dismal science'.[23] Notwithstanding this, every country has its array of economic future-tellers—from the Central Bankers through merchant bankers and currency traders to the university economists. Reports and forecasts abound and should be read with great care.

F. *Institutions and rules of the game*. One thing that the discipline of economics alerts us to is the importance of institutions in the design and development of market economies. Briefly, institutions provide the 'rules of the game' by which individuals and companies interact in exchanges. The institutional environment consists of the formal and informal rules emanating from the macro-level aspects of society—the polity, judicial system, cultural norms, and kinship patterns. It is slow to change and defines the rules of business. As businesses become more global, the range and diversity of the institutional environments they face increases. The transition experiences of the Eastern European countries and the economic difficulties of the East Asian 'tiger' economies are forceful reminders of the impact of institutions on management practices.[24]

It is one thing to list the various forces that shape a market, but quite another to spot trends and identify the turning points that expose market threats and opportunities. Many big companies solve this problem by commissioning special reports and/or private briefings from local and visiting overseas future-tellers. Smaller companies generally do not have this luxury. They are forced to monitor the market themselves. While they read what they can find in the public domain, they should also keep a sharp eye on the people and institutions that can mediate the direction and intensity of change.[25] Some of these mediators are:

- politicians—ones with a key social or business agenda
- regulatory agencies—such as price surveillance and trade practices authorities
- financial institutions—such as the Reserve Bank and the national stock exchange
- mass media publications—with opinions on economic, business, and social issues (e.g. the *Economist* magazine)
- industry associations—especially ones that actively lobby government
- special interest groups—such as consumer groups and people that decide to confront major corporates (e.g. when Greenpeace stopped Shell from sinking the Brent Spar oil rig in the North Sea, and the anti-McDonald's movement during the McLibel trial with its McSpotlight website).

Research has suggested that environmental scanning is often directed towards what is familiar, convenient, and inexpensive. Overall, it is thought that many managers scan their environment to reinforce their beliefs about the organization's current competitive strategy.[26] If this is a natural tendency, then it is important to develop a process to counter this myopic perspective—especially when markets are turbulent.

When organizations face considerable and often multiple sources of uncertainty about their markets, many have turned to scenario analysis as a way to frame this uncertainty.[27] For example, how will the Internet affect a specific market such as that for personal computers, and the structure of its co-opetition? The idea is to create a number of different potential scenarios about the market, each based on a different combination of the

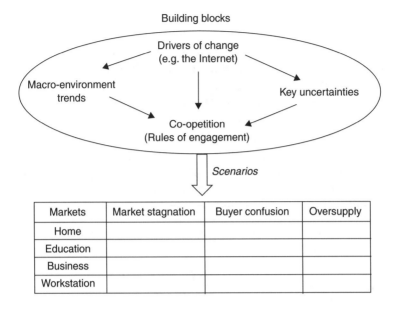

Building blocks

Figure 3.4. Scenario analysis

Markets	Market stagnation	Buyer confusion	Oversupply
Home			
Education			
Business			
Workstation			

forces identified in Figure 3.4. Here, scenario teams identified three market scenarios for PCs (market stagnation, buyer confusion, oversupply) and were interested in how their current market segments (home, education, business, workstation) might fare under each scenario. Each scenario is a description of a fundamentally different future presented in a script-like or narrative fashion. Managers try to identify the critical signposts that signal whether a particular scenario is likely to unfold. They then think through the implications of these scenarios—'What would we do if this happens?' in a particular market. The Royal/Dutch Shell oil company has long been an advocate of scenario analysis.[28] In the world of advertising, the Interpublic group of advertising agencies has used this technique to look seven years into the future.[29]

When organizations face less uncertainty and they are worried about a specific factor in the marketplace (such as how digital technology will replace analogue technology in music systems), some use a variation of scenario analysis called 'roadmapping'. Roadmaps are documents that identify the key factors that define markets (know-why), products (know-what), and the associated technologies (know-how) for one part of an organization. They are generally produced by business units, often in response to a specific threat in the marketplace. They tend to focus only on the next product generation. Motorola has been an advocate of this technique.[30]

When organizations are worried about the occurrence of a specific event such as the granting of a patent, contingency analysis is appropriate. This style of planning presents a base case and an exception or contingency. Another planning tool used for limited uncertainty situations is sensitivity analysis. Here, the effect of a change in one variable is examined when all the others are kept constant. The Du Pont/Marketing-Accounting analysis procedure introduced in Chapter 2 is a good example of this style of planning.

The topics of market trend tracking and monitoring are an emerging discipline. Presently, future-telling consultants occupy the 'high ground'. From this lofty vantage-point, they offer personal suggestions about how markets may evolve. This material is often interesting and engaging, but should always be read with Victor Borge's advice in mind:

> Forecasting is difficult, especially about the future.

#2—The Product Life Cycle

The second market-monitoring framework is the Product Life Cycle (PLC). The belief that many phenomena evolve over time in a predictable way is widespread in business. The human ageing process is often used as an analogy for many so-called 'life cycle' models of evolution. In the case of products, the life cycle is that products and services are born (launched), grow, mature, and die (removed from the market). Some organizations deliberately reformulate their marketing strategy during a product's life. Monitoring life cycle stages and then adapting marketing to these changes is a reactive approach to marketing.

To be useful as a guide to formulating marketing strategy and programmes, a PLC must exhibit three characteristics:

(i) products have a limited life,
(ii) product sales pass through distinct and identifiable stages, and
(iii) each stage requires a different marketing approach for the product to be successful.

Because these three characteristics (especially (ii)) seldom materialize, PLCs are not actually used to formulate strategy by many managers. As shown below, PLCs are more useful for describing the evolution of broad product markets rather than determining the precise marketing strategy of specific brands.

In essence, a PLC is a graph of the sales of a product or service over its lifetime. Plotting sales over time, however, is not a straightforward exercise.

First, it is best to plot unit sales adjusted to a common base. (This removes the effects of package size, price changes, and inflation.) If a very long period of time is involved, as with the PLC for televisions, then it is a good idea to correct for the increase in the size of the population and to keep track of the reason for purchase—first purchase, replacement purchase, and supplementary purchase (e.g. the purchase of a second TV set for the kitchen or a bedroom). The reason for these adjustments is to eliminate their effects on the interpretation of the evolutionary pattern of sales.

There is one crucial factor that affects the shape and the length of a PLC. It is simply the 'definition' of a product. We can define a product as:

- all the products in an industry like computers
- products in various categories (or classes) such as personal computers, workstations, mainframes, and super-computers
- product forms such as desktop and notebook personal computers
- product models like an IBM ThinkPad notebook
- product sub-models like the ThinkPad #2628-PTA.

When sales over time for industries, product categories, and product forms are plotted researchers have discovered several common patterns. Three are shown in Figure 3.5. When sales for (sub)models are plotted they often have no discernible pattern at all. The reason for this is that sales are affected by the day-to-day marketing actions of the organization and its competitors. (For industries, categories, and forms, these effects wash out and what is left is a count of how many units are sold in the market. These sales figures show the combined effects of supply and demand at various points in time.)

The analysis of large-scale industry databases suggests that certain broad trends occur. For example, as an industry grows and matures, (*a*) a smaller percentage of sales comes from new (first time) consumers, (*b*) the difference in relative product quality gets smaller, and (*c*) the market shares of competitor brands become more stable.[31]

The PLC framework is also used to infer the state of consumer knowledge and the nature of competition in a market. For example, in the early stages, consumers will have less experience with the product than at later stages and thus should be more susceptible to marketing messages about the product. In the later stages, competition is intense and many companies compete by expanding their product range—models, package sizes, etc. Also, it is here that price wars are more likely to occur. In a practical business situation, however, it would be better to use market research and competitive intelligence to measure these effects directly rather than rely on such inferences from plotting a PLC.

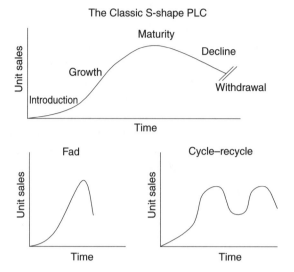

Figure 3.5. Product life cycles

To make the PLC a more useful monitoring framework it is necessary to identify and isolate the factors that determine the pattern of sales. The original assumption underlying the PLC was that products were like humans—they were born (introduction stage in Figure 3.5), grew, matured, aged (decline), and died (were removed from the market). A moment's reflection suggests that this is not a very useful model. By definition, this has to happen—for products, humans, organizations, families, technologies, etc. Also, it suggests nothing about the shape of the lifecycle nor what managers should focus on to understand market evolution. Also, sometimes this analogy can lead managers to observe a decline in sales and terminate the product—a self-fulfilling prophesy.

An alternative to the *human evolutionary pattern* is the *species evolutionary pattern*.[32] Here, the focus is on how products in competitive markets like cars and washing machines evolve over time. When this perspective is adopted, the PLC stages in Figure 3.5 are sometimes renamed as: Introduction, Rapid Growth, Competitive Turbulence, Maturity, and Decline. Then at each stage of the PLC the task is to use the frameworks introduced in Part A of this chapter to model coopetitive evolution.

A third way to view PLCs is to identify the *supply and demand factors* that influence the pattern of sales.[33] Supply-side factors include the new product and service opportunities that new technology provides; the evolution of complementary markets (e.g. more powerful computer chips support more powerful software); the number of companies in the market and the amount of support they devote to the product; the level of competition among these companies; their capacity to meet demand; and government policies that promote certain industries (e.g. IT and tele-communications) and restrict others (e.g. alcohol and cigarettes). On the demand side are factors like changes in the economic and social conditions discussed earlier. There are also many people-factors that affect demand, such as the perceived advantage of the new product, its compati-bility with existing products, the habits of consumers, the ease of switching to the new product, and the person's ability to buy.

It has long been realized that demand and supply factors affect the rate of adoption and diffusion of new products/services. Some years ago a small group of researchers used simulation techniques to reproduce the various shapes shown in Figure 3.5.[34] All that was necessary was to make different assumptions about how fast people adopt and repeat purchase products. These assumptions reflected the combined marketing efforts of suppli-ers and the latent demand of potential customers. For companies that dominate their market like Microsoft and Intel (the Win-Tel standard) in personal computers and Boeing and Airbus in passenger aircraft, this approach to modelling PLCs is very attractive because their joint actions directly affect the shape of the PLC for the industry. In effect, the market dominance of these companies allows them to drive their markets. Other companies not big enough to significantly affect the shape of the PLC are effectively market (PLC) driven.

Modelling the PLC from a supply and demand perspective requires some basic economic modelling—identifying the key factors and combining these into a description of the market. The people who do this most often at the level relevant for marketing managers are the industry analysts employed by management consultants, merchant banks, and stock-broking firms. (This analysis is often sold as an industry report.) Modelling PLCs from a first-purchase and repeat-purchase perspective requires the identification of the key drivers of new product success and constraints to adopting the new product (such as available supply, the costs of switching to the new product, the age of the consumer's existing product, etc.). (A computer-based simulation programme and a good analyst will soon produce plenty of PLCs to discuss.)

Having introduced four perspectives from which to view PLCs, the question arises as to when to use each one. What follows is a strategic principle, or 'if, do' statement.

- Do not use the human evolutionary version of the model as a way to set marketing strategy because:
  - (i) it is difficult to reliably identify which stage a product or service is in (e.g. are books in the growth, mature, or decline stage of their PLC?);[ii]
  - (ii) it assumes that (PLC) sales drive (cause) marketing strategy. (But isn't marketing supposed to cause sales!)

To develop a broad-based understanding of a product-market, use the:

- Competitive Evolution approach in very competitive markets (e.g. Coke versus Pepsi);
- Supply and Demand approach when a market is undergoing structural change (e.g. how will the Internet really change markets);
- First and Repeat Purchase approach when the customer preferences in the market are heterogeneous and customers should be grouped into segments, which when combined will define a market. (Do separate simulations for each segment.)

Before moving on, it is worth discussing one of the popular (among journalists and consultants) myths about PLCs. The myth is that PLCs are getting shorter. If this were true, it would have three significant repercussions for marketing managers, namely, there would be:

- less time to recover the costs of R&D and new product development, which in turn puts pressure on organizations to price their new products higher in order to recoup their investment faster;
- greater pressure to get new products to market faster, which will affect the available time to test products before launch;
- greater pressure to produce more new products, which will affect the scale of new product development activities.

The shortening PLC myth can be analysed in two ways. First, it depends on the level of aggregation at which the product is measured. For example, we cannot say whether the PLC for the computer industry is getting shorter because it has not finished. Also, at the product category and product form levels we have the same problem—the life cycles of super-computers, mainframes, workstations, and the various forms of PCs are still evolving. For models and sub-models the evidence seems mixed. If the product is a poor one, like the IBM PC Jr., it had a short life cycle. However, if the product is better, like the IBM PS/2 range (that was launched subsequently to the PC Jr.), it had a longer life.

[ii] At the time of writing, annual worldwide book sales have never been higher.

The second form of analysis is to review research that directly addresses the issue of PLCs getting shorter. There have been a number of scientific studies conducted and none have found systematic evidence of shortening PLCs.[35] This finding is comforting for practitioners and theorists because it supports the basic tenet that the length of a PLC is primarily determined by how well a product meets the needs of customers (relative to available alternatives). For example, Boeing is still producing 747s, more than thirty years after they were introduced. It also reflects the fact that big market-driving organizations can dictate when new products will be launched and old ones dropped.

This discussion of PLCs leads naturally to the issue of sales-over-time forecasting. Hence, to conclude this chapter, a brief overview of this forecasting is appropriate.

Forecasting PLCs

One could attempt to forecast the shape of a PLC by isolating all the factors that combine to cause sales over time. Given the variety of factors and their interactions, this has proven to be a hopeless task. It has also proven quite difficult to make forecasts of the duration and transition points between PLC stages. Hence, what marketers have done is to simplify the problem by focusing attention on the early part of the PLC—before replacement sales become significant, and when the purchase volume per buyer is one unit. They have developed a number of models with a small number of parameters, which may or may not be based on any assumptions about how consumers make their purchase decisions—the topic of Chapter 4. The early models were based on the well-developed theory of contagious diseases or the spread of epidemics.

One model, published in 1969 by Frank Bass, and refined over the years by a number of researchers, has been used often and with some success.[36] The Bass Model, as the generic version has become known, is a useful starting point for forecasting the long-term sales pattern of new technologies and new durable products under three types of conditions:

(i) no closely competing alternatives exist in the marketplace;

(ii) the company has recently introduced the product and has recorded its sales for a few time periods; or

(iii) the firm has yet to introduce the product, but it is similar to an existing product whose sales history is known.

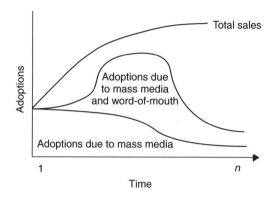

Figure 3.6. Adoptions due to mass media and word-of-mouth Bass Model

The Bass Model attempts to forecast how many people will eventually adopt the new product, and when they will adopt. It assumes that potential adopters are influenced by two types of communication—mass media and word-of-mouth. It also assumes that there are two segments of potential adopters—those influenced only by mass media and those influenced by a combination of mass media and word-of-mouth. Figure 3.6 shows these two groups.

The Bass Model has proven appealing to marketers because it can be linked to the vast amount of research on the adoption and diffusion of innovations.[37] It has also been included in many popular PC-based marketing software packages.[38] However, like all such simple forecasting models, it does have its limitations for marketing managers, such as ignoring the marketing mix elements that drive sales. It is mentioned here because it is the most cited quantitative marketing model of all time, and thus is a part of marketing history. It is also still used by academics and some practitioners.

RECAP

The challenge of analysing markets was captured in the two witticisms that introduced Part B. Also, a river will always flow downhill, but after a heavy storm, it may change its course as it flows across flat country. Thus, the task for the marketing manager is to understand the general flow pattern (evolution) of the river (market) and the conditions that may cause it to change course (such a breakthrough in technology). The frameworks introduced here are useful for charting any of the river-courses that a marketer may encounter. However, like any map-making process, they must be used with understanding and care.

The quote from Sun Tsu at the beginning of this chapter suggested that competing well in a market is built on three sources of knowledge: (*a*) know yourself—Chapter 2;

(*b*) know the enemy—Chapter 3, Part A; (*c*) know the battlefield— Chapter 3, Part B.

In the context of marketing, I add a fourth source of knowledge, namely: (*d*) know the customer—Chapter 4.

KEY CONCEPTS

- *Market Orientation*—an outside–inside view of the organization coupled with the desire to create products and services to satisfy the needs of target segments of consumers.
- *Forecasting*—the use of various techniques such as scenario analysis, roadmapping, and contingency analysis to predict the future. When forecasts are based purely on the analysis of past data, forecasting is a bit like driving a car while looking back through the car's rear-view mirror.
- *Product Life Cycles*—the evolutionary pattern of the sales of a product or service.

KEY QUESTIONS

- Whose responsibility is it to produce, update, and regularly communicate information about the current state and likely future direction of the product-market(s) in which you compete?
- What sources of information are used and how are they collated to produce these pictures of the market?
- Given that futurologists, journalists, and business leaders are prone to make wildly inaccurate forecasts about the future state of markets, what procedures are in place to cross-check these forecasts?
- In your markets, are PLCs getting longer or shorter, and what are the key drivers of their sales?

NOTES

1. M. Porter, *Competitive Strategy: Techniques for Analysing Industries and Competitors* (New York: Free Press, 1980).
2. J. Kavanagh, 'Growth Magic—What Ignites the Spark', *Business Review Weekly* (September 6–12, 2001), 58–71.

3. These are from G. S. Day, *Market Driven Strategy* (New York: Free Press, 1990), pp. 109–19, and P. Kotler, *Marketing Management* (Upper Saddle River, NJ: Prentice Hall, 1997), pp. 228–9.
4. From the *Seattle Times* (April 24, 1994), A1.
5. B. J. Nalebuff and A. M. Brandenburger, *Co-opetition* (New York: HarperCollins, 1996).
6. B. H. Clark and D. B. Montgomery, 'Managerial Identification of Competitors', *Journal of Marketing*, 63, 3 (1999), 67–83.
7. Taken from J. G. Davis and T. M. Devinney, *The Essence of Corporate Strategy* (Sydney: Allen & Unwin, 1997), 300–2.
8. S. K. Keil, D. Reibstein, and D. R. Wittink, 'The Impact of Business Objectives and the Time Horizon of Performance on Pricing Behaviour', *International Journal of Research in Marketing*, 18, 1–2 (2001), 67–81.
9. S. Lubove, 'Get 'em Before They Get You', *Forbes* (July 31, 1995), 88–9.
10. Nalebuff and Brandenburger (1996), 193, op cit.
11. J. R. Hauser and S. M. Shugan, 'Defensive Marketing Strategies', *Management Science*, 2, 4 (1983), 319–60.
12. For a review of this research see T. S. Gruca, D. Sudharshan, and K. Ravi Kumar, 'Marketing Mix Response to Entry in Segmented Markets', *International Journal of Research in Marketing*, 18, 1–2 (2001), 53–66.
13. Some of the more prominent models were: ADBUDB (advertising budgeting); ADCAD (communications); ADMOD (advertising); ADPLUS (advertising wearout); ADVISOR (industrial marketing communications); ASSESSOR (pre-test marketing); BASES (pre-test marketing); BRANDAID (promotions); CALLPLAN (salesperson call planning); DEFENDER (market defence); DETAILER (allocation of selling resources across products); MEDIAC (media buying); NEGO-TEX (international marketing negotiations); NEWS (pre-test and test marketing); PERCEPTOR (design and positioning of new, frequently-purchased consumer goods); PROMOTER (promotions planning); SPRINTER (pre-test and test markets); STRATPORT (allocating resources among business units); and TRACKER (pre-test and test marketing). For reviews of the models, see G. L. Lilien, P. Kotler, and K. Sridhar Moorthy, *Marketing Models* (Englewood Cliffs, NJ: Prentice Hall, 1992); For PC software, see G. L. Lilien and A. Ranaswamy, *Marketing Engineering* (Upper Saddle River, NJ: Prentice Hall, 2003).
14. B. H. Clark and D. B. Montgomery, 'Deterrence, Reputations and Competitive Cognition', *Management Science*, 44, 1 (1998), 62–82.
15. H. Gatignon, T. S. Robertson, and A. J. Fein, 'Incumbent Defense Strategies Against New Product Entry', *International Journal of Research in Marketing*, 14, 2 (1997), 163–76.
16. J. H. Roberts, C. J. Nelson, and P. D. Morrison, 'Defending Market Share Against a New Entrant', in G. Twite and M. O'Keeffe (eds.), *New Directions in Corporate Strategy* (Sydney: Allen & Unwin, 2000), 89–100.
17. A. P. de Geus, 'Planning as Learning', *Harvard Business Review*, (March/April 1988), 70–4.

18. The *Journal of Market-Focused Management* is published by Kluwer Academic Publishers—www.wkap.nl.
19. A. Toffler, *Future Shock* (New York: Bantam Books, 1970); A. Toffler, *The Third Wave* (New York: Bantam Books, 1980); J. Naisbitt and P. Aburdene, *Megatrends 2000* (New York: Avon Books, 1990); J. Naisbitt, *Global Paradox* (New York: W. Morrow, 1994); J. Naisbitt, *High Tech. High Touch* (London: Nicholas Brealey, 2001); F. Popcorn, *The Popcorn Report* (New York: Harper Business, 1992); F. Popcorn, *Clicking: 16 Trends to Future Fit Your Life, Your Work, Your Business* (New York: HarperCollins, 1996).
20. J. Dean, 'Pricing Policies for New Products', *Harvard Business Review*, (Nov.–Dec., 1950), 28–36.
21. See G. R. Dowling, 'Buying is Marketing Too—Japan's Influence on the Australian Coal Business', *Long Range Planning*, 20, 1 (1987), 35–43.
22. See T. Friedman, *The Lexus and the Olive Tree* (London: HarperCollins, 1999).
23. P. Ormerod, *The Death of Economics* (London: Faber and Faber, 1994).
24. For an extended discussion, see S. J. Carson, T. M. Devinney, G. R. Dowling, and G. John, 'Understanding Institutional Designs within Marketing Value Systems', *Journal of Marketing*, 63, Special Issue (1999), 115–30.
25. This idea of mediators was suggested by R. J. Thomas, *New Product Development* (New York: John Wiley & Sons, 1993), ch. 2.
26. D. C. Hambrick, 'Environmental Scanning and Organisational Strategy', *Strategic Management Journal*, 3, 2 (1982), 159–74.
27. P. J. H. Schoemaker, 'Scanario Planning: A Tool for Strategic Thinking', *Sloan Management Review*, (Winter, 1995), 25–40.
28. P. Wack, 'Scenarios: Unchartered Waters Ahead', *Harvard Business Review* (Sept.–Oct., 1985), 73–89; P. Wack, 'Scenarios: Shooting the Rapids', *Harvard Business Review* (Nov.–Dec., 1985), 139–50.
29. See Schoemaker (1995).
30. T. A. Kappel, 'Perspectives on Roadmaps: How Organisations Talk About the Future', *Journal of Product Innovation Management*, 18, 1 (2001), 39–50.
31. Some years ago the Strategic Planning Institute launched a study called 'Profit Impact of Marketing Strategy' (PIMS). C. R. Anderson and C. P. Zeithaml, 'Stage of the Product Life Cycle, Business Strategy and Business Performance', *Academy of Management Journal*, 27, 1 (1984), 5–24; D. C. Hambrick, I. C. MacMillan, and D. L. Day, 'Strategic Attributes and Performance in the BCG Matrix—A PIMS-Based Analysis of Industrial product Businesses', *Academy of Management Journal*, 25, 3 (1982), 510–31.
32. This idea was suggested by G. Tellis and M. Crawford, 'An Evolutionary Approach to Product Growth Theory', *Journal of Marketing*, 45, 4 (1981), 125–32.
33. M. Lambin and G. S. Day, 'Evolutionary Processes in Competitive Markets: Beyond the Product Life Cycle', *Journal of Marketing*, 53, 3 (1989), 4–20.
34. S. Harrell and E. Taylor, 'Modelling the Product Life Cycle for Consumer Durables', *Journal of Marketing*, 45, 4 (1981), 68–75; D. F. Midgley, 'Toward a

Theory of the Product Life Cycle: Explaining Diversity', *Journal of Marketing*, 45, 4 (1981), 109–15; G. R. Dowling and J. Cooper, 'Simulating Product Life Cycles of Products and Services', *Behavioral Science*, 34, 2 (1989), 291–304.

35. For a review see G. R. Dowling, 'Product Life Cycle Traps: Strategic Planning and Shortening PLCs', *Journal of Brand Management*, 4, 2 (1996), 119–32.

36. For a review see V. Mahajan, E. Muller, and F. M. Bass, 'New Product Diffusion Models in Marketing: A Review and Directions for Research', *Journal of Marketing*, 54, 1 (1990), 1–26.

37. D. F. Midgley and G. R. Dowling, 'Innovativeness: The Concept and Its Measurement', *Journal of Consumer Research*, 4, 4 (1978), 229–42; E. M. Rogers, *Diffusion of Innovations* (New York: Free Press, 1995).

38. G. L. Lilien and A. Rangaswamy, *Marketing Engineering* (Upper Saddle River, NJ: Prentice Hall, 2003), ch. 7.

Analysing Buyer Behaviour

To paraphrase an observation of the novelist John Le Carré:

The most dangerous place to look at your customers is from behind your desk!

As in Chapter 3, this chapter takes an outside–inside view of the organization. Understanding consumers is never a simple task because each has his or her own complex psychology that motivates buying decisions. However, this understanding is the cornerstone that joins the organization's marketing strategy (what it wants to achieve) to its marketing programmes (how it will achieve this). Also, good consumer insight is often the factor that reveals market opportunities and exposes false market forecasts.

What is required to attain and retain customers is an understanding of their needs and how they are likely to respond to marketing programmes. Thus, managers need two types of information about consumers—predictions about how they respond to different types of marketing stimuli and explanations about why this happens. Without this information, the design and implementation of marketing programmes is guesswork. Thus, marketing managers are the clients of the academics and professional researchers who analyse customers.

In the discipline of marketing, consumer behaviour (or CB as it is often referred to) is the largest single sub-field.[i] This is not surprising because of the central role that satisfying customers has in the success of any business. Another reason is that the study of CB is extremely interesting to many academics and practising marketers. Over the last fifty years, this interest has generated a vast amount of research and writing on CB. As noted below, it has also resulted in some divisions among scholars about how best to model and predict the behaviour of consumers.

---

[i] The terms buyer behaviour and consumer behaviour are used interchangeably in this chapter.

This chapter looks at buyer behaviour from the perspective of a marketing manager—thus, it will not satisfy the academic or market researcher who adheres to a particular scientific theory of CB. What it sets out to do is to marry the three principal approaches used to study buyer behaviour and introduce relevant facts and explanations that can be used by marketers in B2C and B2B marketing situations.

To motivate the discussion in this chapter, Part A describes some simple data about what brands a consumer has recently bought. The analysis of this type of purchase-history data helps marketers to understand how typical their brand is relative to other brands in their market and in other similar markets. When brands are similar to others, it facilitates learning from other markets. I then describe some of the main general findings that have been accumulated from this type of data over the last forty years. This discussion provides a macro-picture of buyer behaviour. Then follows an introduction to three approaches that are currently used to study CB and how each approach contributes to an overall framework for understanding how individuals, groups, and organizations purchase products and services. The components of this framework are illustrated for B2C and B2B situations. These sections provide a micro-picture of buyer behaviour. Part B of the chapter provides a brief discussion of research techniques for generating insight into consumers.

As introduced in Chapter 1, this analysis of buyer behaviour will use four primary types of marketing knowledge:

- generalizations—what we know from the analysis of purchase-history data and other types of research;
- structural frameworks—what types of data to collect about customers;
- strategic recommendations—what to do;
- market-sensing principles—how to collect data about customers.

These will be supported where necessary with definitions of concepts.

PART A

Market Information

Consider the following ten-week purchase history of brands of instant coffee bought by a single consumer. (These data are often collected from a consumer panel.[1])

A A A B A A C A A B

What can we learn from these data? Apart from the following, not much!

- Brand A fulfils 70 per cent of the customer's category requirements during this period. (Brand B 20 per cent and Brand C 10 per cent.)
- Brands B and C are bought irregularly.
- The consumer seems to buy a portfolio of brands of instant coffee.

To be useful for a marketer, he or she needs to know:

- how typical this pattern of purchasing is for the product category;
- why this pattern occurred.

The answer to the first question can be quite readily determined by aggregating the purchase histories of a number of consumers (coffee in this example), and by comparing this aggregate purchase pattern with the pattern of purchasing of other brands—in other food product categories. This analysis can provide generalizations about patterns of buyer behaviour. As noted in the next section, many of these have proven to be very robust—over time, and across brands, product categories, and different countries.

The second question has proven to be more difficult to answer. Here, we would need information from individual consumers to see which, if any, of the following explanations best describes their behaviour. For example, the person:

- buys their regular brand when it is in stock in their retailer, otherwise they buy another similar brand;
- buys what he or she considers to be the best value at the time (e.g. brands B and C were on special when they were purchased);
- buys different brands for different use occasions, such as a premium brand (B and/or C) for dinner parties and another brand for regular use (A);
- does not care which brand they buy and simply picks the first one that they notice (brand A might have more shelf space in the retailer or the customer remembered seeing it in an advertisement);
- deliberately changes brands occasionally to get some variety.

Here, direct questioning of a representative sample of consumers would reveal what percentage of people best fitted each explanation. When this information has been gathered, the marketer could then think about marketing programmes to reinforce existing behaviour (e.g. if they managed brand A) or change behaviour in order to get a greater share of the customer's category requirements (e.g. if they managed either brand B or C).

On its own, purchase-history data are seldom capable of providing clear insight into the reasons for such buyer behaviour. (They need to be supplemented with data about consumer needs, motivations, decision-making, experience, and the setting in which the purchase takes place.) However, they can be extremely valuable if they are used to develop norms about product category purchasing. This type of information establishes the marketer's expectations about how effective various marketing programmes are likely to be. For example, if there are strong market norms, then the organization will need a *significantly* better marketing programme than competitors to change the well-established pattern of purchasing.

Some General Patterns of Buyer Behaviour, or What Type of Brand are You Selling?

In order to know how well a brand is performing, managers need to benchmark it against other brands—in the market in which it competes, and in other similar markets. The usual way that this is done is to monitor the brand's market share. Market share can be measured in different ways. One of the more common, and least useful, ways of doing this is to measure brand (or company) sales as a percentage of total market (or industry) sales. However, because a brand is seldom targeted at the whole market, market share should be computed as a percentage of the sales of a well-defined target market.[2] The brand can then be assessed as a market leader, challenger, or a minor brand. (For big multi-brand companies like Procter & Gamble and Colgate-Palmolive, this type of analysis sometimes reveals that they have too many minor brands competing in the same market.) Changes in market share over time can be used to calibrate competitive dynamics—especially across the various stages of the competitive-evolutionary product life cycle.

Market share, however, is a relatively crude way of benchmarking a brand. Over the last thirty years, the science of benchmarking brands has evolved considerably. Much of this science has concentrated on developing parsimonious mathematical models to describe the purchase patterns of:

- fast moving consumer goods (FMCG) brands in categories such as food, drinks, cleaners, personal care items;
- consumer durables such as cars and PCs;
- prescription drugs and over-the-counter medicines;
- TV channels, programmes, and episodes;
- retail chains—food, clothing, gasoline; and
- financial services.

This analysis uses data from consumer panels and provides managers with *sales norms* that can be used to predict the performance of a brand in its product category.[3] These panels record the purchase data of households over time so that a long-term purchase history can be built up.[4]

Most FMCG brands, and many business consumables (like office supplies, fuel, maintenance supplies, etc.), are sold in an established market. An important feature of established markets is that they are not subject to radical change, and the changes that do occur tend to be slow. For example, in the market for beer, coffee, hire cars, ready-to-eat breakfast cereals, and watching television, the market leaders tend to persist, and buyers are settled in the way that they buy and use these products. Yes, new brands are launched into these markets, but they tend to look like most of the other existing brands. And sometimes the market grows or declines over time—but usually slowly. The technical term for these types of markets is that they are *stationary*.

There are several reasons why these markets tend to change slowly. One is that individuals consider most FMCG brands to be limited-problem-solving purchase situations. Also, they are experienced buyers and they form stable propensities or habits of purchase that they change only under exceptional circumstances. For example, Robert East and Kathy Hammond found that only about 15 per cent of buyers changed their portfolio of brands during the course of a year.[5] Another reason is that most new brands launched into these markets are very similar to the brands already being sold. Thus, they provide no strong reason for a consumer to change their current brand repertoire. These brands are sometimes called 'me-too' or 'look-alike' brands. (If you remove the brand name and package and present the contents to people in a blind test, they can not reliably identify what brand it is.)

Periodically, these established markets suffer a perturbation. One that is typically short-lived is a brand going on promotion. (The gains from these promotions are typically not maintained once the promotion ceases.[6]) Another type has a longer effect and may be initiated by a market driving company. For example, when cable television challenged the free-to-air television stations, and more recently when the Internet enabled people and organizations to buy a wide range of products and services online. What typically happens in these cases is that some people in the market adopt the new product and then the market settles down again. For example, Amazon.com, Barnes and Noble, and many other major booksellers offer book buying over the Internet. This generated significant interest and publicity, but the sales data for the industry show that the vast majority of books are still bought from bricks-and-mortar outlets.

From the analysis of stationary markets, various sales norms have been observed, for example, over the period of a year:

(*a*) Brands in a product category have very different market shares (e.g. at one time in the US instant coffee market the largest brand had a share of 20 per cent and the eighth brand a share of 3 per cent) and penetration, that is, the percentage of all potential buyers who buy a brand at least once (for these two brands it was 24 and 6 per cent).

(b) Purchase frequencies, which is the average number of purchases made by those people who purchase at least once (per year), vary much less than market shares across all the brands in a category (e.g. 3.6 to 2.0 for the two instant coffee brands).

(c) Most people buy only one item (or multi-item pack) at a time.

(d) The biggest share brands in the category tend to have
  • higher penetration, that is, more buyers,
  • slightly higher purchase frequencies, and
  • slightly more 100 per cent loyal customers
  than the smaller brands.

(e) Most buyers buy a brand infrequently.

(f) For most people, each brand represents only a moderate share of their product category requirements.

(g) Only a minority of people (10–20 per cent) are 100 per cent loyal to one brand over the period of a year.

(h) 100 per cent loyal buyers tend to be light users.

Items (a), (b), and (d) above have been formulated into what is known as the *Double Jeopardy* phenomenon. This states that the less popular brands are not only bought by fewer people (lower penetration) but are also bought less often (lower frequency) by the people who buy them.[7] This is a ubiquitous phenomenon and occurs for all the products and services noted previously—across countries and over many years. Because the empirical research suggests that most brands in stationary markets conform to the Double Jeopardy phenomenon, it provides a useful tool to help classify the brands in a market. This is shown in Figure 4.1.[8]

Figure 4.1 suggests that managers should consider the type of brand they are managing. Most will be small, medium, or large and fall within the Double Jeopardy envelope. There are, however, three less prevalent types of brands. Consider brands like Coke, Intel, and Microsoft. They are big, and a large number of consumers will buy them on the next purchase occasion. This type of brand is labelled a *super-loyalty brand*. There are not many of these super-brands. For example, even brands like American Express, Levi's, and McDonald's that have very high brand recognition and sizeable market shares do not have as high repeat purchase probabilities as a super-loyal brand.

A *change-of-pace brand* is one with a higher than expected market share but a lower than expected proportion of loyal buyers—as predicted by the Double Jeopardy market norm. Many premium beers fit this description.

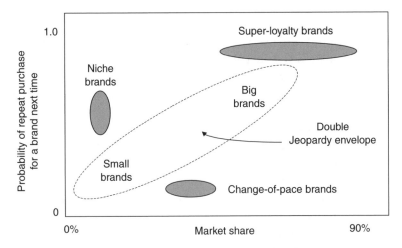

Figure 4.1. Types of brands in a market

People buy them only when they are in a special situation such as having a pre-dinner beer at a good restaurant.

Niche brands are small brands that have a higher than predicted proportion of loyal buyers. Two good examples are Apple Computer and Harley-Davidson. Both have small market shares (5 per cent worldwide for Apple at the time of writing this chapter) and fiercely loyal buyers. In its early days, the Body Shop (cosmetics company) was a niche brand, but as it increased its distribution coverage and appeal, it became a small 'normal' brand. As with most so-called niche brands, those that prosper end up as a small or medium brand within the Double Jeopardy envelope.

Items (f), (g), and (h) above alert marketers to another widespread market phenomenon, namely, that most people are not 100 per cent loyal to a particular brand over a reasonable period of time. Test yourself, do you only ever:

- watch one television channel (or do you cherry-pick the best programme on at the time you want to watch);
- read one newspaper (or read anything within arm's reach);
- eat at one restaurant (or seek variety);
- drink one brand of wine;
- buy only one brand of car.

This list can be quite extensive. What the research shows is that it is unlikely that more than 20 per cent of a brand's buyers are 100 per cent loyal. (Even fiercely loyal Coke drinkers will occasionally try another brand.) Thus, most people and many organizations multi-brand buy. The term used to describe this phenomenon is *polygamous loyalty*.

There are many reasons for polygamous loyalty, for example:

- different brands are used for different occasions (e.g. Moët et Chandon champagne for a special celebration, and Janz with a weekend lunch);
- many brands are complementary not substitutes (e.g. the *Wall Street Journal* for the daily news and *Business Week* for more in-depth company analysis);
- it is necessary to combine various brands in order to create a complete product (e.g. clothing, cosmetics, cooking, travel, etc.);
- some brands do not offer the full range of services desired (e.g. a retailer, radio station, television channel);
- variety is a desirable benefit (e.g. French, Italian, Mexican, Chinese, Thai, and Indian restaurants);
- the desire for novelty (let us try something new or different);
- different members of a household want different brands (e.g. different shampoos for dry, oily, and thin hair);
- in an out-of-stock situation at the supermarket many people buy another brand in the category rather than go to another store;
- the lack of meaningful differentiation and the functional similarity of many brands and retailers in a product category make them easily substitutable for many people.

There are some interesting management implications from the research outlined in this section. For example, in a stationary market, a marketing strategy that seeks to increase the amount that a customer buys of a single brand can be counter-productive. In some cases, like personal investing and eating out where variety is essential for one's wellbeing, or the supply of a critical component in a manufacturing process, it can actually be against the customer's best interests to buy only one brand, or buy from a single supplier. Also, if there are good reasons for customers to have split-loyalty in a product category, then it will be a difficult and expensive process to try to convince them to behave otherwise. It will be even more difficult to achieve a financial return on this type of marketing investment when all the major competitors are trying to do the same thing—such as the airline frequent flyer programmes. (This issue is discussed in more detail in Chapter 11 when the focus shifts to marketing programmes designed to retain customers.)

Another insight from this research concerns how to increase a brand's market share. Market share in this context is:

Market Share = penetration × (purchase frequency × amount bought)

Given that most people only buy one unit of the product on each shopping visit, it would seem that there is scope to increase share by getting people to buy more each time they shop. We see this strategy in a supermarket when a brand is sold in multi-item packs. The hope here is that if there is more product 'within arm's reach of desire', then people will consume more. In B2B situations suppliers often offer a quantity discount. The problem with this strategy is that most people only buy what they (or the family or the organization) need. (They might buy more this time, but then they are out of the market for a longer than 'normal' time.) Hence, in most situations there is only a limited scope to increase market share with this strategy.

Another strategy is to try to increase purchase frequency, that is, get people to buy more often. Again, because all the brands have similar purchase frequencies, and most people tend to only buy what they need, there is limited scope for growth here. In B2B situations, more frequent buying (as opposed to Just In Time delivery) is often discouraged because it increases transaction costs.

The last strategy is to try to increase penetration, that is, get more people to buy at least once. This is the option best supported by the Double Jeopardy research, and, thus, seems to be the one with the most potential. Five tactics to implement this strategy are:

- increase the inherent value of the brand to a wider variety of customers, for example by increasing quality, adding new features, and/or decreasing price;
- get new people to try the brand in the hope that they will like it enough to include in their repertoire, for example by giving away free samples;
- make the brand available to a wider range of potential buyers, for example by increasing the number of retailers that stock the brand:
- increase the salience of the brand, for example by advertising it more to remind (potential) customers that it is available;
- find new uses for the brand, for example Schweppes tonic water as a refreshing soft-drink as well as a mixer with gin; large (Xerox) photocopiers can also be used as a network printer for PCs.

It should be pointed out that these recommendations are frequently ignored by marketing managers. Many marketers favour a strategy that tries to enhance the image of the brand or change its position relative to other competing brands. The idea here is that enhancing the image of the brand will cause an increase in the intention to purchase the brand. Advertising is often used for this purpose. However, it has to be a very good creative campaign to significantly change the image of a 'me-too' brand, because when people are polygamously loyal, they have first-hand knowledge of the strengths and weaknesses of your brand and competitive brands. Advertising tends to work best when there are real differences between brands to promote, or when it can significantly increase awareness about or the salience of the brand.

It is one thing to present research and make strategic recommendations, but the question remains—'How generalizable are these sales norms, and, thus, how robust are the recommendations likely to be?' The market norms have been established for:

- fifty types of food, drink, cleaners, personal care products, and medicines;
- management executive programmes (e.g. at London Business School);
- store chains, individual stores, shopping trips;
- price brands, image brands, private-label brands;
- Australia, Britain, Japan, United States;
- the period from 1950 to 2003.

They tend to be less reliable when:

- the product is addictive (e.g. cigarettes), or
- when there is a very limited range of products available in a market area.

Four main points emerge from the research noted in this section. First, the classification of brands in Figure 4.1 is a useful and (scientifically) supportable way to benchmark a brand. Any of these types of brand can be profitable, because profit is determined by margin, not by the type or size of the brand. Second, multi-brand buying in a product category is extremely common, in both B2C and B2B markets. Thus, marketers would do well to remember that their customers are also likely to be the satisfied customers of a competitor. To reinforce this finding, it is a good idea to use the term *polygamous loyalty* in preference to the common term 'brand switching'. Why? Because most consumers do not deliberately 'switch' among brands in their repertoire—they just choose a different brand because it better suits their needs on this occasion.

The third lesson from this research is that these market norms have a wider application than many marketers readily believe. There is a tendency when reading this type of research to assume that it does not apply to 'my' particular market. The evidence used to justify this position is that it is easy to recall specific consumers (sometimes the person themselves) who do not conform to the norms described here. This perspective is like looking at a forest one tree at a time. Every tree will be somewhat different than its neighbours. However, when the diverse characteristics of trees and buyers are put together, the differences usually average out to reveal the broad purchase patterns described here. And the crucial point is that most marketing programmes are targeted to groups (or segments) of people. (Chapter 6 focuses on this issue.)

The final point that summarizes this section is for marketing managers and their superiors to be realistic about what to expect from their marketing programmes. If the market is characterized as stationary, then it will be quite difficult to design programmes that disrupt the market norms—especially when competitors are vigilant and respond with a counter-programme. This comment applies especially to the launch of new products. For example, to break out of the DJ pattern a new brand would have to differ far more from the existing brands than they differed from each other. Thus, when launching a 'me-too' new brand, set sales goals *low*.

The role of this section in the study of buyer behaviour is to paint the background of an oil painting of buyers. The next three sections paint the foreground.

Studying Buyer Behaviour

> There is an old saying in Spain:
> To be a bullfighter, you must first learn to be a bull.

In its early history, buyer behaviour (or CB) theory was a branch of economics (as, to many economists, it remains). In the 1950s, scholars turned to psychology for enlightenment about how to interpret the behaviour of flesh and blood consumers. In the 1960s, much of this research was summarized in three comprehensive models of consumer decision-making.[9] These three models were based on the principles of cognitive, and to a lesser extent social, psychology and formed the foundation of most of today's CB textbooks. The central concept in this school of thought is the consumer's attitude to the brand—its formation, complexity, and how it is changed.[10] More recently, there have been cries from another branch of psychology—the behaviourists—to incorporate their ideas more formally into explanations of CB.[11] The central concept here is that specific episodes of CB are determined largely by the situation in which the consumer finds herself or himself.

In the academic literature each approach (economics, cognitive, social, and behaviourist psychology) has its supporters and critics. What this debate alerts us to is the value of looking at CB through different lenses, namely:

- *Cognition*—depicting the consumer as a boundedly rational information processor who has (clear) personal goals and who uses evaluative criteria to compare brand alternatives to choose the best brand to achieve those goals.
- *Behaviourist*—understanding the consumer *in situ*, that is, how does the physical, temporal, and social environments of both the purchase and the intended usage situation shape consumer choice.
- *Habit*—treating a purchase as a pre-established behaviour that is triggered by a particular situation, such as a household running out of ready-to-eat breakfast cereal or a business running low on photocopy paper.

The key issue for the marketer is what relative mix of these elements is necessary in order to get a comprehensive and accurate picture of one's target customers. Some research and a little introspection provide a clue to this puzzle.

Despite the popularity (in textbooks) of the cognitive approach, research indicates that it is quite hard to identify behaviour that corresponds to the coherent and elaborate sequences of extended decision-making activities described by this approach.[12] The reason for this is simply that in most B2C purchase situations, the buyers have some experience in making the type of purchase they are involved with. Mostly, they are buying a replacement for an existing product or service or an additional product. Hence, most consumers have some, and often considerable, experience to rely on when they buy most of their products and services. Also, even in unfamiliar situations where a person is buying something for the first time, they tend to suffice.[13] That is, they do not gather all the available information and they do not consider all the available alternatives. (For example, relatively few people read independently published consumer reports before buying even quite expensive items.)

There is, however, one type of situation where purchases are big, risky, and where experience is limited. Here, extensive decision-making is common and takes the form of extensive problem-solving. Examples of these situations are:

- A young couple buys their first house.
- A steel mill decides to replace its oldest blast furnace.
- The government decides to issue tenders for an infrastructure project (such as the Sydney Olympics complex) or to build new military equipment.

In situations such as these, the purchase process can be quite lengthy. In B2B situations, it will typically involve a team of managers who make the buying decision—called the Buying Group (or Decision Making Unit)—and a team of salespeople supported by other experts. In the case of government purchasing the process must also be transparent.

In B2B buying situations, there is often more information collected and more formal processes (or protocols) in place to make buying decisions than in B2C situations. Professional purchasing managers are often assigned the prime responsibility for procurement. At one extreme, suppliers have to 'quote to specifications' if they want to do business, and the focus is on getting a lower price. This style of procurement has been called a 'buying orientation'.[14] Many organizations have adopted an alternative approach to buying. They seek quality improvements and price reductions by working *with* suppliers and by integrating the purchasing function with materials handling and logistics. Internet-based procurement systems such as the General Electric Trading Process Network (http://www.tpn.geis.com) are used to reduce costs and streamline the purchasing process. This type of relationship with suppliers is more cooperative than the hard-line, quote-to-specification type of buying. These organizations are said to have a 'procurement orientation'. A third orientation to purchasing is evolving in organizations that take a very broad business perspective. Here, suppliers become partners in the overall process of design and manufacturing, thus adding value directly to the buyer. Every organization in the network shares research and focuses their activities on making products that customers want. This can be called a 'supply orientation'.

In most cases, the purchasing processes used by ordinary people, and managers in B2B situations, are more subtle than those outlined in the textbooks. And herein lies the challenge for marketers. For each target group of customers, the task is to describe how they go about making their purchase decisions. The major factors that the three approaches to studying CB indicate and that should be considered as the building blocks for these customized models of buying behaviour are shown in Figure 4.2.

Learned Experience

Buyers generally make their purchase decisions with some experience. For example, children learn about buying by watching their parents, and managers learn by being a part of a buying group for their organization. In the case of experienced consumers, this experience can be a formidable

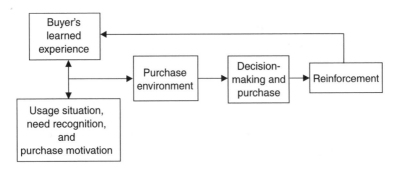

Figure 4.2. A simple model of buyer behaviour

barrier to new marketing initiatives. For example, when buying PCs, there is a segment of buyers who strongly believe that the best time to buy a new PC is 'tomorrow, not today'. Why? Because, they have learned that PC models change so frequently that the longer one can put off buying a new PC, the better value (power, features, and price) they will receive. Thus, one crucial piece of information that shapes buying behaviour is the learned experience of the purchaser.

Related to the buyer's learned experience are the concepts of perceived risk and involvement. Risk is one of the most pervasive concepts in theories of human choice. *Perceived risk* is defined as the individual's subjective assessment of the chance of injury or loss from a product or service.[15] A variety of losses have been measured in B2C and B2B situations—financial, performance or functional, psychological, social, physical, and convenience. The subjective assessment of each type of loss depends on the buyer's experience and the availability of information. The importance of the losses depends on the individual—their wealth, self-confidence, and their innate tolerance to accept or avoid risk. *Involvement* is a concept that is similar to, but more encompassing than, perceived risk. It is the degree to which the buyer is concerned about the product or service being purchased.[16] This concern will be driven by the buyer's perceived risk and interest in the purchase. Involvement is often used as a shorthand way of describing a buying situation, namely, high versus low involvement.

A parsimonious way to summarize the buyer's experience, product knowledge, involvement in the purchase, and perceived risk is their perception of the type of buying situation that they, or their buying group, face. An enduring classification of buying situations was proposed by John Howard, one of the founders of the discipline of marketing.[17] The classification is:

- *Extensive problem-solving*—where the buyer thinks that he or she has little useful knowledge about either the product category or the available brands. For example, an inexperienced photographer buys a digital camera for the first time. The uncertainty here often produces a significant level of perceived risk.
- *Limited problem-solving*—the buyer considers their product category knowledge to be adequate, but brand knowledge is out of date. For example, a weekend tennis player buying a new tennis racket.
- *Routine response behaviour*—the buyer has good product category and brand knowledge. For example, buying one's regular brand of beer. There is little risk with these purchases.

In B2B situations, there is an equivalent classification of buying situations, namely: *new task* buying (similar to extensive problem solving); *modified rebuy* (similar to limited problem solving); and the *straight rebuy* (similar to routine response behaviour).[18] To this list can be added a fourth category, namely, the *system* or *turnkey* purchase. Here, the buyer wants a complete operating product, such as a dam, a road highway, or the main stadium for the Sydney Olympic Games.

The importance of perceived risk and the buying situation is that they have a significant impact on how features of the product such as its brand name, quality, and price are evaluated, and how buying decisions are made. For example, for new low-risk purchases one common purchase strategy is to buy the product or service without too much information search or deliberation—buy, try, and make up your mind about how suitable it is after it has been used. For new high-risk products, the decision may become quite complex and the risk shared among a number of decision-makers— the family or an organizational buying group. This topic is outlined in more detail later in this chapter.

Usage Situations, Needs, and Purchase Motives

How, when, where, and by whom a product or service is intended to be used has a big impact on what (and sometimes where it) is purchased. For example, a car for the family might be new and purchased from a manufacturer-frachised dealer, while a car for a teenager may be used and bought via a trading-post (newspaper) advertisement. Thus, understanding the intended use of a product is important because it will influence the desire for various product features and benefits.

Allied to usage situations is another critical piece of information marketers need, namely, what factor(s) trigger a purchase. Sometimes these are called needs and sometimes motives. A *need* reflects the lack of something that would benefit the person or the organization—a gap between the consumer's actual and desired state. When a need is activated, it becomes a motive for purchase. Thus, *motivation* is an activated state within a consumer that initiates goal-directed behaviour. This activated state can be to 'minimize pain and/or maximize gain'. That is, it can have both a negative and a positive origin. It can also be a negative or positive reinforcement. The classification of needs/motives in Table 4.1 comes from psychology.[19]

Table 4.1. Motives: triggers for purchase

Negative or aversive origin

Problem removal—buyer experiences a current problem and seeks a product or service that will solve the problem

Problem avoidance—buyer anticipates a future problem and seeks a product or service that will prevent the problem

Incomplete satisfaction—buyer is not satisfied with the current product/service and searches for something better

Mixed approach-avoidance—buyer likes some things about the product/service, but dislikes others and will try to find another product/service that will resolve the conflict

Normal depletion—buyer is out of stock or running low and seeks to maintain their supply of the product or service

Positive or appetitive origin

Sensory gratification—buyer seeks extra sensory stimulation (e.g. a stronger taste) from a (similar) product or service

Intellectual stimulation—buyer seeks extra intellectual stimulation (e.g. a more challenging computer game) from a (similar) product or service

Social approval—buyer seeks the opportunity for social rewards (such as personal recognition) through use of the product

---

Purchase of the same product or service can be based on a negative motive for some people and a positive motive for others. For example, clothes shopping is hated by some people but relished by others. The creation of web pages for many companies was seen as the opportunity to improve service to stakeholders (customers, journalists, and others) and expand horizons by some, but as a necessity to keep pace with competitors by many others. Thus, managers need research to find out which of their target consumers are attracted to their products and services by positive or negative motives.

Before discussing the other elements of Figure 4.2, it is useful to explain why involvement and purchase motivations have been highlighted to characterize an individual's pre-buying behaviour. As we will see when discussing advertising (in Chapter 13), the level of involvement (low or high) and the nature of the purchase motivation (negative or positive) of the target customers can be used by marketers to brief their ad agency and evaluate their recommended creative tactics for the advertising to various groups of consumers. The problem that many mangers encounter is that they are asked to commit thousands or sometimes millions of dollars to an advertising campaign, but they lack a research-based framework with which to evaluate the campaign prior to its commission.

Purchase Environment

The third component of Figure 4.2 is the Purchase Environment. This factor can shape the purchase decision-making process of both individuals and organizations. The main characteristics of the purchase environment are:[20]

- Physical surroundings where the purchase (decision) takes place. For example, when the Australian coal producers negotiate supply contracts with Japanese buyers, these are usually conducted in Japan using translators.
- Social surroundings of the purchase—the other people present, their characteristics and social relationships. For example, when shopping for clothes, many people will be accompanied by their spouse or a friend.
- Temporal circumstances of the purchase. The actual time and the place where decisions are made and the purchase takes place. For example, the hours of opening of a store, the duration of a special offer, Christmastime, etc. Also, what is the feeling of time. For example, often individuals or managers feel under pressure to make a quick decision.
- The task definition—what roles are different people expected to play in the purchase decision (e.g. the shop assistant, the buyer and his or her confidant when buying clothes) and what goal is operative (e.g. buying a new garment to be noticed at a special occasion).
- Antecedent and concurrent states of the buyer such as how much money can be spent, and any momentary moods or conditions of the buyer (e.g. anxiety, excitement, fatigue, hunger, etc.).

Another critical aspect of the purchase situation is the scope that people other than the buyer have for controlling the situation in which the purchase (and consumption) occurs. Many purchase and usage situations are governed by a set of quite rigid, informal 'rules of conduct'. For example, there is not much point in trying to negotiate the price of a McDonald's hamburger in a Sydney outlet; there are restrictions about the amount of carry-on baggage many airlines allow; there is a tendering process required to be followed by government; in many markets in Asia and the Middle-East, bargaining is normal; etc. Consumption is also often prescribed by various traditions, for example you sit quietly and applaud at the appropriate time in a classical music concert but you can dance and shout at a rock concert.

In the Asian context, the role of the purchase environment is very important. Research indicates that consumers form situational brand meanings based on the people they are with and the cultural values that are salient. For example, in Shanghai, the modern and youthful image of McDonald's is at odds with the needs of a family birthday party or celebration. Here, tradition and multi-generational concerns like the type of food and the seating arrangement make it inappropriate. However, the modern, youthful, and American brand values of McDonald's are quite appropriate for many young people going out on a date. Thus, young people may evaluate McDonald's in a very negative and a very positive way, depending on the situation.[21]

For a marketer, the task is to understand situational and rule-following behaviour.[22] This can be done in three stages:

- Treat the buying behaviour as (partly) contingent on the purchase situation. (It will also be influenced by characteristics of the buyer.)
- Figure out how past situations have shaped that behaviour.
- Predict how present and possible future situations will influence the continuity of that behaviour.

During the late 1990s, the marketing managers of many dotcom enterprises struggled with this task. Their predictions about how the Internet would radically and quickly change a large number of people's past modes of information search and shopping were hopelessly incorrect. The consequence was that the underlying business model of many dotcoms was ill-conceived—and the era of the dotcom became the era of the dot-comedy!

Decision-Making

The fourth module in Figure 4.2 deals with purchase decision-making behaviour. This area has been the subject of considerable research. However, the findings are not nearly as robust as those reported in the section earlier that dealt with general patterns of buyer behaviour. Hence, what follows should be considered as a starting point for understanding how a specific target group of consumers actually behave. The main elements to consider are:

- *Who makes the buying decision and what roles do people typically play?* A useful classification is:
  —Initiator—the person who first suggests the purchase.
  —Influencer(s)—people whose advice about process, evaluative criteria, and desired outcomes affects the purchase decision.
  —Gatekeeper—a person who controls the flow of information related to a purchase.

—Vetoer—a person who can veto the preferences of other decision-makers.

—Decider(s)—the person or group who makes the final decision.

—Buyer—the person who places the order.

—User(s)—the people who use the product.

In family and organizational purchases, different people often play different roles.

- *What are the stages of the decision-making process?* The number and sequence of stages depend on the buyer's experience and perceived risk. That is, on the type of buying situation. For example, in a routine response behaviour situation the sequence might be: (*a*) need recognition, (*b*) purchase, (*c*) reinforcement. In an extended problem-solving situation, the sequence might be: (*a*) need recognition, (*b*) information search, (*c*) alternative evaluation (and the formation of a tentative brand attitude), (*d*) purchase (or non-purchase if no suitable alternative is found), (*e*) use, (*f*) post-purchase evaluation (and the updating of the brand attitude[23]). When a new low-risk product is encountered the sequence might be: (*a*) awareness, (*b*) consideration, (*c*) purchase, (*d*) post-purchase evaluation (and the formation of a brand attitude), (*e*) intention to repurchase or rejection.

  The crucial point here is that research is needed to determine the sequence of stages and the purchase motives for the target customers. It is often the case that two or three purchase decision sequences are required to summarize how a target group of customers buy. Why? Because of their individual differences.

- *What criteria are used to evaluate a product or service?* As discussed in Chapters 6 and 8, the criteria used can be grouped into three categories of potential benefits: (*a*) functional, (*b*) psychological and social, and (*c*) economic (which includes price). Each potential benefit is delivered by one or more features of the product or service.

- *How do individuals form their preferences and choose among a set of considered alternatives?* This question assumes that the buyer faces either an extensive or limited problem-solving situation. The research that has examined this question suggests that buyers use a simple decision process called a *heuristic.*[24] While there have been many of these proposed, the following two have often been used by marketers to describe their consumers' preference formation:

  — Expectancy-value (or brand attitude)—beliefs about the features of a product or service (such as its perceived quality) are weighted by their importance and summed to derive an overall preference score. The product with the highest preference score is chosen.

—Ideal product—the buyer compares the actual product or service with his or her (hypothetical) ideal brand, and chooses the one that is closest to this ideal.

The decision-making research also indicates that the choice of heuristic depends upon three factors:

—The person—their cognitive ability and prior knowledge.

—The task—what information is available to evaluate an alternative and how it is presented (e.g. the energy rating of a refrigerator), and how many alternatives are being considered.

—The social context—is the person part of a group and do they feel accountable to others (e.g. if they do, then they may use a heuristic that is easy to rationalize and justify to other group members).

Thus, how people make a specific purchase decision depends on the specific circumstances. Also, not everybody who buys a particular product or service at a particular time will use the same heuristic. While this conclusion is not much immediate help to a marketer, its practical significance is to reinforce the need for consumer research.

• *How does a group make its decision?* The group can be a family, some friends, or the buying group of an organization. Again, the heuristic used will depend on the factors just mentioned. And again research is necessary to describe how buyers decide. To illustrate what to look for, consider the following options:

— Single-member choice—one member makes the choice on behalf of the group. (Often, the most senior member of the group or the person with the biggest stake in the outcome of the purchase.)

—Voting—each member has one vote and the alternative with the highest number of votes wins. (In the event of a tie, the least preferred alternative is dropped and the member(s) who voted for this option vote for another.)

—Weighted member choice—each member has one vote, but some members' votes are more important than others. (Often, the people with the most seniority and/or the most expertise, or who have the most at risk, will have more say in the decision.)

— Minimum endorsement—members vote over and over again until one alternative gets the pre-specified number (or quota) of votes.

— Preference perturbation—the chosen alternative is the one that causes the least change to the individual preferences of the group members. (This heuristic explains why some groups choose everyone's second choice.)

The critical point here is that it is not sufficient to know how individuals form their preferences, it is also necessary to know how these are combined to obtain a group decision. Good salespeople are often skilled at uncovering these heuristics.

Reinforcement

The final module in Figure 4.2 deals with consequences of the purchase. Here, the buyer makes a post-purchase evaluation of the product or service. This may be based on the buyer's own experience and/or the evaluations of others. For example, while wearing new clothes, other people may remark on your choice. When a marketing director hires a new advertising agency, other managers may express confidence in the choice. When the organization changes its corporate identity symbols, how do the media react? (Often with mild amusement.[25]) Thus, the purchase and use experience provides either positive and/or negative reinforcement for the decision. And the buyer/user updates his or her learned experience. It is this element of the model that makes buyer behaviour dynamic.

In summary, while we know much about the factors that are important in order to understand buyer behaviour, there is no escape from the conclusion that research is necessary to profile how a target group of customers actually goes about making buying decisions. The next section illustrates why these models of buyer behaviour are important for marketers. The last section then describes some of the common approaches for gathering information about consumers.

Where Marketing Can Make an Impact

Figure 4.2 identifies a number of opportunities for marketers to influence buyer behaviour. To illustrate some of these, let us start with reinforcement. After a person buys a product or service, there is an opportunity to help them confirm that they have made a good choice, and thus provide positive reinforcement. For example, when a car has been awarded 'the car of the year' by a motoring magazine, the manufacturer will often write to recent buyers informing them of the award and congratulating them on their wise choice. Also, research often reveals that advertising 'works' just as well after the sale as before it! Thus, people use the advertising before the sale as a source of information and after the sale as a mechanism for reinforcement—'There is an ad for the car that I have just bought—doesn't it look good!'[26]

An active programme to positively reinforce past purchase behaviour is important for a number of reasons, namely, to:

- have a positive impact on the buyer's learned experience and brand attitude;
- stimulate positive WOM communication;
- reduce any post-purchase cognitive dissonance.

Cognitive dissonance is the psychological discomfort that people often feel after buying something. That is, the buyer feels 'locked in' to the product. It may result because there were few differences between the brands considered ('Did I really buy the best brand?') or because the brand was purchased based on an approach-avoidance motivation (Table 4.1).

Another place where marketing can be effective is in stimulating and sometimes shaping customer needs—the need recognition stage of Figure 4.2. For example, often there is a clear need for an affordable and effective solution to a particular problem, such as helping people to give up smoking. Also, target customers can be reminded of a latent or forgotten need, such as the regular service of their car, a dental check-up, and the intake of calcium (milk) and iron (red meat) in their diet. Two other examples are: Alka-Seltzer's (anti-stomach acid formulation) 'Will it be there when you need it?' and the American Express Card's 'Don't leave home without it' advertising campaigns. In another case, the task is to sell both the product category and the brand. For example, when MBA degrees were first introduced (into Australia), managers had to be convinced first of the value of an MBA, and then the value of the University of X's MBA. Sometimes, however, there is no need for a product or service—even though the people in R&D have discovered something new. Marketing is just a waste of money here.

The crucial issue for the marketing manager is to make sure that the brand name and the (category) need are associated in the buyer's mind. Advertising slogans are often used for this purpose, but some are better at establishing this link than others, for example:

- 'You deserve a break today . . . at McDonald's.'
- 'The American Express Card. Don't leave home without it.'
- BMW—'The ultimate driving machine.'
- GE—'We bring good things to life.'[ii]

[ii] Soon after Jack Welch's departure as CEO, GE changed its twenty-five-year-old corporate slogan to 'imagination at work'.

The purchase environment is another fertile area in which to direct marketing activity. The overall aim here is to ensure that the purchase environment facilitates rather than inhibits purchase. For example, if the product is out of stock or the queue for service is too long, the buyer may not buy. If the salesperson does not like your brand, he or she may switch the buyer to a competitor's brand. If information about your brand is not what the buyer needs, or is less well presented than that of a competitor, the buyer may reject your offer. If the physical surroundings where the purchase takes place clash with the desired image of your brand, the buyer may perceive more risk than necessary. If the buyer cannot pay in a manner that suits them, the sale may be lost. Finally, the overall purchase environment needs to put the buyer in a confident state with a feeling of being in control.

Marketing programmes can have a potential impact on each stage of the buyer's decision-making process. They do this by providing information and sometimes suggesting how a decision should be made. For example, advertisements often suggest features of the product that are important to consider. In new task buying situations, salespeople often conduct a value-in-use (VIU) assessment with the potential buyer to illustrate the economic benefits of their products and services. Also, products offered with a warranty reduce perceived risk. To further illustrate where marketing can influence a decision, consider the B2B situation in Figure 4.3.

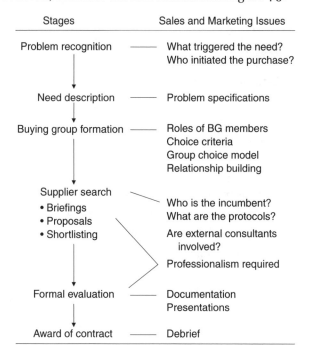

Figure 4.3. Organizational buyer behaviour

In summary, a good description of the characteristics, needs, and motivations of target customers together with insight into how they make their buying decisions is invaluable when considering the design and implementation of marketing programmes. The next part of this chapter describes how information is collected to create the type of model described in Figure 4.3.

RECAP

This part of the chapter provides a macro- and micro-view of target customers. The macro view combines individual episodes of purchase behaviour to reveal common patterns of activity. These are summarized and described in terms of the different types of brands that are commonly found in stationary markets—small, medium, large, niche, change-of-pace, and super-loyal. From this analysis, two clear messages are sent to marketing managers, namely, (*a*) make your brand salient, and (*b*) make it available to as many target customers as possible (i.e. distribute it widely).

The micro-view of CB uses frameworks from psychology to help marketers profile the characteristics and decision-making of their target customers. Developing a rich understanding of customers is essential for formulating marketing programmes and as we will see in Chapters 5, 6, 7, and 13, for new product development, market segmentation, and positioning, and for briefing the organization's advertising agency. In short, understanding customers is central to good marketing practices.

KEY CONCEPTS

As the following list suggests, there is a lot to learn about target customers:

- *Stationary markets*—markets where customer buying is habitual and the market shares of brands are relatively stable.
- *The double jeopardy phenomenon*—small brands (in stationary markets) have fewer buyers who also buy them less often than bigger brands.
- *Polygamous loyalty*—the buying of a portfolio of brands from the same product category to satisfy the person's various needs.
- *Salience*—the ubiquitousness of the brand in the market.
- *Buying group*—the people who make a buying (or not buy) decision.
- *Buying roles*—the functions such as information search and order placement performed by buying group members when making a buying decision.
- *Involvement*—the degree to which a buyer is concerned about the purchase being contemplated.
- *Buying situation*—the amount of knowledge about the brands in a market that the buyer currently has.

- *Purchase motives*—the positive or negative activated need state that motivates a person to consider buying a product or service.

- *Purchase environment*—the physical, social, and temporal surroundings in which the purchase takes place.

- *Usage environment*—how, when, where, and by whom the product or service is intended to be used.

KEY FRAMEWORKS

- *Types of brands*—Figure 4.1
- *Model of buying behaviour*—Figure 4.2
- *Stages of decision-making*—Figure 4.3

KEY QUESTIONS

Marketers need to answer two key questions:

- How typical is my brand (and, hence, what can I learn by studying the marketing practices of other similar brands)?
- Why and how do my target consumers buy my brand (and, hence, what can I change to influence the purchase process and the formation of consumer preferences)?

Marketing managers often face the following paradox. There is a common, shared belief in their organization that customers are important, but there is also a feeling that customer research is not very good at shedding light on their preferences and buying behaviour. Part B now looks at this issue of gathering information about customers.

PART B

Gathering Information about Target Customers

> You don't stand a chance of producing good advertising (marketing) unless you start by doing your homework. I have always found this extremely tedious, but there is no substitute for it.
>
> David Ogilvy

Many marketing managers seem to ignore Ogilvy's advice. They often feel that their natural empathy for their customers and their past dealings with competitors are sufficient to provide the insight necessary to design and implement efficient and effective marketing programmes. Others, however, understand that there is no substitute for monitoring the market, and in particular listening to the voice of the customer—especially if they are in a different stage of life or have a different background to their customers. One marketing director even went so far as to make his staff wear a T-shirt with the inscription 'I am *not* the customer' every time he caught them making unsupported inferences about customers.

Chapter 3 and Part A of this chapter are designed to help marketers gain good knowledge about the environment in which marketing takes place. Knowledge in this context is:

- raw data, for example, the purchase history sequence at the beginning of this chapter;
- information, which is data with structure, for example the frequency with which a brand of coffee is bought;
- knowledge, which is information endowed with meaning, for example the market share of a brand and what type of brand it is (as per Figure 4.1).

Knowledge about the environment in which marketing takes place provides crucial input into the tasks of:

- identifying market opportunities (Chapter 5);
- designing marketing strategy (Chapters 6 and 7);
- creating programmes to implement the marketing strategy (Chapters 8–11);
- writing the marketing plan and specifying controls (Chapter 12).

This role of the organization's Marketing Knowledge System is shown in Figure 4.4. The remaining discussion focuses on techniques for gathering data about customers and the design of the repository of these data, namely, the customer database.

Customer Research

Data about customers can be collected in many ways: observation, customer visits, personal interviews, focus groups, surveys, trade shows, and experiments. There are technical issues involved when gathering data using each approach. Also, each technique has its own particular strengths and weaknesses for providing insight into customers, and data that can be generalized to the market as a whole. (A market research book or a market

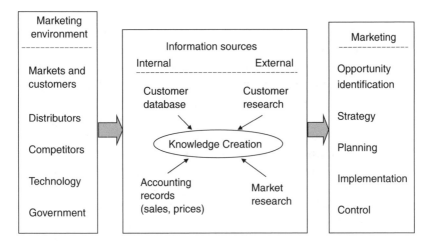

Figure 4.4. The marketing knowledge system

research company will readily outline these.) Thus, multiple techniques will be needed to provide all the information recommended in this chapter.

While data can be gathered from target customers, or people who influence these customers (e.g. friends, partners, and spouses) and experts (e.g. journalists who specialize in a particular field), most is collected from actual and potential customers. In countries like Australia, Britain, and the United States, there is a heavy emphasis on data collected using focus groups and to a lesser extent surveys. Research firms in these countries are also using online market research techniques to gather information from a broad spectrum of people. Internet-based research is becoming known as 'virtual research'. (Interestingly, in many Asian countries, focus group and other opinion-generating research is not as widely used. It is more difficult to collect, and managers place less faith in the opinions of a small group of customers.)

A two-phased approach is often used to gather data about customers in B2C markets. Stage one is to start with some qualitative research—usually focus groups. Here, small groups of customers (six to twelve) are invited to a one- to two-hour discussion about a particular product or service. The discussion is conducted by a trained moderator, and members of the marketing team often observe the discussion from behind a one-way mirror or on closed circuit television. Focus groups are very good for understanding the language, concerns, needs, and motivations of customers. Thus, the information they provide is the feedstock for other types of research. They are also frequently used to provide feedback about new product concepts and to test advertising messages. They are not good for making generalizations to the market as a whole, and they should not be used for strategic decisions such as deciding whether or not to enter a new market, to launch a new product, or to change the price of a product or service.

Stage two in the research process is to follow the qualitative research with quantitative research. Mostly, this involves the design of a survey and its administration to a representative sample of target customers. The aim here is to test the ideas (hypotheses) developed from the qualitative research. Well-conducted surveys are good for making generalizations to a wider population, but not very good for gaining deep insight about customers. Sometimes, the pattern of findings from a survey will require some follow-up qualitative research to help interpret what has been uncovered.

In the world of B2B marketing, the research process just outlined often has a different mix of elements. Qualitative research is conducted on an ongoing basis and often involves open-ended personal interviews with all the people identified in the buying group. Sometimes, these are one-on-one interviews with senior managers carried out by a market research company. (For example, to interview the senior in-house lawyer responsible for the purchase of legal services at a major company can cost in the region of $1000 per interview.) Sometimes, a cross-functional team of managers will visit key customers to 'watch the product in use', discuss new product needs, and talk about the business relationship between the parties.

Salespeople and customer relationship managers can also provide good customer information. Their daily interactions with customers sensitize them to contemporary needs and motivations. Also, the information gained during the selling process can be vital in configuring (new) products and services to fulfil customer needs. One particularly useful type of information relates to the economic VIU of the product/service. This is defined as the maximum amount the buyer should be prepared to pay for the product/service offering. These calculations are based on customer data and are discussed in Chapter 9.

Another place where good information about customer needs and motivations can be found is at trade shows and conventions. Trade shows have a long tradition that go back to the medieval fairs in Europe where buyers and sellers came together to create a marketplace. Today, they are generally big, glittery affairs that are used mainly for introducing new products, generating new sales leads, and maintaining customer contacts. However, the discussions with customers attending the shows and follow-up contact with them can provide good information about emerging needs. They are also a good source of information about competitors.

Survey research in B2C and B2B marketing situations often collects two other types of customer information. One type is the usage and attitudes of consumers to a range of products and services (U&A studies as they are often referred to). This information is supplemented with extensive demographic (or firmographic for organizations) and lifestyle (business issues and conditions) data. It is useful for determining the importance and general concern about issues, and monitoring trends if conducted periodically. Another type of survey gathers customer satisfaction data—or 'feedback after the horse has bolted' as it is sometimes referred to. These data are used (*a*) to help improve the offer made to customers (often), (*b*) as part of the KPIs of managers (sometimes), (*c*) as a reason to praise marketing and customer service employees (sometimes), or (*d*) as a 'stick' to beat employees for poor performance (often).

Research is often conducted at the beginning of the marketing planning process when a description of the competitive market is required, and near the end of this process when recommended programmes need to be validated. However, a better strategy is to conduct research on an ongoing basis. The philosophy here is one of 'sequential learning'—go out and learn something new; digest the learning; go out and learn more; etc.

Finally, it is useful to note that customer research is commissioned for two main purposes. One is to gain insight about consumer buying decisions. For example, how many target consumers are aware, how many of these consider the product/service, how many of these prefer it, and how is this preference converted into first and repeat purchase. The other purpose is political—to justify a decision that has already been made, or as a mechanism to win an internal management argument. (Unethical organizations will also gather data from customers on the pretext that it is for research purposes, but use the data gathering encounter as the lead into a selling process.)

In summary, managers need to set aside a budget for ongoing market and customer research. This research should use multiple methods to collect data to offset the inherent biases in any particular method. The research should focus on gaining customer insight and making market generalizations. Figure 4.5 illustrates the trade-off between these two aims. Managers also need to ensure that the findings from this research are shared throughout the organization. (In many cases, it is surprising to find out how few people actually get to see and discuss research studies.)

More than forty years ago, David Ogilvy offered his colleagues the following advice:

Avoid using research the way drunks use lamp posts: For support rather than illumination.

This is still very good advice.

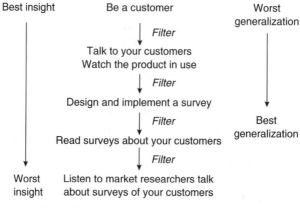

Each filter distorts the picture of your customers

Figure 4.5. Filtering out customer concerns

Customer Databases

A customer database is a collection of data about customers (and sometimes prospective customers) arranged in a logical manner in a computer. The data most often recorded are name, contact details, past purchases, responses to previous special offers, and socio-demographic (for B2C customers) or industry and organization (for B2B customers) data. However, the (previous) discussion in this book suggests that the data that should be contained in the customer database are:

- *Customer characteristics*—name, contact details, socio-demographic (B2C) and organization/industry (B2B) details, media usage, buying role, customer segment membership (i.e. which other customers are they similar to—as discussed in Chapter 6).
- *Customer response to marketing*—what, when, where, how, and why they buy.
- *Customer purchase history*—past purchases and a list of the other brands bought in the category.
- *Customer profitability*—cost to serve, revenue, profitability, (estimated) lifetime value.

If these data are kept in more than one database—such as a sales contact list, order placement and fulfilment, and accounts payable and receivable file—then relational database software is necessary in order to get a comprehensive view of a particular customer. In many organizations with old legacy data systems, this can prove to be a very challenging task.

Over recent years, advances in IT have allowed marketers to track customers individually and then customize marketing efforts to individuals. This form of customized marketing is often called one-to-one marketing or database marketing. For example, in the United States, Lexus has a customer database containing approximately three million names of owners and prospects. They use this to keep in contact with current customers and reinforce their loyalty to Lexus, and to target prospects with information about their new cars.

Customer databases allow marketers to do two things. One is to mine the data using powerful statistical algorithms to uncover new insights about purchase behaviour. For example, a supermarket might use its point-of-sale data to identify sets of products that are purchased at particular times of the day. One such discovery was that between 6 and 8 pm, there was a greater than expected association between beer and paper nappies for babies. Further analysis revealed that young fathers were the buyers. From this type of purchase pattern information it is possible to create new marketing initiatives (such as putting the beer closer to the baby nappies).

Customer purchase-history data are most frequently analysed according to:

- its RFM criteria, namely, the recency, frequency, and monetary value (of the transaction—over the lifetime of the customer relationship) of the purchases;
- cross-buying rates, that is, which products are typically purchased with other products.

The RFM data are used to create customer segments. For example, the catalogue clothing company Lands' End discovered 5,200 different RFM-based segments. The cross-buying data are used to uncover cross-selling opportunities. Here, the marketer identifies people who do not have all the products that are typically bought together and then tries to sell them the 'missing' product(s). However, customers often resent this style of (intrusive) marketing.

In service situations such as airlines, banks, hotels, and restaurants, a good customer database allows any one of a number of customer-contact people to look up the complete history of the customer on a computer. Thus, at the point of service delivery, they can 'recognize' the customer and where appropriate customise the type of service offered. Customers tend to value this and enjoy the experience.

The last decade has seen the rapid growth of database marketing. This industry takes itself very seriously and promotes the virtues of database-driven marketing vigorously. While this style of marketing has many strengths, it also has many weaknesses that need to be considered before it is adopted by an organization. For example:

- Creating and using a good customer database is very expensive. Some of the costs involved are IT hardware and software, data storage, data updating and cleaning, data analysis, skilled personnel, and all the management time involved. These costs can quickly eat up a sizeable market research budget.
- The benefits derivable from mining a customer database focus mainly on increasing the efficiency and effectiveness of current marketing programmes and retaining current customers.
- If a customer database does not also contain a good list of prospective customers, and most B2C databases do not, then any mining of these data provides a very biased view of one's market.
- The data about current customers relate to their past behaviour. Thus, it is a rear-view mirror perspective of the customer, one that is not very helpful for looking to the future or developing new products and services.
- It is often the case that the socio-demographic data collected when a customer is entered into a database are not updated on a regular basis. Also, most databases do not contain data about the customer's media habits, price sensitivity, other brands bought in the category, etc. Thus, the 'picture' of the customer that can be derived from the database is quite limited.

What these weaknesses alert us to is—before investing in database-driven marketing, do a cost–benefit analysis:

- Fully cost the proposed system—its establishment and maintenance.
- Calculate the returns and cost savings from the marketing programmes that will use the database.
- Compare the investment in database marketing with two or more alternatives that would cost approximately the same to implement, for example an increase in advertising, an overall price cut, increasing distribution coverage, etc.
- If one of the primary benefits of the database is to gain a better insight into customers, then compare the information provided by these data with that which would be available from a representative panel of target customers who would be surveyed on a regular basis.

RECAP

Every organization has a marketing knowledge system—it is just that some are more sophisticated and formalized than others. They all try to do what is shown in Figure 4.4, namely, capture data from the marketing environment and turn this into information about what is going on so that more informed and effective marketing decisions can be made. Chapter 3 examined the major factors in the marketing environment. Part A of this chapter focused on consumers. Part B looked at how to gather data about consumers.

Gathering data about consumers and turning it into information useful for marketing decision-making is a complicated process because each research technique has weaknesses. Also, decisions made with respect to one stage in the research process have consequences for the subsequent stages. Hence, using multiple research methods is preferable to relying on information from a single method. To get the best insight about their customers, marketing managers generally gather information with the help of specialists. One such group is market research companies. Briefing these outside suppliers of marketing information is a topic covered in Chapter 13.

Many marketers believe that a customer database is the central part of their organization's marketing knowledge system. It can be if it contains a comprehensive set of data about current and prospective customers, if the skills are available to analyse the data to develop meaningful insights about customer needs, and to enhance the efficiency and effectiveness of marketing programmes. All too often, however, these databases do not contain all the information needed to make informed decisions.

KEY CONCEPTS

- *Marketing knowledge*—information about consumers and markets that helps the marketer make better-informed decisions.
- *Qualitative research*—information derived from individual depth interviews and focus groups.
- *Quantitative research*—information derived from numerical data that is gathered from surveys of consumers.
- *Customer database*—a collection of numerical data about customers (and sometimes prospective customers) arranged in a logical manner in a computer.
- *Database marketing*—the practice of using customer databases to design and implement marketing programmes.

KEY FRAMEWORK

- *Marketing knowledge system*—Figure 4.5

KEY QUESTIONS

Some of the key decisions about research that a marketing manager can make are:

- The size of the research budget—is research a fundamental input into marketing decision-making or is it a discretionary expenditure?

- The style of research—is there an *ongoing programme* of research or is research conducted in response to isolated needs for information about consumers such as the evaluation of new advertising?

- The type of favoured research—qualitative (e.g. focus groups) and/or quantitative (e.g. surveys), and/or research based on mathematical models?[27]

- The accumulation of research—into a comprehensive database or left as isolated reports?

- The dissemination of research—upwards to senior managers or throughout the organization?

- The information in the customer database—limited or extensive?

NOTES

1. A very good source of information about consumer purchasing in a product category is a consumer panel. This is a scientifically selected sample of consumers, households, or businesses intended to represent a larger group—often a complete nation. Data are collected at regular intervals to monitor where, when, and what is bought. Large consumer panels in the United States and Europe may monitor 10,000 + households.

2. Market share calculations are particularly dependent on the definition of 'the market'. They also depend on the unit of measurement—products or revenues. Often, they are calculated using the information that is readily available to the market research company that performs this task.

3. Market research companies such as AGB in Britain, GfK in Germany, IRI in the United States, and Nielsen throughout the world run these panels.

4. The most extensive catalogue of this research appears in A. S. C. Ehrenberg, *Repeat Buying: Facts, Theory, and Applications* (New York: Oxford University Press, 1988). More recently this research has also been summarized in A. S. C. Ehrengerg, M. D. Uncles, and G. J. Goodhardt, 'Understanding Brand Performance Measures: Using Dirichlet Benchmarks', *Journal of Business Research* (2004), forthcoming.

5. R. East and K. A. Hammond, 'The Erosion of Repeat Purchase Loyalty', *Marketing Letters*, 7, 2 (1996), 163–72.

6. See R. East, *Consumer Behaviour: Advances and Applications in Marketing* (London: Prentice Hall, 1997), chapter 4.

7. A. S. C. Ehrenberg, G. J. Goodhardt, and P. Barwise, 'Double Jeopardy Revisited', *Journal of Marketing*, 54, 3 (1990), 82–91.

8. G. R. Dowling and M. Uncles, 'Do Customer Loyalty Programs Really Work?' *Sloan Management Review*, 38, 4 (1997), 71–82.

9. J. F. Engel, D. T. Kollat, and R. D. Blackwell, *Consumer Behaviour* (New York: Holt, Rinehart and Winston, 1968); J. A. Howard and J. N. Sheth, *The Theory of Buyer Behaviour* (New York: John Wiley & Sons, 1969); F. M. Nicosia, *Consumer Decision Processes* (Englewood Cliffs, NJ: Prentice Hall, 1966).

10. See, for example, J. R. Rossiter and L. Percy, *Advertising Communications and Promotion Management* (New York: McGraw-Hill, 1987 and 1997).

11. G. R. Foxall, 'Putting Consumer Behaviour in its Place: The Behavioural Perspective Model Research Programme.' *International Journal of Management Reviews* (June 1999), 133–58.

12. For a specific example see G. R. Dowling and D. F. Midgley, 'The Decision Process Models of Antarctic Travel Innovators.' *Australian Journal of Management*, 3, 2 (1978), 147–61. For other evidence see R. East, *Consumer Behaviour: Advances and Applications in Marketing* (London: Prentice Hall, 1997), pp. 8–12.

13. This concept was first introduced in H. A. Simon, *Administrative Behaviour* (New York: Macmillan, 1957).

14. J. C. Anderson and J. A. Narus, *Business Market Management* (Upper Saddle River, NJ: Prentice Hall, 1999), chapter 3.

15. G. R. Dowling, 'Perceived Risk', in P. E. Earl and S. Kemp (eds.), *Consumer Research and Economic Psychology* (Cheltenham: Edward Elgar, 1999), pp. 419–24.

16. Strictly speaking, this is a definition of personal involvement. Researchers have also studied involvement with decision-making and information search, and the purchase situation. For a description of this concept see P. Laaksonen, 'Involvement', in P. E. Earl and S. Kemp (eds.), *Consumer Research and Economic Psychology* (Cheltenham: Edward Elgar, 1999), pp. 341–7.

17. J. A. Howard, *Consumer Behaviour: Application of Theory* (New York: McGraw-Hill, 1977).

18. P. J. Robinson, C. W. Faris, and Y. Wind, *Industrial Buying and Creative Marketing* (Boston: Allyn and Bacon, 1967).

19. For a review of this research, see J. R. Rossiter and L. Percy, *Advertising, Communications and Promotion Management* (New York: McGraw-Hill, 1997), p. 136.

20. These were suggested by R. W. Belk, 'Situational Variables and Consumer Behaviour', *Journal of Consumer Research*, 2, 3 (1975), 157–64.

21. G. M. Eckhardt and M. J. Houston, 'Cultural Paradoxes Reflected in Brand Meaning: McDonald's in Shanghai China', Research Brief-008, Centre for Corporate Change, Australian Graduate School of Management (2001).

22. From G. R. Foxall (1999).

23. There are many definitions of attitude. Two brand attitude definitions are (a) the learned predisposition to respond to a product, or product class, in a

130   ANALYSING BUYER BEHAVIOUR

consistently favourable or unfavourable way, and (*b*) the buyer's evaluation of the brand with respect to its perceived ability to meet a currently relevant motivation. Some of the key aspects of these definitions are that they are learned, they endure, they are goal-directed, and that they predispose a response. Attitudes are often measured by asking people to rate their beliefs about future benefits from a brand and weighting these by their importance. A person's overall attitude is the sum of the weighted beliefs.

24. J. R. Bettman, E. J. Johnson, and J. W. Payne, 'Consumer Decision Making', in T. S. Robertson and H. H. Kassarjian (eds.), *Handbook of Consumer Behaviour* (Englewood Cliffs, NJ: Prentice-Hall, 1991), pp. 50–84.
25. M. Cave, 'Blobs say it all for BHP Billiton's business of the future', *Australian Financial Review* (21 August 2001), 3.
26. M. L. Ritchins and P. H. Bloch, 'After the New Wears Off: The Temporal Context of Product Involvement', *Journal of Consumer Reseach*, 13, 2 (1986), 280–7.
27. Research using mathematical decision models can be found in G. L. Lilien, P. Kotler, and K. S. Moorthy, *Marketing Models* (Upper Saddle River, NJ: Prentice Hall, 1992), and G. L. Lilien and A. Rangaswamy, *Marketing Engineering* (Upper Saddle River, NJ: Prentice Hall, 2003).

5

Market Opportunities: Finding and Filling Them

> Wherever there is a need, there is an opportunity.
>
> Philip Kotler
>
> I was seldom able to see an opportunity until it had ceased to be one.
>
> Mark Twain

These two quotes capture the dilemma facing many organizations. CEOs and senior managers know that customers have many unmet needs—frustrated customers and golfing companions often suggest what these are. And senior managers look to their marketers to find out how they can be filled. But why is this so difficult to do? And, when a need and its potential market opportunity is uncovered, why do organizations often struggle to assess its potential and create a product or service to tap this market—at a profit?

This chapter explores these issues. It builds on the material in Chapters 2–4. Chapter 2 focuses on the strategic intent of the organization, in particular:

- is it market-driving or market-driven and what is the approach to innovation;
- what are the sources of competitive advantage;
- what is the business model;
- what is the scope of competition.

These characteristics define the constraints faced when attempting to turn an opportunity into a new product or service. They also create a lens through which an organization searches for customer need—opportunities.

Chapter 2 looks at the market through a standard 50 mm lens of an SLR camera. Chapter 3 changes to a wide-angle lens. It looks at broader industry factors and competitive dynamics. It also suggests that market trends and product life cycles be monitored to understand change and to provide the context for thinking about new product opportunities.

Chapter 4 looks at customers using two lenses. The wide-angle lens photographed groups of customers to show the broad patterns of behaviour of many B2C and B2B markets. The wide-angle lens was then replaced with a small telephoto lens that shows some of the details of customer decision-making. This provides insight into how target customers go about evaluating new products and services.

This chapter adopts the Philip Kotler philosophy in the quote that introduced this chapter. It outlines how to identify market opportunities and to create new products and services to respond to customer needs. Part A reviews the main factor that triggers this search, namely, the need to grow. It outlines various possibilities for growth. Part B discusses new product development (NPD), as this is a proven way to drive markets and respond to the increasing expectations of customers. Part C then provides a brief review of how consumers adopt new products and services. This discussion also provides the first detailed look at one of the foundation concepts of marketing—market segmentation.

PART A

Let us Grow!

Successful organizations usually start out by being highly focused on an individual product, service, or market. But success creates the opportunity to branch out in new directions. It also has a tendency to attract the attention of investment analysts. Once organizations attract the attention of the stock market, analysts put pressure on the Board and the CEO to grow. If the organization is in a market(s) that shows no overall growth, this can be a daunting prospect. And, if the organization has no history of innovating, the challenge can be substantial. Predictably, the short-term response to a growth target from the Board is to offer more varieties of what is currently being sold. The product may also be sent to new geographic markets, where it may have to be sold at a different price and through different distributors. Over time, these growth strategies often result in the organization becoming unfocused. It offers too many products and services for too many markets at too many different price points. It loses its sense of direction. Thus, growing while remaining focused is a key challenge for marketing managers and their CEOs.[1]

Losing focus is a worry to marketing people because it signals that the position of the brand and/or organization is becoming blurry—and weaker. A strong, focused position in the minds of customers for a brand and organization are two key marketing assets. For example, for many years millions of dollars were spent trying to convince target buyers that:

- a BMW is 'the ultimate driving machine', and
- a Mercedes Benz is 'engineered like no other car'.

These brand-position statements helped customers to differentiate the two German prestige cars and each acted as an internal touchstone for NPD. For example, BMW improved the handling of their cars and made them 'drive smarter' (an active safety feature/benefit), while Mercedes made their cars 'bullet proof' (a passive safety feature/benefit).

3M is a good example of a company that has grown and retained its focus over many years. 3M's growth is driven by the objective of achieving 30 per cent of sales from products introduced in the last four years (known internally as the '30 per cent rule'). This difficult objective is supported by allowing (encouraging) technical people to spend up to 15 per cent of their time on new product projects of their own choosing (known as the '15 per cent rule'), and offering research grants to help get initiatives past the idea stage (known as 'Genesis Grants'). The organizational culture is supportive of success and equally of failures that contribute to the knowledge base of the organization. 3M has focused all its NPD around the one-word positioning statement 'innovation'.

Where will Growth Come From?

Growth is a powerful motivator to seek opportunities in new and existing markets. To a strategic planner, the problem can be decomposed into the sources of growth shown in Figure 5.1.

The dashed bottom line in Figure 5.1 assumes that as current products/services age they will become less attractive relative to others in the market—hence, a decline in sales. Moving up the figure, the next line assumes some gains to be made by increasing market share. The next

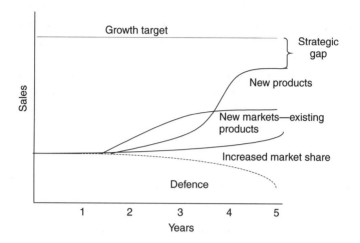

Figure 5.1. Strategies for growth

line shows sales gains achieved by taking existing products into new (geographic) markets. The S-shaped line shows that new products and services will add to overall sales, but they will take some time to develop and to become established in the market (hence, the S-shaped curve). Even with all this activity, sales may still be below the growth target. To close the strategic gap will require either a breakthrough initiative or the acquisition of a competitor.

Figure 5.1 suggests that marketing managers consider a range of strategies to achieve growth targets:

- *Defend* sales to the current customer base. Chapter 3 suggested some strategies for doing this. Chapters 10 and 11 provide an extensive discussion of strategies based on satisfying customers and forming relationships with them.
- *Increase share—of the market or the customer's requirements.* As noted in Chapter 4, increasing share of the customer's product-category requirements typically has only limited potential. The more effective alternative is to increase the number of people who buy the product at least once during the course of a year (defined as market penetration). Another strategy is to cross-sell other related or extra products to customers. For example, banks try to sell as many products and services to their customers as possible—loans, credit card, savings, share trading, funds management, insurance, etc. Many companies report that if they target customers who want 'a one-stop-shop', this can be an effective way to increase sales.

- *More vigorous competition.*[2] This strategy relies on competing smarter or harder. For example, increasing the advertising budget, decreasing price, putting the product on special, revving up the salesforce, offering incentives to distributors, increasing the range of products offered (e.g. Seiko has more than 2000 models of watches) are all ways to compete harder (or head-to-head). However, they are often accompanied by an increase in costs. If these exceed revenues, the outcome is a decrease in profit and the potential wrath of senior managers. Also, directly attacking a competitor, especially a big one, usually invites retaliation. To win with a frontal attack on a competitor usually involves (*a*) having more resources and endurance, or (*b*) using a cost advantage to price significantly lower than the competitor. Often, this second strategy is implemented by launching a separate price-fighting brand into the market.

  Competing smarter often involves a combination of innovation and market segmentation (discussed in Chapter 6). As noted earlier, 3M is a classic innovator. So are Gillette, Hewlett-Packard, Nokia, Philips, and Sony. These companies develop and launch many new products each year, with the knowledge that only some will be successful. (e.g. in the late 1990s, Nokia launched a new model mobile phone every 35 days). A variation of this innovation strategy is the imitation strategy. Here, organizations develop (*a*) a cheaper 'clone' brand to emulate the product they are attacking, or (*b*) a 'me-too' brand to match a successful product, or (*c*) they improve on a successful competitor product and launch it under their own brand name.

- *Move into new markets.* These markets are often new geographical areas—domestic or international. If they are international markets, this will mean that customers are likely to be (slightly) different—in their decision-making and choice criteria. Hence, the need for customer research prior to entry.

- *New uses for the product.* This strategy is implemented by finding new uses for the product among existing customers. For example, an advertisement once claimed that there were 300 reasons how one could use vinegar. (They included things such as to improve metabolism, aid digestion, care for eye infections, treat hair, soothe sprained muscles, relieve headaches, relieve corns, relieve insect bites, destroy bacteria in foods, lower high blood pressure, control weight, improve strength and power, clean the refrigerator, etc.)

- *Enter a new market space.* When the PC market matured to the point when experienced users were buying replacement machines, there were enough experienced buyers to sell PCs direct to this group. Michael Dell was the first person to successfully exploit this new segment of customers. More recently, Dell has used the Internet to sell its PCs. Amazon.com has also successfully (although not profitably) exploited this new market space.

- *Develop new products to satisfy existing or new customer needs.* This strategy depends on being able to find segments of customers with unmet needs, such as Islamic banking, fuel-efficient cars, non-dripping wax candles, computer software to manage customer relationships, and others. The next section discusses this option in more detail.

Marketers often evaluate these strategies in terms of whether they involve creating new products and/or entering new markets. Table 5.1 suggests that there are considerable risks involved when growth is sought by simultaneously creating new products and entering new markets. There is an old saying in management—'take one risk at a time'.

Table 5.1 ranks the strategy that involves existing products and existing markets as the least risky. The reason for this is that the organization has (or should have) good knowledge about its products, customers, and competitors. Thus, this strategy has the lowest overall uncertainty.

Table 5.1. The risks of growth strategies

	Existing products	*New products*
Existing markets	1. Lowest risk	2. Moderate risk
New markets	3. Moderate risk	4. Highest risk

The next lowest risk is assigned to launching a new product into the existing market. Here, customer needs should drive NPD, and the way to communicate (advertising strategy), deliver (distribution and retailing), and price (the price sensitivity of current customers) the new product is well known to the organization. This strategy often involves launching another version of a successful product to current customers. For example, 3M sells yellow Post-It notes and it then decides to sell a range of coloured Post-It notes in various sizes and shapes. Given that the original notes were successful, there is every chance that the new range will also be successful—although it will cannibalize some of the yellow originals. This strategy is called a *product line extension*. Many companies grow this way. For example, Colgate has introduced a number of different varieties of toothpaste that come in different flavours and packages, have different ingredients, or provide different benefits. They all share the respected Colgate name, and thus:

- reduce perceived risk for customers and distributors;
- permit consumer variety-seeking among loyal Colgate customers;

- take up more shelf-space in the supermarket and thus leave less room for competitors;
- increase the salience of the Colgate brand—it is more visible at retail and often advertised more;
- appeal to a wider range of customers, and, thus, increase market penetration.

Sometimes companies use their brand name to enter a new product category used by their current customers, or to attract new customers that respect the brand. For example, Harley-Davidson sells a range of clothing to its customers and to people who want to indulge in the image associated with Harley-Davidson. Swiss Army has capitalized on the success of its pocket-knives to sell watches and then sunglasses. The big accounting firm Arthur Andersen created a firm of consultants called Andersen Consulting to serve the IT needs of its audit clients. (Subsequently, the consultants left the accountants and became Accenture.) This strategy is known as a *product category extension*.[3]

Most new products launched each year in B2C and B2B markets are brand extensions of either the line or category type. While this strategy has many advantages it also has many risks:

- Brand extensions can confuse customers if there is no logical link to the core brand. For example, why does Caterpillar—the heavy earth-moving equipment company—have its brand name on a range of (casual) clothing?
- If the new product is poorly designed or constructed and fails in the market, it can damage the reputation of the parent brand. For example, IBM launched a sub-brand called the PCjr (junior). It was not well received by target customers or well reviewed by industry journalists.
- If the new product is very successful, there is a good chance that it has cannibalized the sales of other products in the line. For example, when Coca-Cola launched Diet Coke with a point of parity with regular Coke of 'good taste' and a point of difference of 'low calories', it certainly lowered the sales of regular Coke.
- Brand extensions can dilute the meaning of the original brand, and, thus, cause a loss of focus. A spectacular example of this is the Gucci brand. Originally, its brand values were luxury, elegance, status, and quality. However, after the product line was extended to cover 22,000 items, many of which were poorly made, it lost much of its brand value. The Virgin brand and its many licensing agreements is also running this risk.

For a marketing manager, the key issue is how to maximize the chance that a brand extension will be successful and minimize the risks. Fortunately, research has uncovered some useful guidelines.[4]

- Successful brand extensions occur when the parent brand lends favourable associations to the extension. These associations may be in terms of offering similar product features and/or benefits, or being used in similar situations, or by similar types of user. That is, there is a logical 'fit' between the original brand and its extension. Thus, the consumer can easily transfer their beliefs and emotions from one brand to the other. For example, Bausch & Lomb has a strong fit between their eyewear and eye-care products. However, when they tried to extend into the mouthwash market, consumers were not impressed.
- High-quality brands stretch farther than average quality brands, although both types of brands have their limits. The reason for this is that high quality is often associated with greater expertise, credibility, and trust.
- A brand that is seen as prototypical of a product category can be difficult to extend outside that category. Some brands define the product category—like Coke for cola soft-drinks, Bacardi for white rum, Ferrari for sports cars, and McKinsey for strategy consulting. These 'master brands' are very difficult to extend outside their category.
- Upward (higher price) and downward (lower price) brand extensions need special care. Often, the anchor-brand name is hidden. For example, when Toyota went upmarket it used the name Lexus. When the Marriott hotel group went downmarket, it used the name Fairfield Inn.

The third most risky strategy in Table 5.1 is to launch an existing product into a new market. The risks here often reside in a management belief that the product's success in one market will ensure its success in another market. However, new customers may have different motivations for purchase, decision-making, brand image associations with the introduced brand, price sensitivity, patterns of product use, etc. A good example of this was the launch of Euro Disney in 1992. For many years, it struggled to meet the financial targets of its backers. This was due, not so much to low visitor numbers, but more to the miscalculations of management (e.g. too many hotel rooms, too many items of merchandize, no wine sold on site, and high prices), and the habits of visitors—they were more frugal and they stayed for a shorter period than expected.[5]

The most risky growth strategy is to launch a new product into a new market. This maximizes the chance that something will go wrong. It should only be considered when the potential rewards are considerable. The more the new product relies on technology that is outside the organization's current field of expertise, the more likely that trouble will be encountered. Also, the less that is known about customers, the more risky the project. Many Internet start-up companies fell into this quadrant of Table 5.1—new technology combined with little knowledge about customer susceptibility to try a new market space. As an increasing number of these companies perished, the industry was often referred to as 'dot-come and dot-go'.

RECAP

Success often creates the opportunity to grow—sometimes by expanding the current operations, but often by branching out in new directions. Growth is pursued by many organizations because their senior managers and investors believe that bigger is better. However, growth comes with many costs and risks. The costs relate to scaling up operations and to managing size and complexity. The risks relate to market failure—new products and services may not work, and/or customers may not want them.

Two key growth-related issues bedevil marketing managers. One is that growth often leads to a blurring of focus. In particular, the meaning consumers give to the corporate name or major brand names becomes blurred. As we will see in Chapter 7, this makes the key marketing tasks of positioning and differentiation difficult. The second issue is the organization's capability to create new products or services. Most organizations are weak in this area. Part B looks at how to improve this capability.

KEY CONCEPTS

- *Focus*—the application of the idea that 'less is more'. An organization becomes stronger by reducing the scope of operations. A brand creates a stronger image by owning a single benefit-related idea in consumers' minds (e.g. Volvo = safety).

- *Brand extension*—when an organization uses an established brand name to introduce a new product or service, in the same product line (a product line extension) or in a new product category (a product category extension).

KEY FRAMEWORKS

- *Strategies for growth*—Figure 5.1
- *Growth strategy risks*—Table 5.1

KEY QUESTIONS

- Is growth an overriding goal for your organization?
- How is growth occurring? And what are the sources of risk that you face?
- Does your organization 'own' an innovative position in the minds of key stakeholders (e.g. 3M = innovation; *hp* = invent)?

PART B

New Products and Services

> Make a better mousetrap, and the world will beat a path to your door.
>
> Ralph Waldo Emerson

Before looking at who is likely to adopt new products and services, it is useful to understand what makes the NPD process and the resulting new products successful. Again, research provides the insight. In this case, it is a meta-analysis (see Table 1.2) of sixty studies that looked at the antecedents of new product success.[6] What the authors found is that the dominant drivers of success are:

- product/service advantage—it is significantly better than current alternatives;
- a product or service that meets current or desired customer needs—as opposed to a developing need;
- there is substantial customer demand (i.e. market potential);
- the marketing and new product launch is done well;
- dedicated human resources in the development process;
- dedicated R&D resources;
- being as early to market as possible but not too early;
- congruency between the technological skills possessed by the organization and those needed to create the new product—'step-out' projects tend to fail.

All these factors seem logical. The one point of tension is having a strong product advantage and being early to market. When the desire to be first to market dominates make sure that the product works as expected (i.e. it lives up to its advertising), otherwise there is a real risk that when it is launched, the product is not bullet-proof. The Apple Newton PDA (personal digital assistant) is a good example of this. It set out to pioneer a new product category. It was early to market, but it was a much publicized failure. (It was expensive and did not work easily or reliably.) Many people referred to it as 'too little and too early'.[7] Today, Palm is the clear market leader in PDAs.

One of the popular myths among senior managers is that firms that are first to market with a new product gain a long-term advantage (such as higher market share and profits) over later entrants—the so-called *pioneer advantage*.[8] This advantage is thought to occur because (*a*) consumers develop stable preferences for early entrants, and/or (*b*) the pioneer becomes the standard in consumers' minds for the product category, and/or (*c*) a pioneer can 'lock-in' consumers in categories that have high switching costs, and/or (*d*) there are network effects in the market such that later adopters want to buy what other customers have already acquired, and/or (*e*) pioneers create barriers to entry for later followers by locking up key resources such as the best distributors, and/or (*f*) early entry enables pioneers to establish economies of scale and learning so that their costs are lower. These are a persuasive set of reasons to expect that pioneers will out-perform late entrants.

The only problem with the pioneer advantage strategy is that a casual look at a few markets shows that sometimes pioneers win, and win big (e.g. the Sony Walkman), but in many instances it is the later entrants that emerge the strongest (as noted above for the Palm Pilot PDA). Such casual observations are supported by systematic empirical research. For example, a study of fifty product categories (mainly consumer goods) found that pioneers had almost an even chance of failing (43 per cent).[9] These findings are consistent with the successful *fast follower* strategy used by many companies to launch new products.[10] The key to success here is to offer: better quality, or more reliability, or improved features, or a cheaper version of the original.[11] Some companies are very skilled at reverse engineering new products and then making them better. This is also a less risky strategy than pioneering a new product category.

One of the above new product success characteristics has been consistently found to be more important than the others. It is *product advantage*. So it seems that, all else being equal, 'if you make a better mousetrap, the world will beat a path to your door'. The reason for this is quite logical. The best way to get people to give up their current product or service is to offer them a *significantly* better one. This advantage can be in terms of more or better features and benefits, and/or a lower price. However, it is possible to have a better product and come second in the market. Sony did this when they launched the Beta video cassette recorder. By all accounts this was a technically superior product, and it is still used when quality is important, for example by many television stations. However, the commercialization and marketing strategy employed by Sony left an opportunity in the market that the makers of VHS machines exploited. (It involved the makers of VHS machines encouraging the release of pre-recorded VHS tapes. This then stimulated demand in the mass market for VHS machines.)[12]

There are two new product success factors that are always important—timing and luck! Sometimes the market is eager for a new product and sometimes competitors take a long time to respond. In other cases, a new product is created well before its time. For example, in the United States, the automobile was invented in 1771, commercialized in 1890, and sales took off in 1909. Most of the early car builders did not survive. (A very high price and no roads meant that cars were just 'rich men's toys'.) Another stumbling block for some products is 'the government'. Often, there are considerable delays for the certification of a new technology—particularly in new aircraft designs and new pharmaceutical products.

As noted in this section, a better product or service that fits the needs of customers are key success factors. The problem for the innovator is how to identify unmet customer needs, while the problem for the imitator is that outlined in the quote by Mark Twain at the beginning of this chapter, namely, to know which new products are likely to be successful—and, thus, be worth investing in. The next section describes some methods for identifying unmet needs. Following this, the focus shifts to the process of developing new products and services to meet these needs.

Sources of New Product and Service Ideas

> You have to kiss a lot of frogs to find the prince.
> Art Fry, inventor of the Post-It Note

The cultures most organizations have developed to maximize operational effectiveness and minimize risk do not automatically encourage innovation. Protecting current business and legacy assets often takes precedence over creating new business. This poses a problem for marketers because others in the organization look to them for innovative ideas, yet they work within a structure that does not naturally foster and reward such effort. In the search for and the development of new products and services, the situation on the right-hand side of Figure 5.2 is all too familiar.[13] To be more innovative, organizations need to redefine work around the creation of customer value (as outlined in Figures 2.4 and 2.6). Functions like marketing and

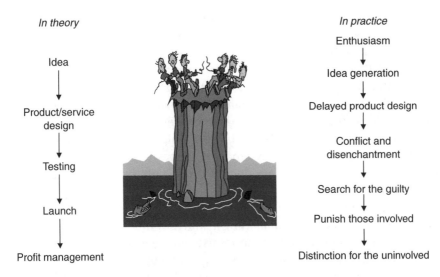

In theory	In practice
	Enthusiasm
Idea	↓
↓	Idea generation
Product/service design	↓
↓	Delayed product design
Testing	↓
↓	Conflict and disenchantment
Launch	↓
↓	Search for the guilty
	↓
	Punish those involved
	↓
Profit management	Distinction for the uninvolved

Figure 5.2. Theory versus practice

technology need to become organization-wide capabilities that support innovation across products and business units.

Organizations typically look for unmet customer needs from three sources. One is the insight of employees, and sometimes experienced people from the organization's advertising agency and market research firm. Another source is the market—often in an overseas location. A third source is consumers themselves. Each has its strengths and weaknesses, and often the best approach is to seek ideas from all three sources. The management task is to consider which employees and customers to talk to (some are better than others), and how to talk to them to elicit the best creative ideas.

Ideas from Employees

Top management, especially the founder of a company, can be a source of new product ideas. For example, on his first trip to the United States, Soichiro Honda became frustrated when trying to find coins for toll booths. His idea was to install coin trays in his cars—a useful innovation. Senior managers, however, have a mixed record of success with their pet projects. Also, these projects can carry a higher than normal risk for the company because many employees are reluctant to criticize them.

Companies that make technology-based products often rely on their scientists, engineers, and designers to dream up new product ideas. For example, Sony puts groups of engineers into teams to work on developing new products. When this type of strategy is employed, it is important to make sure that the team knows who the organization's target customers are, and that design specifications reflect the customers' needs. For example, one of the original design specifications given to the Sony development team for the Walkman was that the device was to fit into the top pocket of a man's shirt. Too often, however, high-technology products are designed to cater to every whim and fancy of any type of potential customer. What results is a product that can only be fully utilized by an expert or a teenager.

When a product is over-engineered to the customer's requirements, people are likely to have trouble using it, and they often resent having to pay for the features they do not or cannot use. (Many video cassette recorders, music systems, mobile phones, PDAs, big photocopiers, personal computer software programs, and TV remote controls fit this description.) In effect, these products have been 'designed to fail' from the customer's point of view. A very good example of such a product is Windows NT or XP (on your PC). It has more than 25 million lines of source code, and is far too sophisticated for most users.

Technology-based products need not intimidate their users. Two such very successful products have been Quicken's electronic cheque-book and financial planning PC software, and the original Palm Pilot PDA—an electronic diary that could communicate with a PC. Both were designed for the unsophisticated user, and both quickly became market leaders in their product categories. Both were designed around the CVP that 'less really is more'. (That is, they had a limited number of easy-to-use functions.)

In service industries, ideas frequently come from front-line service employees. They get regular feedback from customers about what works and what needs improving. Because they have to juggle the organization's service systems and customer requirements, they often have a good idea about what is possible to do and what is not. Other customer-contact people like salespeople, the customer complaints department, and the customer help desk will also have suggestions.

Toyota claims that its employees submit more than one million ideas each year. Many organizations give monetary and other rewards for such suggestions. The 'problem' with such broad-based suggestion schemes is that many do not have a direct connection to unmet customer needs. In order to get more structure to the idea generation process and, thus, a more focused set of ideas, many organizations employ a formal creativity technique to periodically generate ideas for later evaluation and development. These techniques have found favour in companies where a rigid organizational culture makes it difficult to be creative. Some of the more common ones are:

- *Brainstorming.* This technique asks a small group of people to come up with as many (wild) ideas as possible about how to solve a problem, such as find new uses for a product. The idea behind brainstorming is that quantity generates quality. That is, more ideas increase the chance of coming up with a 'winning' idea.[14] Brainstorming is a relatively 'safe' technique that rarely goes into the areas that are uncomfortable for senior managers—especially when they are involved.
- *Feature listing.* This technique calls for listing the major features of an existing product or service and then seeing how modifications of each feature would improve the product's performance or appeal.
- *Evolutionary projection.* Here, the natural evolution of a product or service is outlined and the trajectory of its innovation is identified. For example, Apple sold the first successful 'personal' computer. However, it was Compaq that understood that one important feature of a 'personal' computer was portability. They were much faster to market than Apple and most other PC manufacturers with portable (smaller and robust) machines.
- *Scouting time.* Here, select individuals are encouraged to work on their own pet projects. Companies like Amoco Chemical, Du Pont, Johnson & Johnson, Rohm and Haas, and 3M all encourage this type of activity with seed funding and official time to innovate. 3M's Art Fry who developed the ubiquitous Post-It Note is one of the best known examples of the success of this strategy.
- *Ally with a research university.* It is often surprising to find out what the academics are working on in their laboratories, and what opportunities this basic research might provide.

Ideas from the Marketplace

Market research firms regularly carry out usage and attitude studies for various product and service categories. These provide information about the problems and satisfaction with competing brands that can be useful input into the creativity techniques described earlier. Sometimes, researchers are asked to canvas opinions about innovative new product/service concepts. This is seldom a straightforward task as Scott Adams, business philosopher and creator of the Dilbert cartoon, illustrates:

Airline Survey (1920)

If you had to travel long distance, would you rather:

A. Drive a car.
B. Take a train.
C. Allow yourself to be strapped into a huge metal container that weighs more than your house and be propelled through space by exploding chemicals while knowing that any one of a thousand different human, mechanical, or weather problems would cause you to be incinerated in a spectacular ball of flame.

If you answered 'C', would you mind if we stomped on your luggage and sent it to another city?

Another productive source of ideas is 'what is happening overseas'. For example, many clothing trends are first observed as either street fashion or in the major fashion shows and magazines from London, Paris, Milan, and New York. They are then modified for the mass market. Sometimes the views of anthropologists and sociologists are sought to help companies understand how markets are evolving. This type of future-telling then becomes input into the new product idea generation process.

What competitors are doing is a constant source of new product and service ideas. Few companies, however, have competitive intelligence systems that are capable of tracking what their competitors are working on. Hence, their new products often come as a surprise to managers.

Ideas from Consumers

Often, consumer goods companies will 'go and talk' to some consumers to ask for their suggestions. Focus groups (described in Chapter 4) are a more formal version of this approach. These consumers are asked about current problems with products and services and suggestions for improvement. Another technique is to ask them to describe their 'ideal' product—its features, benefits, and emotional meaning. Sometimes, this direct approach uncovers fairly obvious areas for improvement. For example, many people do not like the process of buying a car, especially the haggle over its price. As a result of this, some car dealers now offer fixed-price cars.

Many market researchers, however, are sceptical about the usefulness of these approaches. The reason is that 'average' or 'representative' consumers generally have trouble articulating their unmet needs, and they are not likely to come up with a breakthrough new product idea. The market research company Research International (in the United States) claims to have a better approach. They recruit a number of SuperGroups® of trained, creative consumers to help companies develop new product ideas. These people, especially as they work with a company over time, seem to be more efficient and effective in creating innovative product concepts.

When industrial companies 'go and talk' to their customers for help and suggestions, they tend to do it in a more intensive and structured way than their consumer goods counterparts. Japanese-style 'design build teams' comprising engineers, production people, salespeople, and representatives from suppliers and subcontractors will converge on a customer for lengthy discussions. They examine the customer's activity cycle to see where they can add value by supplying a better product or service, or reducing costs. When Boeing developed its 777 jumbo jet, they used this approach.[15] They talked to the airlines, baggage handlers, maintenance engineers, airport ground crews, and travellers. In the process, they received hundreds of suggested improvements for the 777. (One was a small pneumatic device for stopping the toilet lid from falling down and making an embarrassing noise—something appreciated by many Asian travellers.)

Market research firms have discovered that not all types of consumers are worth talking to. Hence, the task for marketers and their researchers is to select those who are most likely to provide the best ideas. The SuperGroup approach for consumer products and services is one method. Another is to talk to consumers who are more innovative than their peers. *Innovators* are those people who make a new product/service adoption or rejection decision without needing peer support. They also are often seen to adopt successful new products earlier than other people.[16] These innovators can be both a source of ideas and a test-market for the adoption or rejection of new products. In their test-marketing role they can give a quick, and often quite accurate evaluation of whether a new product concept or prototype will be successful.

In B2B markets, *lead users* are a similar innovative group.[17] These are customers who are generally experts in their field with an ability to offer innovative suggestions about how products and services can be improved. Their organization has a strong interest in finding solutions to its problems and it is willing to help the NPD organization. As a reward for their ideas, the lead user has input into the new product's design, and by getting first use of the new product it can gain an advantage in the market. It may also be offered the product at a lower price. 3M has used this approach and found that it has contributed to finding many breakthrough new products as well as helping to improve current new product concepts and prototypes.

One final source of new product ideas for both B2C and B2B companies is 'observation'. Japanese companies often use this technique to discover new product needs. Product developers watch consumers using the product or service in their natural environment. For example, the design of the original Lexus car was influenced by watching and talking to target customers. One camera company examined 18,000 photographs to see why some did not turn out well. Two common problems were poor focus and a lack of light. The solution was auto-focus and the built-in flash.

As noted at the beginning of this section in the quote from Art Fry, the yield of new products from creative ideas is very low. Some estimates suggest that 50–100 new ideas are required to generate one new product. Thus, it is generally a good practice to get ideas for new products and services from multiple sources. In the overall NPD process (the left-hand side of Figure 5.2), the idea generation stage is cheap—relative to the costs involved in turning them into commercial products and services. The next section outlines the role of a formal NPD process in turning ideas into successful new products.

To summarize, it is interesting to think about when NPD should be driven primarily by customers, competitors, or the company's capabilities (the 3Cs of Figure 2.8). Here are some suggestions:

- *Customer-driven NPD*
  —when there are strong (sub)cultural norms or fashion trends that drive adoption (such as in the teenage market);
  —when lead users are active;
  —when innovators and industry experts can be identified.
- *Competitor-driven NPD*
  —when they obviously lead your target market;
  —if a big competitor's success could seriously impact your business (you have to strike fast to pre-empt their new product or service[18]).
- *Company-driven NPD*
  —when your business process allows you to develop and launch a large number of new products;
  —when you have to certify the design specifications of a product (e.g. pharmaceuticals);
  —when technology allows you to create breakthrough new products;
  —when consumers clearly do not know what is possible.

The Process of New Product Development

Juggling Success Potential and Speed to Market against the Risk of Failure

Over the years, companies like 3M, Eastman Kodak, Hewlett-Packard, and Sony have all developed strong cultures to encourage innovation. Innovation is achieved through individuals and is supported by an organizational culture that rewards people who come up with new product ideas. This culture is, in turn, supported by a formal NPD process. One of the primary roles of the NPD process is to ensure that new product ideas focus on the needs of target customers, and support the strategy of the organization. Another is to ensure that the learning that accrues throughout the development process is shared throughout the organization. Not repeating the same mistakes helps to reduce costs and increase the chance of successful product and service development.

Another equally important role of the NPD process is to help manage the risks involved in product development. These risks accrue to both the organization and the individual (as the right-hand side of Figure 5.2 attests). NPD is risky for organizations because as a new product idea progresses to become a prototype and later a commercial product, significant costs accumulate. NPD is risky for individuals because often managers are blamed for products that fail in the marketplace. In this case, following the formal NPD process is evidence that due process has been followed, and, thus, the process acts as an 'insurance policy' for the individuals involved. It is difficult to get people to be innovative on a scale necessary for an organization to drive its markets if the managers are worried about their careers in the event of the inevitable failures that accompany these risky ventures.

Every organization has its own unique NPD process. While these differ in their detail, many of them have two common elements. One is that there is a series of predetermined, clearly identifiable stages through which a product or service progresses—for example idea generation, screening, concept development, product development, product testing, market testing, and commercialization. The precise number and sequence of stages and the time taken to progress through them varies widely. It depends on the nature of what is being developed. For example, the Boeing 777 was one of the biggest NPD projects ever undertaken, taking five years to complete and at one time employing 10,000 people on the various design and development teams. It also depends on the experience of the organization. For example, Sony has been engaged in NPD for many years. In 1992, it had hundreds of NPD teams working on various projects.

The second common element about the NPD process of many organizations is that there are a number of points during the process (usually four to six) at which the organization formally evaluates whether or not the project should move forward. These have been called 'stage gates'.[19] At each gate a GO or NO GO decision is made by people outside the NPD team. While this process of peer review adds time, and some would say bureaucracy, to the NPD process, it also adds discipline—something that any innovative organization needs in order to control the risks created by their NPD projects. Figure 5.3 illustrates a mini Stage Gate NPD process.

Before discussing the key elements of the Stage Gate NPD process shown in Figure 5.3, it is worth pausing to consider why the initial stage is labelled 'Stage 0'. This is done to remind the NPD team that new product and service development needs to support the overall strategic direction of the organization. This may sound like the 'bleeding obvious', but it is surprising to many senior managers to find out that some of their organization's innovations have little or no relationship to their strategic direction. Consider the case of Xerox in the 1970s and 1980s. Its PARC research facility in Palo Alto, California, invented many of the features that made the original Apple PC such a success, yet neither the Xerox researchers nor their managers knew what to do with these inventions. (Steve Jobs and Steve Woznick, the co-founders of Apple, certainly did.)

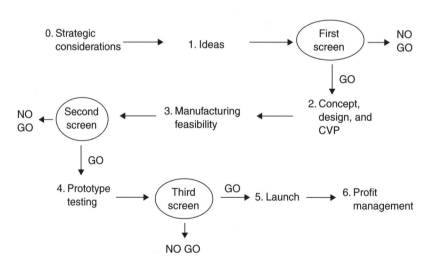

Figure 5.3. Stage gate new product development

The following types of issues need to be considered at each stage of Figure 5.3:

0. *Strategic considerations.* How does the potential new product or service support the organization's overall strategy? What are its key success factors? How will competitors respond? Does the organization have the technical capabilities, culture, and an NPD process to support the intended innovation?

1. *Ideas.* Where will new product ideas come from? (That is, the discussion in the previous section.) For which group of target consumers is the new product or service designed? Is there a gap in the market *and* is there a market in this gap?

   First screen. This stage gate focuses on two criteria, namely (*a*) the overall attractiveness of the market—its size, growth rate, profitability, competitive intensity, loyalty of target customers to existing brands, susceptibility to a price war, the rate of change of technology, etc.— and (*b*) the strength of the business unit—skills and resources, experience in NPD, knowledge of target customers, marketing capabilities, supporting product range, etc.

2. *Concept development.* Here, the core issue is what is the CVP. That is, what functional, economic, and psychological (emotional) benefits will the new product or service offer to the target customers? And how will these benefits be delivered by the design of the product/service? Developing CVPs is covered in Chapter 8.

3. *Manufacturing feasibility.* One of the main weaknesses of sequential NPD is the handoff of the product concept to the design, engineering, and manufacturing team(s). There are two complementary ways to overcome this problem. One is to form cross-functional NPD teams to be involved in all stages of development. (Consultants and researchers often recommend such an approach.) Another tactic is to use a process like quality function deployment (QFD) to manage the potential 'disconnect' between the concept developers and the designers and engineers. QFD is a technique originated by Mitsubishi for use in their Kobe shipyards in 1972. It was later extended by Toyota and more recently has been popularized by US companies and consultants.[20] QFD is a set of inter-functional planning and communication routines to ensure that descriptions of customer benefits are translated into design and engineering specifications that accurately reflect these benefits. (For why this is important see Exhibit 5.1.) QFD is often used as a key planning tool by cross-functional teams.

   Second screen. This stage gate involves building a business case for the new product/service. Is the concept feasible? How does it compare to

Exhibit 5.1. 'Correct' translation of customer requirements

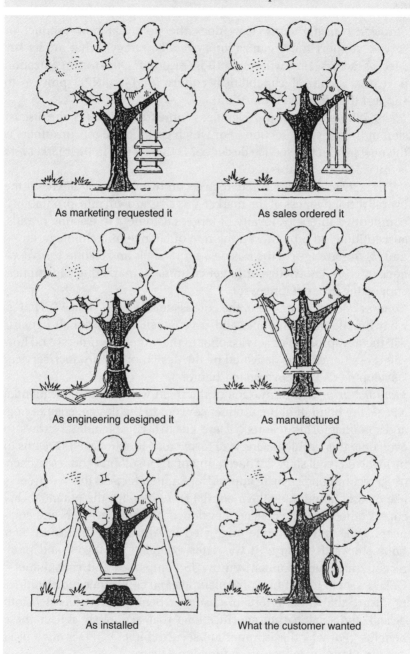

As marketing requested it

As sales ordered it

As engineering designed it

As manufactured

As installed

What the customer wanted

competitive offerings? Will it cannibalize any existing products? Is manufacturing feasible and what are indicative costs? What will be its price? How will it be distributed to target customers? What brand image will be projected? What type and amount of marketing support will it require? What is the profit potential? Are there any legal issues?

4. *Prototype testing.* For consumer products, this stage typically involves developing and testing the launch strategy in the form of a mini-marketing plan—target customer group, product prototype, brand position, advertising, sales and merchandizing, distribution, price level, etc., so that trial sales and any product cannibalization can be estimated. Trial production runs will also be necessary. Extensive market research and test marketing is generally involved. On the basis of these forecasts, budgets (production, personnel, and marketing) can be estimated, and strengths and weaknesses of both the product and its initial marketing determined. Often, this stage of development will alert competitors to the imminent launch of the new product. (They may also try to disrupt the test market by putting their own product on special, increasing advertising, etc.)

For industrial products, this stage may involve what is called an alpha test that is followed by beta testing. Alpha tests involve company personnel using the product as would a target customer. For example, Xerox tests many of its new photocopiers on its own employees before sending them out for beta testing. This involves providing the new product to selected customers for use and critical analysis. This feedback is used to make final adjustments before the new product is launched.

Third screen. This stage gate reviews the results from the prototype testing—sales which are made up of product trial and repeat purchasing (if any), product reliability (and returns), production runs and costs, logistics and distribution, salesforce and retailer support, customer price sensitivity, advertising awareness and brand image formation, etc. The aim is to produce a more reliable (than the second screen) financial analysis of the new product.

5. *Launch.* By this stage, any bugs in the new product and its launch strategy should have been fixed and the task is to roll it out to the wider market.

6. *Profit management.* The aim here is to track awareness, trial, repeat purchase, brand image formation, stock turn, cash flow, customer loyalty, and competitor response. Chapter 12 (Figure 12.6) shows a technique for doing this.

When using a stage gate process such as Figure 5.3, the first step for the organization is to outline the sequence of stages to drive the development of their products and services. Step two is to develop the procedures to be followed at each stage. Step three is to develop the customized screening criteria for use at each stage gate. Agreement about these screening criteria and their relative importance need to be established among the reviewing managers. They are then used to evaluate some past successes and failures to see if the chosen criteria can accurately discriminate between successes and failures. If they can, they form the basis for evaluation. If they cannot, then a new set of criteria needs to be developed.

Not every organization follows all the stages in Figure 5.3. Some adopt a strategy called 'fast failure'. Here, the organization develops a new product to the advanced prototype stage and then launches it into a market. It then iteratively refines the features, position, price, distribution, etc., based on early user feedback and sales results. If the early signs are bad, the product will be withdrawn quickly to minimize losses—both monetary and to the reputation of the organization. This strategy maximizes speed to market but increases the risks of failure. It is more likely to be successful when customers are forgiving and the brand is not likely to be damaged when it evolves.

The key new product screening and, thus, the risk management issue for marketing managers is to achieve a balance between what the statisticians call Type I and Type II errors. A Type I error occurs when what would have been a winning new product is rejected at one of the stage gates, while a Type II error occurs when a bad new product is launched. Why achieving a balance is so difficult to do is because managers are asked to make an investment decision with incomplete information, and to use evaluation criteria at the stage gates that are often unmeasurable and sometimes internally inconsistent. (For example, being fast to market versus launching only high-quality and reliable products.) In cases such as these, populating the stage-gate committees with experienced managers is essential.

In summary, most successful developers of new products and services have their own unique formal and trusted NPD process. The reasons that organizations innovate differently are that they have different core competencies (experience, technology, and funds to invest) and business systems (organizational culture and formal policies). However, many organizations setting out on the NPD trail for the first time do not see the payoff from investing in the development of such a formal process. Robert Cooper's research, however, suggests that organizations that have a formal process tend to have fewer and less costly new product failures.[21]

However, the evidence is mixed about whether these processes contribute significantly to the chance of creating breakthrough new products and services.[22]

While a good NPD process reduces the likelihood of failure, the question remains: 'What is the average failure rate across markets?' Estimates vary, but the common consensus is that most new products and services fail to reach their sales goals. Some studies have estimated an 80 per cent failure rate after products are launched into the market (Stage 5 in Figure 5.3).[23] This is a daunting figure for marketing managers and their superiors.

Exhibit 5.2. Playing the numbers game

Big organizations have the luxury of launching hundreds of new products into their markets each year. For example, in 1992, Sony launched roughly 1000. Approximately 80 per cent of these were low-risk, improved versions of current products and additions to existing product lines. The remaining 20 per cent were high-risk, new breakthrough products. To see how the numbers play out, assume that their new breakthrough products have only a 20 per cent chance of success when launched into the market, and that the new low-risk products have a 50 per cent chance of success. Also assume that the success or failure of each new product is independent of the success/failure of any of the other products. Then, the probability of at least one new product success (P) when n new products are launched is determined by

$$P = 1 - (1 - p)^n$$

where p = probability that each new product will be successful
      = 0.2 for the breakthrough products
      = 0.5 for the low-risk products

n	p (0.2)	p (0.5)
1	0.20	0.50
2	0.36	0.75
3	0.49	0.88
4	0.59	0.94
5	0.67	0.97
6	0.74	
7	0.79	
8	0.83	

Thus, when eight high-risk new products are launched, there is an 83 per cent chance that at least one of them will be a commercial success for the organization. For the low-risk new products, one out of every five launched will be successful.

Three strategies are available to increase the number of successful new products and services an organization launches into the market:

- Improve the NPD process and the marketing of new products. In particular, develop only significantly better products than currently exist in the market.
- Improve the understanding of (unmet) customer needs. This topic is discussed further in Chapter 6.
- Play the numbers game and launch more new products into the market. This strategy is described in Exhibit 5.2.

RECAP

At the risk of oversimplifying a very complicated world, three key success factors of new products and services emerge from the art and science of marketing:

- make them significantly better than existing alternatives;
- make sure they meet a current or desired customer need;
- design them from the target customers' point of view (e.g. the Sony Walkman).

This is such a simple formula for success, but it is so difficult to implement. Why? Because (a) the NPD process that many organizations work through does not promote these success factors, and (b) the risks and uncertainties in NPD require a sustained level of activity that only a relatively few organizations commit to.

KEY CONCEPTS

- *Pioneer advantage*—the (hoped for) higher market share and profits that come from being first to market with a new product or service.
- *Fast follower strategy*—the strategy of re-engineering and improving the new product or service of a market-driving organization and then quickly launching this product under the organization's brand name.
- *Innovators*—people who quickly adopt or reject a new product or service without the need for the support of their peers.
- *Lead users*—sophisticated organizations that are prepared to help co-develop new products with manufacturers. These organizations face a need that will be general in the marketplace well before the bulk of potential adopters, and they expect to benefit significantly by obtaining an early solution to this need.

KEY FRAMEWORKS

- *Drivers of new product success*—page 140
- *Stage-gate new product development*—Figure 5.3
- *Playing the numbers*—Exhibit 5.2

KEY QUESTIONS

- Inside your organization, what are deemed to be the key success factors for a new product or service? And how do these compare to the factors outlined here?
- If you were to draw a map of your organization's NPD process, how would it compare to the stage-gate process outlined in Figure 5.3?
- What is the organization's level of new product development activity? Is this sufficient to drive your markets or to respond to the changing needs of target customers?

To continue the theme of taking an outside–inside look at the organization, Part C examines the characteristics of potential customers for a new product or service.

PART C

Who might Buy Our New Product/Service?

As noted throughout this chapter, not all new products and services have the same degree of newness built into them. Some are breakthrough products designed to create new product categories and, thus, new markets, Amazon.com and the Apple Newton PDA being good examples. Most, however, are brand extensions—of either the product line or product category type. Thus, different types of products are likely to appeal to different types of customers. For example:

- *An upwards brand line extension* may appeal to people who want to trade up (e.g. from a BMW 316 to a 325), or who want more features with the same type of product (e.g. from a Palm Pilot V to a Palm Pilot VII).
- *A downwards brand line extension* may appeal to people who could not afford the better quality product (e.g. the Porsche Boxster), or

who did not need everything that the up-market brand offers (e.g. the Courtyard hotel by Marriott which is targeted at salespeople).

- *A brand category extension* may appeal to people who like the 'family brand' values (e.g. Virgin is a 'challenger' brand for many people), or to people who aspire to the brand values but do not want to fully participate (e.g. buyers of Harley-Davidson clothes who are not motorbike riders).
- *A continuous innovation* such as colour television, safer cars, 3G mobile phones, and notebook PCs often appeal to current users who want more of a benefit that is currently offered. If priced reasonably, they may also appeal to new users of the product category.
- *A breakthrough new product or service* may appeal to people with an unmet need who have the capability to buy and use it (e.g. the first automobiles were very expensive and required the owner to carry out repairs and maintenance).

Breakthrough innovation is an area that has attracted an enormous amount of research—by 1995, more than 4000 separate studies.[24] These new products are of strategic importance to market driving companies because they often create a new market. Also, because all markets start out as new ones, the rest of this chapter looks at the buyers of these products and services.

The evolution of a new market is generally looked at as a two-stage process. First adoption, and then diffusion.

Adoption

People adopt a new product or service if they have a need for it, it is available, and they can afford to buy it. Part B of Chapter 4 discussed the decision-making process involved when buying new (and old) products and services. What was missing from this discussion, and is of importance here, is the timing of the adoption or rejection decision by potential buyers. Why do some people adopt faster than others?

The speed at which people will make an adoption or rejection decision is based on a number of factors—some of which are characteristics of the person, and some which are determined by the organization's marketing. For example:

- When does the potential adopter become aware of the new product or service? Some people have bigger social networks. Some are exposed to more mass media. Some are highly involved in the product category.

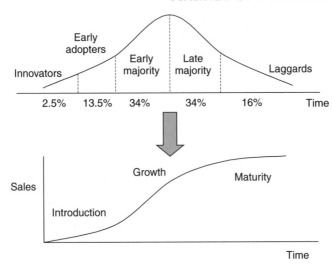

Figure 5.4. Time-based adoption and the PLC

The earlier a person becomes aware and informed about the new product, the earlier they can adopt or reject it. Marketing plays a big role here.

- Some people will not adopt a new product or service without the support of their peers. Because it takes time for their peers to signal that this new product is acceptable to the social group, these people will take longer to adopt than the more innovative buyers. Recall that the innovators are often the first people to adopt or reject a new product. The other people are variously called the 'early majority', 'later adopters', or 'laggards' depending on how long it takes then to become aware and receive enough peer support to adopt. (Peer support can come in many forms. For example, it may be as simple as a friend saying 'I would never buy that', or it may be as subtle as waiting to see whether other similar people or companies have adopted. In other cases, buyers may wait for some type of official endorsement from an industry association or a trusted opinion leader to give the new product their blessing.)

The time taken to adopt a new product has been used as the basis for segmenting people—Figure 5.4. This segmentation scheme forms the basis for the typical product life cycle described in Chapter 3 and shown in Figure 3.4.[i]

---

[i] The adoption distribution is normally distributed and the segments of adopters correspond to the areas under the curve partitioned according to standard deviations either side of the average time of adoption. The S-shaped PLC is the cumulative version of this distribution.

- Some people have a stronger need for the new product than others— thus, they are more motivated to search for it, and they may be less critical of early quality and reliability issues.
- Some organizations offer better new products that are also easier to try before purchase. The ACCORD checklist in Exhibit 5.3 is a very useful guide to evaluating a new product or service.

Exhibit 5.3. ACCORD

One checklist to help evaluate the potential adoption and subsequent commercial success of a new product or service is known as ACCORD. It focuses on the target customer, namely, their needs, perceptions, and current modes of behaviour, rather than the technical aspects of the product/service.

Advantage
What is the *relative* advantage of the new product or service over that being currently used by the target customer? This is measured as the degree to which the product or service is *perceived* to be better than the one it replaces. This advantage can be functional (it does the job better), social and psychological (it fits with status desires of the person), and economical (it comes at a better price or it may reduce the costs of the buyer).

Compatibility
Compatibility is the degree to which a new product or service is perceived to be consistent with the existing values, past experiences, and needs of the target customers. Products and services that are more compatible are less uncertain, and they fit more closely with the target customer's current life situation. Thus, it is easier for the individual to give meaning to these products. Hence, they take less effort to adopt.

Complexity
This is the degree that people think that the new product is easy to understand and use.

Observability
This is the degree to which a new product or its benefits are visible to others. For example, when you buy a new Porsche 911 or the latest fashion garment, people notice.

Risk
Perceived risk is a person's *perception* of their chance of injury or loss when adopting a new product or service. It is a primary factor that inhibits the

adoption of many new products and services. The word perception is important here. For example, bungy jumping and skydiving are perceived as far too risky by some people but not by others.

Divisibility
Also known as trailability, this is the degree to which a new product or service can be experienced on a limited basis before the customer has to commit to the full purchase. Rental cars are a good way to try before buying.

Mobile phones
Why have they been adopted so quickly and widely?

1. *Relative Advantage* over fixed-line phones—no missed calls, mobile communication, status symbol, always handy, etc. Disadvantage—more expensive.
2. *Compatibility*—connects to the existing system thus having a critical mass of other cellphone users was not necessary early in the product life cycle.
3. *Complexity*—it operates exactly the same way as a regular phone.
4. *Observability*—being able to be used anywhere enhanced the perceived status of many users.
5. *Perceived risk*—low for most people although there is some concern about radiation effects. New head-set attachments are designed to ameliorate this.
6. *Divisibility/trialability*—easy for most people, try a friend's phone.

Diffusion

Diffusion is the process whereby information about a new product or service is communicated over time among the potential consumers in a market. The communication channels are the mass media, and/or word-of-mouth, and/or line-of-sight (i.e. by observation). Often, it will be a combination of all three. In a B2B context, managers become aware of, and learn about new products through advertising, salespeople, industry associations, technical magazines, talking to associates, and going to trade shows and conferences. Interpersonal communication is generally thought to be the more influential communication channel.

The mass media is typically good for creating awareness and providing basic information about a new product, such as: What does it do? Where can it be found? How much does it cost? The amount and persuasiveness of this type of communication can also be important. For example, research has shown that the mere fact that a new product is advertised in the mass media is a signal that it is likely to be of better quality than those that are not.[25] I guess that 'money talks'.

In any market segment, some people will be more influential in shaping the opinions of other people. These people are called *opinion leaders* or *innovative communicators*. They are important to identify because they amplify the credibility of information and they may speed up its flow in a market. Thus, they have a disproportionate influence on the adoption or rejection of many new products and services. In B2B markets, consultants, scientists, academics, business leaders, and journalists frequently play this role. In B2C markets, family members, friends, journalists, and celebrities help to shape opinions.

One aspect of diffusion is often misunderstood by marketers. It is that a new product may diffuse both within and across quite different market segments. That is, it is launched into one segment of the market, but other people see it and then decide they can also use it. For example, mobile phones were launched in the United States in 1983 at a price of about $3000 each. The first adopters were male executives whose companies provided them as an office perk. Later adopters were mobile managers, then salespeople and tradespeople, and finally parents, children, and grandparents. They have become one of the true personal electronic products of our time. When a product becomes as widespread as a mobile phone, the companies like Nokia that market them have to be careful to tailor the product to fit the different needs and different price sensitivity of each segment.

To summarize, adoption is an individual decision and is driven by a basic need for the product, its affordability, and its relative advantage over existing products and services that fulfil this need. Diffusion is a process by which information about a new product or service is communicated over time among members of the target market. The marketing strategy of the seller and the evaluation of other people speeds up or slows down the first purchase and subsequent repeat purchase of the product or service. These are the major factors that drive adoption and diffusion. We are now ready to put all this together by segmenting potential adopters into various groups that differ from each other with respect to their susceptibility to adopt a new product or service. Recall that for both market driving and market driven organizations, segmentation is important because it uncovers groups of customers with unmet or under-fulfilled needs. This can stimulate the search for breakthrough new products and services to create new markets or it can lead to improved current products.

RECAP

Look to current customers as the buyers of brand extensions and continuous innovations. Why? Because from the consumers' points of view, the benefits of these new products and services better fulfil their needs. The primary role of marketing here is to promote 'new and improved'.

For new breakthrough products and services, the identification of potential customers is more difficult. By definition, the organization is setting out to offer something to the market that it has not considered before. In this circumstance, it is important to think creatively about which types of customers will benefit from the new product or service. The best way to do this is to resegment the market using the perceived benefits and risks entailed in adopting. Chapter 6 examines this style of segmentation. The roles of marketing here are to identify potential adopters, inform them of the new product, and make it easy to trial and talk about the new product. In this way, marketing facilitates both adoption and diffusion.

KEY CONCEPTS

- *Adoption*—the decision to buy and/or use a new product or service.
- *Diffusion*—the process whereby information about a new product or service is communicated over time among members of the target market.
- *Opinion leaders*—key people who influence the discussion about the merits and demerits of a new product or service.

KEY FRAMEWORKS

- *New product adopter segments*—Figure 5.3
- *ACCORD*—Exhibit 5.3

KEY QUESTIONS

- When developing a new product or service, is its adoption potential assessed against the ACCORD checklist?
- Amongst your target customers, can you identify the innovators and the opinion leaders?
- Is there good information about the potential benefits or solutions to problems and the perceived risks associated with your new products and services?

- When launching a new product or service, are marketing programmes sympathetic to the ACCORD criteria?

NOTES

1. For a good discussion of how growth can unfocus a company, see A. Ries, *Unfocused* (London: HarperCollins Business, 1996).
2. As noted in Chapter 3, many managers adopt a marketing as warfare approach to competition.
3. K. L. Keller, *Strategic Brand Management* (Upper Saddle River, NJ: Prentice Hall, 1998) p.67.
4. Keller (1998), chapter 12.
5. R. F. Hartley, 'Disney—EuroDisney and Other Stumbles', *Marketing Mistakes and Successes* (New York: John Wiley & Sons, 2001), pp. 209–25; M. J. Brannen and J. M Wilson, 'What does Mickey Mouse Mean to You?' *Financial Times* (26 April, 1996), pp. 14–16.
6. D. H. Henard and D. M. Szymanski, 'Why Some New Products are More Successful than Others', *Journal of Marketing Research*, 38, 3 (2001), 362–75.
7. B. L. Bayus, S. Jain, and A. Rao, 'Too Little and Too Early: A Competitive Analysis of the Personal Digital Assistant Industry', *Journal of Marketing Research*, 34, 1 (1997), 50–63.
8. Very little research has been done on the pioneer advantage for services. See, for example, X. M. Song, C. A. Di Benedetto, and L. Z. Song, 'Pioneering Advantage in New Service Development: A Multi-Country Study of Managerial Perceptions', *Journal of Product Innovation Management*, 17, 5 (2000), 378–92.
9. P. N. Golder and G. J. Tellis 'Pioneer Advantage: Marketing Logic or Marketing Legend?' *Journal of Marketing Research*, 30, 2 (1993), 158–70.
10. S. P. Schnaars, *Managing Imitation Strategies: How Later Entrants Seize Market Shares from Pioneers* (New York: Free Press, 1994).
11. Entrants and incumbents primarily compete on the basis of continued product improvements during the early stages of the product life cycle. S. Klepper, 'Industry Life Cycles', *Industrial and Corporate Change*, 6, 1 (1997), 145–81.
12. M. A. Cusumano, Y. Mylonadis, and R. S. Rosenbloom, 'Strategic Manoeuvring and Mass-Market Dynamics: The Triumph of VHS over Beta', in M. L. Tushman and P. Anderson (eds.), *Managing Strategic Innovation and Change* (New York: Oxford University Press, 1997), pp. 75–98.
13. Figure 5.2 is based on G. Urban and J. Hauser, *Design and Marketing of New Products* (Englewood Cliffs, NJ: Prentice Hall, 1993), p. 50.
14. J. R. Rossiter and G. L. Lilien, 'New Brainstorming Principles', *Australian Journal of Management*, 19, 1 (1994), 61–72.
15. K. Sabbagh, *21st-Century Jet* (New York: Scribner, 1996).

16. G. R. Dowling, 'Consumer Innovativeness', in P. E. Earl and S. Kemp (eds.), *Consumer Research and Economic Psychology* (Cheltenham: Edward Elgar, 1999), pp. 111–15.

17. E. von Hippel, *The Sources of Innovation* (New York: Oxford University Press, 1988).

18. J. Trout, *Big Brands, Big Trouble* (New York: John Wiley & Sons, 2001), p. 48.

19. R. Cooper, *Winning at New Products* (Reading, MA: Addison Wesley, 1993).

20. J. R. Hauser and D. Clausing, 'The House of Quality', *Harvard Business Review* (May–June, 1988), 63–73.

21. R. Cooper, *Winning at New Products* (Reading, MA: Addison Wesley, 1993).

22. D. H. Henard and D. M. Szymanski, 'Why Some New Products are More Successful than Others', *Journal of Marketing Research*, 38, 3 (2001), 362–75.

23. R. G. Cooper and E. J. Kleinschmidt, *New Products: The Key Factors in Success* (Chicago: American Marketing Association, 1990).

24. Many of these are noted in E. M. Rogers, *Diffusion of Innovations* (New York: Free Press, 1995).

25. Some of the original research that fostered this viewpoint is: P. Nelson, 'Information and Consumer Behavior', *Journal of Political Economy*, 78, 2 (1970), 311–29; and P. Nelson, 'Advertising as Information', *Journal of Political Economy*, 82, 4 (1974), 729–54.

STRATEGY

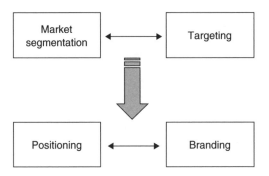

CHAPTER

6

Market Segmentation and Targeting

There is no such thing as an average customer.

Each business discipline has at its core two or three central ideas.[1] Market segmentation is one of these basic ideas on which much of modern marketing is built. For most organizations, market segmentation is a primary way to search for and exploit market opportunities. Part A of this chapter starts by describing three broad types of segmentation—corporate, product-market, and tactical. Big organizations like General Electric practice all three types, while smaller organizations usually practice product-market and tactical segmentation. The chapter then looks at the underlying logic of why most organizations segment their market.

Part B of the chapter examines product-market segmentation and strategic market selection. One of the key questions here is how many segments to compete in? For example, should the organization (or SBU) select a single product-market, or should it seek to develop a product specialization, or a market specialization, or like General Motors, Ford, and Toyota seek to serve every major identifiable segment of consumers—small, medium, and large passenger cars, commercial vehicles, 4WDs, and others.

Part C of the chapter examines tactical segmentation and targeting. Here, the emphasis is to 'get close to customers' by developing a 'rich' understanding their needs, wants, and how they go about buying products and services. The material in Chapter 4 is used to build tactical segments.

This chapter is built around the following definitions:

- *Market segmentation*—is the process of partitioning a heterogeneous market into a number of homogeneous groups of consumers.
- *Market segments*—are groups of actual or potential consumers who can be expected to respond in a similar way to a product or service offer. That is, they want the same types of benefits or solutions to problems

from the product or service, or they are expected to respond in a similar way to a marketing programme.

- *Target markets*—are the segments of consumers that the organization chooses to serve.

These three definitions form the first two parts of the *STP* framework— *Segmentation, Targeting,* and *Positioning* (which is discussed in the next chapter). STP is one of the most important frameworks discussed in this book.

PART A

Segmenting Markets

Three Types of Segmentation

Organizations typically approach the segmentation decision from three broad perspectives. The first is a strategic perspective—as discussed in Chapter 2. Here, the focus is on deciding what industries to compete in and, thus, what broad types of products and services to supply. The organization's set of SBUs and their business models are the mechanisms to implement this type of segmentation. The second type of segmentation focuses on broad product-markets. That is, which types of products and services will be offered in which markets. The third type of segmentation is tactical. The role of tactical segmentation is to implement the customer value approach to marketing described in Chapter 1, Figure 1.3. This type of segmentation is the direct responsibility of the marketing team.

A competition perspective can be used to describe the relationship among the three types of segmentation. Strategic segmentation deals with the 'what' of competition—what industry, what strategy, and what business model. Long time horizons and large investments typically characterize this form of segmentation. Product-market segmentation deals with the 'which' of competition—which types of products and services and which broad type(s) of customers (e.g. business, household, etc). Tactical segmentation deals with the 'who' and the 'how' of competition—who precisely are the target customers and how will they be served. Short time horizons and tactical marketing programmes characterize this form of segmentation.

To illustrate the types of segmentation, consider General Electric. A visit to their corporate website (www.ge.com) shows how they are organized into more than 20 SBUs (e.g. GE Aircraft Engines, Appliances, Lighting, Medical

Systems, Plastics, Power Systems, and others). Each SBU then focuses on various product markets (e.g. Lighting—Home Lighting, Business Lighting, Lighting Systems in Australia, Germany, and others). Within each product-market, the marketing managers tactically segment customers (e.g. Business Lighting—key accounts, major accounts, special projects, and others).

To further illustrate the relationship between the various types of segmentation, consider Porsche Cars North America.[2] The company imports cars from Germany for sale through their dealer network. This is their business model (i.e. their strategic segmentation). In the United States, they offer a limited range of cars that are typically bought by forty-something male college graduates who earn more than $200,000 per year. This is their product-market segment. Consumer research discovered that there were many reasons these people bought Porsche sports cars. These reasons were used to create the following tactical segments:

- *Top guns*—they expect to be noticed.
- *Elitists*—old money, a car is just a car, it is not an extension of their personality.
- *Proud patrons*—the car is a trophy earned from hard work.
- *Bon vivants*—worldly jet-setters, the car is an excitement machine.
- *Fantasists*—the car is an escape, they feel a little guilty about owning one.

With such different segments in the market for a Porsche 911, the marketing team and the dealer salespeople have to be very careful how they advertise the car and talk to a prospect on the showroom floor.

The Logic of Segmentation

The logic behind market segmentation is as follows. It will be to the financial benefit of an organization to offer different products and services to different segments of a market when:

- customers place greater value on different product/service configurations than it costs to create this variety;
- identifiably different groups of consumers exist in the market;
- the organization bases its strategy on economies of scope or economies of focus rather than economies of scale.[3]

The first condition is quite straightforward—consumers must be prepared to pay for different products and services in a category. The second condition is less straightforward. Periodically, market research reveals that segmentation is very limited. One such long-standing example is television. Since the 1970s, in the United Kingdom and the United States television has largely remained a mass medium. While specific non-terrestrial channels do target special interest viewers (such as young children, sports, music, news, and movie buffs), most of these viewers still watch more general entertainment programmes on the free-to-air channels each week than they do their favourite genre channel. Here, the research shows clear viewer segments are hard to identify.[4]

The third condition above focuses on the role of cost in the organization's strategy. When an organization has achieved clearly dominant economies of scale, it can lower its price to such an extent that the customer value created by product variety is (all but) eliminated. (This is one reason for the success of Henry Ford's Model T Ford. It was so cheap, relative to the hand-built cars of its era, that most people would gladly accept its shortcomings.) Such an organization would not be as concerned about segmenting its customers according to their needs as one that bases its strategy on either economies of scope or focus. (Recall from Chapter 2 that economies of scope arise because the organization's costs can be spread across products, and economies of focus arise through specialization.)

The alternative to a segmentation strategy is one of undifferentiated marketing. Here, the organization goes after all the market with one product, and it relies on mass distribution and shotgun advertising to gain maximum salience. Coca-Cola's early marketing of one flavour in one size bottle is a good example. The big free-to-air television channels in Australia, the United Kingdom, and the United States are another example. They all offer a range of general interest, sport, and entertainment programmes to appeal to the broadest possible audience. Intel's early products (the 286, 386, and 486 chips) are another example of mass marketing. With the launch of the Pentium chips, however, Intel segmented its original equipment manufacturer (OEM) market into the segments of home desktops, business desktops, mobile computers, and commercial servers.[5]

There are two broad styles of market segmentation, namely, to (*a*) identify the different types of customers that naturally exist in a market, or (*b*) create artificial groups of customers that better fit the way the organization carries out its business. The first approach groups customers according to their characteristics and needs, while the second approach groups customers according to the organization's capabilities to serve them. This distinction is very important because it can lead organizations to create very satisfied or very dissatisfied customers.

When customers are segmented primarily according to their needs, it is clear how products and services should be designed to satisfy these needs.

When this matching process is done well, the result is satisfied customers. For example, research in the United States discovered that a large number of women who are in the market for a pair of jeans have trouble finding a pair that fit everywhere that they should. One solution to this problem is for the jeans companies to offer a wide range of fittings. A better solution is offered by Levi Strauss. In its Union Square store in San Francisco, a customer can be measured by a body scanner. These measurements are sent to the factory and a perfectly fitting 'personal pair' of jeans is made and sent to the buyer. It takes about ten days and it costs about 30 per cent more. However, if you like jeans and you do not come in a 'standard' size, then this mass customized service is highly valued. Levi's also gains from this service—they have to keep less stock in their shop, they receive market research information about the body shapes of jeans buyers, they have timely information about changes in demand, and they can direct mail their custom customers with new styles and colours. Thus, this example of satisfying the needs of a segment of customers is a win for both parties (but not for the other retailers who sell Levi's).

Instead of focusing primarily on providing value to customers, some organizations use market segmentation to evaluate how customers can provide value to them. For example, for many banks the primary segmentation base is the customer's 'footings' (i.e. the total amount of their debt and deposits). This is the basis of profitability to the bank.[6] From the bank's point of view, this is a sensible way to manage the yield from different types of customers. However, from the customer's point of view it often seems very mercenary. In Australia, one of the most criticized industries by their customers is retail banking.[7]

When managers use an organization-centric classification of customers as their primary mode of segmentation, they see segmentation as an optimization problem. It replaces the search for the needs-based segments with the search for a classification of customers that will lead to the most efficient and/or profitable outcome for the organization. As discussed in Chapter 1, getting a balance between providing value to customers and having customers provide value to the organization is one of the key challenges facing marketing managers. The Levi Strauss example shows that it can be done. It requires a keen understanding of customer needs, often combined with some clever business process innovation. It also needs to be supported by the KPIs of the managers who are responsible for making these decisions. If financial measures of performance clearly dominate customer satisfaction in senior management KPIs, then it should not be surprising to find that customer profitability-based segmentation may dominate customer needs segmentation.

Strategic Choices

The examples of Levi's women's jeans and original Coca-Cola represent two ends of a spectrum of choices faced by marketing managers. The Levi's example is called *mass customization*. The Coca-Cola example is called *mass marketing*. While both strategies can be profitable, there is a feeling among many academics, consultants, and managers that mass customization is the way of the future. Organizations that do not reorganize towards mass customizing their products and services will be left behind. This prediction has been fuelled by a powerful new digital environment that has emerged to facilitate and support market exchanges. Developments in IT and the Internet are two of the more visible examples of this new environment. However, because IT and the Internet have proven to be expensive to develop, and have often not delivered what has been promised, managers need to take care when heading towards a mass customized business model.

Figure 6.1 illustrates four options for marketing managers to consider. At one extreme, a generic product is offered to any interested person or organization. Many industrial products (chemicals, metals, lubricants, fuels, etc.) are sold this way. So are some consumer products. For example, it is possible to buy diamonds (not jewellery) through the website www.aurisa.com. (The resource company BHP Billiton supports this consumer venture.) A variation of this strategy we see in every supermarket is the branded 'me-too' product.

Many big consumer goods companies (like Colgate, Nabisco, Procter & Gamble, Unilever, and Fosters Brewing) produce a number of functionally similar brands in the same product category. For example, in the United States, Procter & Gamble sell nine brands of laundry detergent (Bold, Cheer, Dash, Dreft, Era, Ivory, Snow, Oxydol, and Tide). This is known as

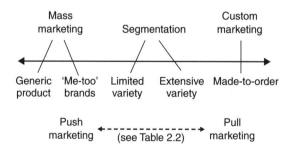

Figure 6.1. Segmentation options

a *product differentiation* strategy—each brand has some unique features, positioning, and packaging, and some may be sold at a different price point. Hopefully, they appeal to different types of customer or they may be preferred for different use occasions. When done poorly, however, product differentiation often resembles mass marketing more than customer segmentation. The reason is that the differences between the brands are more contrived than real. For example, without the packaging, most consumers could not tell which brand of detergent was used to wash their clothes. Also, companies like Procter & Gamble, and the retailers who sell their brands, practice what is known as 'category management'. Here, the emphasis is on managing the profit from the brand portfolio in the product category—a yield management style of marketing. It is a more product-focused than customer-focused approach to marketing.

At the other extreme is *customized marketing* and *mass customization* where every consumer is thought to be unique—either in the way they want to buy and/or their set of needs. Thus, each consumer is a segment of one. Customized marketing is common in B2B marketing—especially for major customers. Here, manufacturing, products, services, prices, logistical arrangements, and financial terms and conditions are often customized for different accounts. Mass customization is becoming more common in B2C markets. Here, organizations try to customize a product in its final stages of manufacture ('what colour would you like'), or with its surrounding service ('could we help you with that'). When an organization has thousands, if not millions of potential target customers, customization can go only so far. In the Levi's example, it was restricted to the product—you get a personalized pair of jeans, but please do not haggle about the price or the delivery.

Most contemporary marketing happens between the two extremes in Figure 6.1. Organizations do not consider all consumers to be the same nor do they have the skills to customize their products, services, and communication to each individual consumer. Some offer a limited range of choices such as Microsoft and Intel. Others, like most automobile and PC manufactures, offer more variety. A few have the capabilities to offer extensive variety, such as Japan's National Bicycle Industrial Company, that can produce any of 11,231,862 variations of 18 models of bikes, and John Deere who can produce more than 2 million different farm seeding machines. The amount of variety offered depends on three factors:

- the number of naturally occurring segments in the market;
- the capability to cost-effectively produce a range of products or services;
- the desired scope of market coverage.

RECAP

One of the key differences between the disciplines of economics and marketing is that while economics talks about consumers, marketing talks about customer segments. By creating groups of homogeneous customers that differ from each other in critical ways, marketing has a richness that eludes much of economics. This makes it more relevant to business—both for the formulation of strategy and for the development of programmes to attain and retain customers.

When an organization creates its segments primarily on the basis of customer needs, it is following the advice of Peter Drucker that was introduced Chapter 1, namely, it is creating (or focusing on) customers. There are many different ways to serve these customer segments. At one extreme, there is mass marketing. Here, there is a basic homogeneity of consumer needs such that most people are happy with a single branded product or service, and, thus, can be considered as being in one big segment. At the other extreme, people have different needs and they are prepared to pay for their individual needs to be satisfied. If the organization has the capability to sense and respond to these needs, a made-to-order strategy will be more appropriate.

KEY CONCEPTS

- *Undifferentiated marketing*—the organization ignores market segment differences and offers one branded product to every potential customer.
- *Product differentiation*—the organization recognizes that segments exist that value different features of functionally equivalently products. Each brand tries to accentuate one or more features to appeal to a certain segment.
- *Mass customization and customized marketing*—the capability to prepare, and deliver on a mass basis, individual products and/or services to meet each customer's requirements.

KEY FRAMEWORK

- *Segmentation options*—Figure 6.1

KEY QUESTION

- In your organization, do managers talk about customers as if they are all similar, or do they talk about different customer segments?

PART B

Product-Market Segmentation and Targeting

Product-market segmentation involves matching broad types of products and services with broad types of customers. The reason for this analysis is to understand the structure of the market in which the organization seeks to compete. Consider the computer market. There are supercomputers, mainframes, servers, workstations, and PCs. Within the PC category, there are desktops, laptops, and palmtops. Consumer groups who buy PCs include government, business, schools, home, and individuals. When serving the PC market, manufacturers know this range of product offerings and these customer segments. Thus, there is little competitive advantage to be gained here.

PC manufacturers, however, can gain insight by looking at the relationship among the segments and products. This is often done by creating a table that cross-classifies products and services against customer segments. Each product by segment cell is then described in terms of its market attractiveness.

Another way to look at the structure of a market is to map the relationship among the customer groups. Figure 6.2 shows three common structural configurations. Consumer segments can be:

- *Discrete*—where consumers have different needs, and/or they use different criteria to evaluate brands in a category. Each customer is in only one segment.
- *Hierarchical*—here individual consumers are combined into groups based on their similarity. For example, in Figure 6.2, consumers D and E

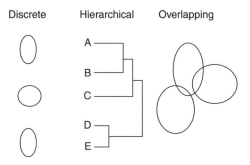

Figure 6.2. Market structures

are the most similar and form the first group; then because A and B are the next most similar, they form a separate group; then C joins the AB group; then D and E join the ABC group. The result is a tree-like hierarchy. This structural configuration is generally used for small numbers of consumers such as key accounts in a B2B situation.

- *Overlapping*—where some consumers may be members of more than one segment. For example, someone who uses his or her PC at home and at work.

For any particular structure, the segments are then described in terms of their attractiveness and the various products and services used. This is a more sophisticated approach to mapping the structure of a market than cross-tabulations and, thus, provides greater insight into how the market 'works'.

There are two pragmatic reasons and one technical reason for a marketer to think about the structure of a market. First, a simple 'picture' of the market (as shown in Figure 6.3) is a good internal communication device. Many managers and other employees need a succinct and commonly shared description of their market structure and the organization's target customers. Organizations tend to have trouble being 'customer focused' when it is difficult to describe who their customers are. The second reason is to uncover the key differences among consumer groups. The discussion of Figure 6.3 below illustrates how important this is.

The technical reason for thinking about the structure of a market is to help brief market researchers when they conduct market segmentation studies to describe the number of segments, their size, and their stability over time. When data about consumers are analysed by a statistical

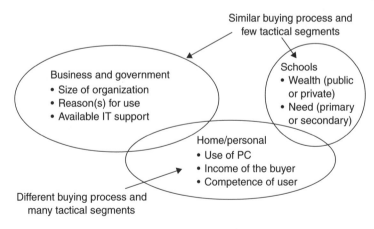

Figure 6.3. Personal computer market segments

algorithm to search for homogeneous groups and to create a market structure, the resulting picture of the market is determined in large part by the
choice of statistical procedure. To produce each of the market structures in
Figure 6.2 requires a different algorithm. Without a discussion of market
structure, what often happens is that the researcher will create a discrete
solution, because this is the most widely available option in many commercial statistical software packages. While this may a good compromise,
in some cases it may be very misleading.

To illustrate the managerial use of market structures, Figure 6.3 shows a
simple map of the PC product-market. In this case, the assumption is that
some of the broad customer segments overlap. For example, PCs used
by teachers and school children travel home each night. Also, PCs used by
office-workers go home. However, PCs used in the office do not tend to be
used at school. The size of the circles in Figure 6.3 represent (my guess of)
the relative attractiveness of each market segment. The other information
in the figure highlights some of the key factors that differentiate each
segment. For example, the assumption is that the wealth of a school, as
signalled by its public or private status and the type of children attending
(primary or secondary), has a major impact on the specific types of
PCs needed and the price sensitivity of customers. These, and other
characteristics, can be used to create tactical segments (as in the Porsche
example earlier).

When segments overlap, as is the case with PCs and mobile phones,
special care is needed when marketing to each segment. The reason is that
the deal (list price, terms of trade, service agreement, etc.) offered to one
segment will be seen by the other segment(s). If a different deal is offered
for essentially the same product, then it may require different branding,
packaging, and the use of different distribution channels to screen the deal
from customers in other segments. Care also needs to be taken that some
enterprising distributors who receive a good deal for products targeted
to one market segment do not buy more than they need and on-sell their
excess to customers in other segments at a lower price. This phenomenon is called a *grey market*, and it is not uncommon for products like
cigarettes and electrical products to be trans-shipped from one country to
another.

When the structure of a product-market has been determined (Figure 6.3),
and the attractiveness of each broad group of consumers has been established, the next task is to determine which markets will be targeted. This
is a strategic marketing decision. It is based on the fit between the attractiveness of the market and the strengths and capabilities of the SBU chosen
to serve this market.

Market attractiveness is often measured, among others, in terms of:

- the five forces in Figure 3.1 (Chapter 3);
- vulnerability to economic conditions (inflation, interest rates, etc.);
- current size;
- growth potential;
- availability of distribution facilities;
- profitability;
- propensity of consumers to switch brands;
- price sensitivity.

The organization's competitive strengths and capabilities are often assessed, among others, in terms of:

- ability to lead a market;
- product quality;
- depth of product range;
- production costs and flexibility;
- brand and corporate image;
- marketing capabilities;
- size of marketing budget.

For the example in Figure 6.3, the differences between the office (government and business) and consumer markets are quite profound. This means that the fit between each market's attractiveness and the capabilities of the SBU will differ. For example, the office market is characterized by:

- bulk buys;
- preferred suppliers;
- service and support from the IT department;
- longer product life cycles (upgrades for most users occur intermittently);
- concern about compatibility and inter-operability;
- total cost (hardware, software, and maintenance);
- experienced buyers;
- conservative marketing.

The consumer market has very different characteristics:

- single purchases;
- direct supplier service and support;
- peak purchasing seasons;
- feature-laden PCs;
- hardware price consciousness;
- both experienced and inexperienced buyers;
- colourful marketing;

- things that are essential in the consumer market are often options in the corporate market (such as CD drives, speakers, and multimedia software).

After their success in the office market, Compaq, IBM, and Hewlett Packard all found it more difficult than expected to move into the consumer market. Their strengths and capabilities were not broad enough to allow easy entry into the new market. They had to change their product range, distribution, sales approach, pricing, advertising, service delivery, and organizational culture to be successful in the new market.[8]

Figure 6.4 maps overall market attractiveness against business and, thus, competitive strength to suggest investment strategies for market development.[i] The diagram shows the relative positions of three SBUs in three different product-markets, and in which direction each may go (the arrows). For example, SBU1 could enhance its capabilities or harvest and make money while conditions are good. SBU2 can try to grow its share of the market (by competing harder or smarter), or it can manage its costs and earnings. SBU3 needs to defend its market (see the section on defence in Chapter 3).

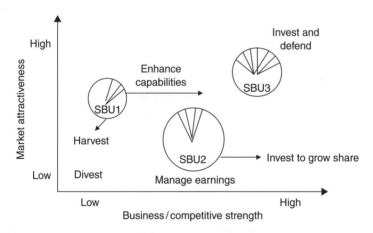

Figure 6.4. Target market selection and development

[i] Managers select a number of factors that describe market attractiveness and business strength. Each of these is then rated for each SBU/product-market being considered (e.g. 5 = very attractive market to 1 = very unattractive). Each of these scores is then weighted to reflect its relative importance (e.g. by distributing 100 points across them). The scores are then summed to produce an overall score for each dimension. The two scores define the centre of the SBU circle. These circles are drawn so that their relative size reflects the relative value of the product-markets. The hatched parts of the circle represent the SBU's market share.

Figure 6.4 can also be used to profile different competitors in a single market (e.g. Porsche, Ferrari, and others in the US sports car market). In this way, it can be useful for anticipating competitor strategies. Used for either reason, the critical issues embedded in this diagram are the definition of the market (e.g. automobiles versus transportation) and the criteria used to profile market attractiveness and competitive strength. These will have a significant impact on where a SBU is located in the market space of Figure 6.4.

The final issue to consider is the degree of market coverage or scope of competition for the organization. A company like Porsche Cars North America has a limited range of cars and essentially targets a single segment of consumers. In contrast, a company like General Motors in the United States has a number of separate divisions, each producing a different range of cars. Their strategy is to have a car for 'every purse, purpose, and personality'. This is known as a *full-market coverage* strategy. Between these two extremes, an organization can elect to adopt a *market specialization* strategy, whereby it has a variety of products and services to serve the needs for the same customer group. For example, many university business schools offer degree courses, open executive courses, and in-company courses to managers. Another strategy is *product specialization*. Here, the organization sells its product to any user. For example, products like aluminium, nylon, steel, industrial diamonds, and pearl shell (for buttons, paint, and the hologram on your credit card) are sold for a variety of uses. Finally, some organizations decide to offer a variety of products or services to different segments. Generally, it is only the big organizations that can support multiple products targeted to multiple segments.

RECAP

Mapping the structure of the product-/service-markets is a crucial exercise. It guides the selection of the product-market(s) in which to compete and, thus, defines the scope of competition for the organization. This then helps to identify the underlying technology that drives the evolution of the market. These are major strategic decisions for most organizations.

Many organizations grow by entering a new product-market. The critical issue here is to build on the organization's strengths and capabilities. For example, becoming a product or market specialist are growth paths that do this. Growth through entering unrelated product-markets has been shown to be more risky. The major reason for this is that it is more difficult to capture the benefits of either economies of scale, scope, or focus. Only a few companies like ABB and General Electric have been able to succeed in the long term with this strategy.

KEY CONCEPTS

- *Market structure*—the number of, and relationship among, customer segments in a market.
- *Market attractiveness*—the potential for a market to provide an above-average return on investment to the organization.
- *Business/competitive strength*—the assets and capabilities of the organization that allow it to compete in a chosen market.
- *Market specialization*—the organization focuses on serving the various needs of a particular consumer segment.
- *Product specialization*—the organization focuses on making a particular product (or service) that it will sell to any consumers who need it.
- *Multi-segment coverage*—the organization serves a variety of market segments, where there may be little, if any, synergy among them.
- *Full market coverage*—the organization attempts to serve all major consumer segments with the various products (or services) that they need.

KEY FRAMEWORKS

- *Market structures*—Figures 6.2 and 6.3
- *Target market selection and development*—Figure 6.4

KEY QUESTIONS

- What is the structure of your market?
- How do your targeted markets rate in terms of market attractiveness and competitive strength?

PART C

Tactical Segmentation and Targeting

Tactical segmentation is the key activity that shapes the development of marketing programmes. If the segments are valid and reliable, then marketing programmes are more likely to be efficient and effective. If they are not, then it is hard to score well on many of the KPIs that the marketing team is rewarded for—customer satisfaction, new product success, effective advertising, sales growth, etc.

This part of Chapter 6 starts by describing some examples of segmentation. The purpose of this is to prime a discussion of the strengths and weaknesses of current segmentation practice. The next section introduces a good way to segment all types of consumers—individuals and organizations. It builds on the three definitions at the beginning of the chapter: market segmentation—the process; market segments—the output; and target markets—the chosen customers. The chapter concludes with two extensive examples of good segmentation in practice.

The Dilemma: How Best to Segment One's Market

As noted earlier, the role of tactical segmentation is to get close to consumers so that marketing programmes can be designed and implemented for each target segment. Given the importance of tactical segmentation to the effective and efficient implementation of marketing, it is not surprising to find that many advertising agencies, consultants, and market research firms have produced proprietary segmentation schemes of consumer markets. (Surprisingly, there are relatively few of these available for B2B markets.) Here are four examples:

- Generation segments—matures (born between 1909–45); boomers (1946–64); Generation X (1965–84); Generation Y (born after 1984). A variation of this is to define a segment based on a significant 'event' in the person's life, such as the *i* Generation for people who have grown up with the Internet.
- MOSAIC (originally from the United Kingdom) is a classification of neighbourhoods into lifestyle types—elite suburbs, average areas, luxury flats, low income inner city, high rise social housing, industrial communities, dynamic families, lower income families, rural/agricultural areas, vacation/retirement.
- Constellation was a segmentation of the Australian population that combined national census data with consumer survey data to produce thirty-eight segments—twenty-four urban, nine town, and five rural. (It is rare to find segments of town and rural groups.)
- VALS (originally from the United States) is a classification of adults based on psychographic attributes (activities, interests, and opinions) that drive buying behaviour. The segments were—innovators, thinkers, believers,

achievers, strivers, experiencers, makers, survivors. Direct marketers use GeoVALS™ to identify zip codes that contain large concentrations of various segments. Other variations include *i*VALS for online consumer segments and Japan-VALS™ that segments Japanese consumers.[9]

These four segmentation schemes are designed to characterize the lifestyles of different groups of people in a community. This type of segmentation is created for its appeal to a wide range of consumer goods sellers. These segmentation schemes are commercial products that a marketing manager can buy access to 'off the shelf', so to speak.

Many other examples of tactical segments have been reported in the academic and business press. Some examples are:

- PCs sold in the consumer market
  —independent young achievers, white-collar affluents, young families (where education is important), small office–home office (known as the SOHO market).
- Retail segments
  —bargain hunters, enthusiasts, cynics, phobics.
- Airline segments for a discount domestic carrier
  —the no-frills, frequent small business traveller; bargain hounds—the no-frills leisure traveller; opportunists—people who pounce on super-cheap deals; one-way commuters.
- Fashion segments
  —professional singles, innovative communicators, hardcore enthusiasts, lifestyle consumers, fashion victims.
- Internet segments
  —Scheme #1—novices, explorers, players, experts. Scheme #2—shopping lovers, adventurous explorers, suspicious learners, business users, fearful browsers, fun seekers, technology muddlers, shopping avoiders. *i* VALS—wizards, upstreamers, socialites, mainstreamers, immigrants, surfers, seekers, pioneers, workers.
- Investment segments
  —delegators, active investors, invest and forget, cautious investors, reluctant investors, beginning investors.
- Retail petrol (gasoline) buying segments
  —F3s (food, fuel, fast), home taxis, price buyers, road warriors, true blues.
- Mobile phone segments for managers
  —hermits, solo practitioners, site bosses, corridor cruisers, corporate wanderers, globe trotters, road warriors.
- Segments of partners in a professional service organization, as created by an internal service group

—'Self-starter travellers'—people who know exactly what they want; 'Lonely planet travellers'—people who will find out for themselves by asking a trusted source; 'Explorers'—people who like to find out for themselves by 'discovery learning'; 'Package tourists'—people who need extensive help to get the job done; 'Stay at homes'—partners who do not want anything to do with the marketing service group.

- Business buyers; segmentation by
  —Size—key accounts, large companies, medium companies, small business, SOHO.
  —Industry—national governments each have their own system for classifying industries; for example, the Australian Standard Industrial Classification (ASIC) codes; the North American Industry Classification System (NAICS).
  —Geography—domestic (and regions), international (and regions), global.
  —Application of the product—OEMs; replacement (or the aftermarket); maintenance, repair and operations. A simpler and better segmentation is whether the product is seen as a cost or a value-add.
  —Customer experience—new buyers, novice buyers, sophisticated buyers.
- Buyers of industrial raw materials
  —service seekers, risk avoiders, non-differentators, minimal involvement, core product/service focused, pushers (high service and lowest cost).

In B2C marketing, but less so in B2B marketing, there are many different segmentation schemes of consumers in the same product-market. For example, every Internet consultant has a different segmentation scheme. Also, both the Constellation and VALS segmentation schemes have claimed to provide a valid representation of the Australian community. One splits the market into thirty-eight segments while the other is comfortable with an eight-segment classification. In fact, for each of the tactical schemes just listed above, it is quite easy to find a variety of competing schemes. Confused as to which scheme to believe? You should be, and you are in good company.

The reason that most tactical segmentation schemes differ is that they are derived from different sets of factors, called *segmentation bases*. For example, in B2C markets the following segmentation bases are commonly used to form segments:

- Geographic—region, climate, density (urban, suburban, rural), etc.
- Demographic—age, family type, gender, income, occupation, education, religion, race, nationality, social class, etc.

- Psychographic—lifestyle, personality, etc.
- Behavioural—usage (heavy, medium, light), benefits sought, usage occasions, loyalty, price sensitivity, shopping frequency, media habits, learned experience, etc.

In B2B markets, organization size, industry, geography, and how the product/ service is used are the most commonly used bases. The reason for purchase, the buyer's experience, and decision-making process are less frequently used—but generally more useful.

The question that a marketer must answer is: 'Which combination of factors should be used to build my segmentation scheme?' The answer to this question most often is: 'It depends'. And this is the marketer's dilemma.

Well, it depends on what the segmentation scheme is designed to do. To illustrate this issue, consider designing a segmentation study (i.e. selecting segmentation bases) from the following points of view. Each group will want answers to a different set of questions from the segmentation scheme, for example:

- *Advertising agency.* What motivates people to buy the product or service? What media do they watch? What will make our ads stand out from the rest?
- *Brand manager.* How can sales be increased? What are the strengths and weaknesses of the current marketing mix? Can customer loyalty be increased?
- *Sales manager.* How can sales and merchandising be improved? Do consumers think that retailers add value to the customer buying experience? Is it possible to cut unnecessary costs?
- *New product development team.* What new products and services do consumers want? What features are important? Who will buy them?
- *Customer service team.* At the point of service delivery, how do we recognize which type of customer we are dealing with? How can service quality be improved? What level of service and support is most efficient?

As these questions suggest, any single tactical segmentation study has a big job to do—if it is to be used throughout the organization.

Marketing managers have three options available when designing a tactical segmentation study. They can buy a syndicated study of their market from a research company—such as MOSAIC or VALS. This is quick, and sometimes special analyses can be done to better customize the results for the organization. Also, advertising agencies are often familiar with these commercial studies and can provide additional insight. However, if competitors are using the same segmentation scheme, there is little competitive advantage to be gained from this approach.

A second option is to commission a customized study that tries to cater to the needs of all users in one big study. This can be time consuming and quite expensive. It may also consume much of the available research budget and, thus, be resisted by managers who need research on other topics. A third option is to design a set of smaller, but related segmentation studies. The crucial issue here is to ensure that one study provides input for the next study, or that the various studies have enough in common so that they can be combined. (For example, each study has the same core set of segmentation bases. The other data collected speak directly to the questions of the primary user group.) With either of these last two options it is important to get input and regular feedback about the study design from the managers who will use the segments that the research discovers. Without this, there is a distinct possibility that the resulting segmentation will be ignored, or in some cases be vilified (often at the expense of the managers responsible).

Tactical Segmentation—The Process

If a manager elects to develop a customized tactical segmentation for his or her market, then it is advisable to create a team to oversee the project. The members of this team will be the marketing manager, representative users of the segmentation scheme (such as brand managers, the ad agency, etc.), and a good market researcher. A good market researcher is necessary to provide guidance about what data are to be collected and how they should be analysed, given the market structure that is thought to exist (Figure 6.2).

The second step in tactical segmentation is to outline a process for segmentation—such as Figure 6.5. It starts with the segmentation team specifying the segmentation problem, and it never finishes. Because consumers change and the products and services offered to them change, tactical segmentation is an ongoing process. In a market such as e-commerce, which is at the early stages of its evolutionary life cycle, the changes may be fast and quite dramatic. In contrast, in the market for fuel oil, the changes are much slower. However, even in these markets unexpected events can trigger a reconfiguration of the market—as evidenced with the oil price rises in the 1970s due to OPEC price fixing and the Gulf War in the early 1990s.

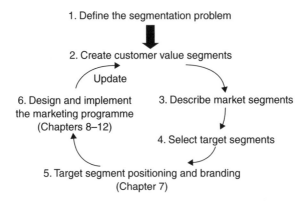

Figure 6.5. The process of tactical market segmentation

Define the Segmentation Problem

Stage 1 in the process of tactical segmentation seeks to understand what questions will be asked of the segmentation scheme. For example, the retail petrol buying segments described earlier were the result of the Mobil Corporation (now part of Exxon-Mobil) trying to increase its share of the US retail gasoline market. They needed to know the number of segments in the market so that they could select target segments and design customized marketing programmes for these segments. Exhibit 6.1 describes the segments and target marketing in more detail.

Exhibit 6.1. Good target marketing

To illustrate tactical segmentation, let us look at the problems faced by petrol retailers. Here, distribution is a key success factor—the more petrol stations, the better the market coverage, and the higher the market share. From the customer's point of view, petrol is a low-involvement product whose purchase is stimulated by a negative purchase motivation (normal depletion) and which the customer seldom actually sees (unless they overfill the tank and spill it down the side of the car).

Consider the following segmentation scheme developed in 1989 by the Mobil Oil Company in the United States.

Retail Petrol Segments

A. *The F3s*—27 per cent of buyers: fuel, food, fast. People who are constantly on the go.

cont.

Exhibit 6.1. *cont.*

B. *Home taxis*—21 per cent of buyers: usually mothers who shuttle children around and use whatever petrol stations are on their route.
C. *Price buyers*—20 per cent of buyers: know in which stations, and on what days of the week, prices will be low.
D. *Road warriors*—16 per cent of buyers: sales-, service-, and delivery-people, truck drivers, and taxis that use a company credit card to buy petrol and food.
E. *True blues*—16 per cent of buyers: people who are loyal to a brand and sometimes a particular petrol station. These people also like their cars and will do some of their own minor maintenance.

One valuable aspect of this segmentation was the realization that about 80 per cent of buyers found value in aspects of the service station experience other than price. At the time of the study, this finding was counter to existing industry thinking that assumed that all buyers were very price conscious.

To develop this example, consider how the marketing team at Mobil might go about selecting some of the segments to target—Stage 4 in Figure 6.5. One thing to do would be to outline a marketing mix (product mix, price level, location, advertising theme) for each segment to see how well it 'fits' each segment's needs.

Designing Marketing to Offer Customer Segment Value

A. *The F3s*
  - Product mix—many self-service pumps with credit card payment facilities; convenience food (e.g. bread, milk, etc.); fast food; papers and magazines.
  - Price level—medium to high.
  - Station location—high traffic, main road locations.
  - Advertising theme—speedy self-service.
B. *Home taxis*
  - Product mix—fewer pumps; driveway service if required; friendly atmosphere; car wash; bread, milk, papers, etc.
  - Price level—high.
  - Station location—suburban through streets.
  - Advertising theme—here to serve you.
C. *Price buyers*
  - Product mix—moderate number of pumps; discount for cash; no driveway service; minimum facilities.
  - Price level—low (e.g. frequent discounting).
  - Station location—secondary high traffic locations.
  - Advertising theme—more kilometres for your dollar.

D. *Road warriors*
- Product mix—same as A above, plus truck access, LPG pumps, and good toilets and washrooms; mechanic on duty.
- Price level—low to medium.
- Station location—high traffic locations.
- Advertising theme—no fuss, self-service.

E. *True blues*
- Product mix—moderate number of pumps; oil, batteries, plus a full range of minor spare parts; mechanic on duty; car wash; driveway service for special customers (e.g. aged, disability, etc.); friendly atmosphere; convenience food and papers.
- Price level—medium to high.
- Station location—suburban locations.
- Advertising theme—the best for you and your car.

Next, the Mobil team would need to assess the attractiveness of each segment. What they found was that price buyers spent the least amount—about $700 per year at a gas station compared to the top spenders who were the road warriors and true blues ($1200 p.a.). They would also need to consider the costs of modifying their existing stations to provide the various marketing mixes outlined above. After this type of analysis, they decided to target the F3s, road warriors, and true blues.

This example reflects many of the realities of petrol retailing, namely, site outlets on any good location that becomes available, and within the general constraints of the overall marketing strategy set by the oil company, fine-tune each station's marketing mix to best fit the type of most passing motorists.

Create Customer Value Segments

Stage 2 in the process of tactical segmentation is often the most difficult because of the variety of segmentation bases available. Thus, it is hard to select a parsimonious set of factors to profile consumers and expose market opportunities. Here, the recommendation is to use the reason for purchase or the intended use occasion and customer needs and benefits as the primary segmentation bases. For example, Band-Aids (those small adhesive bandages) come treated with antiseptics, special Band-Aid strips shaped for finger and knuckle cuts, sport Band-Aids, waterproof Band-Aids, clear Band-Aids, and bright-coloured Band-Aids for children. Each variety has been created for a specific use occasion/need. People do not need any more small adhesive bandages, but they now have a reason to purchase more than one box of Band-Aids for different use occasions.[10]

This style of segmentation is the most consumer-focused type of segmentation and reflects how many consumers (both people and organizations) evaluate products and services—with a mindset of 'what is in it for me!' When used together, these segmentation bases expose opportunities to create customer value—hence, the name 'customer value segments'. Also, this perspective is supported by the notions that (*a*) modern marketing is concerned with creating and capturing consumer value (see Figure 1.3 in Chapter 1), and (*b*) the central role that need recognition and purchase motivations play in consumption decisions (Figure 4.2 in Chapter 4). Thus, reason for purchase and customer needs and benefits become the logical primary segmentation bases.

Table 6.1 shows some of these variables for the photo market. The reasons for taking photos motivate different sets of benefits, and it is these that drive purchase behaviour and subsequent use. Kodak's use of the advertising slogan 'share the moment' reflects this type of segmentation. If research cannot detect different combinations of reasons for purchase and sets of benefits, then customer value segments do not exist in the market. In this case (as for television viewing where 'entertainment' is the overwhelming benefit for most viewers most of the time), the organization would create its segments using the 'descriptor variables' as indicated in Table 6.1.

Table 6.1. Segmentation worksheet for the photo market

Segmentation bases			Descriptor variables		
Reason for taking photos	Benefits		Number of photos taken	Type of camera	Demographics, etc.
	Primary	Secondary			
Celebration	Capture moment Remember	Proof Lasting image	Few	Still Movie Digital	Families Social groups
Travel	Proof 'statement'	Memories	Many	Still Movie Digital	Singles Couples
Nature	Self-expression Enjoyment Demonstrate skills	Memories Affordable	Many	Still (SLR)	Singles Professionals
Portrait	Memory Gift	Archive	Few	Still (SLR) Digital	Professionals

Table 6.1 is really a segmentation worksheet. Its value is to capture the accumulated learning of the organization about customers, and to organize this information in a way that gives prominence to customer value as the best way to create segments. Timothy Bock and Mark Uncles suggest that such a worksheet should contain the following generic types of information:[11]

	Air travel
Segmentation bases	
Reason for purchase	Business; pleasure; emergency; etc.
Benefits—primary and secondary	Comfort; check-in speed; security; direct to destination; etc.
Descriptor variables	
Consumer interaction effects	Flying alone; with a partner; in a group; etc.
Choice barriers	Awareness and knowledge of alternatives; switching costs; frequent flyer membership; budget; etc.
Purchase process and bargaining power	Who decides, influences, and buys; frequent flyer status; etc.
Profitability to the organization	Class of travel; frequency of travel; price sensitivity, etc.

There are three ways that the information in a segmentation worksheet can be used to create a set of usable customer segments:

A. The worksheet is used to brief a market research firm to collect these data, and using various statistical algorithms, the analyst finds the most parsimonious set of segments described by the data.[12] I call this *discovery segmentation*.

B. Using the worksheet and their knowledge of the market, a group of managers 'creatively' form a set of segments. One can think of these segments as hypotheses that will be tested by either (*a*) collecting data from the marketplace (A above), or (*b*) using the segments to guide marketing practice and seeing if they 'work'. When the segments have been developed like this, each one is given a short descriptive name to 'bring them to life'. For example, the 'home taxis' and 'road warriors' in the Mobil scheme. I call this *intuitive segmentation.*

C. Because of time or budget constraints, or simply because it is considered 'too hard' to create customer value segments, those demographic variables in the worksheet and the organization's customer database are used to create a set of fairly sterile segments. The hope here is that the profile of these variables will indicate the needs and wants of the individual (B2C) or the organization (B2B). In some cases, this is a reasonable assumption. For example, when selling life insurance and financial investment products, consumer needs change over the person's life stages. However, for products like travel insurance and retail banking services, such life-stage segmentation would be almost meaningless. I call this *backwards segmentation* (because it goes from right to left, instead of left to right across Table 6.1).

In the real world of short time horizons and limited research budgets, many marketers succumb to the practical difficulty noted above and create their segments using either an intuitive or backwards approach.

The approach advocated in this book is to prefer to search for consumer value based market segments (option A above). *Customer value* is defined as the person's estimate of a product or service's overall capacity to satisfy his or her needs.[13] It can be written as the following equality:

$$Customer\ value = (Benefits - Price)$$

From the consumer's point of view, the components of benefits and price are:

- *Benefits* from a product or service can be:
  —functional—it does the job expected of it, and/or
  —psychological—it provides emotional, intellectual, or spiritual enjoyment (e.g. Nike shoes provide social status), and/or
  —economic—it is acquired at a good price (e.g. Wal-Mart sells branded products at everyday low prices).
- *Price* can be:
  —$, £, ¥, €, etc.,
  —inconvenience, and
  —perceived risk.

Price should be anchored to the target customer's best alternative and their budget—for both money and time. Thus, price is not a simple construct. Chapter 8 outlines how to measure customer value.

To illustrate this value equation, consider the development and launch of the Lexus automobile. First, Toyota identified a segment of potential customers who would like to buy a European brand (such as BMW or Mercedes) but who thought these were overpriced. If they could build a car to the design and perceived quality standards of a Mercedes, and sell it at a significantly lower price, then it should appeal to these customers. With this goal in mind, and the 'smart buyer' as the target segment, the Lexus was developed. In terms of benefits, the engineering, safety, style, and fit and finish of the Lexus were as good as, if not better than, the equivalent Mercedes. In terms of price, the car originally sold in the United States at a discount of $37,000 to the equivalent Mercedes. To reduce the perceived risk of buying an expensive, luxury car from 'Toyota', the car did not carry the Toyota name badge nor was it sold through Toyota dealers. Establishing a separate dealer network and training salespeople to sell to this specific target segment increased the prestige of the brand (a psychological benefit), and reduced the inconvenience of buying and servicing the car. This great value car was an outstanding early success in the market.

Describe Market Segments

Because consumers do not walk around with labels that proclaim which value segment they belong to, Stage 3 in the tactical segmentation process involves describing each segment so that people and organizations can be identified for target marketing. This task involves collecting geographic, demographic, psychographic, and behavioural information (the 'descriptor variables' on the right-hand side of Table 6.1), and correlating measures of these variables with measures of customer value for each segment. Sometimes there is a strong relationship between some of these descriptor variables and the needs and benefits sought by target customers. For example, people of different ages tend to need different drugs and types of medical care; working-class men and university students drink the most beer; 20–40 year olds have the most housing mortgages; open-cut mines are heavy users of fuel oil and explosives; etc.

However, in many cases describing segments for easy identification is tedious because the easy to collect information such as demographics (or firmographics for organizations) is not significantly associated with the value segments. For example, do large or small organizations need PCs? (Both.) Do old or young people buy baby clothes? (People of many ages do—parents, friends, and grandparents.) Do people in the city, suburbs, or rural communities watch the television program *60 Minutes*? (They all do.) And so it goes on. In cases such as these, organizations have to be creative in the ways that they identify which segment a particular consumer belongs to. One simple solution to this problem is to ask the consumer to self-select one of the organization's target segments. For example, briefly describe each of the tactical segments (in a brochure or a web page) and ask the consumer which one best describes them. (Log onto www.sric-bi.com/VALS and go to the VALS Survey option to see which VALS segment you belong to.) Another approach is to ask people to become a member of a customer loyalty scheme. When they join, they are asked about the features and benefits of the product or service that are valued, and from this information they can be assigned to a value segment. As they make purchases and gather points, this information can be used to refine their segment membership.

The critical issue in the second and third stages of tactical segmentation is to segment consumers by moving from left to right across Table 6.1. That is, segment consumers using value bases, and then describe them using any other type of information that is deemed to be relevant for identifying and serving them. This customer value approach to segmentation starts by focusing on what is most important to customers (needs, benefits, price), and only then does it focus on characteristics that can be used to identify consumers for target marketing campaigns.

Recall that many organizations use backwards segmentation. There are two reasons for this. First, it is relatively easy to do. Many descriptor variables (especially demographics and firmographics) are more straightforward to measure than needs, benefits, and price sensitivity. Second, the media (print, television, and radio) profile their audiences using demographics and some other descriptor variables. As noted earlier, if the relationship between descriptors and the value segment membership of consumers is strong, there is no problem here. However, it is risky to assume that 'all females aged between 25 and 40 years, who live in the same geographic area' or 'all small professional service firms in Sydney' have the same needs and preferences.

Select Target Segments

Stage 4 in the process of tactical segmentation involves selecting segments of consumers for whom the organization will develop customized marketing programmes. For Porsche Cars North America, all the segments were chosen. In the Mobil example earlier, three of the five segments were chosen. The reason that Mobil choose the F3s and the road warriors was that they were the two most similar groups. Also, the F3s may become road warriors in the future. The reason for choosing the true blues was that this group, like the other two, valued service attributes that Mobil could offer.

Deciding which segment(s) to target is a critical strategic marketing decision and requires the careful consideration of the following criteria:

- *Market attractiveness*—the segment is large and profitable enough to serve, and competition will not destroy this attractiveness.
- *Accessible*—the segment can be effectively reached and served using available media and distribution channels.
- *Differentiable*—segments are distinguishable from each other and will respond differently to different marketing programmes.
- *Actionable*—effective programmes can be formulated to attract and retain consumers.

Figure 6.6 shows how the Marriott Corp. once identified value-based segments as defined by price (economic value) and quality and features (functional value). They then established a portfolio of branded hotels to serve the segments and span the market. If a consumer traded up or traded down the hope was that he or she would stay at the appropriate Marriott hotel. One of the interesting issues raised in this figure is the name 'Courtyard by Marriott'. Is it or is it not a Marriott hotel? Answer: it is and it is not. Which leads to brand name confusion. (Branding and positioning are discussed in Chapter 7.)

<table>
<tr><td></td><td colspan="4">Quality and features</td></tr>
<tr><td></td><td>Economy</td><td>Standard</td><td>Very good</td><td>Superior</td></tr>
<tr><td>High</td><td></td><td></td><td></td><td>Marriott
Marquis
Top executives,
Wealthy travellers</td></tr>
<tr><td>Above
average</td><td></td><td></td><td>Marriott
Middle managers,
Middle-market
travellers</td><td></td></tr>
<tr><td>Average</td><td></td><td>Courtyard
(by Marriott)
Salespeople</td><td></td><td></td></tr>
<tr><td>Low</td><td>Fairfield Inn
Residence Inn
Economy
vacationers</td><td></td><td></td><td></td></tr>
</table>

(Price — vertical axis label)

Figure 6.6. Hotels by Marriott

It is interesting to compare the structured target marketing of Marriott with the confusing target marketing of General Motors (GM) in the mid-1990s. Al Ries suggests that, in 1921, Alfred P. Sloan developed a single-focus, multi-step strategy for the Oakland Motor Company of Pontiac Michigan.[14] The product range and price points illustrate this approach:

Chevrolet:	$450–600
Pontiac:	$600–900
Oldsmobile:	$900–1200
Buick:	$1200–1700
Cadillac:	$1700–2500

In Sloan's strategy, there were no price overlaps and the divisions only competed with each other when they tried to trade a customer up to the next price bracket. Inside GM, the saying was that: 'Chevrolet is for the hoi polloi, Pontiac for the poor but proud, Oldsmobile for the comfortable but discreet, Buick for the striving, and Cadillac for the rich.' In the 1920s, it was a brilliant way to compete against Henry Ford and his Model T.

But GM managers were a competitive lot, and over the next few decades the various divisions started to compete with each other. By 1996 there was considerable product overlap of price points and brand images among the passenger cars offered by the various GM divisions:

Saturn:	$9995–12,995
Chevrolet:	$8085–68,043*
Pontiac:	$11,074–27,139
Oldsmobile:	$13,500–31,370
Buick:	$13,700–33,084
Cadillac:	$34,990–45,935

(* This price was for their sports car.)

Huge price ranges and overlapping price points are a good way to confuse both customers and the marketing managers in the various divisions of GM. For example, what is the brand image of a Chevrolet? It can be either the cheapest or the most expensive GM car! It can also be a family sedan or a racy sports car!

Segmentation in Action

The following two examples round out the discussion of segmentation. To follow Peter Drucker's advice that was introduced in Chapter 1, one example focuses on marketing and one on innovation.

ABB Electric

In its third year of existence, ABB Electric of Wisconsin faced a 50 per cent drop in total industry sales for its products—medium-size power transformers, breakers, switchgear, relays, and other equipment for power utilities in the North American market. ABB's three main competitors were General Electric, Westinghouse, and McGraw-Edison.

In 1974, ABB engaged the services of Professor Denis Gensch to conduct research about its customers—in particular, their equipment preferences and decision-making process.[15] For example, in this market there were eight independent attributes that consumers used to choose amongst suppliers (presented here with scaled importance ratings):

- Warranty—5.1
- Energy loss—4.6
- Appearance—2.7
- Invoice price—2.1
- Knowledgeable salesmen—1.7
- Maintenance requirements—1.6
- Availability of spare parts—1.5
- Clarity of the bid document—1.0

With this information and the past purchase records of all the major customers, Gensch helped ABB segment its market and design new products and a service programme to better fit customer needs. For example, one of the first actions that ABB took was to offer a full five-year warranty on all its products. The best that competitors were offering was a one-year warranty.

The market segments were of particular interest. The first partition was to create twelve segments of customers according to their geographic location, size, and industry—a common practice with industrial firms. Each segment contained between 148 and 464 potential customers. The basic logic for industry segmentation is the belief that customers in the same industry share similar needs and characteristics, such as their business drivers, technology needs, price sensitivity, decision cycles, and strategic beliefs. Within each of these twelve macro-segments, customers were then segmented based on purchase probabilities. These were computed by comparing ABB's profile on the eight attributes above with its competitors. This resulted in the following segments:

- ABB loyal—ABB is vastly superior to all competitors.
- Competitive—ABB customers who might switch to a competitor because other suppliers are perceived as being very close to ABB.

- Switchable—competitor customers who might switch to ABB because they perceive ABB as being very close to its first-choice supplier.
- Competitor loyal—ABB is significantly inferior to one or more competitors.

Although these segments were developed in a B2B situation, they are equally applicable in most B2C situations.

ABB targeted the 'competitive' and 'switchable' segments with different marketing campaigns that took account of the strengths and weaknesses of the major competitors in each segment. It kept its marketing efforts at the maintenance level for the other segments. To test the effectiveness of this marketing programme, they conducted a controlled test. In one geographic area, the district manager did not want to change his current strategy, while in two other areas the managers were willing to experiment by changing their marketing programmes to defend 'loyal' and 'competitive' customers, and to get a foot-in-the-door for the 'switchable' customers. The result was that in the region where no changes were made sales fell by 10 per cent. In the two regions where the new marketing procedures were implemented, sales increased by 12 and 18 per cent. In the same year, total industry sales fell by 15 per cent!

Moore's Chasms—Segmenting High-Technology Markets

In the field of high-technology marketing, Geoffrey Moore suggests that there are five discrete segments of potential adopters.[16] The following descriptions are based on his original research and consulting:

Product enthusiasts. These people appreciate the architecture of the new product/service and why it is better than existing products; they like being first to get new things; they will search out a new product; they pose fewer requirements on the supplier than other groups and expect to have to sort out some of the bugs in the new product; when they have a question, they want access to the most qualified person to answer; to them risk is not a dirty word, because it automatically implies reward.

Visionaries and pioneers. These people are the ones who immediately see the opportunities that a new product or service offers them or their firm; thus, they see how a new product can solve a problem they currently experience; these people also have the resources and the temperament to follow through with their vision; what drives them is their dream or their need to make a significant improvement in what they are doing, not the cleverness of the new product; they want to use the new product/service as a change agent, in their lives or their firm; they are willing to take risks to achieve their goal; these risks relate more to the product not fulfilling their dream than its cost or functionality; in business, these people have a project, as opposed to the enthusiasts' product orientation; if they can afford the new product, and can be convinced that it will help them achieve their goal, they are less price sensitive than other groups; their success often makes them a highly visible reference point for other adopters.

Pragmatists. These people are into evolutionary change rather than revolutionary change, and want new products to provide a functional, psychological, and/or economical improvement to what they currently do; these people also tend to have a low profile which makes them somewhat difficult to identify; in business, they want sellers to prove (with the numbers) that the new product, process, or service will achieve the improvement that it promises in a short timeframe; they will often pay a modest premium for quality or special service, but in the absence of this differentiation, they want the best deal; to them risk is a dirty word and the improvements offered must be far greater than the risks perceived; while this group may watch the 'visionaries' and 'pioneers', they will not adopt until it is clear that their peers would approve; while they are hard to win over, once they do adopt, they are loyal; the loyalty and buying power of these people is what creates 'industry standards'.

Conservatives and followers. These people tend to avoid discontinuous innovations, because, to them, the traditional ways of doing things are important; many products and services are bought, not because of their inherent value, but because of the feeling that one has to stay on par with everyone else; conservatives often fear many technology- and fashion-driven products, especially when they require new learning; they respond best to simplicity, especially fully integrated and single-function products and services.

Sceptics and less involved. When ice boxes were no longer available, these people finally bought refrigerators; they do not have a great need for what is being offered and may adopt only when economic necessity forces them to; they tend to be suspicious of advertising claims and change agents; when given the chance, they may block the purchase of your new product by other people; the Amish community in Pennsylvania (USA) is a good example of a group that has resisted many innovations.

There are three important aspects about this segmentation scheme. The first is its flexibility. While the segments were developed for the purpose of consulting to Silicon Valley firms in the United States, with some minor modifications they are applicable in a wide range of new product marketing situations. The second critical aspect of this segmentation scheme is

Moore's belief that the segments are discrete. In his terminology, they are separated by Chasms. This discrete market structure suggests two things:

- A new product can be launched into any of the first four segments.
- Because they are needs-based segments, what makes a new product successful in one segment is just as likely to retard its success in another segment.

Consider the launch of the original version of Quicken's personal financial PC software. In essence, its product promise was 'less is more'. That is, it had few features and was very easy to use. While this would make it appeal to 'pragmatists', it would make it extremely dull and boring for the 'product enthusiasts'. To sell to the 'product enthusiasts', it would require many more features. The product configuration, communication strategy (content and media), and price points would be different in order to appeal to each segment.

The third important aspect of Moore's segments is that they can be used to enhance the new product adopter segment scheme described in Figure 5.4 (Chapter 5). Recall that these segments were based on the time taken to adopt a new product or service—the innovators adopted first and the laggards last. This is a fuzzy segmentation scheme because (a) the same factors are thought to drive the adoption of the new product for each segment—some people have more of them than others and thus adopt faster; and (b) it has proven difficult to identify the exact time of adoption that segregates adjacent segments. Thus, this segmentation scheme is difficult to use in a tactical

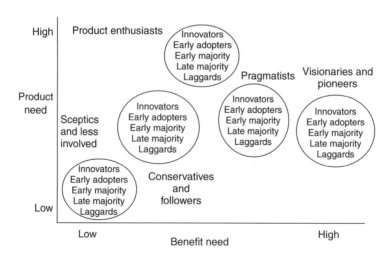

Figure 6.7. New product adoption and diffusion segments

setting. What this type of adoption scheme can be used for is to help marketers think about the dynamics of diffusion within each of Moore's segments. Figure 6.7 shows this double-segmentation scheme.

KEY CONCEPTS

- *Segmentation bases*—the (customer value) variables used to create market segments.
- *Customer value*—the buyer's estimation of a product or service's overall capacity to satisfy his or her needs. It is measured as the benefits offered by the product or service relative to its price.
- *Descriptor variables*—the variables used to describe market segments.
- *Discovery segmentation*—statistical procedures are used to find customer segments from data that profile the need/benefits, solutions to problems, and other characteristics of customers.
- *Intuitive segmentation*—managers judgementally form segments that account for key differences among customers.
- *Backwards segmentation*—the process of forming customer segments using variables other than customer value or surrogates for this.

KEY FRAMEWORKS

- *Segmentation worksheet*—Table 6.1
- *The process of tactical segmentation*—Figure 6.5

KEY QUESTION

- Are your organization's tactical customer segments created using a process of discovery, intuition, or backwards segmentation?

Chapter Summary

Segmentation is the core framework of this book. It can be examined at three levels:

1. *Corporate.* Here, the decision about which industries to compete in and what broad types of products and services to produce guides the

design of the business process for the organization's various SBUs. Also, this segmentation guides investments in the basic technologies that underpin the organization's capabilities.

2. *Product-market.* Here, the products, types of customer, and broad structure of the market together define the competitive arena for marketers.

3. *Tactical.* Here, the (customer-value based) segmentation helps product and brand managers to design marketing programmes that seek to customize the offer made to target consumers as much as possible.

A number of the key issues were also discussed, namely:

- The amount of consumer heterogeneity in the market will determine the number of segments. When most people are satisfied with a commonly configured base product (e.g. television), then a mass marketing strategy is appropriate. Alternatively, when most consumers want, and are willing to pay for, significantly different products, then mass customization is appropriate.
- The type of heterogeneity among consumers determines the structure of the market—discrete segments, overlapping segments, etc. The relationship among segments is important for distribution channel choice (can the same channel be used to serve different segments), corporate and brand positioning (discussed in the next chapter), and for implementing growth strategies (grow by moving into related segments).
- The resources and capabilities of the organization determine the number of segments to target. Bigger organizations can generally target more segments.

NOTES

1. For example, much of modern finance theory is built on two basic ideas, namely, the time value of money (i.e. because it can be invested, a dollar today is worth more than a dollar tomorrow) and diversification (viz. a portfolio of assets balances risk and reward).
2. From W. G. Zikmund and M. d'Amico, *Marketing* (Cincinnati, OH: South-Western College Publishing, 2001), p. 230.
3. These conditions are discussed in more detail in J. G. Davis and T. M. Devinney, *The Essence of Corporate Strategy* (Sydney: Allen & Unwin, 1997), pp. 185–8.
4. M. Collins, V. Beal, and P. Barwise, 'Channel Use Among Multi-channel Viewers', The R&D Initiative, Research Report 15 (March 2003)—available at www.marketingoracle.com.

5. D. Crowe, 'Intel Power Play Looks a Winner', *Australian Financial Review* (4 February 1999), 26.

6. Banks and many organizations that adopt this style of segmentation also segment consumers using a variety of other bases. The point being made here is that this is their *primary* form of segmentation.

7. In Australia, the animosity of customers towards the big banks got so bad that the government appointed an ombudsman to hear complaints.

8. M. Macrae, 'Big Leap for the Big Three', *The Bulletin* (6 July 1999), 72–3.

9. For more detail on these segments, see Zikmund and M. d'Amico op cit., 240–1. SRI Consulting, Menlo Park, California, is the registered owner of this scheme.

10. E. Schulz, *The Marketing Game* (Holbrook, MA: Adams Media Corp., 2001), pp. 94–5.

11. T. Bock and M. Uncles, 'A Taxonomy of Differences Between Consumers for Market Segmentation', *International Journal of Research in Marketing*, 19 (2002), 215–24.

12. For an example, see G. R. Dowling and D. F. Midgley, 'Identifying the Coarse and Fine Structure of Market Segments', *Decision Sciences*, 19, 4 (1988), 830–47.

13. P. Kotler, *Marketing Management* (Upper Saddle River, NJ: Prentice Hall, 1997), p. 10.

14. A. Ries, *Focus* (London: HarperCollins Business, 1996).

15. D. Gensch, N. Aversa, and S. Moore, 'A Choice Modelling Market Information System that Enabled ABB Electric to Expand Its Market Share', *Interfaces*, 20 (January–February 1990), pp. 6–25.

16. G. A. Moore, *Crossing the Chasm* (New York: HarperBusiness, 1991); *Inside the Tornado* (New York: HarperBusiness, 1995).

7

Positioning and Branding

Trading up to image or down to price.

To many businesspeople the letters 'MBA' stand for 'Master of Business Administration'. The MBA is now a recognized business degree in all the major business centres of the world. These three letters on a business card identify that its owner has 'suffered' a number of years of formal business education at the hands of academic (tor)mentors. However, to many people in advertising agencies, the letters MBA stand for 'Murderer of Brand Assets'. In this world, it is often thought that the analytical training that forms the core of many MBAs stifles the creativity necessary to build brands of relevance, fun, and distinction. Sometimes there is tension between the art and science of marketing.

The American Marketing Association defines a *brand* as the combination of a name, term, sign, symbol, or design intended to identify the goods and services of one seller or group of sellers and to differentiate them from those of competitors. The key aspects of this definition are the:

- brand's identity symbols—name, term, sign, symbol, and design; and
- its differentiation—in this case, the brand's position.

Surprisingly, what this definition does not mention is

- the promise the brand makes to consumers about its function, quality, reliability, and the implied social status of the user.

Given that brands are often one of the organization's key strategic marketing assets, the management of brands is of fundamental concern to marketers. For sellers, they are a means of legally protecting their products and services. For consumers, brands help to identify the maker of the product and know who should be held accountable for any problems. When consumers have experience with various brands, it enables them to make faster and more efficient purchase decisions. This matters more and more as choices multiply. Thus, brands reduce the effort and perceived risk of buying products and services. They also add fun and interest to many products—such as Absolut Vodka, Häagen-Dazs ice cream, Harley-Davidson motorbikes, and Levi's jeans.

Parts A and B of this chapter examine three key issues about brands:

- Brand Position and Positioning—where positioning is the management process that leads to a brand's position.
- Branding—the identity and architecture of brands.
- Brand Equity—the value added to a product or service that is endowed by its brand name.

Part A starts where Chapter 6 concluded, namely, with the P-part of the STP framework.

PART A

Brand Position and Positioning: The Battle for Consumers' Minds

> Marketing is not a battle of products, it's a battle of perceptions.
>
> Al Ries and Jack Trout

To put positioning in its broader context, the decision faced by marketers is to design an offer to each target segment of consumers that passes what has become known as the IDU Test. That is, the offer is:

- Important to customers,
- Deliverable by the organization,
- Unique.

Chapter 2 discussed how organizations design themselves to deliver products and services to target consumers. Chapter 8 will discuss the I-element of the IDU Test. This chapter focuses on the unique aspect of this test, that is, position. As outlined below, unique means being able to authentically differentiate the offer from competitive offerings in a way that is important to target customers and sustainable over time.

Let us assume that the organization's NPD process has created a new product or service with something that is important to customers and deliverable by the firm. Unless this is a radical innovation (which is rare), the organization will be launching its product against one or more established competitive offerings. The first task the marketer faces is to understand the positions of these products in the minds of the target customers. His or her second task is to find a way of positioning the new product so that it is perceived as different enough to convince target consumers that it is worth considering at its asking price. Typically, when consumers cannot see any relevant differences between two products, most will choose the cheapest and the snobs will choose the dearest. Hence, if this is not to be the cheapest brand, or its signals of quality will not support the top-price position, then it is necessary to find a non-price position.

To help develop positions for new brands and to reposition old brands, the next three sections describe

- Techniques for auditing the current position of the brand.
- The science of positioning.
- The art of positioning.

Brand Position Audit[1]

Before considering changing the position of a brand, it is necessary to find out how it is currently perceived. The audit process usually starts by reviewing the brand's history. For example, Figure 7.1 shows six generations of the Philips Electronics company's corporate brand. (Each step in the evolution was designed to build on the previous steps. The two corporate tag-lines were used on the advertising during this period.) This historical review may also examine the strength of the brand over time, for example by seeing if it commands a price premium in the market. The audit should then examine what target consumers currently think about the brand. Consumer knowledge can be examined using the structure shown in Figure 7.2.

In Figure 7.2, awareness is a precondition for brand knowledge. As the old saying goes: 'Out of mind, out of business'. Being 'top-of-mind' is best. Having to prompt the potential buyer to recall or recognize the brand is not as strong.

In the middle of the Brand Knowledge pyramid are the components of the target customer's beliefs and associations about the brand. These are the more 'rational' aspects of brand knowledge. Emotions are the less rational aspect that tap into our personal desires for fun, security, social acceptance, dominance, power, recognition, etc. The correct emotional portrayal of the brand (in its advertising) can increase its relevance to the target customer by 'hooking into' the relevant purchase motive. (These were

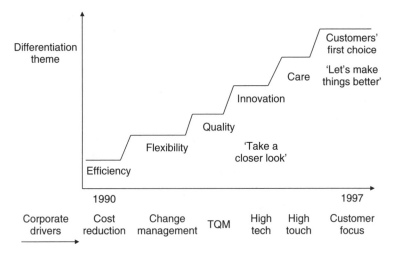

Figure 7.1. History of the Philips corporate brand

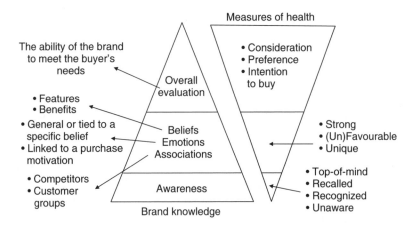

Figure 7.2. The structure of brand knowledge

discussed in Chapter 4.) For example, a hotel may promote that it offers a secure and relaxing environment. Now, if it is targeted to up-market travellers, it might also link the brand to the recognition emotion (e.g. Intercontinental Hotels: 'The place to stay when you know that you have arrived'.)

On the top of the brand knowledge pyramid is the overall evaluation of the brand. (Sometimes this is called 'brand attitude' or 'brand image'.) It is the combined assessment of beliefs, associations, and emotional relevance, and it summarizes the ability of the brand to meet the buyer's needs.

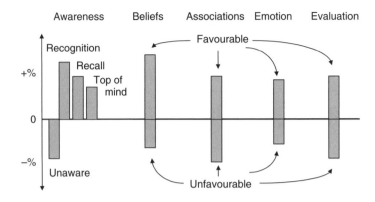

+ or −%: percentage of target consumers who hold either positive or negative beliefs, associations, emotions, or evaluation of the brand.

Figure 7.3. Brand health

Often, this is measured by brand consideration, preference, and intention to buy. (More on this in Chapter 12—Figure 12.6.)

A simple way to measure the strength of a brand is to ask target consumers to rate each element of their knowledge of the brand, that is, the measures of health in Figure 7.2. The results of such a survey can be plotted as shown in Figure 7.3.

The next stage of the audit process focuses on understanding the position of the brand. Position (or perceptual) maps are often used for this purpose and help managers to summarize and visualize the significant elements that differentiate among a set of competitive brands. A map is created from data about people's ratings of a set of brands on a number of the features and benefits that describe each brand. Various statistical techniques can plot these data in two dimensions that best summarize the similarity of the brands. Remember the old saying that 'A picture is worth a thousand words'. Here, this saying is modified to 'A picture is worth 10,000 numbers'.

Figure 7.4 was a position map used by managers of the Buick Division of General Motors in the late 1980s. They wanted to add a new car to their existing product range. It was called the Reatta (a name derived from the Spanish-American word for lariat) and was designed to have a more sporty look than the current set of Buick models. Figure 7.4 shows its desired and actual positions relative to the major current Buick models.[2] (Do you think that the Reatta was a success? The answer is at the end of the chapter.)

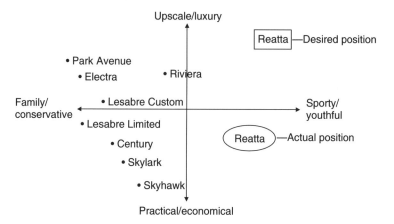

Figure 7.4. Position map of the Reatta and other Buick models

A *position map* like that in Figure 7.4 has the following general characteristics:

- The distances between product alternatives indicate the 'perceived similarities' between any pair of brands, that is, how close or far apart they are in the minds of consumers.
- A vector on the map (shown by an arrow in Figure 7.5) indicates both magnitude (long versus short arrows) and the direction of a brand attribute.
- The axes of the map are a special set of vectors that suggest the broad underlying dimensions that best characterize how consumers differentiate between alternatives. Most frequently, orthogonal axes (straight lines at right angles) are used to represent the two most significant dimensions of the map—in Figure 7.4 these were family/conservative versus sporty/youthful, and upscale/luxury versus practical/economical.

To elaborate the above points, consider the perceptual map in Figure 7.5 that summarizes how a group of consumers once viewed the US beer market.[3] In this map, the perceived distance (dissimilarity) between Budweiser and Miller is about the same as the perceived distance between Coors and Michelob. Further, Beck's and Heineken are perceived to be the closest pair among this set of brands. In looking at the vectors, note that as you move in a north-east direction from the origin, the beers increase in their popularity with men. Budweiser is the most popular with men, and Old Milwaukee Light is the least popular with men. Budweiser (and then Beck's) is the farthest along the north-east direction. To see this most clearly, drop

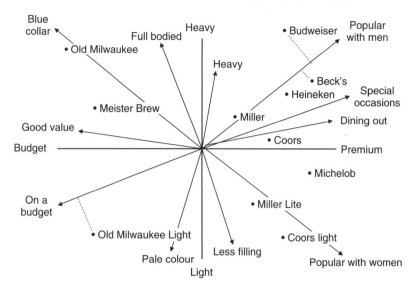

Figure 7.5. A position map of the US beer market

perpendicular lines from the point denoted as Budweiser and Beck's to the vector denoted 'popular with men'. Likewise, if you drop a perpendicular line from Old Milwaukee Light to this vector if it were extended in the south-west direction, you will see that it is the least popular beer with men. Note also that the horizontal axis (in the east direction) is most closely associated with features 'premium', 'dining out', and 'special occasions'. In the west direction, the horizontal axis is most closely associated with the features 'on a budget' and 'good value'. Thus, the horizontal axis (the west to east direction) indicates an underlying dimension of 'budget-premium', along which customers seem to characterize their perceptions of the differences between these beers.

Figure 7.5 captures some of the significant factors defining the competitive structure of the beer market, for example:

- The clusters of beers such as Beck's and Heineken help to identify (sub)categories of beers.
- Michelob is located between the 'Heavy' beers and the 'Light' beers. If its advertising positions it as a 'mid-strength' beer, it has a differentiated position; otherwise, it is likely to be regarded as a 'nothing' beer.
- Old Milwaukee Light has very little direct competition (no other brand is near its location), indicating potential opportunity for a new beer positioned in this quadrant (if there is a large enough segment of customers in this location). To be positioned in this quadrant, a beer needs

to be pale in colour and low priced. For experienced beer drinkers this is probably not a good combination of attributes. For a novice beer drinker, this may be more suitable. Thus, a new brand targeted to new beer drinkers may choose a name that reflects its appeal to this segment of consumers.

- Whether or not a beer is popular with women does not indicate anything about whether it will be popular with men (these two attributes are perpendicular to each other). Thus, although Beck's and Budweiser are equally popular with men; among women, Beck's is more popular than Budweiser (it sits further out along the Popular with Women vector).

In spite of its potential value in offering these insights, the map in Figure 7.5 has two major weaknesses. First, the attributes used to define the map do not seem to be chosen with any underlying theory of segmentation (such as discussed in Chapter 6) or positioning (as discussed later) in mind. For example, the segments are defined in terms of demographic variables (men, blue collar, women), and the brands are described mainly in terms of their features (e.g. price, colour) and some inferred benefits (e.g. less filling, special occasions). The point being made here is that the most crucial phase in perceptual mapping is choosing the set of attributes (and brands) to reveal the key elements of the market structure.

The second weakness of the map in Figure 7.5 is that it says nothing about the brand locations that are most attractive to customers. For example, it does not indicate whether more customers prefer heavy premium beers or light budget beers.[4] Without such insights about demand, organizations risk differentiating products along dimensions that do not increase customer preference. An example of such ineffective differentiation is the Westin Stamford Hotel in Singapore. It once advertised itself as the world's tallest hotel—a feature that was not important to many customers prior to the 11 September 2001 incident in New York, and is now likely to be a negative feature.

Perceptual maps can facilitate brand positioning by helping marketers to summarize and visualize key elements of the market structure for their products and services. For example, the underlying dimensions of *budget–premium* and *light–heavy* in Figure 7.5 capture the combined essence of several features on which beers differ. This helps to think strategically about brand positioning. Two key managerial questions to consider here are:

> Is there a gap in the market?
> and
> Is there a market in the gap?

While most people are better at processing visual than numerical information, some marketers (often called the 'poets' by business school professors) prefer verbal descriptions of their markets. The preference for word descriptions arises because of the richness of the descriptions that a good wordsmith can create, and because some position maps can be a bit of a struggle to understand—especially when consumer preferences are added to a map like Figure 7.5. The marketing managers of Guinness use a verbal approach to understand the relative positions of beer brands around the world—Table 7.1. Their insight relies on the semiotic analysis of beer brand advertising.[5] (Semiotics is the study of the social meanings of signs and symbols.)

The perceptual mapping approach to positioning is really a 'meaning out' approach. That is, what meanings do consumers attribute to and, thus, extract from their brands and its advertising. The study of advertising using semiotics and linguistics is a 'meaning in' approach to studying positioning. That is, what meanings are designed into the advertising of brands.[6] Both approaches are complementary.

Table 7.1. Semiotic analysis of UK beer advertising

Carling Black Label	*Stella Artois*
Key position attributes (or codes)	*Key position attributes (or codes)*
Heritage/roots; beer enjoyment; irreverent masculinity; sporting achievement	Parody; humour; heritage; beer enjoyment
Brand-specific execution tactics	*Brand-specific execution tactics*
Nationalism; 'Rule Britannia' (Dambusters, Union Jacks, 'best-selling beer in Britain'); strength (4.1%); tabloid attitude; Carling (football) Premiership	French language; music; cinematic references; idyllic France; 'reassuringly expensive'
Position themes	*Position themes*
Why—belonging	Why—personal indulgence
What—strength	What—best ingredients = best beer
Who—'lad' user	Who—discerning drinker
Supporting features	*Supporting features*
Brewed to 4.1% alcohol by volume	Premium (reassuringly expensive)
Football sponsorship	
Patriotism	
Popularity	
Advertising proposition	*Advertising proposition*
My Carling confirms me as one of the lads	Stella Artois is the ultimate reward
See www.bass-breweies.com	See www.stella-artois.com

To summarize, the scientific-based approaches to understanding a brand—its history (Figure 7.1), health (Figure 7.3), position (Figures 7.4 and 7.5), and language (Table 7.1)—all help to reveal the strengths and weaknesses of a brand. However, the usefulness of each approach rests heavily on the skills of the analyst who interprets the research. These skills must often be obtained from external consultants.

The Theory of Positioning[7]

When you think of safe cars, the one that probably comes to mind is Volvo. When you want a cold medicine at night, many people think of Nyquil. If you are looking for healthy frozen food, you may reach for Healthy Choice. These are products that have a well-defined position in the minds of many consumers. They are differentiated from the other offerings in their markets on one or more dimensions of importance to consumers. Ries and Trout document many other examples in which a brand's positioning strategy was instrumental to its long-term success.[8]

Most discussions of positioning are more artful than scientific in their approach. They revolve around some well-known examples, such as: Apple—'The power to be your best'; Avis—'We're number two. We try harder'; Coke—'It's the real thing'; BMW—'The ultimate driving machine'.[i] From these are derived a set of generic options with the advice that the marketer pick one that fits the profile of his or her brand—and that is currently not being used by a well-established competitor. Apart from these common-sense rules, there was little logic to guide the choice of a position statement. Recently, however, Professor John Rossiter and Larry Percy developed the theory in Figure 7.6 (and 7.8) to help select a good brand position statement.

Figure 7.6 suggests that three links need to be communicated for a new brand (or new a company). The brand's communication must signal its connection to (*a*) the product category (or if it is a company to an industry), (*b*) the target customer segment, and (*c*) the relevant purchase or usage motivation via its benefits. For well-established brands, or brands with a descriptive name (such as Travelers Insurance), the first link comes

---

[i] At the time of writing this book Apple was using the slogan 'think different'; Avis had slipped to number three so they just claimed that they 'Try harder'; BMW now delivered 'Sheer driving pleasure'; and Coke just keeps changing its promise. To many people, however, it is still 'the real thing'.

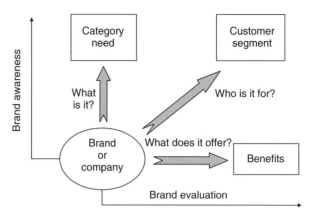

Figure 7.6. Positioning themes

automatically. For a brand such as Boags Strongarm, you need to tell people what it is. (It is a good Australian beer, but you would never guess this from its name.) The second link is often not explicitly made by either the brand name or its advertising message. Sometimes it is obvious, but many times the advertisement does not 'call out' to the target audience, and is thus passed over. Many of those 'obscure' corporate ads found in business magazines get caught by this trap. Are they talking to (potential) employees, (institutional) investors, regulators, politicians, or everybody and, thus, nobody in particular? The third link is all about helping the target customer tune into radio station WII-FM—What's in it for me! Diet Coke's original slogan 'Only one calorie' and later 'Just for the taste of it' were designed to do this.

Figure 7.7 illustrates how two of the world's best business schools— London Business School and the Chicago Graduate School of Business— compare across the three positioning dimensions in Figure 7.6.[9] It also shows how each school tries to pass the IDU test.

Ries and Trout defined positioning as the 'battle for your mind'. That is, what position has the brand or the organization in the mind of the target consumer, and how is it different to competitor brands? Following this theme, Figure 7.6 can be reduced to two decisions about *location*:

- How the brand should be positioned in its product category.
- Whether it should be positioned with respect to the user or the product itself.

Figure 7.8 shows how this is often achieved.

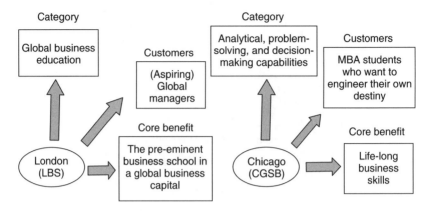

Figure 7.7. London versus Chicago

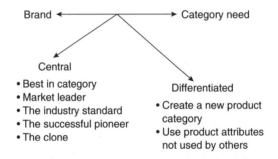

Figure 7.8. Positioning options for category positioning

The first location decision is to determine whether it is feasible to claim the central (or prototypic) location with respect to the product category. BMW's 'The ultimate driving machine' and Coke's 'It's the real thing' were two bold statements of a central brand. Intel's 'Intel inside' and its 'the computer inside' ingredient brand positions were softer statements of a central position. More often than simply stating that the brand is 'it', a central brand will advertise that it 'owns' the category-defining product attribute and/or benefit such as Compaq's 'Inspiration Technology', Miller Lite's 'tastes great, less filling', Mercedes-Benz 'engineered like no other car', and Federal Express's original 'overnight' delivery.

In order to support its claim as *the* brand in the category, a brand may explicitly say or imply that it is 'best in category', 'the market leader', 'industry standard', or the 'successful pioneer'. In essence, central brands try to say that they best represent the core attributes or benefits of the category. The 'power' of this positioning strategy is that it forces all the other brands to be compared to the central (or prototype) brand in the consumer's mind. For example, if Coke is 'the real thing', then every other cola brand must be second best.

The 'clone' position is an interesting variation of the central position. This is an option for a 'me-too' brand, but under a special set of circumstances, namely:

- the brand must deliver the same benefits as the central brand (often the market leader);
- these benefits must be easily and objectively determined by the buyer;
- it must be *significantly* cheaper.

The classic example of this strategy was the IBM clone PCs that flooded the market in the 1980s. For the experienced-user segment who could easily evaluate the performance of these machines, they offered better value than the high-priced market leader IBM. When Fuji Photo entered the US market in the 1980s, it used this strategy against Kodak. Fuji film was significantly cheaper and photographers could 'see' little or no quality difference. Many low-involvement, private-label retailer brands and generic OTC pharmaceuticals also use this positioning strategy.

Because the central position is so highly prized, we see many attempts to link brands to this option. For example, the famous Avis 'We're number two. We try harder' campaign was an example of a number-two brand associating itself with the market leader. Hertz was number one in car rentals at the time—and still is. What made this position so enticing was that it gave a credible reason why the customer could expect Avis to try harder. Another way that challengers try to link themselves to the central position is through a 'club' positioning strategy. For example, we hear about: the 'big 4' accounting firms, the 'big 3' US auto companies, the 'top 10' business schools, and others. Sometimes these clubs can be quite large—such as the Fortune 500. Being a member of one of these clubs is often as important to employees as it is to target consumers.

If a central location is not available, then differentiation is the strategy. Figure 7.8 suggests two such avenues. One such positioning strategy is illustrated by IBM's slogan 'e-business'. What do you do when competitors have staked out positions in the competitive landscape, but you still want to become the *defining* brand for the product category? One solution is to create a new product (sub)category and make a claim for being *the* brand in this (sub)category. Hence, IBM was first to state that it is *the* e-business company. When it launched this branding statement it deliberately did not try to trademark the e-business slogan. There is no point in owning the central position of an industry with nobody else in it.

A second example of this strategy is provided by Apple Computer and the other early 'hobby' computer developers. Having developed their new computers, did they differentiate them by saying that they were smaller than most of the existing computers? No, they started talking about them as 'personal computers'. Thus, they created a new product category that Apple started to dominate as the prototypical example. This fracturing of product categories (and industries) into more and more subcategories offers access to the central position for many more brands. The trick, however, is to first establish a subcategory that reflects the needs of a target segment of consumers. For example, you might sell a *mobile* phone to a salesperson but a *personal* phone to a teenager.

Another type of differentiation strategy is to select an important product attribute that the central-location brand(s) is not using. For example, toothpaste was originally differentiated on the taste attribute (Colgate). Then as competitors entered the market they used other attributes to position themselves: cavity prevention (Crest), brightness (Macleans), fresh breath (Closeup), coloured stripes of paste (Stripe), gel formulation (Aim), plastic package, tartar prevention, fights plaque, with fluoride, with calcium, with baking soda, pump pack, etc. It is getting very crowded here! So crowded, in fact, that Colgate sells a toothpaste in Australia called Total—the container says that it delivers fresh breath, better taste, stronger white teeth, and fewer cavities with its calcium and fluoroguard that fights plaque acids—and all delivered from a pump pack. It has the 'total' set of attributes!

When everybody in the category is claiming to have most of the attributes and deliver most of the benefits, its time to break away from the pack. An interesting example of this strategy was adopted by 7-Up when it announced itself as the 'uncola', and later when it proclaimed that 'it is cool to be clear'. Also, the famous 'think small' campaign for the original Volkswagen beetle car in the US market was an example of what is sometimes called the 'against position'. Going against the trend of the big brands recognizes that there is probably a segment of customers who have different needs and tastes and who will value a distinct alternative from the mainstream brands.

When it is not feasible or not desired to anchor a brand's position primarily to the product category or industry, Figure 7.6 suggests two other alternatives. One that fits comfortably with the main theme of this book is to link the brand directly to a customer segment. A good example of this occurred many years ago when Pepsi labelled its target segment 'the Pepsi generation'. (The compelling idea was to suggest that children do not want to drink the same cola as their parents.) The name 'U-Haul' also links itself to a customer group when it says to target consumers that they can hire a car trailer, but they have to haul their own goods. Another way this link to a consumer segment occurs is when a brand adopts a parochial position. For example, Qantas—'The spirit of Australia'; British Airways; Zurich Insurance; Tooheys Country beer. People who feel a strong attachment to the country or region automatically associate with the brand.

Apple, Microsoft, and the US Army have at times all used a direct appeal to their target customers in their position statements, namely: Apple—'the power to be *your* best'; Microsoft 'where do *you* want to go today'; US Army—'be all *you* can be'. The basic idea behind this type of positioning is to make the user the hero or heroine. Rossiter and Percy suggest this strategy for consideration when either:

- the brand or company is a market specialist such as with Hewlett-Packard's range of 'professional' calculators; or
- a technical product is targeted to a novice user—they will not understand either the enabling technology or the technical attributes so do not focus on these; or
- the purchase motivation for the product is of a reward or positive nature such as intellectual stimulation or social approval, as is the case with many books, computer games, cars, and clothes.

If the user as hero or heroine positioning option is unsuitable, then a product-as-hero positioning strategy can be considered. Here, a key attribute of the product or its performance is the focus of attention. In this scheme, a product attribute 'does something', and performance refers to how well or efficiently this 'something' is done relative to competitors. Advertising that claims that the brand or the company is the best, biggest, most prestigious, highest quality, oldest, lowest priced, has the most attributes, etc., are examples of a product-as-hero positioning strategies.

Some interesting hypotheses are emerging about when it is appropriate to consider using product-as-hero/heroine positions. For example, when advertising to expert customers, tell them about the product attributes and encourage them to generate their own set of related benefits (intellectual stimulation). Experts do not like being 'told' (by an inexpert ad agency) how the attributes of a product produce consumer benefits. Another hypothesis is that when products have the same attributes, purchase motivations, and benefits (e.g. telephones and petrol), attempt to differentiate the brand on emotional associations (e.g. AT&T's 'reach out and touch someone' ad campaign), or create a meaningless attribute so that people can 'see' they are different (e.g. those scientific-sounding motor oil and skin-softening additives).

The other major positioning alternative in Figure 7.6 is to link the brand or the organization directly to a consumer purchase motivation and/or benefit. Rossiter and Percy suggest that there are three situations where this positioning strategy should be considered, namely:

- the brand has a hard-to-imitate benefit such as a satellite phone's worldwide coverage; or
- the brand is designed to relieve a negative purchase motivation such as a laundry detergent removing stains; or
- when the brand must make a logical attack on an entrenched emotion-based attitude such as when advertising condoms.

As we will see in the next section, brand positioning is achieved by combining aspects of the various approaches discussed here. Many marketers believe that such a hybrid approach offers the best chance of creating a powerful brand.

So far the discussion of positioning has focused on individual brands. How do you position a portfolio of brands? If all the sub-brands are sold under an umbrella brand name, such as the range of Healthy Choice meals, then they can be positioned like a single brand. However, if each brand in the portfolio has a different name, then something needs to be chosen as an integrating theme—as Figure 7.6 suggests, this can be a product category, and/or a consumer segment, and/or a benefit. For example, Meredith Corporation bills itself as 'America's leading home and family media company'. It focuses on serving what they call the 'nester segment', namely, people who are interested in their homes and in spending money to make them better. In 1995, their product line consisted of:

- *Better Homes and Gardens*
- *Ladies Home Journal*
- *Country Home*
- *Midwest Living*
- *Wood*
- *American Patchwork and Quilting*
- *Home Garden*
- *Garden, Deck and Landscape Planner.*

Al Ries describes this type of product line positioning as the search for a multi-step focus.[10] To further illustrate it, he provides another magazine example, this time linked to the product attribute 'news':

- *Time*—news of the world
- *Fortune*—news about business
- *Life*—news in pictures
- *Sports Illustrated*—news about sports
- *Money*—news about personal finances

- *People*—news about celebrities
- *Entertainment Weekly*—news about entertainment

To summarize, the major positioning strategies outlined in Figures 7.6 and 7.8 are flexible enough to present a multitude of options to marketers charged with the responsibility of developing a position statement for their brand or their organization. The value of Figure 7.6 is that it identifies the links to be developed in the brand's position statement.

The Art of Positioning

The art of positioning entails turning the previous theory of positioning into a one- or two-sentence positioning statement. This then becomes the script for the brand's advertising. Writing this script is as easy as ABC:[11]

Audience
Benefit
Compelling reason why

Undisciplined marketers try to write a position statement as broadly as possible—to appeal to every potential customer, and to mention all major benefits. However, the art of positioning is the opposite of this. It is about making considered choices to exclude everything except the core benefit of the product and service as desired by the dominant group of customers. The mantra of good positioning is:

Focus!

Consider how car tyres could be positioned. Two options might be:

	A	B
Audience	For parents with young children	For wet-weather drivers
Benefit	XYZ is the safest tyre you can buy to protect the lives of your loved ones	XYZ is the safest tyre
Compelling reason	Because our dual-wall tyres perform exceptionally well in all weather conditions, gripping the road so you will not have accidents	Because our new tread pattern grips the road better than any other tyre currently on the market

Positioning statement A has been used by Michelin with advertising that featured a baby in a tyre and the tag-line 'Michelin: Because so much is riding on your tyres'. Positioning statement B is used every winter by some brand of tyre with a tag-line like 'Better grip in the wet'.

Both the car tyre positions pass the I and D parts of the IDU Test. However, because the Michelin one has a stronger emotional connection to a big group of buyers—those parents who shuttle the children around and who display those 'Mum's Taxi' and 'Baby on Board' signs on their cars—it stands a better chance of passing the U part of the test.

Chapter 6 focused on identifying the Audience or target customer segment part of the ABC positioning script. Chapter 8 presents a framework to help identify the core benefit and the compelling reason why. Tapping into people's emotions, however, is something that is a real art.

KEY CONCEPTS

- *Brand*—The combination of name and other symbols used to identify a product or service and the 'promise' made to the buyer.
- *Brand audit*—The process of reviewing a brand's current standing in the market.
- *Brand position*—The perceptions and evaluation of a brand held by people.
- *Positioning*—The management process used to create a brand position.
- *Central position*—A brand that people think is the prototype of the product category or industry. Because this is thought to be the most powerful position to occupy, other brands often try to indirectly link themselves to this brand—as a challenger, clone, complement, or part of a club that includes the central brand.
- *Differentiated position*—Any position other than the central brand position.
- *Position statement*—One or two simple sentences saying why target customers should buy this brand instead of something else.

KEY FRAMEWORKS

- *IDU test*—The assessment of the brand's position in terms of its 'importance' to target consumers, the organization's capability to 'deliver' the brand promise, the brand's 'uniqueness' relative to competing brands, and the sustainability of the brand position over time.
- *Brand knowledge*—The beliefs, associations, and evaluation of a brand—Figure 7.2
- *Brand health map*—Figure 7.3
- *Position map*—Figures 7.4 and 7.5

- *Semiotic analysis*—Table 7.1
- *Positioning themes*—Figures 7.6 and 7.8

KEY QUESTIONS

- What is the position statement for your brand?
- Does your brand pass the IDU Test?
- What is the current strength of your brand—relative to competing brands?
- For your brand, is there a gap in the market? And a market in the gap?

PART B

Branding

Having conducted an audit of a brand, the task now becomes one of (re)building a strong brand. This part of the chapter describes the basic building blocks that create strong brands. These are the factors that a manager can change in order to build a brand of relevance, fun, and distinction.

Brand Architecture—the DNA of the Brand

There are hundreds of books on branding and hundreds of advertising agencies and marketing consultants who will help to design and manage a brand.[12] Each book and consultant has their own peculiar way of thinking about the key elements of a brand. These can be loosely called the brand's architecture (or its DNA). Figure 7.9 shows the architecture used in this book. Its purpose is twofold, namely, to identify the major factors that a marketer needs to manage, and to organize these into a framework that focuses on understanding the essence of the brand. The reason for this emphasis on brand essence is that successful brands are usually focused around a single dominant positioning theme.

The Offer—the Brand's Core Benefit

As noted at the beginning of this chapter, the next chapter discusses how consumer-focused organizations create products and services that are

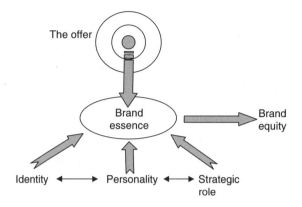

Figure 7.9. The brand's architecture

important to target consumers. The key to the successful development of a desirable offer is to ensure that it creates demonstrable customer value, which was defined in Chapter 6 as

$$\text{customer value} = (\text{benefits} - \text{price}),$$

and that it has a strong positioning statement.

In Figure 7.9, the offer is drawn as three nested circles. In Chapter 8, this is called a 'product/service onion'. It is a framework to help marketers (and the ad agency) to understand which product features deliver which consumer benefits, and to identify the overall core benefit that can be used in a benefit-positioning strategy (Figure 7.6) and that should drive the essence of the brand.

Brand Identity[13]

> That which we call a rose, by any other name would smell as sweet.
>
> *Romeo and Juliet,* William Shakespeare

Shakespeare's line in *Romeo and Juliet* alludes to two important issues about positioning and branding. Where do brand names come from and how do they 'work' to position a brand against its competitors? Why names are important is that they are generally the first point of contact between the consumer and the product or service. And as someone once said, 'You never get a second chance to make a first impression'.

Because names denote and connote meaning, a good name can enhance communication with consumers. This is especially true when a product is new to the market. If the name is descriptive, such as the Australian

Graduate School of Management, Surf, Dive, and Ski, and Travellers Insurance, then it starts the positioning process the first time that it is mentioned. Sometimes governments and not-for-profit organizations understand the power of good names—Fair Trade Laws, Freedom from Hunger, Greenpeace, and the World Wildlife Fund. If the name tells consumers about the core benefit of the product and/or the target consumer group, this is even better:

- Weight Watchers, Lean Cuisine, and Healthy Choice (frozen) foods;
- Head and Shoulders shampoo;
- Intensive Care skin lotion;
- Close-Up toothpaste;
- Budget, Ezi-Rent, and Thrifty car rental.

Sometimes there are literal meanings and inferential beliefs that automatically attach to, or that can be engineered into, corporate and brand identity symbols. For example, the Jaguar car symbol of a jaguar (big cat) suggests 'pace with grace'—one of the company's old advertising slogans. If this imagery exists, and it is favourable to the desired position of the brand/company, then it can help promote the brand to both employees and consumers. (Brands are often more important to employees than they are to consumers.) This school of thought advocates searching for the power of brand identity in semiotics, psycholinguistics (the meaning of words and their imagery), and phonetics (the science of speech sounds). For designers who belong to this *Language School* of brand identity, a new identity 'works' when it helps to build a favourable image or evaluation of the brand.

The opposing school of thought is illustrated by the quote from Shakespeare's *Romeo and Juliet* that introduced this section. Here, the basic driver of a successful brand identity is marketing muscle. That is, with sufficient and effective promotion, most identity symbols can be made to 'work'. For example, over many years, and with the aid of millions of dollars of advertising, packaging, and signage, people have become accustomed to names (and sometimes the logos) of brands like Apple Computer, BMW, Coca-Cola, Exxon, Ford, Kodak, McDonald's, Nike, Shell, Starbucks, and Xerox. It helps that the products and services that these companies offer are regarded highly.

Consultants who argue that a new identity design will significantly improve the overall evaluation people hold of a company or its brands often over-sell the potential contribution that identity symbols can make. This is easily demonstrated by listing the first ten brand names that come into your mind, and then see if you can

- describe the logo;
- recall the brand's colour scheme;

- describe how it writes its name (e.g. upper or lower case);
- recall its advertising slogan (or tag-line or strap-line).

I, and most of my colleagues, regularly fail this test.

An issue that often concerns marketers is how to name a related set of brands. One framework to solve this problem is called a *brand hierarchy*. Here, the company name is used at the top of the hierarchy and the model name at the bottom, for example:

- Corporate brand—Toshiba;
- Family or umbrella brands—Satellite and Portege personal computers;
- Individual brands—Satellite and Satellite Pro;
- Models—Satellite Pro TE2000; Satellite Pro 6100.

Thus, the full name of the PC with which I wrote this book is Toshiba Satellite Pro 6100. The challenge for the marketer is to emphasize those aspects of the brand hierarchy that provide positive associations to target customers. A company like Procter & Gamble places its emphasis on the individual brands (because they often compete with each other on the retailer's shelf), while Toshiba emphasizes the corporate and family brands (because Toshiba is a respected name in PCs, and the family brands are targeted to different segments of users).

The bedevilling question for many managers is 'Is there a "best" way to link a set of brand names?' The short answer is 'no'—if for no other reason than the success of the wide variety of brand names used throughout this book. The decision about which naming system to use usually boils down to whether or not the various products and services should be linked back to the corporate name (so that each entity can 'rent' the positive associations of the other), or whether the organization wants to keep some 'distance' between the various brands (because they compete with each other).

To summarize, brand identity is important, but it is not the most important element of a brand. (The customer value it delivers is the key to its success—relative to that of its competitors.) Identity has three major roles, namely, to help (*a*) create awareness for the brand, (*b*) trigger recognition of the brand—which is especially important when the decision to buy the product is made at the point of purchase (e.g. bottled water, facial tissues, office stationery, etc.)—and (*c*) activate an already stored evaluation of the brand in consumers' minds. In this way, identity is more tactical than strategic. Whether the brand's tactics (the way that it presents itself) supports its strategy (its desired position) is best answered by research. For example, a good way to test a brand's typeface is to write it in several different styles, some of which are used by competing brands. Consumers are then asked to rate each typeface on the attributes that capture the position of the brand. The results can be surprising. For example, a study of audio-tape buyers showed that most target consumers preferred the Memorex name written in the typeface used by Maxell, a key competitor.[14]

There is one time when it is *very* important to understand all the inferences that consumers make from a brand's identity. It is when the brand is taken into a different culture—especially Asia. For example, keeping a Western name and spelling is likely to be more successful in Japan than in China because Japanese consumers are more familiar with the Roman alphabet. If a Western name is translated into Chinese characters, then different writing systems and styles can impact on people's perceptions of the brand. This occurs because the visual characteristics of a name are important to native speakers of Chinese. In short, culture matters—the East is different from the West.

Brand Personality

Brand personality is defined as the set of human-like traits (distinguishing features or qualities) that may be associated with a brand. Like human personality traits that are inferred from an individual's behaviour, expressed attitudes, and socio-demographic characteristics, brand personality traits are inferred from factors such as the brand's features, advertising, price level, retail outlets in which it is sold, and type of customer who uses it. In B2C markets, brands like Disney could be described as wholesome, warm, and friendly, Harley-Davidson as macho and America-loving, and in its day Playboy as outrageous. In B2B markets, General Electric, while under the direction of Jack Welch, was often referred to as aggressive. In the world of management consulting, McKinsey & Company is often referred to as elitist.

Advertising agency creative people like to know what the marketing team's description of the brand's personality is so that they can make sure that this is reflected in the advertising. Sometimes this will change over time. For example, at one time Coca-Cola might have been described as 'Young, healthy and clean-cut'. Then Pepsi came in with 'Witty, streetwise and cynical'. Then Coke countered with 'Gutsy, sassy and challenging'. And so it went on. The ad agency also likes to know the personality profile of the target consumer segment. The reason for this is to assess the fit between the personalities of the brand and the target consumer. Why? Because, consumers usually feel more comfortable with brands that have personalities that are consistent with their own (actual or desired) self-concept.

Research is the key to understanding how target consumers might describe the personality of a brand. For example, some years ago, Perrier's desired brand personality was to be thought of as sophisticated and stylish. However, their research discovered that they were more likely to be seen as flashy and trendy. Jennifer Aaker has developed a Brand Personality Scale to describe the traits that characterize a broad array of brands.[15] The scale uses five personality traits to profile a brand, namely:

1. *Sincerity* (e.g. Campbell's, Hallmark, Levi's, Kodak)
   - down-to-earth, honest, wholesome, cheerful
2. *Excitement* (e.g. Absolut, Benetton, MTV, Porsche)
   - daring, spirited, imaginative, up-to-date
3. *Competence* (e.g. Amex, AT&T, CNN, IBM)
   - reliable, intelligent, successful
4. *Sophistication* (e.g. Avon, Hallmark, Lexus, Mercedes, Porsche, Revlon)
   - upper class, charming
5. *Ruggedness* (e.g. ESPN, Levi's, Nike, Reebok)
   - outdoorsy, tough.

(Cross-cultural research indicates that these five dimensions do not apply outside the United States. For example, in Japan and Spain a 'peacefulness' dimension replaces the 'ruggedness' dimension, and in Spain a 'passion' dimension replaces the 'competence' dimension.[16])

In line with the theme of this chapter for a brand to be differentiated and have a clear brand essence, Aaker's list of personality traits can be used to help build such a personality, and to design the brand's advertising. For example, to build a brand that exudes competence, its communication should emphasize facets such as care, confidence, efficiency, influence, leadership, and technology. To decode a brand advertisement, a good place to start is with the slogan used to sign off the ad. For example, at the time of writing this book, Compaq was using the slogan 'Inspiration Technology'. This would suggest that they were focusing primarily on 'excitement' (through the word inspiration) and on 'competence' (with the word technology).

In many product categories (such as the supermarket products, petrol, industrial supplies, etc. discussed in Part A of Chapter 4), the functional features of the brand are more central determinants of purchase and use than brand personality.[17] In such cases, the personality aspect of a brand's architecture may help as a creative communications device, but it will play a less important role as a creator of brand equity.

Strategic Brand Roles

Whether an organization has a portfolio of brands or a stand-alone brand, the marketer's job is to assign it a particular role in the portfolio or the market. Some of the more common roles are:

- A fashion or excitement brand to maintain interest in the product category (e.g. some of those short-lived new brands of beer).
- A complementary brand to support other products in the portfolio (e.g. the Meredith Corporation's portfolio of magazines targeted to the nester segment listed earlier).
- Some market-coverage brands to saturate a market (e.g. all those news magazines listed earlier in this chapter).
- A challenger brand to appeal to people who do not like the big, market leading brands (e.g. Richard Branson's various Virgin brands).
- A flanker (often a low-price or price-fighting) brand launched to protect a more valuable brand (e.g. used to directly attack a brand that starts a price war).
- A low-end entry or high-end brand to expand the brand's customer base (e.g. BMW's 3-series cars and the Lexus from Toyota).
- A repositioning brand to try to change current perceptions of other brands in the product line (e.g. this was the role of the Reatta in Figure 7.7 and BMW's open-top, roadster sports car).
- An investment brand to claim a stake in a developing market (e.g. this was the role of many Internet brands that were owned by established companies).
- A value brand that offers a good price–quality trade-off (e.g. Wal-Mart's offer of branded merchandise at everyday low prices).
- A 'cash cow' or profit generating brand to provide funds to support the growth and development of other brands (e.g. many mainstream beer brands play this role).
- A factory brand that allows a continuous-production manufacturing process to stay in operation—these products may then be branded by a retailer.
- A high-image or aspirational sub-brand to cater to the needs of a few, and to help sell the less expensive brands in the line (e.g. the old 8-series BMWs).

As can be seen from these descriptions, the role assigned to a brand will have a big impact on how it is presented to target consumers, aspiring consumers, and competitors.

Brand Essence

At the heart of Figure 7.9 is the essence of the brand. It is an amalgam of all the things that work to the brand's unique advantage—particularly its ABC positioning statement. Distilling the essence of a brand is more art than science and is often facilitated by the organization's advertising agency.

Many of history's most famous brands have a clearly discernible essence that they try to express in their advertising tag-line, such as Coca-Cola's 'The real thing', Kit Kat's 'Have a break, have a Kit Kat', BMW's 'The ultimate driving machine', British Airways' 'The world's favourite airline', and 3M's 'Innovation'. Sometimes, the brand essence can be captured in a picture (the Marlboro cowboy), or a logo (the Qantas flying kangaroo).

A strong brand essence emerges when each of the elements in Figure 7.9 combine and focus on a single dominant consumer promise—and this promise is delivered time after time after time. Strong consumer brands are marketed as function plus

- fashion, and/or
- emotion, and/or
- lifestyle.

It is also easy for consumers to verify the brand's promise. For example, SWATCH watches are sold all over the world in interesting shops and worn by fashion-conscious people who seem to enjoy the experience.

Strong business and industrial brands are marketed as function plus

- risk avoidance, and/or
- value creation.

For example, in the days when IBM dominated the mainframe computer market there was a saying among businesspeople that 'nobody ever got fired for buying IBM'. IBM machines did the job they were acquired for, and just as importantly, they did not put the manager's career at risk if anything went wrong.

Brand essence weakens when consumers are confused about the relevance of the brand to their lives or their jobs, and/or when real performance advantages are no longer apparent.

Brand Equity

Brand value emerged as a central marketing concept in the 1980s in the United Kingdom. (The term 'brand equity' emerged in the 1988 at a conference run by the prestigious Marketing Science Institute in the United States. Since then, the two terms are often used interchangeably.) The reason was that companies were being bought and sold for huge sums of money based largely on the estimated dollar value of their brands. Nestlé bought Rowntrees, Segram bought Matel, PepsiCo bought Kentucky Fried Chicken (now KFC), and Grand Met bought Heublein and Pillsbury. These acquisitions triggered a debate among accountants (and marketers) about whether the values of the brands should be included on the balance sheet. The accounting arguments in favour were to record hidden assets and, thus, strengthen the balance sheet.[ii] Marketers were a somewhat more reluctant group. While the valuation of a brand would raise the importance of their marketing programmes to enhance brand strength, it would also mean that the stewardship of their brands would be on public display—and, thus, increase the accountability for their marketing actions. (Some general managers, however, thought this was a great idea.) Today, some companies value their brands and some of these put these values onto their balance sheets—but most do not.

Interbrand Group PLC is acknowledged as a pioneer in, and principal advocate of, financial brand valuation.[18] Their valuation approach is based on identifying the current and future earnings or cash flow from the brand, and then capitalizing this, taking into account inflation and risk. Once a year the magazine *Financial World* publishes estimates of the brand equity value of hundreds of the world's leading brands. (They use a similar, but slightly different, approach to *Interbrand*.) Many brand consultants also offer a brand valuation service—each with its own (best) proprietar valuation method. Thus, like many intangible assets, there is no commonly accepted financial brand valuation methodology.

David Aaker, a founder of the concept of brand equity, defines it as a set of assets (such as name awareness and customer loyalty) that are linked to the brand (through its name and symbol) and add (or subtract) value to the product or service being offered.[19] Aaker's argument is that brands can be considered to be 'strong' or 'weak', and that marketing programmes can build brand equity. Hence, in Figure 7.9 it is shown as the outcome of good branding (and marketing) practice.

The definition of brand equity suggests that a brand has added value, beyond that which comes from the function performed by the product or service. This added value often manifests itself as an increase in one or

---

[ii] In 1984, News Corporation's Rupert Murdoch thought this was a great idea because it significantly improved the company's debt/equity ratio and helped him borrow more money to finance new acquisitions.

more of the following:

- market share,
- price premium/margin,
- customer loyalty,
- trade access and cooperation,
- effectiveness of marketing programmes (such as advertising),
- brand extension opportunities,
- resistance to competitive attacks on the brand.

While brand equity is a hot topic of contemporary marketing, and at first glance it seems to have intuitive appeal, given a second careful look it turns out to be a very 'slippery' concept.[20]

There are two main criticisms about brand equity. One is that there is no underlying theory that relates the drivers of a brand's equity (such as its levels of awareness and customer loyalty) to its outputs (such as greater market share) for a strong brand. The second damning criticism is that most of the attributes of a so-called strong brand can be accounted for simply in terms of its market penetration and the Double Jeopardy phenomenon discussed in Part A of Chapter 4. Thus, brands should be considered as either 'big' or 'small', not 'strong' or 'weak'. From this perspective, brand equity is a concept that adds little to our understanding about how to manage a brand. Because the debate about brand equity is as yet unresolved, it is included in Figure 7.9, but marketers would be wise to treat this concept with great care.

If the idea of brand equity/value is appealing, but a financial measure of brand value is not required, then managers can create a set of indicators of brand equity like those outlined above. One of the most parsimonious sets has been derived from a worldwide study of brands by the ad agency Young and Rubicam (Y&R).[21] According to their Brand Asset Valuator™ model, successful brands are built on four pillars:

- Differentiation (as established by the brand's position and essence).
- Relevance (being personally appropriate to the individual).
- Esteem (being held in high regard).
- Knowledge (the intimate understanding of the brand and what it stands for).

Y&R argue that relevance together with differentiation produce brand strength, while esteem and knowledge combine to produce brand stature.

Two things make the Y&R model worth considering. One is that each of the four elements can be enhanced by a marketing programme—often advertising. (Y&R is a worldwide advertising agency.) A second is that their research suggests that most brands evolve predictably over time. This is

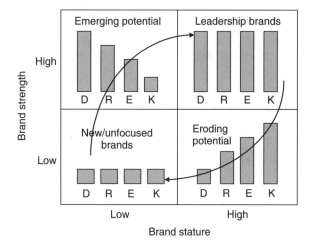

Figure 7.10. The Y&R brand PowerGrid

shown in their PowerGrid in Figure 7.10. Thus, a manager can evaluate the current position of his or her brand by the pattern of the four indicators, and then think about the management actions required to move it to, or keep it in, the north-east quadrant of the grid. For example, the brands that lack differentiation are the ones most likely to start a price war.

In summary, brand equity is a useful concept for marketing managers to the extent that it provides the stimulus and guidance to make better decisions about building brands of relevance and distinction. From this consumer-based perspective (as opposed to a financial valuation perspective), brand equity is the differential effect that knowledge of the brand has on consumers' responses to the product or service and its marketing. Frameworks such as Figure 7.3 and the Y&R brand PowerGrid (Figure 7.10) are useful as a managerial approach to brand building and monitoring. The choice of a particular framework depends on the answer to two questions: (*a*) for whom and (*b*) for what purpose is the measure required?

KEY CONCEPTS

- *Customer value*—the buyer's estimation of a product or service's overall capacity to satisfy his or her needs. It is measured as the benefits offered relative to the price paid.
- *Brand identity*—the name, logo, design, packaging, and other features of a product or service that enable people to correctly identify it.

- *Brand personality*—the set of human-like traits that are associated with a brand.
- *Brand essence*—the intrinsic nature of the brand.
- *Strategic brand roles*—the marketing role of the brand in the organization's portfolio of brands.
- *Brand equity*—the differential effect that knowledge of the brand has on consumers' responses to the product and its marketing.

KEY FRAMEWORKS

- *Brand Architecture*—Figure 7.9
- *Y&R brand PowerGrid*—Figure 7.10

KEY QUESTIONS

- Is it possible to state, in simple terms, the essence of your brand(s)?
- Is it clear how each element of the brand's architecture (Figure 7.9) contributes to the brand's essence and drives its brand equity?
- For marketing managers of multi-brand organizations, has each brand been assigned a specific strategic role so that it enhances the overall equity of the portfolio?
- If you are measuring brand equity, does your measure help to create a stronger brand?

RECAP

No Logo Versus Pro Logo

While the American Marketing Association defines a brand in terms of how its identity symbols differentiate it from competitors, consumers define brands as an assortment of expectations established by the seller, that once fulfilled, form a covenant with them. This is where the real power of a brand resides—inside the mind of the consumer. However, this is also the source of the real vulnerability of brands.

In Chapter 1, reference was made to Naomi Klein's best-selling book *No Logo*. This book outlines many of the social criticisms of the brand-based approach to marketing. In contrast, this chapter presents the Pro-Logo position. The No Logo–Pro Logo debate reveals an interesting marketing irony. Because trust is the basis for all the values associated with a brand, the more companies promote their brands, the more they need to be perceived as ethically pure. And thus, the more they need to be responsive to consumer demands. Hence, the idea in this chapter is not to defend the bad management practices exposed by Klein's book, but rather to focus on brands as a strategic marketing asset.[22] Periodically, business journalists pronounce 'the death of brands'—as happened after 'Marlboro Friday' that was discussed in Chapter 3. So far they have been wrong every time.

Brands are one of the key intangible, inimitable assets of many companies. They usually take years to develop, and like a flywheel, a good brand will deliver a stream of financial benefits to its owner. Consequently, active brand management is a key responsibility for the marketing team.

The following description of Benetton is an interesting case study of the power of branding. It illustrates the development of a global brand and the strategies that Luciano Benetton has used periodically to renew his brand—which are very important when the brand essence involves being fashionable.

Answer to the Buick Question

The Buick Reatta was a failure. It was a good-looking car—something like a Mercedes sports coupé—but the Buick name undermined its new position.

BENETTON

Creating a Sensation Around the Brand (See www.benetton.com for a Selection of these Advertisements)

In 1984, Luciano Benetton commissioned Oliverio Toscani to create a global image for the Benetton brand. This directive would send shockwaves around the world for the next seventeen years. (Toscani's commission was terminated in 2000.)

Toscani's genius was that he presented Luciano with a single, simple idea to position the brand. Originally called 'All the Colours in the World', it soon migrated to the now familiar 'United Colours of Benetton'. This slogan captured the essence of the brand by embracing the colourful character of the clothes and the diversity of the people who wore them. The early advertising featured people from a variety of racial backgrounds wearing the Benetton range of clothes.

Over time the Benetton advertising would migrate from featuring clothing to promoting images that touched very deep emotions in people. Toscani would say that traditional advertising pictures were a bunch of lies. His advertisements were like a Rorschach test—people brought their own interpretation to each image. These ads would win numerous advertising awards and provoke much antagonism—from the public, the Church, community groups, Benetton shop owners, and at one time Luciano's mother. To handle this controversy, Luciano and Toscani would neither strenuously defend nor fully explain the offending advertisements in their press conferences. To ensure that the particularly controversial advertisements did not damage the overall brand evaluation, they would follow a controversial campaign with another that was less offensive—a pattern of confrontation followed by appeasement.

What was innovative about these advertisements was the way that they touched the values of Benetton's target customers. The controversy that surrounded each campaign served to help them break through the clutter of other advertising and to give them more impact. They positioned Benetton as a company that cared about social issues—and one that had a point of view. The main criticism was that they exploited the 'victims' (people and social issues) depicted in the ads.

Main Sources: J. Mantle, *Benetton: The Family, the Business and the Brand* (London: Warner Books, 1999); K. Keller, *Strategic Brand Management* (Upper Saddle River, NJ: Prentice Hall, 1998), p. 155.

NOTES

1. This section borrows from G. L. Lilien and A. Rangaswamy, *Marketing Engineering* (Upper Saddle River, NJ: Prentice Hall, 2003), chapter 4; and G. R. Dowling, G. L. Lilien, R. J. Thomas, and A. Rangaswamy, *Harvesting Customer Value* (State College, PA: Institute for the Study of Business Markets, 2000), chapter 6.
2. Based on G. Urban and S. Star, *Advanced Marketing Strategy* (Englewood Cliffs, NJ: Prentice Hall, 1991).
3. This example comes from W. L. Moore and E. A. Pessemier, *Product Planning and Management* (New York: McGraw-Hill, 1993).
4. To identify meaningful dimensions for differentiation, a position map should incorporate both the perceptions and the preferences of customers. These are called 'joint-space' maps—something that is beyond the scope of this book. For a review of these techniques, see G. L. Lilien, P. Kotler, and K. S. Moorthy, *Marketing Models* (Englewood Cliffs, NJ: Prentice Hall, 1992) and Lilien and Rangaswamy (2003).
5. M. Harvey and M. Evans, 'Decoding Competitive Propositions: A Semiotic Alternative to Traditional Advertising Research', *International Journal of Market Research*, 43, 2 (2001), 171–87.

6. For an example of this approach to the study of advertising, see G. R. Dowling and B. Kabanoff, 'Computer-Aided Content Analysis: What Do 240 Advertising Slogans Have in Common?' *Marketing Letters*, 7, 1 (1996), 63–75.

7. This section is taken from G. R. Dowling, G. L. Lilien, R. J. Thomas, and A. Rangaswamy, *Harvesting Customer Value* (State College, PA: Institute for the Study of Business Markets, 2000), chapter 6.

8. A. Ries and J. Trout, *Positioning: The Battle for Your Mind* (New York: McGraw-Hill, 1986); J. Trout with S. Rivkin, *The New Positioning* (New York: McGraw-Hill, 1996); J. Trout with S. Rivkin, *Differentiate or Die* (New York: Wiley, 2000).

9. This diagram is based on material published in each school's alumni magazine.

10. A. Ries, *Focus* (London: HarperCollins, 1996), pp. 201–32.

11. E. Schultz, *The Marketing Game* (Holbrook, MA: Adams Media Corporation, 2001), chapter 4.

12. Here are some examples: D. A. Aaker, *Building Strong Brands* (New York: Free Press, 1996); D. A. Aaker, *Managing Brand Equity* (New York: Free Press, 1991); J.-N. Kapferer, *Strategic Brand Management* (London: Kogan Page, 1992); K. L. Keller, *Strategic Brand Management* (Upper Saddle River, NJ: Prentice Hall, 1998); C. Macrae, *The Brand Chartering Handbook* (Harlow: Addison-Wesley, 1996); L. Upshaw, *Building Brand Identity* (New York: John Wiley & Sons, 1995); Anspach Grossman Enterprise (www.enterprisegrp.com); FutureBrand FHA (www.futurebrand.com); Landor Associates (www. landor.com); Lippincott and Margulies (www.lippincott-margulies.com); Wolff Olins/Hall (www.wolff-olins.com): Young and Rubicam (www.yr.com).

13. For an extensive discussion of corporate as opposed to product brand identity, see G. R. Dowling, *Creating Corporate Reputations* (Oxford: Oxford University Press, 2001), chapter 8.

14. D. L. Masten, 'Logo's Power Depends on How Well It Communicates with Target Market', *Marketing News* (5 December, 1988), 20.

15. J. Aaker, 'Dimensions of Brand Personality', *Journal of Marketing Research*, 34, 3 (1997), 347–56.

16. J. L. Aaker, V. Benet-Martinez, and J. G. Berrocal, 'Consumption Symbols as Carriers of Culture: A Study of Japanese and Spanish Brand Personality Constructs', *Journal of Personality and Psychology*, 81, 3 (2001), 492–508.

17. J. Romaniuk and A. Ehrenberg, 'Do Brands Lack Personality?' The R&D Initiative, Research Report 14 (May 2003), available at www.marketingoracle.com.

18. See, for example, M. Birkin (Group Chief Executive of Interbrand), 'Assessing Brand Value', in P. Stobart (ed.), *Brand Power* (London: Macmillan, 1994), pp. 209–24 or K. L. Keller, (1998), pp. 359–67.

19. D. Aaker, *Managing Brand Equity* (New York: Free Press, 1991), p. 4.

20. See, for example, P. Feldwick, 'Do We Need Brand Equity?' *Journal of Brand Management*, 4, 1 (1996), 9–28 and A. S. C. Ehrenberg, 'B. E. or not B. E.', ARF 43rd Annual Conference and Research Expo, New York, *Advertising Research Foundation* (7–9 April, 1997).

21. An advertisement in the *Economist* stated that Y&R had invested $50 million researching 13,000 brands in 32 countries. In the process, Y&R have interviewed 95,000 adults. It is described in Keller (1998), pp. 625–32.
22. For the Pro Logo case see 'The Case for Brands' (page 9) and 'Who's Wearing the Trousers?' (pp. 26–8), the *Economist* (8 September, 2001).

PROGRAMMES

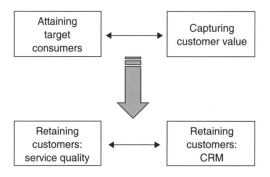

8

Attaining Customers: Creating, Communicating, and Delivering Customer Value

Nobody ever got fired for buying IBM.
(The key to IBM's success in the 1970s and 1980s.)

When IBM was the king of the mainframe computer market, they discovered a wonderful paradox that made them successful—IBM sold their mainframe computers, operating systems, and service, but many of the buyers were not really interested in the hardware, software, or, for that matter, the support. Consider the situation faced by an organization buying a big mainframe computer. The buyer was typically a big organization acquiring the mainframe to run its mission-critical operations and accounting. This was an extensive problem-solving situation and the buying group who were assigned responsibility for making the choice of computer consisted of a variety of managers (including representatives from user groups and the CEO), only a few of whom knew much about hardware or software. Also, the purchase was risky—in terms of the amount of money involved, the lock-in to the vendor's equipment, and the chance that the system would not deliver what a variety of different users wanted. As tenders were called and the evaluation process unfolded it became clear that IBM was one of the more expensive options—their price was high relative to competitors, and they were reluctant to offer any form of discount. There was often a technically better option on the shortlist of prospective vendors. But, more often than not, IBM got the sale. Big Blue (as they were called) was the clear market leader.

As a member of the buying group who did not have extensive knowledge about computers, software, or computer vendors, consider how you would have felt. You are about to make a buying recommendation that will have a major impact on the organization's competitiveness and future viability—and regardless of how much homework you do during the buying process, you are still not completely confident that you are on top of every aspect of this complex decision. If the purchase turns out to be a good one, some people may remember that you played a part in the correct decision. If the purchase turns out to be a bad one (as many IT purchases do), then many more people will remember your participation, and some will blame you for it. If *highly respected* IBM, the *market leader*, puts up a reasonably competitive proposal, it is quite an easy decision to award them the contract—even though the IT people on the buying group might say that Vendor X has a better cost–performance package. Why? Because, by awarding the contract to IBM you are buying the new IT system *and* an insurance policy for your personal reputation. ('If the highly respected, market leader's system would not deliver, then no other system would either! Hence, don't blame me—we bought the best on offer at the time'.)

Another example of 'making an offer that can't be refused' occurred for the purchase of the main stadium for the 2000 Olympic games in Sydney. The organizing committee wanted a world-class facility for the opening and closing ceremonies and for the athletics competition. The stadium would be used after the games by the citizens of Sydney for various sporting events. A stadium to seat 100,000 patrons is a very expensive piece of infrastructure. Tenders were called and proposals submitted. All the short-listed proposals could provide a world-class facility. However, one proposal stood out from the rest. Not only would it build the stadium and its fit-out (lighting, catering, public address system, etc.), but it would also arrange for the financing of the venture. As a member of the buying group for this project the choice is easy—you get a world-class stadium *and* you do not have to worry about financing the deal. This package won the contract.

B2B situations often provide clear examples of offers that have demonstrable value to buyers. In the IBM example, the value was functional (for the organization) and psychological (for some key members of the buying group, including the CEO). In the case of the Olympic stadium, the value was functional (it is a great stadium), economical (it did not strain the budget for the games), and psychological (the buying committee members did not need to worry about the financing). When you are involved in making a big sale, there is a powerful incentive to undertake two critical marketing tasks, namely, (*a*) understand the latent and expressed needs of the customer, and (*b*) think creatively about how to satisfy these needs.

This chapter examines the issue of customer acquisition. That is, how does an organization make an offer to its target consumers that will entice them to buy (and keep buying)? In Chapter 1 (Figure 1.3), this was labelled creating and capturing customer value. Part A of this chapter focuses on value creation, Part B on value communication, and Part C on the delivery of customer value. Chapter 9 examines assessing the value of the offer (i.e. calculating the maximum amount the customer should be willing to pay), and how to capture this value (i.e. setting the appropriate price and in B2B situations using the appropriate selling strategy).

The Customer Value Proposition

Figure 8.1 presents the overall framework that links these three activities together. When combined they create what is called the customer value proposition (CVP). A CVP is the consumer's set of resulting experiences from using a product/service.[1] For example, consider the CVP of a laser printer for a PC, relative to a dot-matrix printer. It is faster, offers sharper contrast, and it is more expensive than a dot-matrix printer. These are some of its key features. The sharper contrast makes the images produced easier to read and it allows for more complex images to be clearly reproduced (two benefits). The faster printing speed saves time (another positive benefit). The higher price is a disadvantage and it can only be offset if the benefits are valued more than the higher price. Because we see many laser and dot-matrix printers being sold, this is evidence that sometimes the benefits exceed the price and, thus, the laser printer offers added value to only some consumers.

For a salesperson selling laser printers, the task is to discover which group of potential buyers might see the added value provided by the more expensive printer. This is where the definition of a CVP is important to revisit. For the type of consumer that makes a price–quality trade-off when buying PC peripherals, what is the *resulting set of experiences* from having one's documents printed on the laser printer? OK, clearer and easier-to-read documents. But this will often not be everything. What experiences do these benefits really deliver? Often, it is 'better communication'

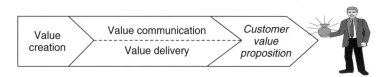

Figure 8.1. Acquiring customers

that can lead to 'greater persuasion' and 'increased likelihood of success'. Now the value of these three experiences is often considerable. And when they come for only a few extra dollars, this is a small price to pay. (Sale made!)

In many B2B marketing situations, CVPs need to be formulated to take into consideration the direct customer *and* the customer's customer. These situations occur when a product or service sold to an organization enables it to add value to the products and services of its customers. For example, Intel makes a more powerful computer processor and sells it to Compaq. Compaq's PCs can now run more advanced software that, in turn, enhances the experience of the user of the Compaq PC. Thus, the CVP of an Intel processor enhances the value of Compaq's PCs and the end user's experience. Hence, we see Intel marketing to the PC manufacturers, and advertising directly to PC users to tell them of the benefits of their various processors. This is an example of a combination of 'push' and 'pull' marketing.

It is interesting to consider how Internet/web-based technology can enhance the CVP offered to target consumers. There are at least six sources of value-add from this new technology:

1. *Convenience.* The target consumer need not leave his or her PC to shop—twenty-four hours a day and seven days a week. This benefit can be mitigated, however, if the process of locating websites and navigating through them is difficult.

2. *Cost.* Costs are of two types. One type is the cost of information search. In extensive problem-solving situations this can be substantial and manifest itself in terms of time, physical search, and the inconvenience involved. Surveys are showing that many people are using the Internet at the start of their shopping process to select a set of products and services for further consideration. They then revert to their normal mode of shopping to examine the products and make the final selection. The second type of cost is the actual price paid. Often, cost savings here are illusory. While the posted dollar price may be (slightly) lower, when delivery and the perceived risks associated with other issues such as secure payment are added, the total is often similar to that in a traditional outlet.

3. *Service.* For the segment of consumers who are happy to serve themselves, the Internet has proved to be most useful. (For the old-fashioned consumer who seeks personal service, it has largely been ignored.) For example, Dell Computer has set up Premier Pages on its website for many of its most valuable business customers. Together, Dell and the customer agree on a number of standard configurations for the customer's employees such as administrators, mobile managers,

and power users. (These are internal customer segments.) These employees then access their organization's Premier page to order their PC and preloaded software at a pre-negotiated price.

4. *Choice*. Choice has two dimensions—the breadth and depth of assortment. In the electronic 'marketspace', these two dimensions expand to the point where the amount of choice can overwhelm many people. Search engines are then necessary to help find exactly what one is looking for. For those people who like more 'choice', the Internet has proven to be of great value.

5. *Customization*. This is the ultimate form of customer value creation for many, though not all, products and services.[i] (It is also a powerful way for organizations to differentiate their products and services, and it is often associated with customers being less price sensitive.) Recall, however, from the discussion in Chapter 2 that mass customization is difficult for most organizations to deliver.

6. *Coordination*. For many B2C and B2B consumers, being able to interact with an organization through one portal that provides a total picture of the customer's relationship with the organization is a valuable service. The amount of value provided, however, is tied directly to the comprehensiveness of the customer's information on the organization's database. Such portals can help to reduce the costs of doing business with an organization.

To summarize, the key to acquiring consumers is the strength of the CVP offered—relative to the strength of the CVPs offered by competitors. The more precisely that a CVP can be described, the

- less chance there is for confusion inside the organization,
- more focused the communication about the CVP can be, and thus the
- less chance for uncertainty in the minds of target consumers.

Thus, a good CVP helps to manage the expectations of both the target customer and the employees responsible for creating and delivering customer value. What CVPs are not is a list of attributes of the product or service, or platitudes such as offering better quality, providing great service, exceeding customer expectations, having satisfied customers, or forming a relationship with customers. Nobody can disagree with these platitudes and nearly every organization is trying to achieve these goals.

---

[i] For products and services that are valued because other people are also owners, mass customization adds little value. Many clothing fashions fall into this category. For example, some people want Levi's 501 jeans and Nike Air Jordan shoes precisely because their peer group has them.

Customer acquisition (and retention—Chapters 10 and 11) is implemented through a set of marketing programmes. A *marketing programme* is the coordinated set of functions that are necessary to create, deliver, and communicate the offer made to consumers.[ii] Part A now focuses on creating customer value.

PART A

Value Creation

The more that is put into an advertisement, the less that the audience takes out of it.

Old advertising proverb

A CVP comprises a set of resulting experiences from using a (branded) product or service. The advertising proverb above suggests that it is the most important resulting experience that is crucial to focus on. This single experience is usually driven by only a handful of (core) benefits delivered by the product/service. Thus, the value of the offer made to target consumers is derived from the benefits and the resulting experience delivered by the product/service. This customer value theme was introduced in Chapter 6, when consumer benefits were advocated as one of the primary tactical segmentation bases. It was illustrated with the claim that most consumers tune into the radio station with the call sign WII-FM—'what's in it for me!' This section presents a framework for uncovering what the core benefits of the offer made to target consumers really are.

Understanding the benefits and experiences that people want and may derive from a product or service is not an easy task. To do this requires a manager to *become the consumer*—a task that goes beyond listening to them. (This issue was raised in Chapter 4—Figure 4.5.) To further illustrate this point, consider the senior automotive executive who could not understand why so many car buyers disliked the experience of buying a car.[iii] When asked about his car buying experience, he confessed to not having bought a car (or for that matter having his car serviced) for the last twenty years. In his case, the car manufacturer provided him with a new car as part

---

[ii] Many marketing textbooks refer to these programmes in terms of the 'marketing mix', which as Chapter 1 indicated is some combination of the 9Ps. Here, I use a simpler and more customer-focused framework as shown in Figure 8.1.

[iii] This is a true story told to me by the manager described here.

of his salary package. When he had driven the car for 1500 kilometres, someone automatically replaced it with a new one so that his old car could be sold as a 'demonstrator'. It was impossible for this senior manager to empathize with most car buyers about the frustrations involved during the car buying experience. Some experienced marketers adopt the opposite perspective. They practice the mantra of 'buy your own dog food'—or better still, 'buy and eat your own, and your competitors' dog food'. The idea here is that all managers should experience their own and competitors' products and services as their customers do. (This is easy to say, but it seems to be seldom practised.)

Another difficulty often experienced with developing a deep understanding of target consumers is when managers assume that their experience enables them to know what the target consumer needs. Many new (technology-based) products are designed this way. The thinking goes along the following lines: 'If the target consumer is a typical household (two adults, two children, one pet, etc.), then they will need all the following features on their video cassette recorder—X, Y, Z, etc'. This is an example of what is variously called either the 'engineer's lament' (sorry engineers) or the 'academic's lament'. It is stated thus:

> It is hard to give someone what they want, when *you* know what they need.

The engineer's lament highlights two management traps. The first is to focus on what is offered to target consumers rather than the benefits and experiences derived from the product/service. (Recall the IBM example at the beginning of this chapter.) The second is to describe the offer made to consumers in terms of its features—'our $299 VCR has super-fast forward and rewind, can be programmed up to 16 days in advance, can play tapes recorded in both PAL and NTSC, etc'. The problem with presenting a product or service to target consumers in terms of its features is that people seldom (if ever) really buy these features. What they actually buy is the benefits and/or solutions to their problems delivered by the product's features. For example, in the 1990s, Apple Computer understood that people were not buying its PCs. What they were really buying was captured in the Apple advertising slogan that signed off all their advertisements, namely:

> The power to be your best.[iv]

[iv] In terms of the discussion in Chapter 7 on Positioning, the Apple slogan failed the U-part of the IDU Test. It was not unique because it referred equally to all brands of PCs. Apple subsequently changed the slogan to 'Think different', in part to reflect its heritage as being different from the early IBM/DOS PCs.

That is, many people buy a PC to enhance their (and/or their organization's) capabilities. Yes, it has to have a certain configuration of features to do this, but most users know almost nothing about how the hardware and software is configured to write the report that they have just completed. (And nor do they care.)

The distinction between features and benefits is a crucial one to appreciate. The following definitions were provided by a salesman:

- A *feature* does something.
- A *benefit* gives something.

In many cases, advertising and salespeople will refer to the features of their products and services in order to show how a resulting benefit is delivered or problem solved. For example, an advertisement for an Asics running shoe stated (and illustrated) how the 'newly developed GEL material placed in the forefoot of the shoe (feature) provided extra cushioning and protection (benefit)'.

It is useful to pause here to recall the discussion in Chapter 7 about 'brands'. In the context of features and benefits a brand name is a feature of the product or service. It may be a very powerful feature if it has been imbued with a lot of meaning by consumers. In this way, the brand may deliver (extra) benefits such as trust and reassurance.

The key to being customer-focused is to concentrate on the benefits and/or solutions to problems that the consumer wants from the product/service. As noted in Chapter 6, these can be:

- functional (the product/service does the job expected), and/or
- psychological (it provides emotional or intellectual rewards), and/or
- economical (it is offered at a good price).

To illustrate the difference between what is bought and what is sold, consider the examples in Table 8.1.

The task for markers is to design the offer to target consumers so that the emphasis falls on what is bought rather than what is sold. The role of the features of the product/service is to 'prove' that the benefits or solutions to problems promised can be delivered. For example, it is the Intel Pentium 4 processor in the PC that delivers those great graphics. There is one exception to this strategic principle of focusing on the benefits that will be discussed shortly.

Figure 8.2 provides a framework that has been used by many marketers to show the role of features and benefits and to focus the offer made to target consumers on one or two core benefits/solutions. It is called a Product–Service Onion—to suggest that one often has to peel away the

Table 8.1. What is sold and what is bought

What is sold	What is bought
A cordless, electric drill	Holes of various sizes made safely almost anywhere
National Geographic magazine	Cheap travel
Banking products and services	Wealth creation, enhancement, and protection
Revlon cosmetics	'Hope'
A place in a school	Education for 'life' (i.e. life skills and knowledge for the rest of your life)
An MBA degree	Enhanced career prospects and increased confidence
The services of an advertising agency	Increased sales, and a better chance of promotion for the responsible manager

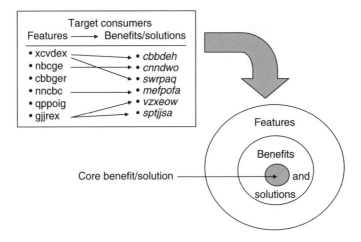

Figure 8.2. Product–service onion

outer layers of the onion (the features of a product) to find the edible part (the benefits). Also, the sweetest part of the onion is found in the core. The onion metaphor is also used because it is often quite a difficult task for managers to shift their focus away from what they are very familiar with (all those great product features) to what customers really want (the benefits). (As you peel an onion, you also get tears in your eyes.)

Product–service onions are created by first specifying the (tactical) target segment of consumers (from Chapter 6). Then, a list of the key features of the product and/or service is created. Stage three then involves linking these features to benefits or solutions to problems that target consumers want. This process is shown in the top left part of Figure 8.2. Note that some of the features listed will not link across to a customer benefit. When this happens, it suggests that this feature will play no part in the communication of the offer to the target consumer. That is, the feature is not necessary to 'prove' that the benefit will be delivered. For example, while great PC graphics are produced by more than a Pentium 4 chip, it is only the chip that is featured in Intel's advertising. (Recall that the more information—in this case, features—that is put into an advertisement, the less information the consumer will take out of it.)

Once a list of feature–benefit links has been created, they can be arranged into an onion as shown at the bottom-right of Figure 8.2. The reason for reconfiguring the lists of features and benefits into an onion is to force the marketing team to *focus* on the core benefit/solution. (Recall the discussion of focus in Chapter 7—Positioning and Branding.) These onions are a very good way to summarize a product/service, and communicate its essence to other non-marketing managers—especially CEOs. (They can also be used to brief the advertising agency and the market research firm—the topic of Chapter 13.) The best way to illustrate these three functions (summary, focus, and communication) is via some examples.

Figure 8.3 presents an onion for the watch that saved the Swiss watch industry—SWATCH (Swiss watch). The essence of what made this brand

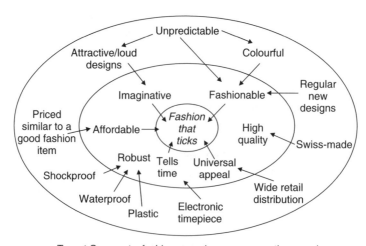

Target Segment—fashion conscious, young, active people

Figure 8.3. SWATCH

successful was its focus on the target segment of young, active, and fashion conscious people, and its redefinition of what a watch should be, namely, 'fashion that ticks'. Prior to this, a watch was a timepiece for most people. It was also a product that most people kept for many years. Once fashion became a prime feature–benefit of a watch there was a good reason for target consumers to buy a new watch every fashion season. To facilitate this behaviour SWATCH kept the price at a level similar to a garment for its target market. Notice in Figure 8.3 that some of the functional benefits (e.g. high quality and robust) do not directly support the core benefit. What they reflect are benefits that are 'givens' for the product category—the watch fits the lifestyle of the target user. The link between Swiss-made and high quality is an implicit association for many people and, thus, it comes as a free benefit from the brand name for those people who associate quality with Swiss watches. Not trying to link every possible benefit to the core illustrates the discipline of focus. SWATCH is also a good example of marketing innovation (in particular, segmentation and positioning) in action.

Figure 8.4 shows a generic onion for the ubiquitous debit/credit card. Notice the two negative features—the interest charge and the annual fee. The problem here for marketers is that all these cards have a similar set of features, and for many people they are just a commodity. If they are linked to a customer loyalty programme (discussed in Chapter 11) they may acquire some differentiation (until the other cards copy this initiative).

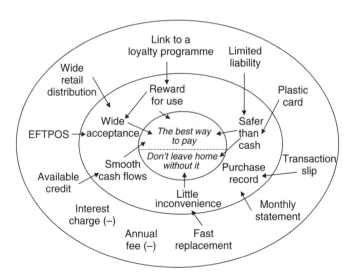

Figure 8.4. Bankcard

The marketing innovation required is to identify a target consumer segment and choose a benefit that this segment will relate to.

Figure 8.4 has two core benefits to reflect how two companies viewed this market. Citibank in the United States at one time positioned its cards as 'The best way to pay'. This would appeal to people who place high value on functional performance. In contrast, American Express once positioned its cards using the slogan 'Don't leave home without it'. This would appeal to people who are highly risk averse—a psychological appeal. Visa has used wide acceptance as its core benefit and expresses this with the slogan 'We're everywhere you want us to be'.

Figure 8.5 presents an onion for an industrial product called Flo-Top. This is a liquid that is used to create a rock-hard, perfectly level surface on concrete and other floor surfaces. For example, when high-precision equipment is to be installed in a factory, it needs a level surface. Flo-Top can be poured over the concrete floor to provide such a surface. It turns out that this product can also be used to repair damaged floors—often at a considerable cost saving to resurfacing the floor with its original material. Thus, there are two core benefits of this product. The Flo-Top onion suggests that you can sell either:

- the branded commodity product Flo-Top (through industrial distributors), and/or
- the service of new floor finishing (using Flo-Top and a floor-finishing crew), and/or
- the service of old or damaged floor repair.

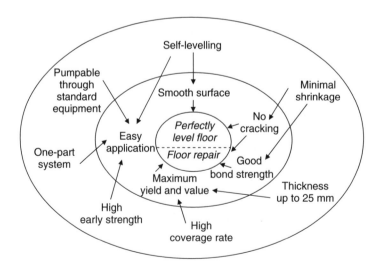

Figure 8.5. Flo-Top

That is, you can be in a commodity market (with low margins, aggressive competitors, etc.) or a value-added service market. Better still, be in both markets. This is possible because there are different segments of customers involved in each of these businesses. (This is an example of how the onion framework can help to think about strategies for growth—a key topic in Chapter 5.)

Before concluding this section, it is necessary to return to the issue of features and benefits. The overarching recommendation here is to focus on the benefits and solutions to problems more than the product and its cute features. However, the topic of segmentation suggests that there are likely to be exceptions to any such blanket recommendation. In this case, one such exception occurs when communicating with consumers who have extensive knowledge and experience with the product/service being acquired. (See Chapter 4—Figure 4.2—and the discussion of the Product Enthusiasts in Chapter 6.) These people often know as much, and sometimes more, about the product/service than the seller. Also, this expertise makes them acutely aware of, and interested in, the product's features and how these deliver the unique benefits they desire. Thus, they do not like being 'talked down to' by advertising or salespeople about how a feature delivers a particular benefit. What they like doing is to interpret the communication for themselves. For this type of target consumer, it is often a good communication strategy to focus on the product—in particular its special features, reliability, and quality. Thus, it may be necessary to create different advertisements and place them in different media for this segment of consumers.

To summarize, the concept of a CVP and the framework of the product/service onion combine to describe the offer made to acquire target consumers. In a competitive and over-communicated world, there are two keys to success. First and foremost, the research on the adoption and diffusion of new products (reviewed in Chapter 5) suggests that winning products and services make a significantly better (more valuable) offer to target consumers than competitors. If this is not possible, then Chapter 7 (Positioning and Branding) suggests that a brand that passes the IDU Test is the key. The onion framework is useful here because it helps to focus on the single, most compelling reason for the target consumer to buy.

Overall, the offer to target consumers can be described using four equations:

- The offer = the onion and CVP
- The value of the onion = the value of the benefits − price
- Price (relative to competitors) = $ + inconvenience + perceived risk
- Marketplace advantage = our offer and CVP ≤ or > competitors' offer and CVP.

KEY CONCEPTS

- *Customer value proposition*—the consumer's set of resulting experiences from using the product or service.
- *Product feature*—an attribute of the product (or service) that helps deliver a benefit or solve a problem for the consumer.
- *Benefit or solution to a problem*—the satisfaction of a need or want of the consumer delivered by the various features of a product or service.
- *Price*—the combined dollar paid plus any inconvenience suffered and risk perceived.

KEY FRAMEWORK

- *Product/service onion*—Figure 8.2 (and Figures 8.3–8.5)

KEY QUESTIONS

- What is your CVP—for each different target segment of customers?
- What is your CVP-based marketplace advantage?

PART B

Communicating Value—IMC

When you have a good offer to make to target consumers, the next task is to let them know about it. The traditional approach for B2C companies was to use broadcast, mass-media advertising if the marketing budget would support it. (If it did not, then print and radio were used.) In B2B situations, the media mix might involve some corporate image (print) advertising, but the main emphasis was on the salesforce, brochures and catalogues, advertising in specialist industry publications, and trade shows. In professional services 'advertising' was a dirty word—and often banned by the industry association. These firms spread their message through WOM, supported by some discrete entertainment (or relationship building), and a firm brochure that featured all the partners and their achievements.

Today, there are few conventions about what types of communication B2B, B2C, or professional service firms should use. Also, there are some new options to choose from such as the Internet and sponsorships, and some of the old options have been renamed, for example WOM is now sometimes called BUZZ marketing.[v] Few conventions and more choice combine to make designing marketing communication programmes an exciting task. Unfortunately, it also often results in messy communication. The concept of IMC, which stands for Integrated Marketing Communication, is now used to remind marketers that all elements of their communication with target consumers and the distribution channel members that deliver the offer should be coordinated to support the CVP.

IMC can be both strategic and tactical. At the strategic level, IMC programmes are designed so that the various types of media support the brand positioning (Chapter 7), and capture any interactions between types of media communication. For example, up-market brands should be promoted in up-market media. Also, some media are good for providing information about a brand—such as websites—while other media are better for generating an emotive response—such as television. Over the years, advertisers have discovered that certain types of media are best used in sequence. For example, it has been found that publicity should precede advertising. (The publicity generates interest, and the follow-up advertising provides information.) Microsoft has used this strategy for the launch of Windows 95, 98, and 2001 (XP). Another more recent discovery is that broadcast television advertising can be used effectively to provide the legitimacy of Internet sites that are themselves vehicles for advertising.

At a tactical level, IMC means making sure that the public relations firm, the ad agency, the salesforce, the merchandisers, the web designers, the event sponsorship firm, and others actually work together. It also means ensuring that the central message in all forms of communication is the same, and is presented in a consistent style and tone with the same brand identity symbols.

The following elements need to be coordinated when planning an IMC programme.

1. *Marketing Objectives.* In this chapter, the main marketing objective for the IMC programme is to attain target consumers. These consumers,

---

[v] This is another example of clever marketing. The (brand) name WOM sounds a bit staid when compared to the images evoked by the name BUZZ.

however, could be of three types:

- new category users, that is, people or organizations that do not currently buy from the product category—such as people buying frozen dinners for the first time, or organizations buying pagers for their employees for the first time;
- brand switchers, that is, single-brand loyal consumers who are to be enticed to switch to our brand;
- polygamous loyals, that is, people who buy a portfolio of brands and are to be enticed to buy our brand for the first time (or more of our brand).

The communication message would be different for each type of target consumer. For example, for new category users it may be necessary to 'sell' the product category as well as the brand. When MBA degrees were first introduced into Australia, the task was to sell the benefits of an MBA (to both prospective students and employers), and the benefits of choosing University X's MBA. For brand switchers, the task is to demonstrate that your brand is better than their current brand. For polygamous loyals, the task is to get your brand included in the portfolio, possibly by showing that it is appropriate for a particular use occasion.

2. *Target Consumer Action Objectives.* The second factor that needs consideration is the target consumer action objectives desired from the programme. These action objectives are usually trial, first purchase, or repeat use. Trying the product/service might entail free use of the product (such as test-driving a car), using a free sample of the product (e.g. a small packet of washing powder left in the mail box), or imagining the use of the product such as watching a video for a holiday destination.[vi] First purchase may involve some type of extra incentive—such as buying a new product during its launch week at a lower introductory price. Repeat use might involve asking consumers to use the product several times (e.g. use this hair shampoo every day for one week), or use multiple varieties of the brand (e.g. different frozen dinner meals). Specifying the action objectives at this early stage of planning helps to determine the mix of promotion activities that will be needed in the IMC programme.

3. *Communication Objectives.* The heart of an IMC programme is its communication objectives. These depend on three things, namely, (*a*) the

---

[vi] Some interesting research in psychology and marketing has discovered that the longer people are allowed to try a product (test drive the car for three days as opposed to twenty minutes), the more likely they will become attached to it. This is called an Endowment Effect. It also seems that it is often stronger for women than men.

type of consumer, (*b*) the action objectives for the consumer (both of which were just discussed), and (*c*) whether the target consumer considers the product/service to be high or low involvement (as discussed in Chapter 4). The communication objectives for low involvement products and services are generally to create awareness for the brand and link it to the relevant category need, and then to entice trial. A (un)favourable evaluation of the brand is usually formed after it has been used.

For high involvement products and services, the communication objectives are more complex. Here, the idea is to move target consumers through a 'learn–feel–do' sequence of effects. For example, the AIDA model that was originally developed as a sales training approach is: Awareness, Interest, Desire, Action.[2] The innovation-adoption model is: (awareness), knowledge, persuasion, decision (adoption or rejection), implementation (i.e. use), confirmation (or reinforcement).[3] The hierarchy-of-effects model is: awareness, knowledge, liking, preference, conviction, purchase.[4] As noted in Chapter 4, what typically happens in practice is that these sequences of effects are not found exactly as they are presented here. Different people go through different decision-making sequences. For example, in a study of the decision sequence of people deciding to take a joy-flight to see the Antarctic continent, 57 per cent went through the sequence: awareness, decision, and confirmation (i.e. talk to their friends about what they intended to do); 15 per cent went through the sequence: awareness, knowledge, decision, and confirmation; 11 per cent: awareness, evaluation, decision, and confirmation; and the remaining 17 per cent used other sequences.[5] Hence, the communication objectives are always to create awareness and then to move people through whatever sequence of stages are necessary to achieve action. Figure 8.6 contrasts the low and high involvement IMC objectives. (It suggests that the evaluation of a brand is formed and updated during each stage of the adoption process.)

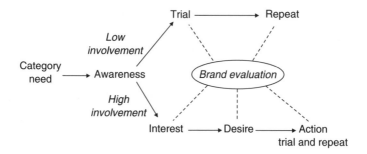

Figure 8.6. Communication objectives

4. *Communication Mix.* The next task in developing an IMC programme is to specify both the reach of the programme and the mix of communications that will be used to meet the marketing and communication objectives. There are many alternatives—public relations, advertising (on television, radio, print, outdoor, catalogues, narrow-cast, broadcast, etc.), direct marketing, sales promotions, personal selling, samples, sponsorships, package design, point-of-purchase displays, the Internet, etc. Each medium has a different 'fit' with target consumers' media habits, and each has its advantages and disadvantages for achieving the desired communications objectives. Often, a 200-page book is required to explain the art and science of choosing the appropriate mix. Hence, what will have to suffice here are some references, some interesting observations, and three examples—Exhibit 8.1.

Exhibit 8.1. Examples of IMC programmes

The following short examples illustrate what three organizations have done to communicate their offer to their target consumers:

- The Healthy Choice range of frozen dinners was launched in the United States with television advertising and both consumer and trade promotions. The position for the product used the benefit claim of 'healthy for your heart' to the target consumers who were both new category users and brand switchers. The sales promotion offer was an introductory trial coupon distributed during Heart Month via Sunday newspapers and direct mail. This was supported by a public relations event—free cholesterol tests in stores. (Both these consumer promotions supported the brand's position and contributed to building a favourable brand attitude.) Trade promotions consisted of a sales video shown to retail buyers and the usual buying allowances to get the product into the already crowded supermarket freezer displays.[6]
- Akzo Nobel is a leading paint maker in Europe. It launched Sikkens Cetol Novatech, a translucent paint (wood stain) into the Austrian market. The target consumers were professional painters and architects (who were used to create 'pull'). Advertising appeared in trade magazines for both the target groups. The painters were encouraged to try the new paint by being offered a free paint kit that included a letter and leaflet that explained the advantages of the new paint and one litre of paint worth $15-20.[7]
- In 1996, Pharmacia & Upjohn (one of the top ten pharmaceutical companies in the world) launched a non-prescription hair regrowth product called Rogaine into the United States with a budget of $75 million.

The objective was to create a new product category and achieve annual sales of $250 million. The target consumers were men and women aged 25–49 years. Rogaine was to be positioned as the only medically proven hair regrowth product. Separate thirty-second television advertisements were created for men and women and the media schedule was designed so that 92 per cent of the target consumers would see the ads seven times during the four-week launch period. The advertising was complemented by an extensive trade promotion campaign—40,000 physicians and 20,000 pharmacists were given promotional material. A direct marketing campaign was also developed for target consumers. Distribution included pharmacies and the hair-care sections of food, drug, and mass-merchandise retail outlets. Separate packages were developed for the men's and women's products even though the formulations were exactly the same.[8]

While there are hundreds of books about (how to do) advertising, two that fit the art and science philosophy of this book are:

- David Ogilvy, *Ogilvy on Advertising* (London: Pan Books, 1983). (It is still in print.)
- John Rossiter and Larry Percy, *Advertising Communications and Promotion Management* (New York: McGraw-Hill, 1997).

Ogilvy's book is an easy read that is full of common-sense advice. (David Ogilvy was one of the founders of modern advertising.) The Rossiter and Percy book is a scientifically based look at advertising.

The following observations about advertising come from a variety of sources—only some of which I can remember:

- 'Good advertising is always written from one person to another. When it is aimed at millions, it rarely moves anyone'. (Fairfax Cone, a founder of the Foote, Cone & Belding advertising agency.)
- Advertising works best when it is written for radio first.
- Media clutter is increasing. For example, the average US household received more than three credit card offers each month in 2000—there were 3.54 billion pieces of direct mail sent. The response rate dropped to an all-time low of 0.6 per cent. (*Marketing News*, 10 September 2001, p. 9.)
- Some repetition of a message increases its persuasive impact, but very high levels of repetition prompt a decline in impact—and may actually annoy people. (Hence, beware of that great deal to run your single advertisement eighteen times during the one football match!)

- If the product is chosen at the point-of-purchase, then show it in the advertising (so people can recognize it).
- Link the brand benefit to the brand name. That is, make the brand name prominent. (People often remember an ad but cannot recall the brand.)
- What target consumers currently believe about a product is the starting point for developing the communication message. (Do not use advertising or salespeople to argue with consumers, they will tune out or argue back, either of which is unlikely to be successful.)
- Do not talk down to your audience. Make sure the copy is honest and has something to say. (William Bernbach, creator of the now-classic Avis campaign 'We're number 2, we try harder' and the original 'think small' and 'Lemon' campaigns for Volkswagen in the United States.)
- Each brand should develop and constantly communicate its own USP, such as 'Colgate cleans your breath as it cleans your teeth'. (Rosser Reeves, another founder of modern advertising.)
- Communicate the hidden drama of a brand, that is, the key reason why the manufacturer made it and why people buy it. (Leo Burnett, another founder of modern advertising.)

It is at the stage when communication objectives have been linked to marketing objectives that cost estimates can be developed and managers can determine if the organization can afford the planned programme. IMC, which is essentially a pull marketing approach, should only be used if the marketing manager is confident that it will contribute to profit over a reasonable period. (The effects of many IMC activities like advertising may take some time to pay off.) Otherwise, the brand should be pushed through the distribution channel to target consumers. For many FMCGs and B2B supplies, what seems to happen is that the manager estimates what he or she needs to spend on trade promotion (e.g. slotting allowances, quantity discounts, and cooperative advertising) and consumer promotions (e.g. free samples and cash rebates), and whatever is left over from a predetermined budget allocation is allocated to advertising. This is not the most 'scientific' way to set an IMC budget—a point returned to in Chapter 12.

5. *IMC Programme Monitoring.* The final part of the IMC programme is evaluation and tracking. Here, an audit trail of how money is spent should be developed—such as the monitoring of how trade promotions have been used by channel members, how many consumer promotions were redeemed, and where and when advertisements were placed. It is also

necessary to evaluate the effectiveness of the overall programme. This is usually done by taking measures of the consumer response steps and the evaluation of the brand (Figure 8.6)—before, during, and after the programme. Thus, measures of inputs and outputs provide an overview of the effectiveness of the programme to communicate the value of the offer made to target consumers.

IMC and the Web

Of particular interest to many marketers is their organization's website and its role in creating and communicating customer value. Organizational websites are designed to engage target consumers with interactive communication and move them (closer) to a purchase decision. These websites come in two general forms:

- *Transactional sites*—are electronic storefronts like those operated by Amazon.com, Cisco, and the clothing brand Gap (gap.com). In B2C markets, these sites try convert an online browser into an online buyer. For example, the Gap website sells more clothes than most of its individual stores.[9] These sites are successful when potential buyers know the brand and the merchandise. In B2B markets, transactional websites often start out as an electronic brochure, then progress to an order-taking system, and sometimes evolve into a quite sophisticated marketing system. Cisco Systems, the company that sells routers and networking gear that powers the Internet, is a good example. Its site blends technical support with each step in the selling process and the post-sale service of its equipment. Its Configuration Agent software walks its business customers through the components and design configurations necessary to build a customized product. Its Status Agent software lets customers track the status of their order online. In 1999, more that half the orders placed with Cisco were not touched by a human hand—Cisco just shipped the product and collected the money.[10]
- *Promotional sites*—are effectively digital brochures. While they can be very engaging (by using games, contests, and quizzes), their primary role is to provide information about the organization (e.g. to school children, journalists, investors, and potential employees) and about its products and services. Some are also used for consumer research, such as the Cathay Pacific Airline site (cathay-usa.com) that interviews frequent flyers.

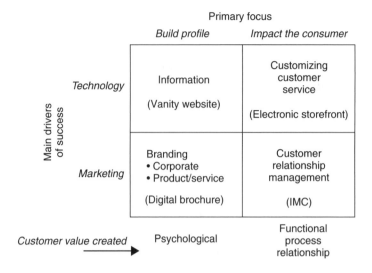

Figure 8.7. Organizational websites

Figure 8.7 shows how many organizations have configured their websites. In the context of IMC, websites are still most often used as a complement to the direct selling activities of the B2B salesforce, and as a supplement to broadcast advertising in B2C markets. The CRM sites are the ones where IMC plays a major role.

Marketers who have specialized in designing marketing programmes for the Internet have rekindled interest in how to stimulate favourable WOM about a company and its products. Earlier this was called BUZZ marketing—to create community-based interest about a product, service, or event. Research has consistently shown that personal recommendations are more persuasive than mass media advertising in getting people to change their minds about ideas and to consider purchasing products and services.[11] Hence, the marketer's task is to encourage people to do what they like doing, namely, talking to each other—but in this case, about their organization's product or service. On the Internet, Amazon pioneered chat groups, book reviews, and recommendation engines ('other people like you have read these books').

In an e-commerce world, where people sometimes form virtual communities and a small number of experiences can quickly become a large number of attitudes, monitoring WOM is an important task—one that is often the responsibility of the marketing or public relations group. Some marketers, however, are adopting a more proactive strategy. They are trying to 'shape' the conversations in these virtual communities. One technique is to identify the 'opinion leaders' in the community and to *co-opt* them to help develop and/or market the product. For example, some software developers give early versions of their programmes to selected people to 'test' prior to its public release. Their (positive) reactions are posted into the marketspace for others to see. Another tactic is to e-mail the opinion leaders with information and updates about the product—it keeps them informed and provides a feeling of being a valued customer.

On a broader scale, one technique that has been shown to be effective is to discover what people are buying and to use this information to make recommendations to other similar consumers. Prior to the Internet, this type of information was often published as a 'best-seller list' (of books) or the 'top ten music singles'. (Many people like to 'follow the herd'.) In the Internet age, this type of information can often be published by customer segment, that is, 'people like *you* are buying XYZ'. Another opinion forming tactic for the masses is to seed information into chat rooms and onto bulletin boards—something that is easy to do in many virtual communities.

In summary, in an over-communicated marketplace, it is becoming harder for organizations to break through the clutter with their offer. By focusing and integrating their brand communications, organizations are finding that the cost-effectiveness of communication is improved relative to a scattergun approach. While the logic of IMC seems clear to both marketing managers and advertising agencies, it has proven to be more difficult to implement than expected. One reason for this is that IMC plans are not adequately developed. Another reason is that the overall responsibility for marketing an organization or a brand is often split among several people.

KEY CONCEPTS

- *IMC*—the design of a marketing communications programme where all the elements are integrated and coordinated to deliver a clear, consistent, and compelling CVP about the organization or a brand.

KEY FRAMEWORKS

- *IMC programme*—(a) Marketing objectives; (b) Target consumer action objectives; (c) Communication objectives; (d) Communication mix; (e) Programme monitoring
- *Communication objectives*—Figure 8.6
- *Organizational websites*—Figure 8.7

KEY QUESTIONS

• Does your organization or brand have an IMC plan? If yes, is it focused on the CVP for the organization/brand?

• Do various managers have responsibility for different aspects of marketing the organization/brand? How do they coordinate their plans and programmes?

PART C

Delivering Value

Push and/or Pull Marketing Strategies

To introduce this section, it is useful to reflect on the organization's preferred approach to attaining (and retaining) consumers. Some use what is called a *push* marketing approach whereby most marketing activity is directed at distributors and retailers in order to get them to carry the product and promote it to target consumers. The salesforce, price incentives, cooperative advertising, and other forms of trade promotions are used to push the product through the distribution channel (agents, wholesalers, retailers, and others) to consumers. In B2C markets, push marketing is often used for FMCGs where buyers are familiar with the products and exhibit polygamous loyalty, and brand choice is made at the point of purchase. In B2B markets, push marketing is often used for MRO (maintenance, repair, and operations) products.

In contrast, the *pull* marketing approach directs most of the marketing activities to target consumers. (In the case of B2B, there are often two types of target consumer—the organization actually buying the product/service, *and* that buyer's customers. That is, the customer and the customer's customers. For example, Flo-Top may be marketed to a company that repairs floors and the organization having its floor repaired—and the consulting engineers who recommend how the floor should be repaired.) The purpose is to create interest in and desire for the product/service, and to motivate consumers to ask distribution channel members to stock it. Thus, demand is 'passed back' through the distribution channel. Advertising and promotions are commonly used to achieve this effect. The General Motors (USA) 'Ask for genuine GM parts' advertising campaign is a good example. Pull marketing

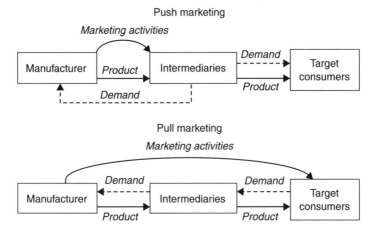

Figure 8.8. Push and pull marketing

programmes tend to be used when a strong brand is an important part of the CVP, and it is chosen before the shopping trip is undertaken. Hence, consumers are more familiar with pull marketing.

Figure 8.8 compares the two styles of marketing. In practice, most organizations use both push and pull, with more emphasis on one style of marketing. Also, companies in the same industry may use a different emphasis between push and pull marketing. For example, while Procter & Gamble (P&G) promote their individual brands and the idea of everyday low prices to target consumers—a pull strategy—they also spend considerable time and effort working with retailers—push marketing. On the other hand, Lever Brothers relies more on pushing its brand through the distribution channel than pull marketing activities to stimulate consumer demand.

The Distribution Channel

Now that target consumers know about the organization's offer, where do they find it? The answer to this question depends on the answers to the following questions:

- Where and when do target consumers expect to find the product available?
- Where are target consumers (geographically) located?
- How can intermediaries add value to the customer buying experience?

- In getting products from the manufacturer to the end user, where is it most cost effective to carry out the logistical operations of transportation, inventory handling, warehousing, breaking bulk, and packaging?

The answers to these questions result in a distribution strategy. (In Chapters 1 and 2 this was the 'place' P of the marketing mix.) Answering the last question provides the foundation for answering the other three.

Channel Functions

A *marketing channel* is a set of interdependent organizations or people (such as agents and salespeople) involved in the process of making a product or service available to target customers.[12] These intermediaries are necessary to bridge the discrepancy between the assortment of goods and services produced by the manufacturer and the assortment demanded by the consumer. To bridge this discrepancy, somebody—either the manufacturer, the intermediary, the salesperson, or the consumer—must accept responsibility for the following functions:

- *Collecting information*—about customer needs and demand, and making this available to other channel members.
- *Promotion*—of the products and services.
- *Negotiation*—about prices, volumes, delivery, and the transfer of the title to the product or service.
- *Ordering*—placing orders to initiate delivery.
- *Taking possession of the goods*—to move them from manufacturer to consumer.
- *Financing*—the various transactions as the goods move through the channel.
- *Risk taking*—with each of the tasks above.

To illustrate these functions, consider the purchase of a garment from the Gap website. The buyer would take responsibility for (*a*) collecting information by searching the website for the appropriate garment, (*b*) placing the order, (*c*) arranging finance for the transaction—usually by a credit card. Gap is responsible for the promotion and setting the terms and conditions for the purchase (negotiation). A courier company will deliver the garment to the buyer. All parties, including the bank that issued the buyer's credit card, will assume part of the total risk of this transaction. Contrast this with the purchase of black coal by the Japanese steel industry. Here, the Japanese buyers collect information about coal quality, costs of production, and the available supply from various mines around the world. Promotion is negligible because coal is bought according to its specifications—ash content, sulphur content, calorific value, etc. The serious negotiations take place in Japan and orders are placed through formal contracts. Production is transported from the mines to the shipping ports (mainly) by rail. Shipping is organized by a stevedoring company and the coal is transported to Japan in the ships of a big Japanese trading company, which also arranges finance for the buyers. Risks are shared by the trading companies (bulk shipping and buyers paying their debts), the government (safe rail transport), the stevedoring company (getting the correct coal onto the correct ship), the buyers (the coal is what they expected), and the sellers (the buyers will pay on time and adhere to the terms and conditions in the contract).

When thinking about the seven activities above, there are two key issues to consider. One is to understand that all the activities are necessary for some person or organization to carry out. The term 'disintermediation' is used to refer to the removal of an organization in the channel arrangement, or the substitution of one channel member by another more efficient member. In the world of e-commerce, this is becoming a common occurrence. For example, when Amazon sells direct to customers, it removes the bookstore from the channel—*however*, it has to perform the operations of the bookstore (acquiring books from the publisher) or arrange for another organization to do so (such as the company that ships the books to the buyer). Disintermediation occurs when an organization thinks that it can reduce costs and/or increase the efficiency of the overall channel system by reconfiguring the basic tasks.

The second issue to understand is the complexity of the channel system. The best way to do this is to draw a map of the system and to identify where value is added, costs occur, time is taken, and conflict may occur. Figure 8.9 shows such a map. It depicts the traditional situation for the sale of new cars through a company-owned or franchised car dealer. The map starts with the manufacturer and ends with the buyer. Thus, it is a part of the value chain described in Chapter 2 (Figures 2.5 and 2.6).

The map in Figure 8.9 could be enhanced, and also made more complex, by looking at the flow of information and the organizations responsible for promotion. For example, car manufacturers do market and consumer research that is (sometimes) given to the dealers. Dealers provide sales data to the manufacturer and they report on their satisfaction with the transport company that delivers them their cars. Manufacturers undertake image advertising for the car while the dealer conducts 'retail' advertising to attract customers to the dealership. (The image and the retail advertising often contradict each other—'this is a great-looking, state-of-the-art car'

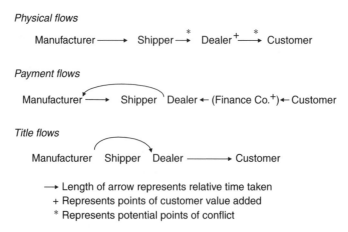

Figure 8.9. Mapping the distribution channel

says the manufacturer, but 'there is a stock-clearance sale on this weekend' says the dealer. This is an example of the breakdown of IMC.)

To summarize, managing distribution channels can be enhanced by understanding the functions of all intermediaries. It is also necessary to know who has the most power in the distribution channel (e.g. supermarkets and chain stores for many FMCGs); the issues that generate conflict (e.g. manufacturers having to pay slotting fees to get their products on the supermarket shelf); the 'choke points' in the channel (i.e. where delays and bottlenecks occur); and what, if any, added customer value each channel member contributes (e.g. the transport companies that ship new cars to the dealers sometimes damage the cars).

Designing Distribution Channels

The first three questions posed above focus on how best to deliver value to target consumers. The actual design of distribution channels is a compromise between what is ideal, what is feasible given the organization's size and budget, and what opportunities and constraints exist in the market. Generally, the design process starts by considering the needs of target consumers. These are:

- *Availability*—is it necessary for the product to be everywhere the consumer is, or will the consumer search for and travel to a specific location to buy. For example, the Coca-Cola distribution system is designed to make Coke available 'within arm's reach of desire'. This is an *intensive distribution strategy* that provides functional value (location convenience) to mobile Coke drinkers. At the other extreme is an *exclusive distribution strategy* where consumers are happy to travel to the only outlet in their area. For example, there are not many Porsche dealerships and Tiffany jewellery stores about. Part of the psychological value of buying these products is the effort involved in going to the outlet. Most distribution can be described as *selective*—enough outlets are used for target consumers to find the product or service without too much trouble.

- *Service help*—what help does the target consumer need when buying the product. As noted in Chapter 4, this will depend on the type of buying situation faced by the consumer. In extensive problem-solving situations, buyers often need the help of good salespeople. In routine response behaviour situations, they are largely self-reliant.
- *Service backup*—what add-on services are best provided by channel members other than the manufacturer. For example, credit, delivery, installation, insurance, and repairs are often provided by various intermediaries.
- *Product assortment*—does the target consumer need to buy one or a collection of products and services to fulfil their needs. For example, when shopping for groceries and office supplies a broad assortment is desirable. When shopping for clothes and PCs a different type of assortment is important. Here, multiple styles and brands offer the opportunity for people to 'shop'—that is, compare products and choose the one that best meets their needs. Thus, assortment can be described in terms of its breadth and depth.

A second channel-design decision involves considering whether each target segment of consumers can be served through the same distribution channel and, if not, whether using a multi-channel strategy will cause conflict among channel members. For example, Dell Computer's target consumers are predominantly experienced PC users. They know enough about PCs to be confident buying direct. Compaq, IBM, and many other PC manufacturers would like to sell to both experienced and inexperienced buyers. The inexperienced buyer needs service help—often in person—and thus a computer retailer can add value here. The experienced buyer may be happy to buy direct—and as Dell has demonstrated, this can result in cost savings. However, as many PC manufactures have discovered, trying to sell direct and through retailers at the same time upsets the retailers—channel conflict results!

One time when a multi-channel strategy is likely to work is when the target consumers are distinctly different—in terms of their needs, buying process, and demographic characteristics. (In Chapter 6, this was referred to as a discrete market structure—Figure 6.2.) Consider the situation faced by the Polaroid camera company. In Chapter 1, it was noted that 18–30-year-old buyers were buying Polaroid instant cameras as a social lubricant. However, Polaroid also sells cameras to professional photographers, and scientists and engineers—two other very different groups. Professional photographers use the camera to help set up their shot and avoid the risk of taking poorly composed pictures, while the scientists and engineers use them as a device for instant data recording (e.g. showing the leaking of fluid from a machine during its inspection). Because each of these groups gain a different type and amount of value from the same camera, it would be possible to sell it through different distribution channels, in different packages, and at different price points. For example, professional photographers might be offered one model sold through photographic stores at the top end of the price range (it will be a one-off, tax-deductible purchase). Scientists and engineers could be offered the same camera under another model name sold by Polaroid's salesforce and shipped direct to the organization that may buy in bulk. The 18–30 year olds would be offered a third model at a cheaper price than the professional photographer, which they could buy in department stores, chemist shops, or photo processing shops. The same camera is sold at three different price points, in three different 'packages' (models and packaging), through three different retail outlets.

The next channel-design decision involves identifying the available options. What might be an ideal distribution arrangement might be too expensive or already taken by a competitor. For example, the US Time Company originally tried to sell its inexpensive Timex watches through jewellery stores, but most refused to carry them. It finally found that mass merchandizers would sell them. Avon chose door-to-door selling because it was not able to convince department stores to sell its cosmetics.

Figure 8.10 illustrates the basic structural channel configurations in B2C and B2B markets. Examples of the direct-to-customer channel in B2C markets are door-to-door sales, website and mail order (catalogue) sales, and telemarketing. Direct marketing in B2B situations generally occurs through the company salesforce. Sales agents are used in both B2C and B2B markets—especially when goods are imported. These are people or firms that search for customers and negotiate the terms of trade on behalf of a manufacturer. They generally do not take title to the goods. Wholesalers and industrial distributors are companies that buy (in large quantities), take title to, store, and physically handle goods before reselling them (in smaller quantities) to retailers.

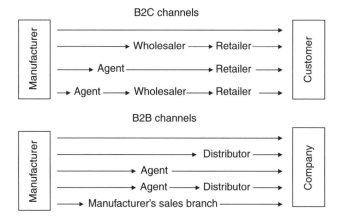

Figure 8.10. Types of marketing channels

From the manufacturer's perspective, the more intermediaries there are, the more opportunities there are for coordination problems to arise, the more difficult it is to get information about consumers, and the less control the manufacturer has in ensuring that the right products are available, at the right price to support the product's CVP, at the time the consumer wants them.

Traditionally, the relationship between the various intermediaries in a distribution channel was focused around the ordering and physical distribution of goods. Business was conducted 'at arm's length', and sometimes it was quite adversarial. The manufacturer's objective was to move the greatest possible volume of goods at the highest price. The intermediary's goal was to buy at the lowest price and to negotiate the best trading terms and conditions. These were not always compatible economic objectives.

In 1985, Wal-Mart and P&G initiated a partnership arrangement built on trust and a shared vision to meet their consumers' needs, while driving out excess costs in the system. Aided by IT technologies such as electronic data interchange, bar coding, scanning at the point of sale, and database management, and with the help of cross-functional account teams staffed by managers from both companies, the two companies re-engineered their supply chain. P&G's on-time deliveries to Wal-Mart improved significantly, as did inventory turnover. Wal-Mart moved closer to the goal of many retailers, namely, replenishing the stock of fast-selling items rapidly while reducing the prices on slow moving items as early as possibly. The P&G–Wal-Mart partnership provided the stimulus for other distribution channels to think about how they could achieve the twin goals of lowering costs and improving service to the ultimate customer.

Forming a strategic partnership like that of P&G and Wal-Mart relies on trust and collaboration for its success.[13] Another approach has been to form a *vertical marketing system* (VMS). These comprise the manufacturer and the intermediaries acting as a unified system. VMSs initially developed when a strong channel member sought to impose its control on the behaviour of other channel members. Sometimes the powerful channel member was the manufacturer and sometimes the retailer. Today, VMSs are designed using a corporate, administrative, or contractual model:

- *Corporate VMS*—involve the single ownership of two or more organizations in a channel.
- *Administered VMS*—coordinates production and distribution through the economic power and/or covert control (through joint promotions, sales training of the staff of the intermediary, provision of market research data for the dealer's trading area, etc.) of one of the channel members.
- *Contractual VMS*—consist of independent organizations that contract with each other to move goods from producer to consumer in an integrated manner. Wholesale and retail cooperatives are examples of this system as are franchise arrangements like those of Avis, Ford, and McDonald's.

To summarize, the design of a distribution channel needs to generate consumer demand and create time and place utility for target consumers. To do this requires that the roles and responsibilities of channel members need to be understood by all the parties. For example, manufacturers and retailers may be involved in joint promotion activities. Retailers may assume responsibility for product assortment decisions. Warehouses and distributors may be primarily responsible for quick deliveries to minimize retail stock outs. The 'channel captain' needs to manage the long-term working relationship among channel members, and minimize any conflict between members that arises from manufacturing imperatives (e.g. car manufacturers pushing inventory into car dealerships), and the marketing tactics of channel members (e.g. different car dealerships in the same city will often bid against each other to make a sale).

Service Channels

The final topic of this section is service channels. Recall from Chapter 1 that pure services are characterized by the interaction of the consumer and the provider. Thus, service delivery must be designed to take into account the needs and capabilities of the target consumer. A key channel design issue here is the mix of 'high tech and high touch'. For people who consider themselves to be fully-paid-up members of the 'Digital Generation', many services like banking, book buying, insurance, investments, music, and travel reservations can be delivered through electronic marketing channels such as the Internet. For partially paid-up members of the Digital Generation, interactive voice response (like a telephone help service) and self-service machines (like an ATM) may be the most cost-effective alternative. For the technology challenged or fearful consumer, interacting with another person is the key to successful service delivery.

The 'allfinanz' or 'bankassurance' (banking, investment, and insurance) market provides a good example of the key service channel issues facing many marketers. A company develops or inherits a channel structure that must be reconfigured to be made more efficient and effective. For example, in 1998, Citicorp and the Travelers Group merged to gain access to each other's distribution network: Citicorp had a worldwide network of branches and Travelers had 10,300 Salomon Smith Barney stockbrokers, 80,000 Primerica Financial Services insurance agents, and 100,000 agents selling Travelers insurance. Together with both companies' electronic marketing and service channels, every type of target consumer could be served. Thus, this new distribution network was a valuable strategic asset, but one that needed (*a*) pruning to take out excess costs and redundancies, (*b*) training to accommodate the sale of a broader assortment of products and services, and (*c*) refocusing to migrate customers to the most profitable channel for the company.

Arguably, the biggest challenge for many organizations is to migrate customers from one distribution channel to another. The key to success here is to try to entice (or pull) people across to the new (more cost-effective) channel rather than to push them. The pull strategy should be based on the added customer value offered by the new channel. Often this is overlooked and a strategy based on charging for what used to be a free service is used to push customers. The result is often many disgruntled customers.

KEY CONCEPTS

- *Distribution (Marketing) channel*—a set of interdependent entities that coordinate to move products or services from producer to consumer.
- *Channel conflict*—disagreement among marketing channel members about roles and/or goals: who should do various activities and for what rewards.

- *Disintermediation*—the removal of an entity in the channel arrangement or the substitution of one channel member by another more efficient member.
- *Distribution strategy*—*exclusive*—giving one dealer the right to distribute a brand in a particular territory; *intensive*—stocking the brand in as many outlets as possible; *selective*—stocking the brand in multiple outlets in a territory.

KEY FRAMEWORKS

- *Push and Pull marketing*—Figure 8.8
- *Distribution channel map*—Figures 8.9 and 8.10

KEY QUESTIONS

- Who is your 'channel captain'?
- Where in the channel (*a*) is conflict likely to occur? (*b*) are the choke points located? (*c*) is customer value added (or subtracted)?

RECAP

Few products and services, IMC programmes, or channel structures remain competitively dominant over all the stages of the product life cycle. Products improve, consumers learn and, thus, need different types of information and help, and competitors change their strategies. Thus, there is an underlying evolution to markets. As noted earlier, Dell exploited this when it designed its go-to-market business model to serve the more experienced PC buyer. Figure 8.11 illustrates how both IMC and the distribution channel can change as a product market evolves.[14] In the early stages of the PLC the challenge is to create a market. Educating and helping target consumers are important functions for marketing programmes. In the later stages the challenge is to manage the profitability of the offer made to target consumers.

To summarize, the hidden fulcrum of every marketing programme to attract target consumers is the CVP. There is an old saying that 'a good offer will often sell itself'. Having developed such an offer, the task is to tell target consumers about it. The real success of IMC comes when the organization's or brand's promises are aligned with its performance. These promises are not just to target consumers, but just as importantly to employees, business partners, and distribution channel members. The key marketing function for the distribution channel is to deliver the value offered, and in the process to support the CVP and brand position.

Value added by IMC and the channel

		High	Low
Market growth	Low	IMC—build awareness and trail Channel—selective distribution and provide help to consumers	IMC—remind consumers about the brand and CVP Channel—manage costs
	High	IMC—build the brand; stress importance and delivery of benefits Channel—broaden distribution coverage	IMC—stress the uniqueness of the brand Channel—search for new or additional channels

Market creation   Profit management

Strategy

Figure 8.11. Changes across the PLC

NOTES

1. This definition is from M. J. Lanning, *Delivering Profitable Value* (Oxford: Capstone, 1998).
2. E. K. Strong, *The Psychology of Selling* (New York: McGraw-Hill, 1925), p. 9.
3. E. M. Rogers, *Diffusion of Innovations* (New York: Free Press, 1995), chapter 5.
4. R. J. Lavidge and G. A. Steiner, 'A Model of Predictive Measurements of Advertising Effectiveness', *Journal of Marketing*, 25, 4 (1961), 59–62.
5. G. R. Dowling and D. F. Midgley, 'The Decision Process Models of Antarctic Travel Innovators', *Australian Journal of Management*, 3, 2 (1978), 147–61.
6. This example is from Rossiter and Percy *Advertising Communications and Promotion Management* (New York: McGraw Hill, 1997), chapter 1.
7. From J. C. Anderson and J. A. Narus, *Business Market Management* (Upper Saddle River, NJ: Prentice Hall, 1999) p. 245.
8. From R. A. Kerin and R. A. Peterson, *Strategic Marketing Problems* (Upper Saddle River, NJ: Prentice Hall International, 2001), pp. 560–76.
9. 'Clicks and Mortar at Gap.com', *Business Week* (18 October 1999), pp. 150–2.
10. 'Cisco@speed', in the *Economist* (26 June 1999), Survey—*Business and the Internet*, 10; Kerin and Peterson (2001), p. 465.
11. E. Rogers, *Diffusion of Innovations* (New York, Free Press, 1995).
12. This definition is from L. W. Stern and A. I. El-Ansary, *Marketing Channels* (Upper Saddle River, NJ: Prentice Hall, 1996).
13. R. D. Buzzell and G. Ortmeyer, 'Channel Partnerships Streamline Distribution', *Sloan Management Review* (Spring 1995), 85–96.
14. This diagram is based on M. M. Lele, *Creating Strategic Leverage* (New York: John Wiley & Sons, 1992), pp. 249–51.

9

Capturing Customer Value: Pricing and Selling

It is easy to know the price of something, but much harder to know its value.

It is increasingly being recognized that pricing is one of the most crucial functions of marketing management. One reason for this is that price is the element of the marketing mix that directly drives revenue. Also, some research by Robert Dolan suggested that if the following companies could realize a 1 per cent improvement in their prices, they could boost net income by a significant amount: Coca-Cola by 6.4 per cent; Fuji Photo 16.7 per cent; Nestlé 17.5 per cent; Ford 26 per cent; and Philips 28.7 per cent.[1] These are impressive numbers and they have once again focused the attention of senior managers on prices.

While price is a very important marketing function, Dolan's research also indicates that marketers struggle to come to grips with setting prices to capture the value created by their organization's offer to target consumers. In short, pricing is a headache. It is often a key feature of strained relations with good customers; the weapon competitors use to steal market share; and a source of conflict between salespeople, marketing managers, and the internal accountants. One reason for this is that the responsibility for pricing functions (such as setting trade and retail prices, changing prices, offering discounts, developing promotions, etc.) is often allocated to different people. Another reason is that most organizations do not do much, if any, serious research on pricing. Hence, in an environment that lacks good information about the prices of competitors and the price sensitivity of various segments of customers, it is easy for different people in the organization to have their own (firm) views about what the price of a particular product or service should be.

Before discussing the fundamentals of pricing, it is helpful to pause to think about how pricing 'problems' often present themselves inside the organization. What is often initially perceived as a pricing problem may not always be the best way to frame the issue. The following examples suggest that many so-called pricing problems are positioning and/or innovation problems in disguise. For example:

- When consumers cannot tell the difference between two products or services, which one do you expect them to choose? The snobs will choose the dearest, but most people will choose the cheapest. Thus, when a product fails the Unique part of IDU test introduced in Chapter 7, what may seem to be a pricing problem is really a positioning problem in disguise.

- The pricing of commodities provides other examples. Many organizations try to reduce their production costs in order to compete on price. Unless the organization has a cost advantage over its competitors, this is generally a hard strategy to maintain. If the organization does not have a direct cost advantage it might try to reduce the 'delivered cost' to consumers by asking the buyer to assume some of the production function (e.g. IKEA furniture is assembled at home by the buyer). This will work if the target consumer is prepared to serve themselves and the lower price is sufficient to compensate for this effort. Sometimes, however, organizations set out to differentiate their commodity. They might add a special ingredient to their product or describe it with a meaningless feature (e.g. Shell XMO motor oil). Others use some clever advertising and/or packaging (e.g. Absolut vodka). Sometimes, a commodity product is delivered with special service (e.g. Southwest Airlines' fun in-flight service). Thus, the focus shifts from function, costs, and price to making it easy for target customers to choose a suitable product. ('If all vodka is the same, then why not choose the one with the distinctive bottle and the creative advertising.')

- Brands of Irish crystal like Waterford are well respected and very highly priced—so high that the potential for breakage becomes a purchase inhibiting factor for table items like wine glasses. There is no shortage of less expensive crystal from which to choose (and occasionally break). To overcome this 'sticker shock' problem (as the US automobile industry calls it), Waterford introduced a less expensive line extension 'By Waterford'. Consumers who want the Waterford name can now pay less and get it in small print. However, this strategy will cause two problems. One is that the new line of crystal will cannibalize some of the sales of the original Waterford. (Hopefully, this will be offset by attracting a sufficient number of new buyers.) A second problem is one of brand image. Is the new crystal real Waterford or is it not? An innovative strategy that could have been considered is to offer a lifetime replacement for accidentally broken glassware—at say one-half of the retail price. Waterford crystal could then be positioned as a lifetime investment.

- In 1990, forest products giant Weyerhaeuser's particleboard business had a smaller market share and was less profitable than its major competitor Georgia-Pacific. Particleboard was a commodity used to make less expensive furniture. Customers made it clear to Weyerhaeuser's salespeople that they wanted the product to meet industry quality standards, be cut to thin dimensions, be delivered on time, and above all, be cheap. However, a little research showed that the customers' insistence on securing a low price was wrong! A team of Weyerhaeuser managers discovered that customers could save the considerable costs of gluing smaller pieces of particleboard together if they used larger dimension board. They could make further savings if the surface of the particleboard had a better finish because this reduced the costs of lamination. Both these innovations resulted in a higher cost per board foot, but a lower total cost to the furniture manufacturer.[2]

The essence of setting of prices in many B2B situations is reflected in the proverb at the beginning of the chapter. It is also illustrated by the Weyerhaeuser example. The essence of good pricing is to understand the value of a product or service as expressed in its CVP (Chapter 8), and then post a price that captures this value. Weyerhaeuser is an example of what is known as 'value-based pricing' based on 'consultative selling'. It is customer-focused and starts with the basic question:

What is the maximum amount that the customer should be prepared to pay for this product/service?

The answer to this question sets the upper limit on the posted price for a product or service. The product's cost sets the lower limit. Figure 9.1 shows

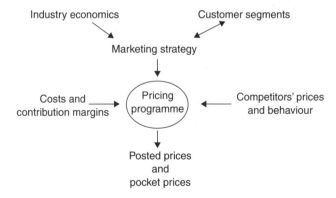

Figure 9.1. Factors that determine prices

the major factors that need to be considered when setting a price between these two limits.

Figure 9.1 is the blueprint for this chapter. Not only does it provide an organizing framework for thinking about pricing, but it also identifies the key information requirements on which good pricing practice is built.

Industry Economics

Many big management consulting firms start to examine pricing by understanding the basic economics of the industry in which a product or service competes. Chapter 3 looked at many of these factors under the headings of industry analysis and competitive rivalry, market analysis, trend tracking and monitoring, product life cycles, and price wars. The key issues to understand are:

- The current price level in the industry, and the spread of prices across industry participants.
- The overall direction of prices (up or down) as driven by technology and competition.
- The critical industry and marketplace factors that are driving industry price levels, such as *supply*—overall industry capacity, plant openings and closings, new competitors, imports, etc; *demand*—demographic changes, substitute products, etc.; *costs*—new technologies, scale effects, etc.; *stage of the product life cycle*—in the early stages, prices tend to be higher than in later stages; *regulation*—price surveillance authorities, trade practices legislation, government expectations about social responsibility, trade barriers, subsidiaries, etc.

The PC industry illustrates the role of technology in setting industry price levels. Moore's Law is the principal driving force here. More than thirty years ago, Gordon Moore, a founder of Intel, suggested that every eighteen months the processing power of a computer chip doubles while cost holds constant. (This law also applies to other aspects of PC technology such as computer memory and data storage.) It has driven the evolution of the hardware side of PCs and many consumer appliances—more powerful PCs and more intelligent electrical products produced at lower costs and priced more cheaply.

Customer Segments

A key difference between the way that marketers and consultants examine pricing is that marketers spend a lot of time examining the segments of consumers in the market. Chapter 6 was devoted to this exercise. The key factors here are to understand how consumers think about price. This information provides crucial insight for pricing decisions and focuses on the following:

- price sensitivity,
- price elasticity,
- customer value,
- reference price,
- budgets and mental accounting.

Each of these factors focus on different aspects of determining the level of demand in a customer segment, and, thus, they will affect the marketing objectives of the product/service—hence the double-headed arrow in Figure 9.1.

Price Sensitivity

Price sensitivity refers to the potential for an individual to notice and then react to a change in price. Consumers may not notice a change in price because (*a*) they are not interested in or informed about the product or service, (*b*) they shop so infrequently that they have forgotten the price they paid last time, or (*c*) someone else buys the product for them. A person's reaction to a price change can be psychological (such as re-evaluating the brand) and/or behavioural (such as buying less).

Thomas Nagle has identified a number of factors that are thought to effect how sensitive individual consumers are to the price of the product or service they are considering:[3]

- *The unique value effect.* Buyers are generally less price sensitive when the product is perceived to be unique, and when it best fits their particular needs.
- *The substitute awareness effect.* The more substitute products or alternative suppliers that a consumer is aware of, the greater their price sensitivity. It is thought that the Internet will increase this awareness and, thus, increase price sensitivity. Reducing the time available for

consumers to search is a tactic used to dampen this effect. For example, car dealers often say that their price is valid only for that day.

- *The difficult comparison effect.* The more difficult it is to compare prices, the less price sensitive buyers tend to be—all other effects being equal. This is why organizations make it difficult to directly compare the price-performance of many products and services such as a mobile phone and its call plan. The hope is that if price-performance is difficult to calculate accurately, then the buyer will focus on other features of the deal, such as the look of the handset.

- *The total expenditure effect.* The lower the price relative to the total income of a person or budget for an organization, the less price sensitive the buyer tends to be. Leasing a product is often used to mitigate this effect because each lease payment is much smaller than the total price.

- *The shared cost effect.* Price sensitivity is less when the cost is shared with another party. For example, the price of many prescription pharmaceuticals is not seen as great as it is because they are often subsidized by the government or a health-benefit insurance company.

- *The price quality effect.* Buyers are less price sensitive when the product is thought to have greater quality, prestige, or exclusiveness. Luxury goods exploit this effect.

A simple segmentation scheme based just on these factors is created by partitioning them into two sets—those that affect the perceived value of the brand's differentiation (such as the unique value and difficult comparison effects), and those that affect the perceived pain of its cost (such as the total expenditure and shared cost effects). Figure 9.2 shows four price-sensitive segments, namely, (*a*) Price Buyers do not value specific features

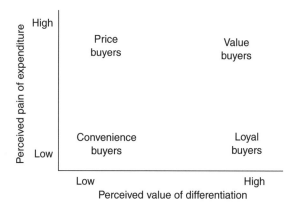

Figure 9.2. Price-based segments

and cannot be convinced to pay more for uniqueness, (b) Convenience Buyers seek their required level of quality and are not overly concerned about cost—any suitable brand will do—(c) Value Buyers are price sensitive but are prepared to pay for added value, and (d) Loyal Buyers have strong preferences based on the uniqueness of a brand and will buy it if it does not exceed their price threshold.

Price Elasticity

Price elasticity of demand is a measure of the reaction of a market (segment of consumers) to a change in price. It is measured as the ratio of the change in quantity demanded to the change in price, as follows:

$$E = \frac{\text{percentage change in quantity demanded}}{\text{percentage change in price}}.$$

In most cases, E is negative, that is, price increases result in less demand. However, for some luxury goods (like perfume), it can be positive. When $E = 1$, total revenue is not effected by the change in price. (Revenue is price $\times$ quantity.) When E is greater than 1 the price is said to be elastic. If E is also negative, then total revenue rises. Conversely, if E is less than 1, the price is said to be inelastic, and if E is also negative, total revenue falls.

The price elasticity of a segment of consumers will depend on:

- their price sensitivity;
- whether they are motivated to search for a lower price;
- whether they think that higher (or lower) prices are a natural trend (e.g. they are driven by broad economic conditions like inflation).

Price elasticity will also depend on the magnitude (small, medium, or large) and direction (up or down) of the price change. And it can be affected by how the price change is presented to consumers (e.g. as a price promotion or a sale price or an everyday low price, etc). Thus, price elasticity is a quite complicated concept. The crucial issue for marketers is to conduct research to find out (a) the sign and the value of E, and (b) what factors drive price elasticity.

Customer Value

Price is what you pay, value is what you get.
Warren Buffet

In Chapter 6, customer value was advocated as a primary basis for forming tactical segments. Customer value was defined as benefits minus price. Here, the task is to describe how customer value can be measured and, thus, bring more precision to this concept. Five such measures are briefly described, namely, (1) internal engineering assessment, (2) field value-in-use, (3) stated importance ratings, (4) conjoint analysis, and (5) choice models.

The first two measures are objective measures of customer value. They rely on a careful study of the target customer's needs, and the purchase and usage process. These measures provide an important point of reference for better understanding how perceptions can enhance or reduce the actual value estimates that people make. Methods 3 and 4—stated importance ratings and conjoint analysis—are perceptual measures. They will often differ from objective value measures because of psychological considerations such as risk perception. Perceptual measures are obtained by questioning consumers about their perceptions of and preferences for features and benefits. Method 5—choice models—is a behavioural measure. This type of measure uses observations of actual past purchase behaviour as the basis for estimating value. (The other four measures rely on information or judgements before a purchase.)

1. *Internal engineering assessment* In many B2B situations, the organization's own scientists, engineers, and managers will conduct an internal engineering assessment of the customer's operations, needs, and buying process. The Weyerhaeuser case was an example of this approach. The success of this method depends on (*a*) how well the team really understands the customer, and (*b*) how well this understanding is translated into economic aspects of customer value. To help this understanding, many organizations supplement their own analysis with customer input about the value of satisfying a need or resolving a problem. The SPIN selling technique described later in this chapter has proven to be a useful framework for eliciting this information.

2. *Field value-in-use* Another value assessment technique used in many B2B situations is Field Value-in-Use Assessment. (This is also known as economic value to the customer.) For a supplier's current product or service, VIU is defined as the price that would make the customer indifferent (i.e. economic break-even) between continuing to use their current product versus switching to another option. For a new product, VIU is the maximum amount that the customer should be willing to pay for the new product given the extra benefits (over those provided by the current product) that it offers. Exhibit 9.1 illustrates how VIU can be calculated for two products.

Exhibit 9.1. Calculating value-in-use

Consider an organization that is currently using a machine that cost $300 to buy, $200 to install, and $500 in maintenance and operating costs over its lifetime. Thus, it has a life cycle cost of $1000. This is the 'reference product' in the following diagram (Figure 9.3). A seller approaches this organization with two new products. One has the same set of features as the reference product, but it costs less to install ($100) and operate ($300). The second new product is an enhanced version of the first new product—it contains new features that the seller considers offers $300 worth of enhanced value to the customer. It costs $200 to install and $300 to operate. What is the maximum amount that the customer should be prepared to pay for these new products? Given the definition of VIU earlier, namely, the total price of the new products should not exceed that of the equivalent reference product, then the answer is $600 for product 1 and $800 for product 2.

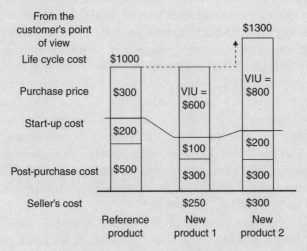

Figure 9.3. Value-in-use calculations

The seller should set its price for these products somewhere between its costs and the VIU to the customer. Exactly where will depend on the ability of the salesperson to capture the value that the product delivers.

From the seller's point of view, the critical issues when using a VIU approach to pricing such as illustrated in Exhibit 9.1 are:

- Choice of the reference product—should it be the customer's current product, a physically similar product, or any product that fulfils the same need.

- Calculating the costs of the reference product. This will often require the customer revealing sensitive information to the seller. Also, if the target cost is the full, life cycle cost, it may be necessary to convince the customer that this is the appropriate cost to be using—as opposed to simply the purchase price. (Budgets often force buyers to focus on the purchase price, not life cycle cost.)
- Identify customer resistance points. These are usually (a) uncertainty about the new product's benefits and performance advantage, (b) a reluctance to change suppliers, and (c) concern over the length of the payback period to recover the higher price.

3. *Stated importance ratings*   This method is one of the most popular approaches to measuring customer value. Typically, in a field research survey, respondents are given a set of features and/or benefits that describe a product or service and are asked to rate (or rank) each feature-benefit on their importance to them or their organization. Respondents are also asked to rate a set of competitive products on each of the feature-benefits. What results is an importance–performance analysis of the customer value provided by the competitive brands or suppliers. While this approach is easy to develop and execute, it has a number of weaknesses that limit its usefulness. First, respondents will often give (nearly) all the feature-benefits a top importance score on the ratings scale. Thus, there is little discrimination. Second, the approach does not give any clear indication of willingness to pay for the feature-benefits. Third, the trade-off between one feature and another that characterizes most real choices is not measured. Fourth, there is only a weak link between importance ratings and choice behaviour because many, and sometimes all, the options have a minimum, acceptable level of this feature (e.g. airline safety).

4. *Conjoint analysis*   Conjoint analysis is one of the best value assessment techniques that a marketer can use—in either B2B or B2C situations. It takes explicit account of the trade-offs that people make when they choose among a set of options. Also, if price is one of the features used to describe the product or service, then the importance of each feature (called its utility or part-worth) can be rescaled to reflect how much the buyer is willing to pay for different amounts of the various features. Exhibit 9.2 provides two examples of conjoint analysis used to assess customer value.

5. *Choice models*   Many organizations keep extensive records of customer purchases in their databases. Sometimes these data can be cross-matched with survey data about the characteristics of customers (typically demographics). From this type of data analysis, tactical segments can be formed. For example, American Express produce tactical segments based on ARPU (Chapter 2), customer profitability, and the portfolio of products acquired.

Exhibit 9.2. Conjoint analysis

Suppose that the two most important features of digital cameras are price and the clarity of picture.[4] Further, assume that three different levels define price ($600, $800, $1400) and three define clarity (high, medium, low). Taken together, these two features describe nine different digital camera concepts (A to I) in Table 9.1. Also, assume that an individual ranks each of the concepts from '9' as most desirable to '1' as least desirable as per Table 9.1. These rankings reflect the individual's trade-offs between price and clarity.

Table 9.1. Digital camera concepts

Price	High clarity (3.2 megapixels)	Medium clarity (2.5 megapixels)	Low clarity (1.3 megapixels)	Average score
$600	A	D	G	
	9	7	3	6.3
$800	B	E	H	
	8	6	2	5.3
$1200	C	F	I	
	5	4	1	3.3
Average Score	7.3	5.7	2	

Using what is called an additive utility model, we can compute the total utility for each camera concept:

$$U(A) = 7.3 + 6.3 = 13.6 \quad \text{1st preference}$$
$$U(B) = 7.3 + 5.3 = 12.6 \quad \text{2nd preference}$$
$$U(C) = 7.3 + 3.3 = 10.6 \quad \text{5th preference}$$
$$U(D) = 5.7 + 6.3 = 12.0 \quad \text{3rd preference}$$
$$\text{etc.}$$

The relative importance of each feature is given by the range of the feature divided by the sum of the ranges:

Clarity $7.3 - 2.0 = 5.3$ Relative importance $5.3 / 8.3 = 64\%$
Price $6.3 - 3.3 = 3.0$ $3.0 / 8.3 = 36\%$
Total utility range $= 5.3 + 3.0 = 8.3$

Notice that this procedure allows us to infer how much it is worth to this individual to move from a low to medium to high clarity picture. For example, the difference in utility of $800 (5.3) to $1200 (3.3) is 2 utility units. Thus, in this

cont.

Exhibit 9.2. *cont.*

price range each unit of utility is worth $100. Because the difference between medium and high clarity is (5.7 − 2.0) 3.7 utility units, and each unit is worth $100, then this person should be prepared to pay $370 to move from medium to high clarity. Here we have an explicit measure of the person's price sensitivity.

When product/service concepts are described by more than two or three features then the simple procedure illustrated above is not really feasible. What now happens is that a special set of product concepts is developed to be rated by the respondent, and a special form of regression analysis is used to calculate the importance weights (utilities) of the features from these ratings. For example, suppose that a laptop personal computer is described as follows:[5]

Size of the hard disk	2, 4, or 6 GIG
Manufacturer	IBM, Compaq, or DELL
Price	$2250, $3500, $5250
Weight	6 lbs or 7.5 lbs
Processor speed	Pentium II CPU of 233 or 300 MHz

Of the (3 × 3 × 3 × 2 × 2) 108 possible combinations, only eighteen are needed to capture all the major trade-offs in the individual's decision. From these eighteen ratings, a (dummy variable) regression analysis can be estimated to reveal the importance of each feature for an individual. These importance ratings (regression coefficients) can then be used as a segmentation base and clustered together to form (benefit) segments of target consumers. Thus, conjoint analysis is often used to help create tactical consumer segments.

Many market research firms use conjoint analysis to help their clients understand their target consumers' decision-making. Also, for the more quantitatively literate marketer, PC-based computer software is available to design and estimate conjoint models. See, for example, G. L. Lilien and A. Rangaswamy, *Marketing Engineering* (Upper Saddle River, NJ: Prentice Hall, 2003), chapter 7.

This approach to indirectly estimating customer value is called data mining. It is widespread but has three important limitations:

1. Non-customers are ignored (they are not on the customer database). These may often be a big source of potential growth.
2. Polygamous loyalty (Chapter 4) is ignored.
3. Data mining says what has happened, but only rarely does it suggest why this has happened or what to do to change consumer behaviour.

Given the limited picture that internal data can provide about customer value segments, data mining is best used as a supplementary form of customer value assessment.

The direct-marketing industry routinely uses an experimental form of purchase behaviour analysis to measure customer value. For example, with a new product offering, the direct-marketer chooses samples of customers from its database and sends out a number of different versions of its offer. It then records who purchases and how much they purchase of each version of the offer. This information is then used as input to the right-hand side of the following equation:

$$\text{Probability of purchase} = f(\text{type of offer, type of customer}) \qquad (1)$$

Special purpose statistical models are used to estimate the importance weights of each variable on the right-hand side of equation (1). For example, the type of customer may be profiled by their demographic profile and past purchases of other products from the direct marketer. The type of offer will involve different prices. Thus, these models *observe* choice and then *infer* the value that different types of customers attach to each type of offer. (This was the approach used by ABB Electric in the example of segmentation reported in Chapter 6.)

Given an estimate of the probability of purchase for each respondent for each offer, the analyst can then estimate the profitability of each offer:

$$\text{Expected customer profit} = \text{probability of purchase} \times \text{likely purchase volume if a purchase is made} \times \text{profit margin for this customer} \qquad (2)$$

As suggested in Chapter 2, this is just the type of information a marketing manager needs to link marketing actions to financial outcomes.

Reference Prices and Other Psychological Aspects of Prices

Marketers need to understand the psychology of pricing in addition to its financial economics. For example, few managers think about the pricing reference points that their consumers carry around in their heads. Two such reference points are the quality level of the product or service (as expressed in the saying 'you get what you pay for'), and price points expected for various types of products and services. These reference points are formed through the buyer's learned experience (Chapter 4), and also depend on the amount of money available for the purchase. Thus, they will differ across segments of consumers.

In the contexts of negotiation and price setting, it is important to know the reference price or 'expected price' that target consumers have for a particular product or service. In negotiation situations the reference price is often called the 'reservation price', and it is the upper limit for what the buyer is willing to pay. Sometimes, in consumer settings, these prices are expressed as 'I will never pay more than ($20) for a (bottle of wine).' Pricing too far away from the target segment's reference price can result in lost sales. For example, luxury brands that are sold too cheaply are often perceived to have something wrong with them (such as being a fake or damaged). Some retail stores try to manipulate these reference points by showing a product with an inflated 'recommended retail price' that has been marked down for sale. The high price is supposed to signal high quality and the words 'on sale' are thought to motivate the buyer to limit their search and buy now.

Another psychological tactic is to end prices in an odd number, such as $299 for a television set and $2.95 for a box of breakfast cereal. Many years ago there was a practical reason for this type of pricing—it made the sales assistant give the customer some change from the cash register and, thus, produced a record of the sale. This helped to minimize employee theft. Today there are various arguments presented for the use of this tactic. One is that there is a heightened sensitivity to prices that end in odd numbers, especially nine or ninety-nine, and that they are perceived as being lower than the rounded-up price. However, even though many retailers are fond of using odd-price endings, the published research findings in this area are inconclusive about their effect on increasing sales.[6]

An intriguingly important psychological aspect of pricing is to know whether the target consumers consider price to be either

- a measure of sacrifice (such as petrol for the car), or
- an index of quality (such as a diamond).

This perception will colour the person's reaction to the posted price.

Budgets and Mental Accounting

All consumers and organizations face the problem of allocating their income to expenditures. In the organizational context, the budget process is formalized, and good marketers and salespeople know about their customers' budget allocations. For example, what is the budget cycle, which expenditures are designated as capital expenditure, which are MOR, etc.

The prices charged for a product or service have to fit into the customer's budget cycle and allocation. Otherwise, the seller may need to arrange a time varying payment schedule.

For consumers the budget process is equally important to understand but it takes a more subtle form. The term 'mental accounting' is now used to describe what seems to happen.[7] Economist Richard Thaler suggests that people tend to categorize money into three types of mental accounts based on when it is received and when it is to be used: current income, assets, and future income. Current income is the most spendable while future income, such as a retirement investment, is generally deemed untouchable. Also, it has been found that the payment patterns of consumers may vary depending on the account from which the money is to be withdrawn. For example, vacations and parties are often prepaid (from the current account), while many durable goods are bought on credit (from the asset account). The key issue here is that price setting and the facilitation of payment often depends on the target consumer's mental accounting.

In summary, the factors considered in this section are important segmentation criteria when the focus turns to setting the price for a product or service. Without good insight into the price sensitivity, customer value, and psychological aspects of pricing, it is difficult to set prices to capture customer value and to meet the objectives described in the next section.

Pricing Strategy

The strategic aspect of pricing manifests itself at two levels. First, there is how the price level of products and services reflects the overall corporate strategy of the organization. For example, companies like IKEA, Southwest Airlines, Wal-Mart, and the Korean automotive companies try to win in their markets through a strategy of low-price leadership. In the case of Wal-Mart, they have the lowest costs of all the major retailers, and they back their 'everyday low prices' with a policy of 'satisfaction guaranteed'. At the other extreme, some organizations are positioned as exclusive. For example, the Caribbean island of St Barts is outrageously expensive for most tourists. It has an informal policy of 'to keep it exclusive, we'll keep things expensive'.

The second strategic aspect of pricing refers to the role of price in defining the level of customer value offered (Chapters 6 and 8), positioning the product or service (Chapter 7), and its support of other marketing programmes to attain and retain target consumers. If the organization has selected its target market and positioning carefully, then its pricing should follow logically from these decisions. For example, traditionally brands positioned as high quality (or exclusive or prestigious) have a high price (and excellent presentation, classy advertising, etc.). Brands positioned as 'good value' should be priced at a reference point slightly lower than their perceived quality. 'Economy' brands should have low price and standard quality. In retailing the emergence of the category killer stores in the United States (Home Depot, OfficeMax, Sportmart, Toys 'R' Us) that feature the largest product assortment within a category at the lowest prices have redefined traditional price–quality relationships. Overall, the key to success is for the elements of the marketing mix to fit together to present a unified and distinctive image for the company and its brands.

The next strategic pricing issue to consider is the role of price in achieving the marketing and financial objectives of the organization. The two extreme cases are to survive and to maximize current profitability. Many other objectives exist between these two.

In some cases the objective is as simple as survival. In periods when there is over-capacity in their industry, many continuous-production manufacturing companies (such as aluminium and steel) price most of their production in order keep the factories running. As long as prices cover variable costs and make a contribution to fixed costs, the companies stay operating. In the late 1990s, survival pricing was a key consideration for many start-up dotcom companies. It is also not uncommon for not-for-profit organizations to adopt a variant of survival pricing, namely, full cost recovery.

The objective of maximizing current profit is as much a theoretical ideal as it is a practical reality. (Sometimes this approach is known as setting an 'all the traffic will bear' price.) It assumes that the organization has accurate knowledge of both its demand and its costs. In reality, these are difficult to estimate. Hence, a compromise profit-oriented pricing objective is to achieve a target return on investment. The return is profit while the investment can be the assets tied up in an SBU, a product line, or a brand. Other financially oriented objectives are to maximize revenues or cash flow. The hope with these two is that they will ultimately lead to increased market share and, thus, pricing power in the marketplace.

Here are some other pricing objectives. Some organizations have explicit sales volume goals. For example, in the automotive industry many marketing plans prescribe volume targets that reflect plant capacity thresholds. For reasons of pride as much as financial return, some companies seek to price to maintain their market leadership—Budweiser beer and Coke being two examples. In technology markets, being the (clear) market leader (and, thus, the least risky choice) is very important. Thus, the posted price must support this objective. To obtain market dominance, or to hurt a competitor, an organization may set a temporary predatory price (below average or marginal cost) for a product or service. To avoid price wars, an organization may set the price of a product to maintain parity with a competitor.

When introducing a new product or service, two pricing approaches are commonly considered:

- *Set a skimming price.* Here a new product is launched at a high price to 'skim the cream' off the market. That is, only the less price sensitive consumers will buy the initial product. When demand falls away, the price can be lowered to attract more price sensitive buyers. Du Pont has used this strategy when launching cellophane, nylon, and teflon onto the market. Intel has also used this strategy with its new PC-chip designs. Many entertainment products like video cassette recorders, compact disc players, and digital cameras are launched at a skimming price. Often companies who use this strategy will create another lower-priced model of the product for later market entry.

  Market skimming makes sense when (*a*) there is a sufficient number of target consumers who are prepared to pay the high price, (*b*) the high price will not attract competitors (the product may be protected by a patent), and (*c*) the organization needs a high price to recover its R&D investment and the costs of bringing the product to market. The high price may also provide status value to the consumer.

- *Set a market penetration price.* Here the price of the new product is set as low as possible to quickly enable the product to become established in the market. Conditions that favour market penetration pricing are (*a*) when there are more users the product is more valuable to each buyer (e.g. the Windows operating system for PCs), (*b*) the market is very price sensitive, (*c*) production and distribution costs fall with volume, (*d*) when market segments are not pronounced, and (*e*) a low price will discourage competitors.

The pricing objective that fits best with the overall philosophy of this book is *perceived value pricing*. Here, the value assessment techniques described earlier are used as the primary input into price setting. The marketing team calculates the value of a product or service to an individual customer (B2B) or market segment (B2B and B2C). When using a technique like conjoint analysis, this value assessment can contain all the main aspects of the offer to customers such as brand name (and thus position), quality, special features, different price points, etc. From this research, marketers estimate the sales volume and then unit costs. If the product satisfies the organization's financial objectives at the planned price and costs, it is launched.

Perceived value pricing is a great idea 'in theory', but it is often difficult to implement in practice. There are three reasons for this:

- The product or service has to have a clear CVP. (Here the CVP concept and the product onion framework are helpful.)
- Competitors will often be offering a similar product or service at a lower price. (Hence, passing the IDU test is important. Recall that if the product is not unique, many target customers will buy the cheapest.)
- The advertising agency has to be able to communicate convincingly the CVP. Communicating perceived value prices often involves a feature–benefit style of advertising. Consider the copy of an advertisement for the EIZO professional computer monitor:

THIS IS THE CHEAPEST COLOUR MONITOR ON THE MARKET.
(THAT'S WHY IT COSTS AT LEAST US$500 MORE THAN THE REST.)

When you pay for an EIZO Flexscan T660i colour monitor, you actually get a lot less.
Less problems. Less hidden costs. Less headaches.

The T660i can easily lower its normal electricity consumption by an incredible 93%. That's because it comes with the unique PowerManager™ feature, which automatically shuts off the monitor when you aren't using the system. And since the in-built microprocessor does not stop running, you can resume work by simply touching the keyboard or the mouse.

However, this is merely one of the cost-cutting benefits that the T660i has to offer.

To ensure a flicker-free image, the T660i can refresh the image on the screen up to an amazing 90 times a second. Also, the special ErgoPanel™ is bonded directly to the screen. This eliminates glare, improves focus and reduces eye strain.
Etc.

For a marketing manager, the key issues with pricing objectives are that:

- The objectives should be stated explicitly in the marketing plan.
- All managers should know what the objectives are.
- When hybrid objectives such as 'increasing sales volume and profit' contain elements that are incompatible, there is a clear policy to guide making a trade-off between the objectives.
- Prices are set with full regard to all of the following: customer value, then costs and competition.

Costs and Contribution Margins

As noted earlier in this chapter, cost provides the 'floor' on which to build a pricing strategy. But the vexing question is, which costs? Well, direct variable costs set the short-term price floor. Sometimes these are close to zero, for example, when an airline sells an unused seat on a plane that is about to depart—a tray of food and a slurp of fuel is the direct variable cost. In the short term, when price exceeds the variable unit cost, it provides a contribution to fixed costs. In the long-term, however, the price floor is the full (fixed plus variable) unit cost. Some Internet companies have discovered that these costs are greater than the price of the products they are selling. The result is a good deal for customers, high sales revenues, but large financial losses.

For a marketing manager one of the key issues is not to set short-term prices for the long run. That is, they have to ensure that the overall pricing schedule exceeds the long-run average cost of the products and services sold. The case of hotel pricing illustrates this issue. Assume that a boutique hotel has an occupancy rate of 70 per cent and that at this rate the average cost of a room is $100 of which the variable cost of a used room is $20 (cleaning, bed linen, administration, etc.). The short-term price floor is $20 and the long-term floor is $100. If the average room rate during the week is $150, then the hotel can drop the weekend rate below $100 (but above $20) and remain viable.

The pricing tool of contribution margin is indispensable when setting prices. Contribution Margin (CM) is

$$CM = \frac{\text{Unit selling price } - \text{ Unit variable cost}}{\text{Unit selling price}} \qquad (3)$$

In the hotel example for a weekday room it is ($150 − $20)/$150 = 87%.

A key question that marketing managers are often asked is by what percentage must sales rise (or fall) after a price cut (increase) to achieve the same total dollar sales revenue? This calculation can be made as follows.[8] Consider the following example where the price (P), variable cost (VC), and contribution margin (CM) are all calculated on a unit basis. If we start with a price per unit of P = $1 where the variable costs are 60 cents (VC = 0.6P) and the contribution margin is 40 cents (CM = 0.4P), then sales changes can be calculated as

$$\text{Sales revenue change } = \frac{\text{Old\$CM } - \text{ New\$CM}}{\text{New\$CM}} \times 100 \qquad (4)$$

Table 9.2. Variable costs and contribution margins

		20% Price change	
Current price		Decrease ($)	Increase ($)
Price	P	0.8P	1.2P
VC	0.6P	0.6P	0.6P
CM	0.4P	0.2P	0.6P

For the sake of illustration, let us assume that variable costs stay the same regardless of whether the price is raised or lowered. For a 20 per cent price change, the P, VC, and CM are shown in Table 9.2.

For a 20 per cent decrease in price sales have to rise by $\{(0.4P - 0.2P)/0.2P\} \times 100 = 100\%$. For a 20 per cent increase in price the acceptable decrease in sales revenue is $\{(0.4P - 0.6P)/0.6P\} \times 100 = -33.3\%$. This type of analysis is a critical part of every decision to change prices. The example used here is simplistic but it illustrates the asymmetric nature of many price changes.

Many organizations anchor their pricing decisions to their costs—and, thus, ignore the perceived value of their offer. A good example of this approach is the cost-plus practice of pricing. Among construction companies, professional service providers, and retailers, this is a common pricing method. The costs should be direct variable costs (not full costs), and the 'plus' (or multiplier) can be based on industry tradition, individual experience, or rules of thumb. This approach to pricing has a number of practical advantages, namely, (*a*) it is simple and easy to apply, (*b*) it is based on cost data which pleases the accountants, and (*c*) it seems to be a 'safe' pricing method as it covers costs. Only when costs are fairly constant—at different levels of demand and over time—does this form of pricing have theoretical merit. These conditions characterize many retailing situations, but are less common for durable consumer products and industrial products.[9]

In summary, because most marketing managers are not trained in cost accounting, it is best to involve the organization's (friendly) accountant in calculating contribution margins and resulting sales changes from a proposed price change.

Competitors

Chapter 3 discussed price wars and market defence, two key factors to consider when setting prices. Here, the focus was on understanding a competitor's likely response to a price change. In many markets, a price change invites a competitive price response—especially where the product or service is perishable and the variable costs are very low (such as an airline seat). The downward price spirals that regularly occur in these markets have prompted many competitors to try to shift the focus of competition to other elements of the marketing mix. What is driving this new strategy is the elevation of profitability above market share as the primary pricing objective.

In this section, the focus is on pricing strategies that are anchored in some way to the prices of competitors. The most blatant of such strategies is *Going-Rate-Pricing*. In commodity industries like base metals, chemicals, fertilizer, fuel oils, and others, organizations tend to charge the same prices for the same grade of product. The best that can be done in many of these industries is for a few organizations to establish small points of difference (often based around customer service) that enable them to charge a slight premium. One or two organizations are regarded as price leaders, and these are watched closely by the other competitors. For small organizations, the reason for setting their price like this is largely one of survival. Higher prices will not attract customers, and lower prices may be perceived as starting a price war and result in retaliation from a big competitor. The supposed rationale for this type of pricing at the industry level is that going-rate prices reflect the collective wisdom of the industry and this strategy is less likely to start a price war.

Some manufacturers and retailers use a strategy called *everyday-low-pricing* as a way to signal 'value' to target consumers and 'stable prices' to competitors. These stable prices eliminate the price fluctuations that result from constantly putting products on promotion. They also bring a degree of certainty to pricing for both retailers and consumers. Often, this may also result in creating an image of fairness and reliability. This strategy stands in contrast to price-promotion competitors that follow a policy of *high–low pricing*. When this strategy is implemented by retailers, one or two brands in the product category are always on promotion, while the rest may be priced (slightly) higher than the everyday-low-price competitors. The retailers use these price promotions as loss leaders to generate store traffic. For the manufacturers whose brands are rotated through the cycle of being on and off promotion, this policy can cause problems such as diluting the value of the brand ('Is this a high-price or a low-price brand?'), heightening sensitivity to price (when retail advertising talks about price, consumers focus on price), and creating peaks and troughs in production and logistics operations.

The bottom line is that an organization's prices are judged against those of its competitors. Factors like the reputation of the producer, consumers' evaluations of the brand, special features of the product, functionality, perceived quality, etc. can all help to substantiate price differences, but these differences will be calibrated against the price of competitive offers. This is especially true for polygamous loyal customers.

Pricing Programmes and Policies

In many small- and medium-sized organizations, the responsibility for setting a price resides with the CEO, after advice from the marketers. Sometimes, formal pricing policies have been developed, but in many cases pricing is an ad hoc activity that fits the circumstances of the day and hopefully the strategy of the organization. Price setting in this type of environment is more often art than science. The danger of 'artful price setting' is described in an old Russian proverb:

> There are two kinds of fool in a market.
> One charges too much.
> The other charges too little.

Bigger organizations are more likely to have formal policies and procedures for setting and changing prices. These reflect a combination of industry experience, art, and science, and act as a control mechanism and risk monitoring process. Big organizations often have a specialist group that works with the marketers to set prices, administer price changes, and offer discounts and allowances to selected (business) customers. For example, in a big Australian telecommunications company this group is staffed with accountants, economists, lawyers, and researchers. The group takes responsibility for understanding the regulatory restrictions on pricing; gathering information about competitors—their advertising, cost structures, strategic intent, key personnel, price schedules, and competitive reactions; modelling the price sensitivity and elasticity of various target consumer segments; and estimating the potential cannibalization of price changes in one area on the demand in other areas (such as changes to fixed-line telephone prices on the demand for mobile services). When prices are set or changed, the various sales, marketing, and brand managers are required to have their suggestions reviewed by this group. Needless to say, the specialist pricing group is often perceived by the brand managers as a bureaucratic impediment to a fast market response. However, over the years, it has saved the company from many pricing disasters. (One occurred when a junior brand manager misinterpreted a major competitor's retail advertisement as a price decrease when, in fact, it turned out to be a price increase.)

One of the key areas where it is important to have a formal pricing programme is when pricing a line of products or services. (A product line comprises a set of products that are marketed together.) Consider the task faced by the marketing manager of one of Australia's leading red wine brands—Penfolds. The lowest priced brand in the range is Rawsons Retreat and sells for about $A10 per bottle. The highest priced brand is Australia's most distinguished wine, Grange Hermitage. In 2003, the current release of this wine sold for $A350 per bottle. There are twenty other brands in between these two. How should the prices be set across the full range? Kent Monroe, one of the world's leading academic pricing experts, suggests that the relationship between price and quality should be that the price differentials become wider as the quality increases over the product line. This is illustrated for a selection of Penfolds red wines in Figure 9.4. Monroe suggests that people tend to remember the highest and the lowest prices of the line more than others, and that the higher priced products are perceived as higher quality but lower value than products at the lower end of the line.[10] (A branding consultant might also suggest that Penfolds have to think about some of the brand names used.)

In Figure 9.4, notice that all the brands fall on a curved pricing line. This is an easy way to check if the posted prices 'fit' the theory—in this case for a product line, and also for a set of competing brands in a product category.

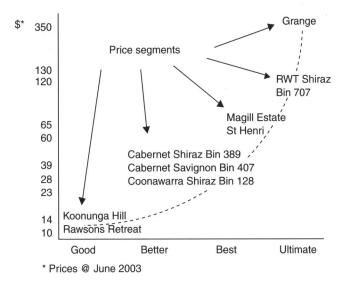

Figure 9.4. Penfolds—reds

Posted Prices and Pocket Prices

A posted (or sticker or ticket or list) price is the public price that appears on the organization's price schedule. A pocket price is the actual amount of money that gets into the bank account. What causes the difference between these two prices are the discounts (for cash, quantity, or by season) and/or allowances (e.g. for a trade-in) that are given to the buyer. As we will see in Chapter 12 (Figure 12.5), the difference between these two prices can be substantial, and something that must be controlled by the internal pricing group or the marketing manager.

The key issue for the marketing manager is how to 'design' the posted price seen in the marketplace. One practical heuristic is to:

> make posted prices easy to understand
> but
> hard to compare.

A good example of this design principle is known as 'postal pricing'. The current rate for a letter is 50 cents anywhere in Australia. The US Postal Service had a flat rate of $3 for a small package anywhere in the United States. At the same time, FedEx and UPS had a range of prices depending on the size and the desired delivery time for their packages. The US Postal Service used its postal price to reinforce its position of 'cheap' and simple (remember it is the government). The other major courier companies had a pricing schedule that was complex and difficult to understand for many people—a fact that US Postal used in some of its advertising.

Another piece of advice about communicating posted prices from pricing consultants is to always link one's price to a benefit. In this way, the emphasis shifts from price to customer value. A good example of this has been used by a number of telephone companies around the world. Their research suggested that many (most) people saw a phone call as a commodity—and, thus, the cheaper the better. Many phone company advertisements reinforced this view with the offer of cheaper prices. The marketing task was to shift the focus from cheap phone calls to something else. One strategy that had some success was to remind people about why they often used the phone, namely, to keep in contact with family and friends. Advertising campaigns with a theme of 'reach out and touch someone', 'call home', and 'friends and family' for a time began to shift the focus away from discount plans.

To summarize, to a large extent the posted price of a product or service will determine the types of customers and competitors a brand or an organization will attract. Selecting the price of a product is a moment of truth in formulating marketing programmes to attract and retain target consumers. The right price complements the other elements of the marketing strategy. The wrong price can ruin a product's chance of success in the marketplace. The problem for the marketing manager is that price setting is an extremely complex endeavour. Figure 9.1 provides an overall framework to guide the development of a pricing programme. Embedded in it are the 3Cs of pricing—customers (their characteristics and the value they place on the product or service), costs, and competitors. Different combinations of these factors ensure that each pricing decision will be unique. Because of this, many marketing managers will use two or more approaches to setting a price in order to cross-check their decision-making.

In order to set a price that will capture the customer value engineered into the organization's products and services, it is worthwhile looking in a bit more detail at how to discover the value that customers place on products and services. The approach described in the next section is used in face-to-face selling. From it, marketers, in both B2B and B2C situations, can learn more about how to assess customer value, and then set a price to capture this perceived value.

Personal Selling—the Art of SPIN

Purchasing agents are people who know the price of everything and the value of nothing.

(The salesperson's lament.)[i]

A coarse way to classify selling situations that confront salespeople is that they are either Commodity Sales or Consultative (Relationship) Sales. This classification is useful in both B2B and retail situations. The way to distinguish between these two types of selling situations is to apply this simple test—'Would the prospect be willing to pay for the sales call?' In a consultative situation, the answer is a clear 'yes'. Hence, the quote above suggests a commodity selling situation.

Commodity sales are characterized by the products or services providing almost identical functional benefits and they are bought mainly on the basis of price. Many insurance policies, office supplies, and book titles fit this description. Buyers are motivated by paying a low price and acquiring the product with a minimum of effort. The salesperson usually concludes

---

[i] This saying is also often used to denigrate accountants and economists.

the sale in one session. In some cases, the customer may even see the sales representative as a barrier to achieving a successful result. This occurs when the salesperson has a poor selling technique.[11] Today, some buyers are going onto the Internet to search for the lowest price and to consummate the transaction.

Consultative sales are characterized by buyers wanting some hands-on assistance to help make their decision. Investment products, industrial machinery, and new forms of electronic products such as a DVD player fit this description for many buyers. In Chapter 4, these purchase situations were described as Extensive Problem-Solving. Often, the role of the Internet here is to help the buyer to gather background information on the product or service before talking to a sales representative. This information allows the buyer to ask the salesperson 'sensible questions' about the product. The sale may take a number of sessions to complete. Good salespeople can bring added value to these purchase situations. They do this by offering expertise, by 'listening' to the customer, and/or by creating a customized solution to the problem if this is possible. Thus, their role is to both communicate value and add value.

Neil Rackham is one of the leading advocates of consultative selling.[12] His SPIN Selling technique is grounded in an extensive research programme and is used by many B2B salespeople around the world. His argument is that the key to good consultative selling lies not in persuading, but in understanding the customer. The sale starts not with the products and services the sales team is rewarded for selling, but rather with understanding the business that the prospect is in. Rackham's approach to selling is outlined in Figure 9.5. Each sales call, from the most sophisticated to the simplest, goes through four distinct stages:

1. *Preliminaries.* These are the background research (if needed) and the warm-up events (such as how you introduce yourself) before the serious selling starts. Sometimes these will be perfunctory and sometimes they may take hours or days to conclude. For example, in many situations, there is a careful 'feeling out' process to establish the things that are essential in order to do business with the other party. This is often required before any serious business can take place in various Asian countries.
2. *Investigating.* This is the process of asking questions to find out further information about the buyer and his or her particular needs. In extensive problem-solving situations, this is the most important stage of the selling process. The SPIN technique of questioning described below is how good salespeople uncover the value inherent in the

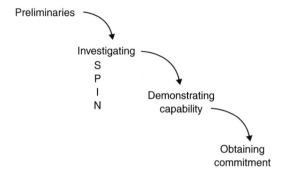

Figure 9.5. The four stages of a sales call

products and services they are selling. In the process, they may uncover new ways to add value to the customer.

3. *Demonstrating capability.* Here, the salesperson convinces the customer that they have something that will help to solve a problem and/or add value to a customer's business. Doing a VIU calculation would be such an activity as would be demonstrating the product or service for the customer.

4. *Obtaining commitment.* In small sales, commitment is usually exhibited by taking an order or making the sale. Good salesperson closing skills are important in these sales. In larger sales, it may be to schedule another sales call, to visit a factory, or to attend a product demonstration. These intermediate steps all lead towards the final purchase decision.

The real insight of Rackham's approach to selling is his SPIN sequence of asking questions in the investigation phase of the sales call:

1. *Situation questions.* At the start of the sales call, salespeople ask data-gathering questions about facts and background. For example, 'How long have you had this piece of equipment?' and so on. Good salespeople do not use too many of these questions because they can become tedious for the buyer.

2. *Problem questions.* After the situation has been established to the common agreement of the buyer and seller, the good salesperson moves on to asking questions that explore problems, difficulties, and dissatisfaction in areas where the seller can help. For example, 'How much has the machine cost in maintenance?' 'What percentage of defects does the machine produce?' Inexperienced salespeople tend not to ask enough problem questions.

3. *Implication questions.* These questions can be quite subtle to ask. They are designed to take a customer problem and explore its

effects and consequences. For example, 'How would a machine with a reliability rating of 97 per cent reduce the number of defects produced?'

4. *Need-payoff questions.* These questions are designed to get the customer to tell the salesperson the benefits that the salesperson's solution could offer. For example, 'How much cost would be saved if a more reliable machine was used in place of the current machine?' Rackham's research suggests that top salespeople ask more than ten times as many need-payoff questions per call as do average performers.

Rackham's consulting company (Huthwaite) runs courses on SPIN selling and his fieldbook provides examples of the SPIN questions.[13]

The insight gained from the SPIN questioning technique is useful for helping sales and marketing people to discover the value embedded in their products and services. While it forms only a small part of the overall sales process, it fits this book's emphasis of understanding, creating, and capturing customer value. A full treatise on selling and sales management can be found in the book of Andris Zolters and Prabhakant Sinha.[14]

KEY CONCEPTS

- *Price sensitivity*—the potential for an individual to notice and react to a price change.
- *Price elasticity*—a measure of the effect of a change in price on the quantity demanded, as measured by (per cent change in quantity/per cent change in price).
- *Customer value*—the buyer's estimation of a product or service's overall capacity to satisfy his or her needs. It can be measured by: an internal engineering assessment; field value-in-use; stated importance ratings; conjoint analysis; choice modelling.
- *Value-in-use*—the maximum amount that the customer should be prepared to pay for the product or service.
- *Skimming price*—a relatively high price charged at the beginning of a product or service's life cycle that is systematically lowered over time.
- *Penetration price*—a relatively low introductory price meant to quickly establish a product or service in the market.
- *Posted price*—the official price listed for public display.
- *Pocket price*—the actual amount of money banked from the sale of a product or service. It is the posted price minus discounts and allowances.

KEY FRAMEWORKS

- *Factors that influence prices*—Figure 9.1
- *The 3Cs of pricing*—customers, costs, competitors
- *SPIN*—Figure 9.5
- *The customer value approach to pricing*—Exhibit 9.1 and Table 9.3 (following)

KEY QUESTIONS

- Does your organization base its pricing decisions on good marketing information (viz. the industry economics, customer segments, marketing strategy, competitors' prices)?
- Do you really understand the psychology of your target customers' reactions to price (e.g. their mental accounting, reactions to odd-price endings, etc.)?
- Are costs and contribution margins known and accepted by the people responsible for setting prices?
- Does the organization have a formal pricing policy to manage pricing?

RECAP

As noted at the beginning of this chapter, price setting is one of the most complicated of all the marketing activities. Because of this, there are no simple and robust rules for pricing. In practice, it is best described as art based on science.

The science of pricing focuses on using research to understand the price sensitivity of individuals and the price elasticity of markets. The art of pricing focuses on setting sensible pricing objectives, understanding the interactions of price with other elements of the marketing mix, and predicting competitor reactions to price changes. Linking both art and science is the management of pricing.

The management of pricing involves:

- Working with the organization's accountants to understand costs and contribution margins.
- Developing a pricing policy and assigning responsibilities to people for setting prices, changing prices, offering discounts and allowances, preparing invoices, etc.
- Making sure that the KPIs of people who have authority for the organization's prices are aligned with the organization's pricing objectives (e.g. do the salespeople's KPIs support the pricing objectives of the brands they sell?)

Table 9.3. Two broad approaches to setting prices

Cost approach	Customer value approach
What are our costs?	Estimate the target customers' VIU.
What mark-up do we need to meet our (financial) target?	Adjust VIU up or down based on the quality of the company's reputation.
How does our price compare with our direct competitors? (Does it need adjustment?)	Compare this price to direct and indirect competitors' prices. (Does it need adjustment?)
Launch the product/service and see who buys.	Can we make the brand at a cost to meet our target profit?

• Establishing measures to monitor how price (*a*) interacts with other elements of the marketing mix (e.g. price and quality), (*b*) supports marketing objectives (e.g. to inhibit a new entrant), and (*c*) drives sales.

The overarching recommendation of this chapter is for marketing managers to approach pricing from a mindset anchored on customer value as opposed to cost. The contrast between these two approaches is shown in Table 9.3 for a new product or service.

NOTES

1. See R. J. Dolan and H. Simon, *Power Pricing* (New York: Free Press, 1996), p. 4.
2. From M. J. Lanning, *Delivering Profitable Value* (Oxford: Capstone, 1998), pp. 26–7.
3. T. Nagle and R. Holden, *The Strategy and Tactics of Pricing* (Upper Saddle River, NJ: Prentice Hall, 1997), pp. 77–93.
4. This example is from G. R. Dowling, G. L. Lilien, R. J. Thomas, and A. Rangaswamy, *Harvesting Customer Value* (State College, Penn State University: Institute for the Study of Business Markets, 2000), chapter 2.
5. This example is from L. Krishnamurthi, 'Pricing Strategies and Tactics', in D. Iacobucci (ed.), *Kellog on Marketing* (New York: John Wiley & Sons, 2001), chapter 12.
6. R. M. Schindler, 'Relative Price Level of 99-Ending Prices: Image Versus Reality', *Marketing Letters*, 12, 3 (2001), 239–47.
7. S. O'Curry, 'Budgeting and Mental Accounting', in P. E. Earl and S. Kemp (eds.), *Consumer Research and Economic Psychology* (Cheltenham: Edward Elgar, 1999), pp. 63–8; R. H. Thaler, *The Winner's Curse* (New York: Free Press, 1992), chapter 9; R. Thaler, 'Mental Accounting and Consumer Choice', *Marketing Science*, 4, 3 (1985), 199–214.

8. This approach is from Dolan and Simon (1996), chapter 2, and Krishnamurthi (2001).

9. See G. L. Lilen and A. Rangaswamy, *Marketing Engineering* (Upper Saddle River, NJ: Prentice Hall, 2003), p. 418.

10. K. Monroe, *Pricing* (New York: McGraw-Hill, 1990), chapter 13.

11. The 'standard' selling approach in these situations contains a series of steps such as: opening the sales call, investigating needs, giving benefits, handling objections, and closing the sale. The rule seems to be that it is OK to be pushy if you can take the order during the call, but if this does not happen, then your pushiness reduces your chance of final success.

12. N. Rackham, *SPIN Selling* (New York: McGraw-Hill, 1988).

13. N. Rackham, *The SPIN Selling Fieldbook* (New York: McGraw-Hill, 1996).

14. A. A. Zoltners, P. Sinha, and G. A. Zoltners, *The Complete Guide to Accelerating Sales Force Performance* (New York: American Management Association, 2001).

CHAPTER

10

Retaining Customers: Customer Value, Satisfaction, and Service Quality

As in Chapter 11, this chapter focuses on programmes to increase the likelihood that a customer will continue to buy the organization's products and services, or to use the more common expressions, to develop customer loyalty or reduce customer churn. The motivations for developing loyalty/ reducing churn are threefold. One is the notion of amortizing the costs of acquiring customers—the longer they are retained, the more likely that the profits from each sale will (eventually) exceed these costs. For example, it may take as long as six years for the premiums on an insurance policy to cover the costs of acquiring that customer. A second motivation is to reduce the volatility of cash flows. A third motivation is to provide a solid foundation for growth. Sometimes, this is called the 'leaky bucket' theory of marketing. If customers can be retained (plugging the leaks in the bucket), then new customers grow the company's customer base (raise the level of water in the bucket). As noted in Chapter 2, all these effects can contribute directly to increasing shareholder equity.

When thinking about customer retention, the two key questions are:

- Who to retain?
- How to retain them?

Part A of the chapter looks at which types of customers to retain. The key issue here is that some customers are likely to be unprofitable. For non-profitable customers to be retained, they must make a contribution to the organization's business performance in another way. Part B then examines how to retain the chosen customers. Three strategies are outlined, namely, customer value, customer satisfaction, and service quality. Chapter 11 looks in detail at CRM as a more holistic approach to customer retention.

PART A

Desirable Customers

When thinking about customer retention, managers often start by using some rudimentary 'back-of-the-envelope' calculations to understand the nature of the problem they face. This section illustrates three such measures, namely, (*a*) the impact of losing/retaining customers on individual customer profitability and growth, (*b*) the lifetime value of customers, and (*c*) the distribution of current customer profitability (i.e. what percentage of current customers are profitable).

Customer Churn

Consider three brands (A, B, C) each with 100,000 customers. Assume that each brand attracts 10,000 new customers each year for ten years. Assume also that brand A has a 10 per cent annual churn, that is, it loses 10 per cent of its customers each year; brand B has 20 per cent churn; and brand C 30 per cent churn. The average length of time that a customer will buy a brand is calculated as the reciprocal of the churn rate. That is, for brand A this is 1/10 per cent or 10 years; brand B 1/20 per cent = 5 years; brand C 1/30 per cent = 3.3 years. These figures are used to help calculate the break-even profitability of customers. For example, if it takes five years of annual premiums to recover the costs of acquiring the customer, then brand A will be profitable, brand B break-even, and brand C a loss-making brand.

If growth is the objective, some simple customer flow calculations reveal that after ten years, brand A will have 100,000 customers, brand B will have 55,368 customers, and brand C will have 36,217 customers—despite each brand adding 10,000 new customers each year. If brand A wanted to double the size of its customer base after ten years, it would need to add about 25,300 new customers per year. (Brand B would need to add slightly more than 42,000 new customers annually.) Thus, without a high retention rate it is very hard to grow the size of the customer base.

Customer Lifetime Value

The definition of a profitable customer is a person or organization whose revenues over time exceed the full costs of attracting and retaining them.

This concept is often called customer lifetime value (CLV). To calculate the CLV, project the net cash flows expected from each customer (segment) over time, and then calculate the present value of that stream of cash flows.[1]

The two key factors in this definition that largely determine customer profitability are:

- How will revenues be allocated to customers?
- How will the full costs be defined and measured?

While most management accounting systems keep track of revenue from different customers, the same cannot be said about the allocation of costs to customers. The allocation of costs to different customers, products, distribution channels, and marketing programmes is a constant source of debate in many organizations. For example, surveys of marketing managers often show that they do not view distribution and general administration costs as falling within their domain.[2] The point here is that, without agreement on the definition of marketing costs and rules for their allocation, it is impossible to work out the full costs of a marketing programme, and, thus, how marketing drives the profitability of various products and customer segments.

Because marketing costs are a large component of the cost structure of many organizations, the organization's accountants need to work with their marketing counterparts to develop better measures of CLV, and the effectiveness of the various marketing programmes (like CRM) designed to enhance CLV. Some of the key issues that are being discussed in the management accounting literature that impact on this task are:[3]

- Activity-based costing that focuses on activities as the fundamental way to assign costs to customers (and often products and distribution channels). Figure 10.1 shows four types of indirect activity costs, namely, A—costs that are spread across all products such as time spent monitoring quality; B—costs spread across all customers such as call centre support; C—costs spread across products and customers such as warranty support; and D—costs necessary to analyse markets such as market research.
- The use of cost hierarchies to assign costs to products and customers—such as pre-sale costs, selling costs, and post-sale costs. Also, how strategic marketing decisions (such as rushing a new product to market) affect up-stream and down-stream costs.
- New ways to classify costs such as value-added costs. That is, consumers see some costs as adding direct value to the product or service (e.g. increasing quality) while for other costs, there is little value added (e.g. the sponsorship of an art exhibition). A related, and just as interesting, concept is value-added time. Exhibit 10.1 provides some examples.

In short, there is a need for a stronger dialogue between marketing management and management accounting.

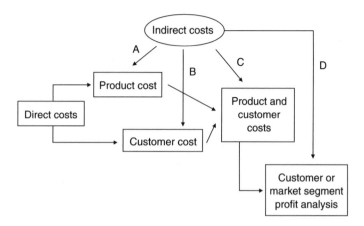

Figure 10.1. Activity based costing

Exhibit 10.1. Value added time (VAT)

Federal Express is a company that attempts to achieve 100 per cent VAT in its customer service. By keeping the express packages moving towards their destinations at all times, it provides a quicker service and greater customer satisfaction.

VAT is the percentage of time in which customer value is being added to the product or service. The following figures show how little this percentage can be for some products and services. For example, while a life-insurance policy application is with the insurance company for ten days for processing (its cycle time), only seven minutes of this elapsed time deals with actually issuing the policy to the customer.

		Cycle time	VAT	%
Life insurance	New policy application	10 days	7 min	0.15
Product package	New design	18 days	2 h	1.4
Bank	Loan approval	2 days	34 min	3.5
Hospital	Patient billing	10 days	3 h	3.8

A company that focuses on speed of response will attempt to remove time delays from its business systems. These are typically caused by jobs waiting in queues, jobs moving from one process to another, inspections, and rework.

Source: J. Davis and T. Devinney, *The Essence of Corporate Strategy* (Sydney: Allen and Unwin, 1997), p. 144.

Because of the complexity of calculating CLV, many organizations resort to very simple forms of analysis. For example, one type of customer profitability analysis is to calculate the contribution (revenue less variable costs) from each customer (or customer segment). This is a relatively poor measure because by ignoring fixed costs, it overestimates customer profitability. As the number of customers grows, so do many costs such as database support, distribution, salesforce, inventory, warehousing, etc.

Another back-of-the-envelope calculation often used is to focus on revenues, and then to classify customers as either high, medium, or low cost to serve. For example, if someone spends approximately $100 per week on food in their supermarket and they stay in the area for an average of ten years, then they have a revenue stream of approximately $50,000. If they make positive recommendations about the supermarket that get other people to shop there, their lifetime value is even higher. Given the way that they actually shop (such as one trip per week or daily visits buying few items), and the types of groceries they buy (such as a heavy emphasis on brands on special), the costs of serving them can be classified as high, medium, or low. Then their profitability can be estimated.

The main rationale for using such simple methods of profitability analysis is that the organization's management accounting system is not sophisticated enough, or sufficiently trusted, to provide better data. Also, these rough calculations are often sufficient to provide a reasonable rank ordering of the profitability of customer segments.

Sitting behind any measure of CLV are a set of factors that drive customer profitability. They refer back to issues covered earlier in this book. There are four aspects of the customer's situation that typically impact on their value to the organization. For example, in B2B markets:[4]

- *Customer economics.* Customers are more sensitive to price when the product is a big part of their business. They are more sensitive to service when it has a big impact on operations. Small businesses and providers of professional services like accountants, lawyers, and retail pharmacists are groups who salespeople say are typically very price sensitive and often reluctant to pay for ancillary services.
- *Buying power.* Big customers (especially government agencies and departments) have greater ability to extract price concessions and service support from vendors. Sometimes, high-profile customers, such as an innovative, lead-user company, may be able to negotiate a better deal because of its opinion-forming role in the market.
- *Buying process and the decision-making unit.* Some organizations have very detailed and time-consuming purchase processes. Organizations

with a formal purchasing department such as hospitals or government agencies and departments are typical. The costs of selling to these customers can be very high—both in terms of the time taken and the supporting documentation required.

- *Competitive activity.* In many mature industries consumers are experienced purchasers and the marketing actions of many vendors have 'trained' them to focus on price. Here, price cutting is common and the provision of 'extra' services becomes expected by buyers.

A good example of the interaction of these four factors occurs in the purchase of routine legal services by banks, insurance firms, and telecommunications suppliers. Each company generally maintains a panel of law firms and shares its work among them. There is a very detailed and time-consuming tendering process in order to win a place on the panel. The firms are evaluated by the buyer's in-house lawyers—an expert decision-making group. They often ask for, and expect to receive, extra services such as having one of the client lawyers seconded to their company for a period of time. As the work is done, the in-house lawyers receive regular information about relative prices and service levels of each firm on the panel. Because of the volume of legal work required by these big companies and the status of being a member of these legal panels, the big law firms are aggressive competitors for this type of work. Margins on this routine work are typically lower than the more high-profile cases reported in the business press.

How Many Customers are Profitable?

To profile their customers, marketers can also look at the distribution of customer profitability. This is often done by assuming that the '80:20 rule' approximates this distribution, namely, 20 per cent of customers account for 80 per cent of the profits. This rule-of-thumb was first noted by the eighteenth century economist Pareto, who observed that a small number of people own most of the money and wealth in a society. Since then, this phenomenon has been found in many other areas. In marketing, it is a common assumption about customer profitability and sales (e.g. 20 per cent of the products also produce 80 per cent of the sales). However, like many such rules-of-thumb, this one turns out to be a good guide in principle but *incorrect* in its application. When companies actually examine the distribution of their customer profitability, they are often surprised by what they find. For example, some big retail banks have found that more than 60 per cent of customers are unprofitable, and that less than 20 per cent provide all the profit.

The crucial issue here is not to assume the 80:20 rule but to *examine the actual distribution of customer profitability* and the reasons for this. For example:

- What types of customers are more/less profitable? How is this related to factors such as ARPU, the size of customer, and their geographic location, etc? (Some B2B companies are finding that it is the mid-sized customer that is the most profitable. The ARPU of small customers is too low relative to the costs of serving them, while the big customers are too demanding—for both more free service and lower prices.)
- Why are the unprofitable customers unprofitable? Is it because some customers are being over-serviced? Is it because the distribution channel the customer is using is too costly? Are the products and services they are buying incorrectly priced? Are price discounts being offered indiscriminately? And so on.

Many retail banks around the world have done this type of analysis and discovered that if they can encourage their unprofitable customers to use cheaper types of service outlets (such as phone banking, Internet banking, and ATM machines), then they become close to break-even profitability. (Exhibit 10.2 outlines some of the key issues involved with migrating customers to a more cost-effective service delivery platform.) Banks and other organizations have also discovered that if they can sell customers a wider range of products and services, APRU increases and churn decreases.

In summary, the above types of analysis help marketers to grapple with the issue of which customers to retain, and which customers should be encouraged to leave. An additional criteria to guide this choice is the customer's strategic fit with the brand or organization's business process and/or corporate position.

Strategically Important Customers

The strategic importance of a customer can be looked at in a variety of ways. One is to serve customers who have a natural fit with the organization's or the brand's desired position and customer value proposition. These customers should be relatively easy to attain and retain. Another dimension of strategic importance is to focus on customers who are important in their market. There may be the opportunity to 'rent' the reputation of these customers in the company's marketing communications. For example, many professional service firms list their high-profile clients in their corporate

Exhibit 10.2. The challenge of moving customers from A to B

Customer profitability analysis and the opportunities made available by new forms of technology have stimulated many organizations to try to migrate their less profitable current customers to cheaper service platforms. For example, airlines are encouraging Internet booking, electronic ticketing, and self-service check-in; banks are encouraging the use of ATMs and Internet banking; while some US grocery stores are using self-checkout lanes.

What these organizations are discovering is that many customers do not want to move to a new mode of service delivery. Some of the key reasons for this reluctance are:

- While the new service platforms may offer enhanced value over time, many are not reliable when they are first launched, and, thus, they actually degrade service quality.
- The move can require learning new information and engaging in new behaviours that often involves high technology.
- In order to be successful, the customer has to take more responsibility for both the service delivery and recovery after a service failure.
- Customers are uncertain about the reasons for change, new benefits to them, risks involved, and the process of changing.

The key to moving customers across service platforms is segmentation. That is, form current customers into migration segments based on factors such as their prior experience using other forms of self-service technologies in other situations; their needs for personal 'hand-holding' service; the length of time they have been a customer and, thus, their service expectations; their propensity to accept change; etc. This analysis will reveal that some types of customer will be more susceptible than others. These can be targeted for the initial migration, and they can then be used as examples of success for the other more reluctant groups.

brochures. Some consumer brands use celebrities to help 'sell' their products. A third criterion is to retain customers who will actively promote the organization or the brand. These are often referred to as opinion leaders. For example, in the world of women's fashion, opinion leadership can be both verbal (talking about fashion with one's peer group) and visual (look what the beautiful people are wearing). An important criterion, often overlooked, is to retain customers who will help define the future of the company. For example, banks often fight to open a branch office on the campus of a university because the poor student customers of today have a good chance of evolving into the high net worth customers of tomorrow. Finally, some customers are good to retain, even if they might not be profitable, because they can provide insight into how the next generation of products should be formulated. As noted earlier in the book, these customers are variously called innovators and/or lead users.

Many big organizations whose business is built around a continuous-production process (such as hotels, car manufacturers, and steel mills) have another group of strategically important customers. These are the high-volume customers who provide the base load for the 'factory'. For many car manufacturers, the car rental companies are one such customer. For some hotels, they are the tour groups.

In summary, each customer (segment) should be profiled by its profitability and strategic importance. Then, depending on the nature of the organization's operations, other factors can be added to this list to determine which customers to try to retain and which to lose.

KEY CONCEPTS

- *Customer churn*—how many customers a brand or organization loses each period of time (often a year).

- *Customer lifetime value*—the difference between customer revenues over their lifetime and the full costs of attracting, servicing and retaining them.

- *Value-added costs*—costs that add direct customer value to the product or service.

- *Value-added time*—the percentage of time customer value is being created as a product or service is produced.

KEY FRAMEWORKS

- *Activity-based costing*—Figure 10.1

- *Distribution of customer profitability*—The percentages of customers who fall into the categories of high, medium, and low profitability, break-even, and unprofitable

KEY QUESTIONS

- Does the organization produce regular measures of customer churn, customer loyalty, customer lifetime value, and a distribution of customer profitability? If things are not measured, they are unlikely to be well managed.

- How are costs allocated to customers (and marketing programmes)? Does this form of cost allocation help to identify desirable and undesirable customers (and marketing programmes)?
- What percentage of the cycle time of product/service production is value-added time?
- Has the organization identified its strategically important customers, and are the reasons for their classification known and accepted?

Having established some guidelines for selecting the most desirable customers to retain, the focus now shifts to how to keep them.

PART B

How to Retain Desirable Customers

This part of the chapter looks at three approaches that organizations use to retain their customers:

1. Offer better customer value than their competitors.
2. Develop programmes to enhance customer satisfaction.
3. For service organizations—enhance service quality.

Customer Value

> Make a better mousetrap and the world will beat a path to your door.
>
> Ralph Waldo Emerson

By far the simplest and most straightforward customer retention strategy is to offer *superior* value to customers. Superior value drives a number of desirable outcomes such as attaining more customers, customer retention, high ARPU, loyalty, and high market share. To offer superior customer value, however, often means that considerable effort has to be directed to:

- understanding the latent and expressed needs of customers;
- improving the product or service—quality, features, availability, etc.;
- reducing costs in order to reduce prices.

In many cases, decisions involving improving the basics of a product or service are beyond the mandate of the marketing team. This is especially true when products designed and manufactured overseas are sent to a branch office for sale. For example, the world's big electronics companies (like Canon, Hewlett-Packard, Philips, Siemens, and Sony) practice this form of global marketing in many of their smaller markets. The basic product is designed for the world market, and minor adaptations to things like the power system are the only concessions to local market conditions.

When the basic offering to customers cannot be changed and it is sold at a similar price and level of perceived quality to its competitors, marketers often start a desperate search for tactics to develop customer loyalty. One such tactic that is discussed in the next chapter is to link the product or service to a customer loyalty scheme. Another is to provide some type of additional service with the product. For example, new cars are sold with a service warranty; hotel accommodation is provided with free airport transfers, etc. The idea here is that the service component of the offer to customers can in some way compensate for a 'me-too' product.

What both these strategies (a better CVP and additional services) are designed to do is to increase the level of customer satisfaction in the hope of developing loyalty and reducing churn.

Customer Satisfaction

I am easily satisfied with the very best.

Winston Churchill

Customer satisfaction is thought to be a major driver of customer retention. It is also thought to contribute to the enhancement of a brand's evaluation, repeat-purchase intentions, and positive WOM communications. While claims have been made that satisfaction lowers price sensitivity and leads to increased purchase volumes, these effects depend on the type of customer (e.g. are they price sensitive and do they need more of the product). Thus, the reliability of these last two marketing generalizations is considerably less than the first three mentioned here. This, in turn, suggests that each organization use research to calibrate the flow-on effects of (dis)satisfaction.

Another claim made is that customer satisfaction automatically leads to customer loyalty. This suggests that satisfied customers will not defect to a competitor. Research and casual observation suggest that this is also not a reliable generalization. For example, Chapter 4 outlined how many customers buy a portfolio of brands in the same product category. This phenomenon was called multi-brand buying and/or polygamous loyalty. Thus, customers can be satisfied and loyal to variety of competing brands at the same time. Customers can also be satisfied with a product or service and switch to another brand because:

- a new and better brand enters the market;
- the brand is temporarily unavailable; or
- the customer's circumstances change and the old brand is no longer available (e.g. relocation to another city or country), or it is no longer needed (e.g. the children have all left home).

Thus, customer satisfaction is an important determinant of customer retention, but it should not be considered the Holy Grail. However, what can be said with a good deal of confidence is that the more satisfied customers an organization has, the better. (This is, however, a rather self-evident statement.)

Customer satisfaction can be formally defined as a person's felt state that results from a product or service's perceived performance relative to its expected performance. This definition is grounded in the expectancy-disconfirmation theory of customer satisfaction.[5] Its key components are *perceived performance* and *expectations*. If performance falls below expectations the customer is dissatisfied. If performance meets expectations, the result is satisfaction, and if performance exceeds expectations, the customer is very satisfied and sometimes may be delighted.

The definition of customer satisfaction alerts marketers to consider three issues in order to develop programmes to enhance satisfaction, namely:

- how do customers define (perceived) performance;
- how are expectations formed;
- what are the costs incurred when expectations are not met, and what are the gains for exceeding expectations.

Defining Perceived Performance

Customers typically gauge the performance of a product or service against a set of criteria similar to those they used when evaluating whether or not to buy it in the first place. These evaluations will be in terms of the three broad customer values discussed extensively throughout this book, namely, functional performance (e.g. the product does the job expected of it), economic performance (e.g. it was a good buy), and psychological and social performance (e.g. I feel good when using the brand).

In many cases, marketers want to know how the features of the product, and its accompanying service, drive these three customer values. When this level of detail is required, customers are asked to rate the *product* on a range of features. These will depend on the product in question, but will generally include: performance (how well it works), design (its ease of use), 'packaging' (its presentation), fit and finish (the look and feel of the product), conformance with specifications (was it all there), reliability (does it work properly each time it is used), durability (how long it will last), and serviceability (is it easy to service). For *personal services*, the main evaluation criteria are: empathy (does the person receive caring, individualized attention), responsiveness (is the service prompt and timely), competence (is the job done correctly), reliability (is the service dependable and are problems solved), assurance (the knowledge and courtesy of employees and their ability to convey trust and confidence), and tangibles (are the physical facilities, equipment, and the appearance of people appropriate). For *self-services*, criteria such as the following need to be considered: is the interface technology easy to use, reliable, and available when and where needed? Do people perceive that the savings inherent in self-service result in lower prices or a better resulting experience? Also, does the technology interface 'recognize' the customer? For example, ATM machines give every user the same set of options—even though the bank knows that a customer probably does not have access to many of them.

One issue that is often troublesome for many marketers is understanding how their customers *perceive* the features of a product and service. Consider the feature of quality. Many companies have spent a fortune implementing TQM programmes and gaining quality assurance certificates (e.g. from the International Organization for Standardization—ISO), but have been unable to get a (financial) return on their improved quality.[6] Quality has been engineered into the product and certified, but the customers cannot 'see' the quality difference. Often, the reason for this is because competitors also have the same certified quality. Another reason is due to poor marketing communication.

Communicating quality can be done in a number of different ways, not all of which are obvious or intuitive. Consider the following:

- Communicate quality in the advertising positioning slogan—Mercedes Benz 'engineered like no other car'; BMW 'the ultimate driving machine'.
- Link the product or service to a reputable quality assurance monitor, such as ISO or the J.D. Power and Associates customer satisfaction index—Lexus built its US business around the Power surveys.
- Understand the 'signals' of quality used by customers—the sound from a car exhaust pipe signals engine power; the sound of the car door closing signals build quality; a higher price signals better conformance quality (less variation across product features) and performance quality

(you get more); suds means cleaning power for detergents; dark beer is 'stronger'.

- Ensure that the 'packaging' reflects the quality—in Australia, Lexus salespeople wear a suit; premium beer is not sold in cans; and premium wine is not sold in flagons or casks.
- Offer a warranty—'satisfaction or your money back—no questions asked'; guarantee the resale value of the product (another tactic used by Lexus when it launched its cars).
- Sell through quality distributors—they generally provide a better atmosphere and the product can 'rent' their image; or sell from an up-market location—the top professional service firms often locate in the most prestigious part of the 'city'.

Forming Expectations

The second half of the customer satisfaction equation is expectations. This is the target against which performance is measured. The key questions here are how are they formed, can they be managed, and how high are they usually set?

People form their expectations using information from a number of different sources, namely:

- What the organization says to expect, through its advertising, salespeople, public relations, and the layout of its service facilities. This can be explicit—a bank advertisement saying that nobody will wait more than five minutes in the queue; and implicit—the number of check-in counters and the queuing area at the airport.
- What competitors say to expect from themselves and others. This may be communicated using comparative advertisements.
- The customer's past buying experience and their polygamous loyalty. The last encounter with a product or service is often the single best predictor of what to expect on the next occasion. Also, the amount of experience with a set of products and services in a category (or industry for B2B customers) is a powerful benchmark against which the performance of each new product and service is evaluated.
- What other people are saying—friends, associates, journalists, and rumours.
- The reputation of the organization. For example, when people are dealing with 'the government', they will often lower their expectations relative to the same product or service provided from a private organization.

Some of these sources of information are controllable by the organization and others are not. Notwithstanding this fact, marketers should do everything they can to set the level of expectations that their organization can meet. When expectations are set too low, the company runs the risk of not attracting enough customers. When set too high, the risk is not being able to meet them. This important issue is discussed further in the next section.

The management of expectations is often a primary role of the organization's advertising. When the Accenture consulting firm signs off all its advertising with the slogan 'Innovation delivered', this is what their clients come to expect. When Qantas says that it embodies 'The Spirit of Australia' then passengers expect a certain 'Australianness' in the way that service is delivered.

To manage expectations when a zero-defect product or service is undeliverable, many organizations institute a policy of 'no unpleasant surprises'. As the airlines have (finally) discovered, a little bit of timely information about why a flight has been delayed can reduce the anxiety of travellers. A variation of the 'no unpleasant surprises' policy is often used by managers who deal directly with CEOs and Board members. Here, the policy is 'no surprises'—pleasant or unpleasant. (Setting the expectations of other managers is one of the most difficult internal marketing tasks managers face in their jobs.)

The final issue to consider is how high expectations are usually set. This is determined by three factors. One is a cultural norm. For example, in Japan, the customer is elevated to quite a high level in society and the expectation is that very high service levels are the norm. This stands in stark contrast to many other countries. A second factor that sets the level of customer expectations is the position of the product or service. Labels such as 'first class', '5-star', 'luxury', 'premier', 'budget', 'economy', and 'standard' are all designed to set the level of expectations. A third factor is the posted price. Is it at the top, middle, or bottom of the range of similar (quality) products and services? For example, the price of business class seats for many of the long-haul airlines can differ by up to 50 per cent. Thus, there is cheap, average, and expensive business class—and the service varies accordingly.

Falling Short or Exceeding Expectations

A much promoted customer service initiative is to try to 'delight the customer'. As noted in the definition of customer satisfaction, this would entail exceeding, as opposed to meeting, customer expectations. Customer

Exhibit 10.3. Delighting the customer

Many consultants argue that the best way to form a strong relationship with customers is to consistently delight them. Delighting customers is done by exceeding their expectations. As any primary school teacher will tell you, this is a dangerous strategy. Here is the reason why. (Grandparents should also please take note.)

When you exceed the expectations of a customer, what is very likely to happen is that the person raises their expectations about what the next service encounter will deliver. In other words, you have clearly raised the expectations regarding what you can and will deliver. If this better standard is not delivered next time, disappointment may follow.

If you want to keep delighting customers, look at the task you have set yourself. To delight them you have to keep exceeding their ever increasing expectations. For most organizations, this is actually quite difficult to do. It strains both their customer-contact people and their business systems.

Delighting customers is wonderful rhetoric. It is a commendable goal. (It is also a good consultant sales pitch.) But it is difficult to sustain without some clever business process innovation. (And as parents discover when they pick their children up from the grandparents, delighted and excited children can be a real challenge to manage.)

The alternative strategy to delighting customers was stated by a senior executive of Du Pont:

'I am not out to delight my customers. I just want to become indispensable to them so that they can't live without me.'[7]

delight is thought to be a guaranteed way of achieving very high customer satisfaction. The mantra of 'delight the customer' is worth examining for two reasons. First, as outlined in Exhibit 10.3, it is a somewhat dangerous strategy for most organizations to adopt. Second, it suggests that managers consider the more general issue about the shape of the response function of customer satisfaction.

Figure 10.2 shows some research that looks at the issue of the gains and losses from exceeding or falling short of expectations.[8] It shows that satisfaction is not a linear function of (dis)confirming the customer's expectations, and that falling below expectations is more serious than the gains possible from exceeding expectations. The research also shows that experienced customers have a (slightly) different reaction than inexperienced customers. For the experienced customers, there is a small 'flat spot' when expectations are exceeded by a small amount. That is, there has to be a significant

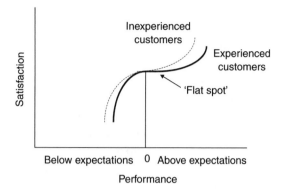

Figure 10.2. The gains and losses from disconfirming customer expectations

'surprise' before this group's satisfaction is raised above that expected. Thus, for a manager, delighting customers is not as important as making sure that performance does not fall below expectations—and if it does, then having a service recovery programme in place to limit the damage.

Measuring Satisfaction

There are four main reasons why organizations measure customer satisfaction:

- For diagnostic purposes in order to drive improvements and to identify the factors that matter to the customer.
- To reward and encourage the customer service staff.
- For benchmarking purposes—against competitors and across the units of a multi-divisional business (e.g. which branches are better than others).
- It makes the respondents feel good. For example, sometimes when a customer is mildly dissatisfied, having the opportunity to record this feeling in a formal communication to the organization is a cathartic process.

When organizations set out to measure customer satisfaction, they are presented with a range of alternatives, and a variety of research firms willing to help. Each measurement technique has its strengths and weaknesses that depend on how the data are collected and how they will be used. For example, customer complaint schemes are good for highlighting areas of dissatisfaction. Interviewing lost customers can help to identify the factors that triggered the customers to switch to a competitor. Focus groups are good for understanding the emotional aspects of performance and expectations. Mystery shoppers are good for uncovering the strong and weak points experienced when buying the company's and competitors' products and services. Customer satisfaction surveys are good for calibrating the overall distribution of satisfaction and dissatisfaction among customers. If the items from these surveys are analysed in terms of both their importance and performance, this can help managers to identify if they are under-performing in important areas and/or over-performing in unimportant areas.

One of the best known customer satisfaction surveys is the J.D. Power and Associates Customer Satisfaction Index for US automobile companies. The index is constructed by weighting respondents' scores on a wide range of factors relating to a vehicle's ownership experience (such as dealer service, the finish of the car, its reliability, quality, etc.), and combining them into an overall index score. Brands that score well on the overall index or selected aspects of it often refer to their J.D. Power's ratings in their advertising (http://www.jdpa.com).

Customer self-reports are often used to measure changes in service quality and customer satisfaction at different points in time. However, managers should be warned that measuring these types of change is quite difficult to do in a valid and reliable way. The main reason for this is that many service quality improvement programmes create a new service culture that needs to be measured with a new set of performance attributes. Thus, simply comparing the same set of measures at two points in time can provide a misleading picture of what, if anything, has changed.[9]

A final issue to consider is how the results from customer satisfaction surveys that form part of a person's KPIs can affect his or her behaviour. In these circumstances, the measures can be used as much as a mechanism to punish people for poor performance as to reward him or her for good performance. Being evaluated against customer satisfaction numbers can motivate people to manipulate the measures. For example, a partner in a professional service firm who had received an average of 3 on a 5-point scale from a group of clients suggested to a new client that the average score for the service that was being offered by his firm and its competitors was 4. He then instructed the new client to rate his service as a 4 if they thought it was average for the industry and 5 if they thought it was better. His average rating improved to 4 with no change in service quality.[10]

In summary, the key issue with customer satisfaction is to get excited about it, but not so excited that its pursuit and measures distort the organization's

culture. Few organizations have the will or the ability to fully satisfy every customer all the time. This is especially true for large organizations that serve a
wide range of customers (such as an airline, bank, hotel, telecommunications
company, or government agency). As noted in Chapter 2, there is often a fine
line between being customer focused and being customer compelled. There
has to be a balance between the following two clever-sounding customer satisfaction policies:

> Rule #1—the customer is always right.
> Rule #2—if the customer is wrong, see Rule #1.[11]
> And
> The customer is Number 2 (employees are Number 1).[12]

Service Quality

In order to effectively monitor customer service and consequently deliver
high-quality service, it is important to develop a model of service delivery.
Organizations like Disney, Southwest Airlines, and McDonald's have successfully differentiated their services from their competitors based on their
quality. Service quality is, therefore, of particular importance to many organizations in their search to gain a competitive advantage. As noted earlier,
service quality, or the lack of it, results from a comparison of perceived with
expected performance.[13] This section looks at the following areas important to customer service delivery:

- how organizations deliver service;
- how customers evaluate service;
- identifying service quality gaps.[14]

How Organizations Deliver Service

Figure 10.3 summarizes a range of factors that influence how organizations
deliver service to customers. The process starts with the culture and management orientation of the firm. A customer-focused orientation will have
a direct affect on the management of customer expectations and the set of
systems developed to deliver customer service. For example, some years
ago, a well-known computer company in Australia thought that its PCs
were so technically good (both hardware and software) that service and

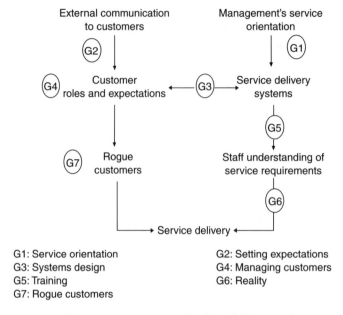

G1: Service orientation
G3: Systems design
G5: Training
G7: Rogue customers

G2: Setting expectations
G4: Managing customers
G6: Reality

Figure 10.3. How organizations deliver service

support should play a secondary role. They allocated few people to the customer support function and because these staff were often overworked, they periodically stopped answering their telephones. (This company demonstrated a product focus and steadily lost market share.)

The next task of management is to design and develop a service system that:

- meets the expectations of customers for this type of service;
- if possible, differentiates the organization from its competitors;
- is capable of being delivered by the business systems of the organization;
- delivers this service by staff who feel socially comfortable and enthusiastic.

When such a system has been designed, then managers need to set the expectations of customers as to how the service will be delivered, its quality, and the role that the customer must play for the service encounter to be successful. For example, when visiting a dentist the customer's role is to sit still and keep one's mouth open (and grunt occasionally when the dentist asks a question). On an airline, customers are expected to arrive early, board in an orderly manner, consider fellow passengers when eating and moving around, etc.

All of these aspects combine to produce the actual service a customer receives. The staff have to be confident of the organization's commitment and ability to deliver promised customer services, and they have to be given the authority to make decisions in cases where customers present them with non-standard requests.

There are a number of areas in the delivery process where organizations need to be particularly careful to ensure that service is delivered to the standards expected. The potential 'gaps' in service delivery are shown in Figure 10.3.

Gap 1 deals with the customer focus and service orientation of the organization. Sometimes problems occur because different parts of the organization deliver a different quality of service. For example, customer-contact employees 'over promise' and back-room employees 'under deliver'. Another potential gap can appear when an organization does not consistently deliver a style and quality of service. For example, sometimes the customer really is King or Queen, and the orientation of staff and the service system are designed around a model of *skilled servitude*—responsiveness, customization, and empathy from skilled and experienced staff. In other situations, customers are regarded as a distraction to what employees see as the major function of the organization. Many public sector organizations such as metropolitan transport, police, roads and traffic authorities, and post offices have been accused of having a limited service orientation. They are often designed around a *service factory* model—efficiency, consistency, cost-effectiveness, and service delivered through standardized and tightly controlled systems.

Gap 2 occurs when the organization fails to communicate what to expect from the service encounter, especially during times of change. Consider the MBA programmes in many business schools. Years ago, faculty considered that students were akin to products. The coursework and experience during the programme moulded a certain type of (tough) graduate. In more recent times, as many types of organizations developed a customer focus, students came to the programme expecting to be treated as customers. Often, customer-focused students and product-focused faculty had a clash of ideology. An alternative service model is the 'learning partnership'. Here, both faculty and students have clear roles—the faculty guide students through an up-to-date curriculum and the students take prime responsibility for their own learning.

Gap 3 focuses on system design. The crucial issues here are:

• can the system consistently deliver its desired quality level;
• can it cope with peak demand;
• can it cope when parts of the system unexpectedly break down?

With a complex system such as an airline, the service design requirements can be formidable. Also, with large numbers of customers, it is inevitable that many customers will be unhappy with (some aspect of) the service they receive. For example, consider a large airline like Qantas. For every passenger flown, there are a number of service encounters at: check in, baggage handling, in-flight service. If we assume a minimum of five service encounters for each passenger, then for every one million passenger journeys flown there are five million possible service failure points. If Qantas could achieve a level of 99.9 per cent service excellence, they will still upset 5000 people per one million passenger journeys. Hence, it is easy to see why a complaints handling department, and a set of formal procedures for dealing with complaining customers, is an essential part of the design of all large-scale service delivery systems.

The fourth potential failure point—Gap 4—occurs when customers do not know their role in the service delivery process (such as when a child first visits the dentist or a hairdresser). It can also occur when organizations do things that change customer expectations relative to what the organization can deliver. A good example of this occurs when a company announces that it will retrench Xooo employees, but customers should not expect any fall in service levels.

Gap 5 focuses on training. Companies like Disney put their customer contact people through extensive training prior to any contact with a paying customer. This training involves basic procedures, deportment, and 'attitude'. Other organizations believe that 'on the job training' is the best (and cheapest). You encounter this form of training when you are served by someone with 'trainee' on their name badge. When an organization proclaims that it delivers great service, then training staff on the customers can be a dangerous strategy—most customers do not like it even though they are too polite to complain. The worst form of this type of on-the-job training is to put the new staff behind the 'enquiries counter'. Here, you have matched the most inexperienced staff with the most difficult customers—and both tend to dislike the experience.

Gap 6 occurs when one or more of the following occur:

- staff do not understand or cannot use the service delivery system; and/or
- staff have a bad day.

Either of these can cause the delivered service to fall short of customer expectations.

Gap 7 in Figure 10.3 focuses on the issue of the rogue customer. Organizations often encounter people who push their systems and customer service people to the limit of (and beyond) their tolerance. These 'customers from hell' (as they are often referred to by staff) do not 'fit' the organization's preferred service delivery systems. Some can be extremely disruptive and attract the attention of the media, causing negative publicity. A formal set of procedures for handling these customers needs to be established to manage these situations.

Delivering quality service is like a two-sided coin. Now we look at the other side, namely, how customers evaluate the service they receive.

How Customers Evaluate Service

Figure 10.4 inverts the priorities in Figure 10.3 and replaces management's intentions with the actual service experienced by the customer. This analysis produces two additional potential problem areas, or 'gaps', as shown in the Figure 10.4.

As outlined earlier, perceived service quality is the difference between expectations and actual performance. Also, after each service encounter, customers typically update their expectations about what to expect during the next service encounter. Thus, Gap 8 is a moving target that only continuous research can track.

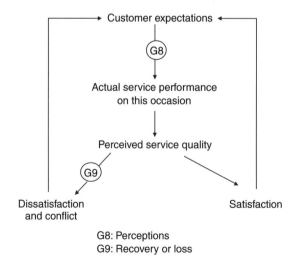

Figure 10.4. How customers evaluate service

Research indicates that when customers are satisfied with a service encounter, they tend to:

- speak favourably about the service and the organization that delivered it—if the opportunity arises;
- use the service again—if the need arises;
- think more favourably about the organization that delivered the service (i.e. enhance their overall evaluation).

Notice that the first two outcomes are presented as contingent outcomes. That is, customers who receive good service, or even delightful service, do not automatically run around broadcasting their satisfaction to anybody within earshot. People simply do not have the time or interest to become outspoken advocates for every organization that serves them well. However, if a relevant situation arises—such as being asked by a friend or acquaintance—they will probably respond with good WOM. Many service quality consultants over-claim that positive WOM is an automatic outcome of good service when they are touting for work.

Gap 9 occurs when customers are dissatisfied. They may:

- complain to the people responsible for the service or the organization's formal system for handling complaints;
- complain to a public authority, industry association, or the media;
- speak unfavourably about the organization and/or the service encounter;
- stop using the service, if they have other available options;
- downgrade their overall evaluation of the organization.

There have been some interesting studies about how customers react to bad service. Many have been conducted by consultants and lack the scrutiny of peer review. Hence, the findings are difficult to generalize. Notwithstanding this, some of these findings have entered marketing folklore. For example, it is not uncommon to hear that one dissatisfied customer will tell up to twenty other people about their bad experience. If this were universally true, it would not take long for a company's overall evaluation to be critically damaged. What is more likely to happen is that *some* customers who receive bad service will broadcast their displeasure. These are likely to be the more experienced customers who can make better judgements about the service they should have received, and the reasons for its failure. Less experienced and/or less self-confident customers are often less vehement in their damnation of poor service. (Some will even blame themselves.)

In summary, Figures 10.3 and 10.4 identify nine potential problem areas in the delivery of quality service. These 'gaps' represent potential management hazards that can largely be overcome by astute forward planning and periodic review of the service performance of the organization.

KEY CONCEPTS

- *Customer satisfaction*—the extent to which a product or service's perceived performance matches a customer's expectations. If expectations are not met, the customer is dissatisfied. If expectations are met, the customer is satisfied. If expectations are exceeded (by a significant amount), the customer is delighted.
- *Service model: Skilled servitude*—individually customized service delivered with responsiveness and empathy usually by skilled and experienced people.
- *Service model: Service factory*—service delivered through standardized and tightly controlled systems.

KEY FRAMEWORKS

- *Gap model of service delivery*—Figures 10.3 and 10.4

KEY QUESTIONS

- Is yours really a better mousetrap? Or do you have to rely on other efforts to gain loyalty and reduce churn?
- Do you try to delight customers? If so, is this really possible over the long term?
- Do you know how target customers form their expectations and at what level these are set?
- Do you try to actively manage the expectations of target customers?
- Is customer satisfaction regularly measured? For what purposes?
- When analysing customer service, are praise and complaints motivated by particular incidents, particular people, your delivery mechanism, customer expectations, or random events? (Responses to fixing problems will differ depending on the source of the dissatisfaction.)

RECAP

Retaining desirable customers provides the foundation for growth and long-term profitability. The single best strategy to retain customers is to offer a better customer value proposition than competitors. Sometimes this will be based on a better quality and/or lower-priced product or service. In other cases it will involve following guidelines such as:

- Create a customer database and IT system to provide a comprehensive, real-time picture of the customer.
- Set customer expectations high enough to attract target customers, but not so high that they cannot be achieved—consistently.
- Always deliver the promises made by the people and the communications of the organization. That is, 'Walk your talk'.
- When problems occur, fix them quickly.

NOTES

1. For a review of various approaches to calculating CLV, see P. D. Berger and N. I. Nasr, 'Customer Lifetime Value: Marketing Models and Applications', *Journal of Interactive Marketing*, 12, 1 (1998), 17–30.
2. See, for example, G. Foster and M. Gupta, 'Marketing, Cost Management and Management Accounting', *Journal of Management Accounting Research*, 6 (Fall 1994), 43–77.
3. Foster and Gupta (1994).
4. B. P. Shapiro, V. K. Rangan, R. T. Moriarty, and E. B. Ross, 'Manage Customers for Profits not Just Sales', *Harvard Business Review* (September–October, 1987), 101–8.
5. R. L. Oliver, *Satisfaction: A Behavioural Perspective on the Consumer* (Boston: Richard D. Irwin/McGraw-Hill, 1997).
6. A survey by A. T. Kearney claims that in Britain, less than half of all TQM programmes show any demonstrable results at all. Reported in 'An Inside Job', the *Economist* (15 July 2000), p. 61.
7. J. Weber with L. Bernier and E. Updike, 'For Du Pont Christmas in April', *Business Week* (24 April 1995), p. 130.
8. S. Burton, S. Sheather, and J. Roberts, 'An Exploratory Approach to Study the Effects of Disconfirmation on Customer Satisfaction', Australian Graduate School of Management, Working Paper 97–001 (January 1997).
9. For a review of the issues involved in using self-report measures to calibrate changes in service, see G. R. Dowling, 'The Alpha, Beta Gamma Approach to Measuring Change and its Use for Interpreting the Effectiveness of Service Quality Programs', *Australian Journal of Management*, 26, 1 (2001), 55–67.
10. The industry average was 4, but this manager was performing below his colleagues. What he did was to provide an artificially high (for him) anchor point for the rating scale. When most clients adopted this higher anchor point, his average rose. Very clever—but very naughty!

11. Stu Leonard, US supermarket owner.

12. H. F. Rosenbluth and D. McFerrin Peters, *The Customer Comes Second* (New York: William Morrow, 1992).

13. For a review of the original models of service quality and the more significant updates, see M. K. Brady and J. J. Cronin, 'Some New Thoughts on Conceptualising Perceived Service Quality: A Hierarchial Approach', *Journal of Marketing*, 65, 3 (2001), 34–49.

14. This 'gap-type' framework was originally developed by A. Parasuraman, V. A. Zeithaml, and L. L. Berry, 'A Conceptual Model of Service Quality and its Implications for Future Research', *Journal of Marketing*, 49, 4 (1985), 41–50.

11

Retaining Customers: Customer Relationship Management

As noted in Chapter 1, Customer Relationship Management (CRM) is one of the new approaches to marketing management and a hot topic for consultants. It is premised on the belief that developing a relationship with customers is the best way to get them to become loyal. And, it is argued, loyal customers are more profitable than non-loyal customers. Support for this proposition has been eloquently advanced by Frederick Reichheld and consultants such as Peppers and Rogers and PriceWaterhouseCoopers.[1] CRM has also been the driving force behind the introduction of many customer loyalty programmes.

The work of the consultants suggests that a company can achieve significant increases in profits (e.g. 25–50 per cent) from only small improvements (e.g. 5 per cent) in customer retention rates. (Again, this is research that is difficult to verify because little of it has been peer reviewed before publication.) Hence, the strategy is to engineer increased customer retention, often with strategies labelled as CRM or Customer Loyalty Marketing. Research indicates that these schemes are generally liked by customers.[2] Anecdotal evidence suggests that they are seldom fully costed when presented to the general managers who are asked to fund them.

This chapter takes a critical look at CRM. It does so because these programmes are gaining in prominence and there are concerns that they are now being implemented in areas where their cost-effectiveness is questionable. The section on 'How CRM programmes are supposed to work' reviews the origins of CRM programmes and in doing so illustrates many of the conditions required for CRM to be successful. The section on 'How CRM does work—B2B' reviews CRM programmes in B2B markets. This is where CRM has a long history of success. The section on 'How CRM does work—B2C' reviews CRM programmes in B2C markets. Here, the potential success of these programmes is more problematic. The section on 'Customer loyalty programmes' then examines customer loyalty programmes—something that many people belong to, but about which there is growing controversy regarding their success. The final sections of this chapter focus on the key question facing marketing managers, namely, are CRM programmes likely to be a cost-effective use of marketing funds—relative to the programmes outlined in the previous chapters?

How CRM Programmes are Supposed to Work

CRM had its origins in two unrelated places. One was driven by technology—most often developed in the United States.[3] Under the direction of marketers, information technology and statistical algorithms are used to capture data about customers and to use this to increase the efficiency and effectiveness of selling what the organization currently makes—a classic push-marketing strategy. CRM systems such as call centres, websites, e-mail, customer service and support teams, and loyalty programmes are used to manage the relationship with customers. Good examples of this approach can be found at http://www.cyberdialogue.com; http://www.siebel.com.

Database-driven CRM has claimed significant improvements in

- identifying profitable and unprofitable customers;
- increasing the efficiency and effectiveness of direct marketing;[i] and
- increasing customer satisfaction.

However, critics argue that

- gathering an extensive amount of information about customers ('a 360 degree view' as it is sometimes called) raises concerns about privacy;
- managers concentrate less on what customers really want (their latent and expressed needs) and more on what the data patterns suggest their organization should be able to sell them; and
- relationships seldom develop beyond satisfaction into rapport because they start with the seller 'targeting' customers and then attempting to 'capture' them.[4]

---

[i] For example, the average response to an unsolicited direct mail marketing offer is only about 2 per cent, and seems to be falling.

CRM programmes have also experienced some significant implementation problems. Examples include the high turnover rates of staff in call centres, the frequent cost blowouts associated with constructing a data warehouse, problems implementing new information technology systems, and the high cost involved in designing a new information architecture to support more customized selling. Forrester Research has estimated that implementation of a fully configured CRM programme can cost between $60–100 million and requires at least two years to bring into full operation. Also, the Gartner Group, a leading technology research and advisory firm, has estimated that more than 50 per cent of all CRM projects do not show a positive financial return.[5]

Figure 11.1 presents a snapshot of how (database-driven) CRM is designed to work. The top sequence of effects shows the customer relationship path to success. Depending on the type of product (e.g. high or low involvement), this relationship can be based on an affective association ('I really like this brand'), or it may simply be the result of convenience and self-interest ('There is nothing special about the brand, but it's always available when I need it'). The bottom effect in Figure 11.1 involves mining the customer database to identify customers who may be susceptible to buying more of the company's product. When such customers are identified, a cross-selling programme is often implemented. *Cross-selling* seeks to sell additional products or services to customers who already buy something from the organization. For example, when the banks joined forces with

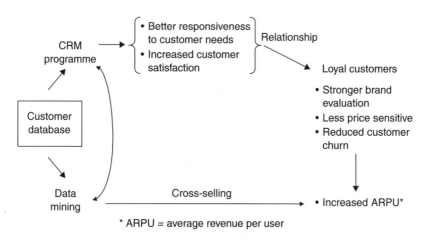

Figure 11.1. How it is hoped B2C CRM will work

insurance companies they often tried to sell their home mortgage customers home insurance, contents insurance, loss of income insurance, and life insurance. Together, the outcomes in the figure have stimulated many companies (both manufacturers and retailers) to invest in creating a database-driven CRM system.

The other place CRM developed was in B2B marketing. In Scandinavia and northern Europe, the Industrial Marketing and Purchasing Group has been studying three types of relationships, namely:

1. programmes that are aimed at customer retention (similar to those in Chapter 10);
2. programmes that involve special supply and delivery arrangements with key suppliers;
3. relational partnering programmes that are designed to leverage the resources of other businesses (such as the co-development of new products).[6]

The overall aim of B2B relationships is to help both firms develop a sustainable competitive advantage in their marketplace.

Relationships between businesses are typically based on trust, service, and the effective coordination of doing business between the parties. They rely for their success on both parties having their economic incentives aligned with each other (more on this in Chapter 13), the structural ties between companies (such as the electronic exchange of data), and the personal relationships among managers. Here, the emphasis is on understanding customer needs and then solving problems or delivering benefits that create functional and economic customer value. While information technology is important in this style of CRM, it is designed to support, rather than drive, the customer relationship as it does in many B2C markets. The types of relationship that develop here are often deep and meaningful—both for the companies and the people involved.

CRM has always been an integral part of B2B marketing. In fact, its success in this field was a key stimulus for B2C marketers to develop their CRM programmes. As shown later in this chapter, as CRM migrated from B2B to B2C, it did not travel as well as expected. The prime reason for this is that the nature of a relationship is quite different when a company sells to hundreds of thousands and sometimes millions of customers, than when it sells to a few key accounts or a couple of hundred major customers. Because B2B CRM provides the design template for these schemes, the next section reviews how they work in a B2B setting. Then it is easy to see the strengths and weaknesses of CRM as implemented in consumer settings.

How CRM Does Work—B2B

Key Accounts

When companies have a number of 'key accounts', the primary responsibility for managing the relationship between the customer and the organization is typically assigned to an Account Manager. Good account managers focus on four key issues:

- defining and reiterating the purpose of the relationship;
- setting the boundaries for the relationship and managing its style;
- establishing the mechanisms for creating and capturing value;
- evaluating outcomes.

The first two issues are really about managing the roles and expectations of the parties involved. Sometimes this is described as:

'Who gives what.'
'Who gets what.'
'When are things due.'
'How will disputes be resolved.'

The third issue is concerned with the day-to-day working relationship between the parties. How are benefits created and problems solved (e.g. through cost savings or productivity improvements), and how will the gains from this collaboration be shared (e.g. through a straightforward fee for service arrangement or through some type of performance-based contract).

The final issue focuses on demonstrating *actual value added* to the customer. This is often done in only a superficial way. For example, many organizations use satisfaction surveys to measure the client's perception of the mechanics of the relationship—how quickly the firm responded to a client request, was promised material delivered on time, were the account team members easy to work with, was the invoice transparent and correct, etc. This is helpful information about the hygiene factors of a relationship, but it does not address the core reason why such relationships are built and maintained, namely, the joint creation of a sustainable competitive advantage.

Some companies, however, have procedures that demonstrate to the client the actual value added by an assignment. Thus, when reviewing assignment outcomes, they can 'prove' that they have more than paid for the fee that they have received. When this happens, clients are generally satisfied. And, there is less emphasis placed on, and less need for, those tiresome satisfaction surveys mentioned above. The reason for this is that if a manager can be confident in demonstrating to his or her peers that the organization is clearly better off, then they will be more accommodating of the supplier's preferred way of working.

Not every assignment lends itself to calculating the dollar value of its outcomes. However, in many B2B situations, it is possible to make such a calculation. The best way to demonstrate the added value of an assignment is to agree on its calculation at the *beginning* of the relationship. The true story in Exhibit 11.1 illustrates what happens when this is not done.

Exhibit 11.1. Missing the opportunity to change the pricing rules

The overseas client of a large law firm rang the engagement partner with a major problem. They were an insurance company and had just been issued with a claim for $100 million. If the insurance company challenged the claim and this went to court, there would be considerable fees involved and the potential for negative publicity. If the claim could be settled quickly by alternative dispute resolution, then a lot of time and money could be saved.

On receiving the phone call from the client, the partner dropped the matter he was currently working on and he and a senior associate flew to the client's office. Three long days later, they reached a settlement with the claimant's lawyers for $20 million. The client was delighted. For the lawyers, it was then back on the overnight plane home.

The first thing the partner did when he returned to the office the following morning was to prepare two invoices—one of which would be sent to the client. One invoice charged the client the standard, blended head-rate of fees, plus expenses. The other invoice contained the same total amount plus a 'performance' bonus. The client was delighted and there was a demonstrable saving of $80 million. Which invoice should be sent?

After discussing the matter with the firm's managing partner, the standard invoice was sent—there was to be no performance bonus from this job despite the clear amount saved. The incident, however, worried the managing partner—in engagements such as this, how much money, if any, was the firm leaving uncollected?

To explore the issue further, the managing partner invited three very senior CEOs of major companies to the firm's next partner retreat. They were asked how much they would have been prepared to pay in these circumstances. Without hesitation, each one said 'something less than $80 million'. One CEO, however, did add the following caveat—'make sure you send the invoice directly to me'.

So, it seems that the firm did not capture all the value from this engagement that they were entitled to.

The story in Exhibit 11.1 is a really a pricing issue. In this case, it highlights a cost-based pricing scheme (e.g. many professional service firms charge out at approximately three times direct labour costs) as opposed to a performance-based scheme (e.g. what amount of the reduction in the insurance claim can the law firm expect to receive). In these circumstances, is it ever possible to charge above the standard fee? And not jeopardize the client relationship?

In the situation described in Exhibit 11.1, the answer is probably no. The reason being that the partner did not change the 'rules of the engagement' *before* he left his office to work on this job. Had he asked that this emergency be treated differently because of the work that had to be left unattended while he was away, the client may have agreed to some different payment scheme. However, once he and the senior associate boarded the plane, the client's expectations were that it was 'business as usual'.

There are, however, some clear-cut situations when it is likely that added value (over that initially expected) can be created. These situations are more likely to occur when the relationship between the parties is more involving. To illustrate this idea, consider three types of sale that frequently occur in B2B situations:

- *The price/performance sale.* In this situation, the customer often invites bids from various companies to supply certain quantities of product to its specifications. Price is a key element of the bid. Performance is measured by the merchandise being delivered—to specifications, on time, every time, a full order, accompanied by the correct paperwork, and with a smile.
- *The relationship sale.* Here, the supplier makes various changes to their product and/or service to accommodate the customer's special needs. Just-in-time delivery is an example.
- *A strategic partnership.* Here, both parties pool complementary skills and resources to collaborate on a specific project. These arrangements go well beyond joint venture and licensing agreements. Often, it is necessary for both parties to make significant investments of non-salvageable assets—equipment, personnel, and knowledge—in order to create a joint competitive advantage.

With price/performance sales, there is often little scope to create or capture any added value that may accrue from the exchange. However, if the situation does arise, an organization may seek to negotiate a performance-based contract. The key issue with these contracts is how will performance be measured—to the satisfaction of both parties.

In relationship selling, there is a good chance that added value can be created. Sometimes this is given away in order to secure the contract. Smarter suppliers, however, capture the added value by bundling their product and service together, and negotiating a special price for the bundle. The way to approach a bundled-pricing problem is to ask the now-familiar question:

What is the maximum amount that the other party should be prepared to pay for the product and service that is being offered?

As we saw in Chapter 9, the answer to this question is called the EVC or the VIU price. When this calculation is agreed to at the beginning of a relationship, it sets the upper limit on value created. How this value is then shared will depend on how the two parties negotiate, and what precedent exists for bundled pricing in the customer company and in the industry. In many situations, there is no such precedent. In this case, one must tread carefully when suggesting a VIU-based price.

In strategic partnership arrangements, there is considerable scope to create added value. (This is the prime reason that they are established.) The difficulty here is to write a contract to share the added value that will not tear the partnership apart. This can happen because the relationship between business partners includes both common and conflicting interests. Also, many of the actions of the parties in the relationship that create joint value are not freely observable by the other party. Under these circumstances, either party can choose to pursue his or her private interests at the other's expense. This contractual opportunism is what economists call a 'moral hazard'.[7] It is one of the prime reasons that many partnerships fail—either because it is unwittingly designed into the collaborative arrangement (as we will see in Chapter 13 when discussing working with advertising agencies), or it emerges over time as the goals of the parties change.

In summary, the thing that makes CRM a cost-effective programme in a Key Account situation is the nature of the relationship between the parties. These relationships involve structural ties between the organizations, two-way trust, commitment, the sharing of sensitive information, power sharing, equal work, risk sharing, and the involvement of people of equal standing. In short, they involve 'having skin in the game' and seeking to create demonstrable added value. As we move further away from this style of relationship, it becomes more difficult to capture the benefits of CRM.

Other Accounts

Typically, organizations have relatively few key accounts. Most of the business involves customers who are not as big, profitable, or strategically important as the key accounts. Selling on the basis of the product or service's price/performance, and some relationship selling, is common with this larger group. Segmentation by customer profitability is often used to determine the type of relationship that will be offered to various customers.

The key issues here are to *define* and then *manage* the types of commercial relationship that different segments of customers can expect to receive. When this is not done, one of two things typically happens. Either the customer keeps pushing for more service and lower prices, or *they* define the characteristics of their desired relationship. In the first case, many of these pushy customers evolve into 'customers from hell'. In the second case, it is easy to antagonize the customer because of something that was done that the CRM staff did not realize was important to the customer.

Defining commercial relationships involves a clear statement of the CVP. The customer can expect 'this and this and this' for 'this price'. Managing customer relationships is all about consistency. Consistently delivering what is promised, and not creating special circumstances where more is given than promised in the CVP. (Recall the discussion about delighting customers in Chapter 10.)

Fortunately, B2B marketers have been dealing with the problem of establishing different types of relationship with different segments of customers for many years. During this time, they have learnt how to build CRM systems to deliver a standard of service commensurate with the profitability or strategic importance of their customers. Figure 11.2 shows a model of such a system.

There are two critical factors that make a system like the one shown in Figure 11.2 work. One is the nature of the data in the customer database. The

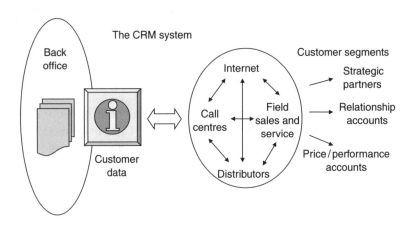

Figure 11.2. A stylized CRM system

information about customers that is needed was discussed in Chapter 4. Recall that the crucial issue here is whether the data actually provide a comprehensive picture of *all* the 'relationships' the customer has with the organization. For example, in their dealings with CEOs, banks and telecommunications companies often find that their service to the person as a business customer far exceeds their service to the person as a private individual. When very senior managers get relatively poor service 'at home', it can contaminate their perceptions of the relationship in the business environment.

The second critical factor is the ability of the various touch-points between the customer and the organization to coordinate with each other. For example, when a customer interacts at different times through, say, the corporate website, e-mail, and a call centre, does the information from each encounter get passed throughout the CRM system so that each customer touch-point has access to accurate, timely, and comprehensive information about the customer. If this does not occur, then there is a good chance that customers become frustrated—'I told the person I dealt with last time that information'. There is also a good chance that the customer database may not be updated.

When organizations have a few thousand customers, all of whom are other businesses that understand 'how business works', CRM systems of the style shown in Figure 11.2 are a cost-effective way to tailor marketing effort to customer profitability. However, when such a system is scaled up to use in a B2C situation, companies like Aspect, Compaq, Epiphany, Oracle, PeopleSoft, and Siebel Systems are often called in to help design and implement the CRM programme. While problems with large-scale CRM systems can be caused by poor information technology, the problems of interest in the next section are the result of poor marketing thinking.

How CRM Does Work—B2C

In recent years, the academic marketing community has questioned some of the key premises that are used to support B2C CRM in general, and the relationship marketing and customer loyalty programmes used to help implement these programmes. The academics base their scepticism on two sources of information. One is the thirty-year research tradition that focuses on the empirical patterns of purchasing for a wide variety of consumer products and services. (This research was reviewed in Part A of Chapter 4.) The second is some emerging research that tests (*a*) the key assumptions that underpin relationship marketing, and (*b*) the effectiveness of the CRM tactic of customer loyalty programmes.

One of the keys to evaluating the potential cost-effectiveness of B2C CRM is to explore the nature of a relationship that a customer might want to develop with a brand—for example, Nescafé instant coffee. (For many years, Nescafé has run television advertisements suggesting that its target customers form a deep-seated emotional relationship with the brand.) Once we have a good understanding of what a 'relationship' means to the buyers of various mass-market brands, it is then possible to design an appropriate CRM programme.

Relationships in B2C Markets

There is considerable anecdotal evidence to suggest that many customers simply do not have the time, interest, or emotional energy to form relationships with a wide variety of products and services they buy. Exhibit 11.2 suggests that there will be four segments of customers in most markets, only one of which should be targeted by the organization. Also, the *Partner* segment will be composed of a number of tactical relationship segments defined by different combinations of the characteristics of a relationship: trust, commitment, the sharing of information, partnership among people of equal standing, open and honest communication, keeping promises, being fair, not acting opportunistically, etc.

Exhibit 11.2. Who wants a relationship with the organization

Some recent research about CRM suggests that four customer segments exist in B2C markets:[8]

Sleepers—people who are yet to be convinced that entering a 'relationship' with the organization would be to their benefit.

Transacters—people who know that they do not want a relationship, and who will avoid any interactive contacts with the organization.

Opportunists—people who do not want a relationship, but who will exploit any offers made by the organization.

Partners—people who believe they will benefit from a closer association with the organization, and who are willing to contribute to the relationship.

Given the diversity of customer expectations about the nature of a potential relationship with an organization, it is likely that there will be a variety of desired styles of relationship with the organization.

Also as we move away from B2B markets towards mass B2C markets, the nature of a seller–customer relationship becomes somewhat paradoxical. The paradox is the problem of trying to form a 'relationship' with large numbers of customers, while at the same time trying to make a profit by selling mass-produced products and services to them. The social nature of a relationship juxtaposed with commercial reality suggests that only in certain types of situations will special types of 'relationship' be achievable. Recent research suggests that customers understand this paradox. They do not confuse commercial exchanges and the illusion of mass customization offered by companies as an interpersonal relationship.[9]

The counterpoint to this argument is an interesting stream of research started in the 1960s. William Wells and others suggested that there were deep psychological motivations underlying the evaluations people formed of the brands they bought.[10] Following on from this research, Jennifer Aaker proposed that brands have distinct personalities defined along the dimensions of sincerity, excitement, competence, sophistication, and ruggedness.[11] (This was discussed in the Brand Personality section of Chapter 7.) From the perspective of interpersonal relationship theory, Susan Fournier also suggested that consumers form different types of explicit emotional relationships with their brands.[12] Sometimes these forces converge to create distinct subcultures of consumption—as with bikers, golfers, runners, skydivers, and surfers. An extreme version of this position is illustrated in Exhibit 11.3.

When people like the head of Saatchi & Saatchi stretched the relationship view of marketing to low-involvement products, it caused others to attack this relationship theory of marketing.[13] One poignant avenue of attack was

---

Exhibit 11.3. Lovemarks

Mr. Kevin Roberts, the colourful chief executive of Saatchi & Saatchi Worldwide is in love with his clients, in brands that show him love, and his theory of love—because love is everything in the battle for brand supremacy. Mr. Roberts wants to pump emotional juice into brands, and have a primal, lustful, sensual, intimate experience with them. On www.lovemarks.com he outlines what he sees as the Holy Grail for marketers—making brands into "lovemarks". A brand as a "trustmark" is no longer enough. He argues that marketers, and especially his advertising agency has to turn trust into lust and love—the ultimate relationship.

Source: R. Burbury, 'Who loves you baby—Kevin does, grrrr', *Australian Financial Review* (9 February 2001), p. 27.

the evidence presented by Susan Fournier to support her theory. In one case, she interviewed three respondents for 12–15 hours each (in four or five in-house sessions).[14] In another case, she used 2–3.5 hour interviews with eight coffee drinkers as feedstock for her theory of consumer–brand relationships.[15] This style of research is often used to generate propositions that are subsequently empirically tested. However, to date there has been a paucity of empirical research to indicate the generalizability of her findings.

A second avenue of concern about FMCG and brand-relationship marketing is that to many people it seems fatuous. Do many buyers of Maxwell House, Sanka, Tasters Choice, High Point, Folgers, Nescafé, Brim, and Maxim really develop an emotional bond with their instant coffee? Or the retailer where they buy these brands? Our sense would suggest that some customers might use their coffee brand for the roles outlined earlier, but most people would not. Research supports this scepticism. For example, two recent studies (in 2000) of Australian and UK consumers by the Carlson Marketing Group suggest that only 11 per cent of people say they felt 'extremely close' to brands.[16] Also, research suggests that the major decision when buying grocery brands is whether or not to buy from the product category. Brand choice, for most people, is a much less important decision.[17] Hence, when evaluating the qualitative research by Fournier and others, it is important to think about where the respondents were selected from on the overall distribution of customers (e.g. highly involved with coffee brands through to no interest at all).

There are, however, situations where anecdotal evidence indicates that forming a relationship with a brand, and/or the retailer selling it, will be relevant. In markets where psychological and social value dominate function (such as luxury goods, cosmetics, and lifestyle brands) there may be a significant 'brand component' that drives consumer choice and commitment. Some consumers may attribute a personality to the brand and want a relationship with it. For example, if you are Harley-Davidson selling big motor cruisers and the feeling of being free and somewhat rebellious, then forming a relationship with your customers makes sense. Here, much of what is being bought is social and psychological in nature. The motorbike is really a 'ticket to entry' to one of the various Harley-Davidson subcultures. The company creates much of the 'product' by fostering the core values of personal freedom, machismo, patriotism, and American heritage.[18] They manage the customer relationship with a CRM programme that involves bike rallies, services, clothing, collectibles, and their Harley Owners Group club.

If customers do not want a relationship with a product or service, they may still appreciate a relationship with the retailer that sells them. Many CRM schemes have been launched across a range of retail formats. In areas where product bundling is important to help the customer construct the desired outcome (e.g. with clothing, housewares, cosmetics, and travel), such a programme may add value to the customer experience, and, thus, there is a significant quid pro quo for both parties. However, even for the oft-cited success of the UK retailer Tesco's CRM scheme, it is difficult to get a good measure of success. The reason is that the loyalty scheme was introduced as part of a much broader programme of new business development.[19] The paradox here is that good business practice requires an integrated approach to marketing that will give rise to confounded measures of CRM success.

Another potential value-adding avenue for CRM programmes is to help customers establish a dialogue with the company. Many customer call centres, loyalty programmes, and websites have been used to create a communication channel between the organization and its customers. But real dialogue is two-way communication. And it requires up-to-date, accurate, and comprehensive customer data—and a personalized response. The current state of many legacy customer data systems undermines having a dialogue with 'the masses'.[20]

Another type of 'relationship' to have with customers is not to have a relationship with them at all. Here, the strategy is to just provide good products and services at competitive prices, and be easy to do business with—with no strings attached. The organization's focus is to provide the best customer value—through its products and service. Nothing more, nothing less. Many customers will respond to this offer with the best type of loyalty imaginable—repeat purchase, and sometimes positive recommendations to others. These 'transaction' customers will also be less costly to serve than many 'relationship' customers.

Research suggests that in these non-relationship markets favourable evaluations can develop about the brands, but they are more likely to be based on frequent satisfied use than any personality attribute of the brand or a relationship with it.[21] Also, the over-time stability of these expressed evaluations is not high. This evidence suggests that they do not reflect commitment or brand loyalty.

In summary, both anecdotal and research evidence suggests that customers who form a relationship with their brands, especially FMCG brands and the retailers that sell them, are the exception not the rule. Even so, it may be the case that there are enough of these customers for an organization to develop a very profitable CRM strategy with them. What makes such a strategy desirable is if these relationship customers stay with the organization longer, and the economics of serving them make this group more profitable.

On the Profitability of Long-Life Customers

A basic assumption of relationship marketing is that long-life customers are more profitable than short-term customers. Although arguments and case studies are plentiful, systematic empirical evidence is rare.[22] Also, much of the evidence is based on cases that involve fixed-term contracts (such as for mobile phone services) or memberships (such as with a book club) with customers. In these situations, the cost to acquire customers is amortized over the lifetime of the relationship and the company need only spend funds to ensure customer satisfaction. In the more common non-contractual setting (such as buying from a department store), acquisition costs are repeated and the company must also spend money to keep the relationship alive.

Contrary to the line of argument that long-life customers are more profitable, it has been argued that loyal customers will often be less profitable.[23] One reason for this is that they may expect a reward for their loyalty. This may be in the form of a price discount (for accumulated volume) or extra free services. Also, short-term (or spot-market) customers may be prepared to pay the asking price and expect little extra from the seller. In particular, the four basic assumptions that underpin the profitability of long-life customers have been questioned, namely:

- It costs more to acquire a new customer than to retain one. (It depends on whether they come naturally to the product, service, or store—'I always shop here because it is so convenient'—or whether they have to be seduced to come.)
- The costs of serving these customers is less. (It often costs the same to serve each customer who buys the same amount of product.)
- They pay higher prices. (It depends on how price sensitive they are.)
- They spend more. (Only if they need more.)

Werner Reinartz and V. Kumar studied the customers of a large catalogue retailer to see if they could find support for these assumptions.[24] They found no substantive support for them and their overall finding was that 'long-life customers are not necessarily profitable customers'. To illustrate their findings, the correlation between lifetime duration and lifetime profit was 0.2. In other words, only 4 per cent of the profitability of a customer is explained by the length of time that the person was a customer with the company.[25]

What this study indicates is that it is the amount that a customer spends with a company that drives their lifetime value to the company—regardless of how long they have been, or are likely to be, a customer of the company. Hence, marketing strategy should be focused on revenue generation (ARPU in Figure 11.1 and Chapter 2) and transaction-cost management—in preference to the creation of 'loyal' customers. The tactics for this are quite different from those used to create loyal customers. For example, given a budget that would support either a cross-selling or a customer affinity programme, cross-selling would be preferred.

One way to cross-check the findings of the Reinartz and Kumar study, and the recommendation that managers should focus more on revenue enhancement than customer retention, is to look at the ability of customer loyalty programmes to enhance customer profitability. There is little argument that these programmes keep their customers 'on the books' for an extensive period of time. But the crucial question is: 'Are these customers more profitable?'

Customer Loyalty Programmes

Recall that Chapter 4 suggested that most people exhibit multi-brand buying or polygamous loyalty when they buy most of their products and services. In situations such as these, what can a Customer Loyalty scheme hope to achieve? If it is designed as an offensive weapon, it may secure a temporary first-mover advantage. However, if it looks as though it will change customer purchasing patterns, it will soon be countered, often by the introduction of a similar or (slightly) better scheme. For example, two weeks after American Airlines launched the first frequent flyer programme (AAdvantage), United Airlines launched its Mileage Plus programme.[26]

Once these programmes become established in a market, their patterns of use often mirror the purchase patterns of the products and services they support. For example, most *frequent* flyers in Europe are members of three to four frequent flyer schemes—they exhibit polygamous loyalty to the schemes as well as the airlines. Typically, the infrequent flyers are members of only one scheme.[27] It seems that these 'golden handcuffs' neither induce single-brand loyalty among the heavy users nor significantly more purchases by light users. First and foremost, customers want a product or service that does the job required. If there is an add-on benefit offered by a Customer Loyalty programme, then people will join if it is 'free', and in the case of frequent flyer programmes, they will use convenient airline alliance partners to get every entitlement they can—the Opportunist customers in Exhibit 11.2.

People tend to participate in loyalty schemes for a variety of reasons. For example, because they like to collect entitlements and/or because they see these schemes as a form of (delayed) price discount. Few, however, seem to participate because they want to change their established patterns of purchase or form a deep-seated relationship with the company involved. Research by Robert East and Wendy Lomax in the United Kingdom suggests that customers join the schemes of the companies they already use—rather than use the companies whose schemes they have just been offered.[28]

This perspective suggests that only modest changes in consumer behaviour can be made from even a well-designed Customer Loyalty programme. Bryon and Anne Sharp set out to test this contention.[29] They studied Australia's biggest loyalty programme and one of the world's largest in terms of per capita market coverage. The programme is called *FlyBuys* and at one stage the retail outlets involved were responsible for more than 20 per cent of Australian retail spending. Two years after launch, it had more than two million members and an annual operating budget (not including customer rewards) in excess of $20 million. The programme offered points for department and supermarket store patronage, credit card use, and petrol buying that could be redeemed for free air travel and accommodation.

The Sharp and Sharp study employed the brand benchmarking approach discussed in Chapter 4. They used consumer panel data and statistical modelling to establish 'normal' patterns of repeat-purchasing, and then looked for departures from these predictions as evidence of the impact of the *FlyBuys* programme on creating 'excess' loyalty. Two conclusions from this study are noteworthy. First, the authors state that they 'do not observe the consistent finding of brands in the *FlyBuys* programme showing higher levels of average purchase frequency given their individual levels of penetration' (p. 479). Second, they state that 'Of the six loyalty program brands, only two showed substantial repeat-purchase loyalty deviations and both of these showed this deviation for non-members of the loyalty program as well as members'. (p. 485) Given that *FlyBuys* was one of the biggest, loudest, and boldest attempts to use a loyalty programme to re-engineer patterns of repeat purchase, these results are not encouraging for marketing managers and consultants extolling the virtues of such programmes.

The research cited in this section suggests that most Customer Loyalty programmes will have neither a substantial nor a long-lasting effect on customer purchasing habits or the amount of product purchased. Added to this finding are persistent rumours from the business world that suggest that many loyalty schemes have 'completely failed'.[30] Also, research done by McKinsey & Company is suggesting that companies should re-evaluate their loyalty schemes as a matter of urgency.[31]

Notwithstanding this negative publicity, the schemes remain in place. Why they are likely to persist, is a result of three factors:

- Once they are launched, they are difficult to unwind.
- There is an industry of consultants and programme providers that push these schemes.
- Many airlines make a profit by selling 'air-miles' as rewards for these programmes.

Putting Customer Relationships in Perspective

For most of the products and services we buy on a regular basis, brand preference exists. The crucial question is whether it can be attributed to some type of relationship we develop with the brand or whether it is driven by salience (we know more about some brands than others), availability (it is in stock where we usually shop), and/or habit (it is the brand usually bought). Extensive empirical research for FMCG brands suggests that for most people it is these last three factors.[32] As noted above, there are some exceptions to this finding (such as Harley-Davidson motorbikes, the VW Beetle motorcar, Apple Macintosh personal computers, Marlboro cigarettes, and possibly Levi's jeans and Body Shop cosmetics). However, given the tens of thousands of brands in the market, even a hundred or so such brands represent the exception, not the rule. Hence, a CRM programme designed to build a deep-seated relationship with the 'typical' consumer of a 'typical' brand is more likely to be a romantic distraction than a cost-effective marketing strategy.

The inherent problem with CRM is identified in its name by the words *relationship* and *management*. It will be difficult for consumers to have much influence in the relationship if companies seek to manage it—to their profitable advantage. A vivid example of this 'management' is shown in the frequent flyer programme application form of Australia's major airline—Qantas. See Exhibit 11.4. It has a section on 'Terms and Conditions' from the airline's legal department. It is interesting to speculate on the type of customer relationship that starts out with 'a talk from our lawyers', requires a joining fee, and has a membership fee.

The simple way to check the nature of a brand is to segment customers according to the strength of relationship *they* would like to have with it (from strong to none), and then for the 'willing' *Partner* segment in Exhibit 11.2, determine the type of relationship they would like to have with

> **Exhibit 11.4.** Qantas manages the expectations of its hoped-to-be loyal customers
>
> Here is a summary of *some* of the terms and conditions of membership of the Qantas Frequent Flyer programme:
>
> - a once-only joining fee;
> - an account-service fee charged every two years in advance;
> - retain all boarding passes, airline tickets, receipts, and documentation for point adjustment requests;
> - the Qantas Frequent Flyer membership card provides no benefit other than identification;
> - Qantas Frequent Flyer expressly reserves the right to terminate or materially alter the programme at any time, without notice;
> - Qantas Frequent Flyer reserves the right at any time, in its absolute discretion, and without notice, to revoke membership of any member to utilize any reward or benefit;
> - Awards are subject to capacity controls and availability is limited. Some flights may not have any award seats available. Seats for Award travel are booked in special classes of service.
>
> *Source*: Qantas Frequent Flyer brochure (in Australian travel agents at 01/08/02).

the brand. For example, in the case of Harley-Davidson we would expect that a large proportion of buyers would have a strong relationship with the brand, and this would be deliberate and positive (as shown by the care taken of these bikes); enduring (sometimes evidenced by the owner wearing the company name and logo on their clothing and occasionally as a tattoo); social (Harley owners recognize each other); and two-way (they would expect special treatment from the company in return for their support of it). In contrast, we would expect a much lower proportion of instant coffee buyers to have a strong relationship with their brand(s).

Figure 11.3 summarizes the thesis on CRM. The bold arrows that are crossed out represent the conventional wisdom that recent research suggests is dubious. That is, that CRM programmes have a significant, direct effect on market share, and/or a strong, indirect effect via increased customer loyalty on sales. The dashed arrows indicate the likely weak effects of many CRM initiatives such as the ubiquitous customer loyalty programmes. For example, any small increase in sales or market share would result from the modest increase in brand salience. And it is brand salience, not customer loyalty, that is likely to lead to any increase in the share of the customer's category purchases. The role of a customer loyalty

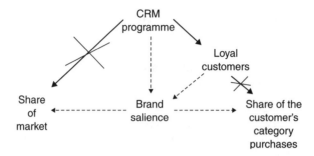

Figure 11.3. How CRM really works

programme in this scheme is to act as an additional attribute to promote. It may also appeal directly to a small number of the brand's customers and, thus, enhance its perceived value. However, the more significant effect is likely to be that it raises the profile of the brand in the marketplace—until it is copied.

Given that CRM is likely to have a relatively weak effect on both share-of-market and the share-of-customer purchases in the product category, it is legitimate to suggest that their overall cost-effectiveness is doubtful on this basis alone. Hence, the question: 'Why do companies persist with these programmes?'

Apart from trying to build strong relationships with large numbers of customers, there are two ways in which CRM programmes may be an effective use of a marketing budget. First, in many cases they are a purely defensive tactic. If a direct competitor launches such a programme, other competitors match it. In this scenario, a CRM programme is part of the price the company pays for being in the market.

The second reason has been suggested by two game theorists, Barry Nalebuff and Adam Branderburger, whose idea of co-opetition we looked at in Chapter 3.[33] They suggest that CRM programmes are a strategy that competitors use to help avoid starting a price war. For example, when all the airlines have a frequent flyer programme they all increase the switching costs of their customers—and the higher percentage of flyers who belong to any programme, the better for all. When these programmes become established, it takes a bigger price cut to entice a competitor's customers to forsake their points. It also makes it somewhat easier for the major airlines to raise their prices—especially for travellers with large numbers of points. Thus, price cuts are less effective and price rises less risky.[34] In effect, the airline programmes are a good example of co-opetition, that is, *co-op*eration and comp*etition*.

Regardless of the reason for launching a CRM programme, one of the major problems for schemes that are based on redeeming points is the long-term liability this creates for the company. The accounting for these points has been a particular problem for the airlines. Having expiration dates on the miles and making them difficult to redeem are only part solutions. These tactics just transfer an accounting cost to a brand-equity cost. That is, when a customer gets angry because they cannot redeem their points for their preferred alternative, they tend to blame both the programme and the brand.

Evaluating the Potential of a CRM Programme

The previous section suggests that in highly competitive markets, a CRM programme may be a defensive strategy used by many competitors and a way to dampen the level of price competition in a market. If these are not the objectives of the programme, but rather it is to re-engineer customer purchasing patterns, then the following evaluation procedure could be followed.

The first step is to conduct an audit of the market in which the brand competes. Can this market be described by the Double Jeopardy law we reviewed in Chapter 4? If it is one where the competing brands are functionally similar but differ in their popularity, then there is a good chance that the Double Jeopardy law will hold. Recall that it has been found for the repeat buying behaviour in markets such as: most grocery packaged goods, store choice, television programme and channel choice, newspapers, some durable goods (e.g. automobile makes), some educational services (e.g. business school executive programmes), and some industrial products (e.g. contracts for aviation fuel). It has been found for these brands in Australia, Britain, continental Europe, Japan, and the United States over the last thirty years.

When a Double Jeopardy brand is recognized, research suggests that a penetration (share-of-market) strategy is appropriate. The objective here is to increase the number of buyers of the brand, but not how often or how much they naturally buy. (The assumption here is that people will only buy what they need.) Marketing programmes that increase the salience of the brand, such as more advertising and wider distribution, should be cost-effective. Sometimes the publicity surrounding a new customer loyalty programme, such as *FlyBuys* mentioned earlier, will also provide a temporary increase in salience. Another tactic is to increase the inherent value delivered to the customer. A better CVP can be delivered by enhancing the product/service (more features, better quality, etc.) or reducing the 'price' (the amount paid, make it easier to buy the brand, reduce the perceived risk of the brand), relative to competing brands. These are traditional ways to allocate a marketing budget.

If the brand does not conform to the Double Jeopardy law, then research suggests either a penetration strategy or loyalty strategy. (It is always a good idea to have as many potential buyers as the organization can service.) The objectives of a loyalty strategy can be to enhance the value of the brand and/or to increase the amount or how often current customers buy. (Recall that there seems to be little point in fostering customer retention unless it actually leads to increased spending by these long-life customers.) Customer clubs, rewards for purchases, extra services for members, and product bundling programmes are often used to increase sales. Cause-related marketing has also been tried. (e.g. 'if you buy our brand, we will donate some money to a worthy cause.') As Figure 11.1 suggests, the motivation here is relationship-based—of either the affective type or one based on convenience and self-interest. Sometimes, it is also possible to increase the amount of a product used by suggesting other use occasions, for example, tonic water as a mixer (with gin) and as a straight soft drink.

The crucial issue addressed in this section is to be clear about the marketing objective. It is seldom possible that a marketing budget will stretch to implement all possible programmes to attain and retain customers. Hence, with a limited budget and the current plethora of suggestions from consultants, it is essential to be clear about the objective of a CRM programme—and to be realistic about what is likely to be achieved.

Designing a CRM Programme—B2B and B2C

For those companies that set out to design a CRM programme to target potential *Partner* customers, the following guidelines should prove helpful. They are based on the research reviewed throughout this book and aim to maximize the programme's chance of success.

A. Specify the objectives of the CRM programme. For example, is it to practice a form of co-opetition or is it to counter a competitive offer? Is it to try to increase sales? In short, be specific about the hoped-for gains from the programme.

B. Given A, identify the tactical segments of relationship customers for whom a CRM programme is most applicable. That is, how will the programme add most value to both the organization and the customer. For example, in B2B situations, it will be customers who will benefit from a closer working relationship with the organization. *Transaction* customers seeking price/performance sales would not be as desirable. In B2C situations, it will be customers who want to develop a dialogue with the organization (and thus may be a source of valuable information), or who can be 'handcuffed' to it (or its brands) through such a scheme, or who want a deeper emotional connection to the organization. Customers who are already 'loyal' to the organization or its brands, or who are low volume users, are less desirable.

C. Design the CRM (Loyalty) programme to directly enhance the value proposition of the product or service. For example, the General Motors rebate scheme and the GM Card that allow participants to build up savings towards the cost of a new General Motors car is better than a scheme that awards frequent flyer points for the purchase of gasoline. The reason for this requirement is to direct loyalty to the brand (a direct effect) rather than to the programme, or to the current deal (indirect effects). For many low-involvement products, the incentives offered by the programme become the primary reward. Once the incentives are removed (or used up), the prime reason for purchase disappears.

D. *Fully cost* the CRM programme. There are a number of highly visible costs, such as those associated with the programme's design and launch—especially the IT and database costs. However, there are also many hidden costs, such as management time, changes to operational structures and procedures, and the costs associated with countering the launch of a similar programme by a competitor. Possibly the biggest of these hidden costs is the opportunity cost of spending the money on a CRM programme as opposed to other marketing activities. The total cost of these programmes can be quite large, for example it has been suggested that the cost of the airline frequent flyer programmes is 7 per cent of annual revenue. This is substantial when it is realized that many airlines peg their advertising at approximately 3 per cent of revenue.

E. Project revenues and other non-financial benefits of the programme over its anticipated life. When doing this take explicit account of competitors' reactions to counter the scheme.

F. Compare the full costs and anticipated benefits of the CRM programme with the effects of a similar expenditure of money on other marketing programmes—such as a price cut, an increase in advertising, enhancing product/service quality, obtaining more distribution coverage, etc. If the CRM programme will deliver the best return, it should be implemented; if not, one of the other programmes should be implemented.

In summary, the idea is to design the best scheme possible, specify the likely financial and behavioural outcomes of the scheme, fully cost this scheme, and then evaluate the cost-effectiveness of this programme against other marketing programmes costing a similar amount of money. If the CRM programme passes this test, then launch it. Otherwise, use the money elsewhere.

KEY CONCEPTS

- *Customer relationships*—the connection between the organization or a brand and its customers. This connection usually involves trust, commitment sharing, information, partnership, risk sharing, etc.
- *CRM*—activities designed to build a long-term relationship with target customers.
- *Data mining*—the search for purchasing patterns in the customer database.
- *Cross-selling*—the tactic of trying to sell additional products or services to customers who already buy something from the organization.
- *Key accounts*—the small number of most important (big, profitable, strategic) customers.
- *Product bundles*—combinations of products and/or services offered to customers at a single price.
- *Customer loyalty*—the commitment (attitude and/or purchase behaviour) of a customer to a brand, service, store, or organization.
- *Customer loyalty programme*—a scheme offering some type of delayed, accumulating economic benefit to people who buy the brand.

KEY FRAMEWORKS

- *CRM systems*—Figures 11.1 and 11.2

KEY QUESTIONS

- If you are thinking about implementing a new CRM programme, have you followed the six steps outlined in the section on 'Designing a CRM programme—B2B and B2C'
- If you already have a CRM programme in place, have you recently examined its cost-effectiveness?

RECAP

The basic idea of CRM has been a foundation concept of B2B marketing for decades. Practised here, it is an integral part of successful marketing. However, as the *practice* of CRM has moved into various B2C markets, it has encountered many difficulties. Some of these are structural, such as (*a*) the customer databases and management accounting systems of many organizations cannot deliver the outcomes desired, and (*b*) while the CRM name suggests that this should be a pull-marketing strategy, it is often implemented as if it is a push-marketing strategy (e.g. by cross-selling other products to customers and/or trying to up-sell customers to a more expensive model). Other difficulties are tactical, such as trying to engineer and then manage different types of relationships with different segments of customers—some of whom like *Opportunists* want to exploit the relationship.

The keys to success of any type of CRM programme are twofold, namely:

- manage the expectations of target customers about the type of relationship being fostered;
- link all the features of the CRM programme to the overall CVP and the positioning of the brand.

The rhetoric of CRM (and loyalty programme marketing) suggests that this concept will anchor the future of marketing. The practical and financial realities, however, suggest it will continue to be an integral part of B2B marketing and an interesting possibility for the segment of *Partner* customers in B2C marketing.

NOTES

1. F. Reichheld with T. Teal, *The Loyalty Effect* (Boston: Harvard Business School Press, 1996); the Peppers and Rogers Website is http://www.1to1.com.; a summary of the PWC approach can be found in S. A. Brown, *Customer Relationship Management* (Toronto: John Wiley & Sons, 2000).
2. See, for example, R. East and W. Lomax, 'Do Store Loyalty Programmes Really Work', *Marketing Week* (2 December 1999).
3. D. Schultz, 'Learn to Differentiate CRM's Two Faces', *Marketing News* (20 November 2000), p. 11.
4. S. Fournier, S. Dobscha, and D. Mick, 'Preventing the Premature Death of Relationship Marketing', *Harvard Business Review*, 76,1 (1998), 42–51.
5. D. K. Rigby, *Management Tools 2001: Annual Survey of Chief Executives* (Boston: Bain & Company, 2001); C. Gillies, D. Rigby, and F. F. Reichheld, 'The Story Behind Successful Customer Relationship Management', *European Business Journal*, 14, 2 (2002), 73–7; D. K. Rigby, F. F. Reichheld, and P. Schefter, 'Avoid the Four Perils of CRM', *Harvard Business Review*, 80 (February 2002), 101–9.

6. D. Ford, *Understanding Business Markets: Interaction, Relationships and Networks/The Industrial Marketing and Purchasing Group* (London: Academic Press, 1990).

7. See P. Milgrom and J. Roberts, *Economics, Organization and Management* (Englewood Cliffs, NJ: Prentice Hall, 1992) for a general discussion of moral hazard.

8. K. Fletcher, 'Consumer Power and Privacy: The Changing Nature of CRM', *International Journal of Advertising*, 22 (2003), 249–72.

9. L. O'Malley and C. Tynan, 'Reframing Relationship Marketing for Consumer Markets', *Interactive Marketing*, 2, 3 (2001), 240–6.

10. W. Wells, F. Andruili, F. Goi, and S. Seader, 'An Adjective Checklist for the Study on "Product Personality"', *Journal of Applied Psychology*, 41, 5 (1957), 317–19; W. Wells, *Lifestyle and Psychographics* (Chicago: American Marketing Association, 1972).

11. J. Aaker, 'Dimensions of Brand Personality', *Journal of Marketing Research*, 34, 3 (1997), 347–56.

12. S. Fournier, 'Consumers and their Brands: Developing Relationship Theory in Consumer Research', *Journal of Consumer Research*, 24, 4 (1998), 343–73.

13. M. Uncles and G. Laurent, 'Editorial', *International Journal for Research in Marketing*, 14, 5 (1997), 399–404; B. Sharp, 'Is This Love? Stretching the Bonding Metaphor Too Far', *Professional Marketing* (December 2000/January 2001), pp. 13–14.

14. Fournier (1998).

15. S. Fournier and J. Yao, 'Reviving Brand Loyalty: A Reconceptualization within the Framework of Consumer-Brand Relationships', *International Journal of Research in Marketing*, 14, 5 (1997), 451–72.

16. R. Burbury, 'Brand Commitment on Wane', *Australian Financial Review* (3 July 2001), p. 22.

17. G. Foxall, *Consumers in Context*, The BPM Research Project (London: Routledge, 1996).

18. J. W. Schouten and J. H. McAlexander, 'Subcultures of Consumption: An Ethnography of the New Bikers', *Journal of Consumer Research*, 22, 1 (1995), 43–61.

19. R. East and A. Hogg, 'The Anatomy of Conquest: Tesco Versus Sainsbury', *Journal of Brand Management*, 5, 1 (1997), 53–60.

20. T. H. Davenport, J. G. Harris, and A. K. Kohli, 'How Do They Know Their Customers So Well?' *Sloan Management Review*, 42, 2 (2001), 63–73.

21. F. Dall'Olmo Riley, A. Ehrenberg, S. Castleberry, T. Barwise, and N. Barnard, 'The Variability of Attitudinal Repeat-rates', *International Journal of Research in Marketing*, 14, 5 (1997), 437–50.

22. See, for example, N. Bendapudi and L. Berry, 'Customers' Motivations for Maintaining Relationships with Service Providers', *Journal of Retailing*, 73, 1 (1997), 15–37; R. Morgan and S. Hunt, 'The Commitment-Relationship Theory of Relationship Marketing', *Journal of Marketing*, 58, 3, (1994), 20–38; J. Sheth and A. Parvatiyar, 'Relationship in Consumer Markets: Antecedents and

Consequences', *Journal of the Academy of Marketing Science*, 23, 4 (1995), 255–71; F. Reichheld with T. Teal, *The Loyalty Effect* (Boston: Harvard Business School Press, 1996).

23. G. Dowling and M. Uncles, 'Do Customer Loyalty Programs Really Work?', *Sloan Management Review*, 38, 4, (1997), 71–82.

24. W. Reinartz and V. Kumar, 'On the Profitability of Long-Life Customers in a Noncontractual Setting: An Empirical Investigation and Implications for Marketing', *Journal of Marketing*, 64, 4 (2000), 17–35.

25. Squaring a correlation coefficient indicates the amount of variance explained from one variable to the other.

26. B. J. Nalebuff and A. M. Brandenburger, *Co-optetion* (New York: HarperCollins, 1996), p. 131.

27. *OAG Business Travel Lifestyle Survey* (1998) (Dunstable: Official Airline Guides).

28. East and Lomax (1999).

29. B. Sharp and A. Sharp, 'Loyalty Programs and Their Impact on Repeat-Purchase Loyalty Patterns', *International Journal of Research in Marketing*, 14, 5 (1997), 473–86.

30. B. Sandilands, 'More leg room and a walk-up bar', *Australian Financial Review*, (12 July 2000), Special Report, 3.

31. J. Cigliano et al., 'The Price of Loyalty', *McKinsey Quarterly*, 4 (2000), 68–77.

32. A. Ehrenberg et al., 'Brand Loyalty', in P. Earl and S. Kemp (eds.), *The Elgar Companion to Consumer Research and Economic Psychology* (London: Edward Elgar, 1999), pp. 53–63.

33. Nalebuff and Brandenburger (1996).

34. See also B.-D. Kim, M. Shi, and K. Srinivasan, 'Reward Programs and Tacit Collusion', *Marketing Science*, 20, 2 (2001), 99–120.

IV

ADMINISTRATION

Planning
and
control

Working with
suppliers

12

Planning and Control

If you fail to plan, you are planning to fail.

Anonymous

A good deal of planning is like a ritual rain dance.
It has no effect on the weather that follows.

James Brian Quinn

These two quotations reflect the broad spectrum of opinions about planning. Every guide to management says to plan is a good thing, but the reality of business suggests that the best conceived plans often fail to eventuate. The resolution to this dilemma is found in the *process* of planning. For many managers, especially ones with limited experience in their organization and/or the market in which they are working, the process of planning can be invaluable. Planning requires a disciplined approach to thinking. It forces the planner to develop a framework to integrate information, expose assumptions, and spell out how targets will be achieved.

A marketing plan, like any written document, is a selling device. Thus, to 'make the sale', the plan needs to gain the confidence of both its target audiences—the senior managers who will sign off on the plan and the people who will implement it. To do this it needs to:

- have a clear structure;
- accurately and concisely reflect the current situation;
- link marketing strategy to the organization's overall strategy and business model;
- be clear about its assumptions;
- be supported by evidence—preferably data and information that other managers understand and accept;
- link programmes to financial outcomes;

- be well presented—simple, clear, easy to read, and of the length expected by senior managers;
- have a positive overall tone, such as how business will be enhanced or done better.

Some of these criteria have been discussed in previous chapters. For example, the Du Pont analysis outlined in Chapter 2 is a technique for linking programmes to financial outcomes. One criterion comes from Jack Welch, the legendary CEO of General Electric. He suggests that a plan with a positive 'spin' (to use the public relations term) is often more favourably received than one that reflects 'doom and gloom'.[1] The criterion that suggests that opinions be grounded in evidence comes from personal experience. (One of our colleagues here in the business school always asks for the evidence that we have used to form our opinions. Over the years it has proven to be a good practice to present it along with our opinions.) The suggestion that the marketing plan has a clear structure is elaborated in the following section.

There are, however, two (potential) downsides to planning. One is the time it takes. Some organizations have a ritualized process for planning that entails seemingly endless meetings and may involve the production of a massive, formal plan. The second downside is a result of organizational culture. In some organizations, managers may be reluctant to develop a formal, written plan because it stands as a testament to their strategic thinking, proposed actions, and commitment. In the event that the plan's targets are not achieved, it can be used by others to expose their shortcomings. In the event that objectives are surpassed, the manager is on record as being too conservative. Thus, some managers prefer to have verbal plans that subtly change as the year progresses. This type of situation is an example of a lack of fit between the organization's work process and culture.

It is also necessary to remember that planning decisions will not be made independently of the personal values and career goals of the individuals concerned and the organizational structure. For example, many companies use the position of Brand Manager as a training ground for more senior marketing positions. Brand managers know through their KPIs that if they meet budget targets and do not cause a major catastrophe, they are likely to be promoted. This environment conditions much of their decision-making. It is sometimes called the Brand Manager Lifecycle and can be described thus—when taking over a brand, the new manager proceeds as follows: *research, repackage, relaunch,* and then *resign* (hopefully to a more senior position or the ad agency).

Part A of this chapter presents a marketing planning framework that gathers and organizes the information in this book. The framework contains a number of feedback loops to reflect the fact that a great deal of the process of planning involves a compromise between what is desirable and what is feasible. Part B of the chapter then looks at the issue of making marketing work. While there has been a great deal written about designing marketing strategy and programmes, there is much less known about actually implementing marketing.

PART A

Marketing Planning

Figure 12.1 is a simple and flexible planning process. The top part of the framework deals with understanding the gap, if any exists, between the current situation and the objectives that drive the plan. When these objectives are set by other senior managers, sometimes in an overseas office, there is often a gap between what is desired and what may be achievable. Over the years I have seen a number of CEOs tour around their organizations broadcasting their growth objectives and then anchoring them into the planning process. If these are 'stretch' objectives, what often follows is a negotiation

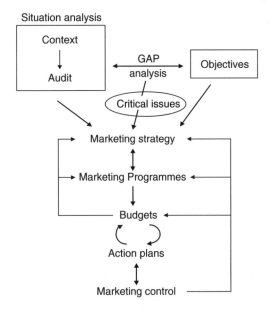

Figure 12.1. Framework for a marketing plan

along the lines of 'prove to me that you can't meet my expectations'. This is a somewhat confrontational approach to planning. Sometimes this works. Sometimes it is ridiculed by the staff who have to participate.

The central part of the marketing planning framework deals with strategy and programmes—the material covered in Chapters 6–11. The bottom part of the framework is about the iterative process of budgets, action plans, and control systems.

The planning framework in Figure 12.1 needs to be flexible. It may be used to plan for the organization, a particular brand, complementary brands (e.g. fuels and oils), a product line (such as a range of health foods), a new product, a customer segment, or a key account. Also, organizations differ in their needs for planning and their culture about planning. Thus, one size or type of planning does not fit all. It is rare to find two organizations that use an identical approach to planning their marketing. Thus, Figure 12.1 should be considered as a guide not a formula.

One further note about any framework used for marketing planning. To follow Peter Drucker's advice that introduced Chapter 1, the central focus of a marketing plan should be the target consumers, not the product or service. Later in this chapter, when the discussion moves to organizing the marketing function, I return to this issue.

Situation Analysis

Chapters 2–5 provide the frameworks and ideas with which to review the current situation and growth prospects of the organization. This is called 'context' in Figure 12.1. In particular, a good plan will contain a brief review of important industry factors and competitive rivalry. This should be followed by a brief statement of the organization's strategic intent, business model, and style of innovation. Also necessary to include here is a brief description of the current market structure and the tactical segments targeted by the organization. The use of one or two key characteristics of buyer behaviour can make the description of these segments come alive. How the product and target customer segment around which the plan is formulated support the organization's strategic intent and style of innovation should then be clearly stated.

The next section of the Situation Analysis is a Marketing Audit. The 4Ps and 3Cs framework (Figure 2.8) is ideal for this purpose. The rows of the matrix (capabilities, competitors, and customers) summarize the information contained in the Context section. The columns present a snapshot of the current (or desired if the plan is for a new product) offer to target consumers. Depending on the amount of detail required, some or all of the cells in this framework can be described.

Use of the 4Ps and 3Cs framework highlights two things. First, it is at the intersection of the rows and columns that one uncovers SWOT. Hence, if a SWOT analysis is used, it should be derived from and linked back to this framework. (In many cases a good 4Ps and 3Cs analysis will make SWOT superfluous.) The second thing that the 4Ps and 3Cs framework alerts us to is that every plan should remind its readers that timing and luck play a big role in successful implementation. Managers responsible for implementing strategy and launching new products acknowledge this. It is revealed in the 4Ps and 3Cs framework because eight out of the twelve cells in Figure 2.8 are beyond the (direct) control of the organization.

Objectives

Objectives appear in various forms. As noted earlier, broad organizational objectives come from the CEO or other senior managers. They generally have a corporate flavour to them, such as 'increase return on assets by 2 per cent', or 'grow the business revenues to $50 million'. This type of objective sets the broad parameters for marketing planning. However, these corporate objectives need to be translated into marketing objectives, such as 'increase market share', 'increase margins', 'improve customer satisfaction', 'increase the number of key accounts', 'reduce marketing costs', 'reduce customer churn', etc.

To be operational, however, marketing objectives need to be measurable. Thus, a *marketing target* is the marketing objective stated in terms of magnitudes and dates. For example, the objective 'to increase market share' becomes 'increase the current 10 per cent market share to 15 per cent by December 31'. The objective of 'reducing marketing costs' may become 'reduce the costs of acquiring new customers from an average of $200 per customer to $150 per customer in three months, and reduce the annual retention costs from $300 to $250 by the end of the financial year'.

For an organization or SBU to manage by objectives (MBO), the objectives (and their targets) need to (*a*) be arranged in a hierarchy of importance, (*b*) be realistic, and (*c*) be internally consistent. For example, in many mature and competitive markets it is unrealistic to expect significant growth—yet this is often an objective. Also, the objectives to simultaneously reduce costs and increase customer service levels are often incompatible. In many cases, so are the objectives to increase sales and margins.

Gap Analysis

Commuters on the London Underground railway system hear the warning 'mind the gap' at many stations. The same warning is applicable to marketing planners.

The Gap Analysis in Figure 12.1 summarizes the nature and magnitude of the task facing the marketing manager. When a considerable gap exists between objectives and organizational capabilities, either objectives need to be revised, or capabilities need to be enhanced, or new initiatives need to be considered. The first two options suggest that 'we cannot get to there from here'. One way to close the gap may be to consider changing the mindset of the organization's approach to marketing. In Chapter 3, the 'marketing as warfare' approach was contrasted with the 'co-opetition' approach. Alternatively, added investment in the organization's marketing capabilities may be necessary. This may mean an increase in the marketing budget, the implementation of better marketing systems, or may require an increase in the skill base of the marketing team. The third option suggests that innovation may be the best strategy. In Chapter 2, the innovation approach of market-driving and market-driven organizations was described. In Chapter 5, the NPD route to growth was outlined.

Critical Issues

Flowing from the gap analysis will be a number of *critical issues* that need to be addressed in the body of the marketing plan. A *critical issue* is anything that is currently, or that can, impact on achieving the objectives of the marketing plan. An issue may emanate out of the organization's internal operations or the external operating environment. It can have a positive or a negative affect on achieving objectives.

The process of identifying critical issues can be facilitated by convening an issues workshop. The marketing team, their direct-report senior manager, and possibly the account managers from the ad agency and market research firm convene to review the situation analysis, objectives, and gap

Potential impact

Urgency	Low	Significant	Major
Low	Periodic monitor	Periodic review	Develop action plan
Significant	Periodic review	Third priority response	Second priority response
Pressing	Develop action plan	Second priority response	First priority response

Figure 12.2. Critical issues priority grid

analysis over a one to three year time horizon. The aim is to identify and prioritize the eight to ten most critical issues that will impact on achieving the objectives of the marketing plan. An issue priority grid as shown in Figure 12.2 is a good way to summarize the outcomes of the workshop.

Marketing Strategy

The marketing strategy of an organization is based around its strategic and tactical market segmentation. Chapters 6 and 7 used the STP framework to outline how to think through the issues of segmentation, targeting, and positioning. In these chapters and in Chapter 1 (Figure 1.3), the underlying theme through this process was how to create and capture customer value.

A good marketing plan will contain a:

- statement about the role of segmentation (e.g. Figure 6.1);
- description of the market structure (such as Figure 6.3);
- target segments and why they are selected (e.g. Figure 6.4);
- rich description of each targeted tactical segment (using the information in Chapter 4);
- description of the brand's actual and desired position (Chapter 7);
- description of brand health (Figure 7.3);
- position map for competitive brands (e.g. Figures 7.4 and 7.5);
- description of the brand's architecture (Figure 7.9).

Without all this information it is difficult for senior managers to understand how the marketing programmes described in the next section will implement the marketing strategy.

Marketing Programmes

Marketing programmes are the basic reference point for marketing practice. Figure 12.1 has a double-headed arrow joining the Marketing Strategy and the Marketing Programmes sections of the plan. This reflects the fact that strategy and programmes are often developed jointly. The programmes were outlined in Chapters 8–11. The focus was on attaining and retaining target consumers. The various programmes use a combination of the marketing mix elements (the 9Ps) introduced in Chapter 1. Also, as outlined in the next chapter, these programmes will be implemented and sometimes partly designed by outside suppliers of professional marketing services such as the organization's advertising agency.

One theme that should run through this section of the marketing plan is how each programme influences sales and makes a financial contribution to the profits and fixed costs of the organization. The Du Pont framework introduced in Chapter 2 and/or other financial modelling techniques (such as break-even and contribution analysis) can be used for this purpose. Without some type of financial modelling it is difficult to substantiate budgets, and to convince senior non-marketing managers of the effectiveness and efficiency of the proposed programmes.

A good way to link the discussion of strategy and programmes back to the earlier sections of the marketing plan is to update the 4Ps and 3Cs framework introduced in the Situation Analysis section. Highlighting changes to the various cells of the matrix will focus attention on key aspects of the plan, and will signal where changes to last year's budgets and action plans are to occur.

Budgets

In most organizations, the budget section of the plan is 'where the rubber meets the road'. When strategy and programmes degenerate into dollars, it is easy to see how well the product or service is expected to do. In many organizations, the budgeting process starts with a sales forecast. This provides an estimate of market potential and is also useful to help work out the costs necessary to support various levels of sales.

Sales forecasting and budget setting is often based on past performance. This process may start with last year's actual sales and expenditures and adjust these by some percentage to reflect corporate objectives or anticipated market realities. (For example, this could be 'sales up by X per cent and costs down by Y per cent'.) This approach is appropriate when markets are stable, the current marketing is working, and the organization is not seeking significant change. However, if the marketing plan needs to close a significant gap, and this requires a change in marketing strategy, then sales forecasting, and the resultant budget setting, is quite difficult. The reason is that buyer response will differ according to where expenditures are made (e.g. advertising versus sales promotions) and how much is spent (e.g. match or exceed competitor spending).

To illustrate the vagaries of budgeting consider the various approaches used for setting an advertising budget.

- If a new product is being launched, then the *Objective and Task Method* may be used. Here, the manager starts with the sales goal and works backwards through a series of steps to achieve this goal. For example,
  —sales objective (in units);
  —number of repeat users necessary and the amount they will buy;
  —number of triers of the brand;
  —potential customers who have a favourable brand evaluation;
  —customers who see the advertisement and become aware of the brand;
  —number of advertisements inserted in the media.
  The key here is to specify the correct sequence of steps for the new buyers (and thus the advertising tasks), and the conversion ratios (the number of potential buyers moving between adjacent steps). The size of the budget is determined by the cost of producing the ads, placing the required number in the media, and paying the agency for its services. If the brand is entering an existing product category, then the manager should use another method such as the product category or industry advertising-to-sales ratio to cross-check the amount of money estimated.
- In markets where there is evidence of a strong relationship between the volume of advertising, which is often referred to as share-of-voice (SOV), and market share, also known as share-of-market (SOM), then the budget can be set by specifying the market share required and budgeting the same percentage of the product category or industry's total advertising. Airlines, retail banks, and telecommunications companies (who sell essentially the same product or service) often use this *SOM–SOV Method* as one of their approaches to budgeting. If the product is new, some advertisers recommend spending a higher percentage for the first year or so.[2]

- A (too) frequently used method of budget setting is called the *Affordable Method*. Sometimes this amount is calculated as a percentage-of-sales—last year's sales or this year's forecast. The problem here is one of backwards causation, that is, sales is 'causing' advertising expenditure. In other cases the amount to spend on advertising is simply calculated by asking the marketing director or the financial controller 'how much money can we afford?' Setting a budget like this is tantamount to saying that there is only a tenuous relationship between advertising and sales.

- Another dubious method of budget setting is the *Competitive Parity Method*. Here, the budget is set to match that of the main competitor. The arguments for using this method are that it reflects the collective wisdom of the industry and that it helps prevent advertising wars. However, there are no a priori grounds for believing that competitors are setting their budgets correctly, and there is no scientific evidence that this method stabilizes competitors' advertising expenditures.

- Marketing scientists prefer to use a model-based procedure as one of the budgeting methods. These models base the budget calculation on the relationship between advertising and sales (called the sales-response-to-advertising function). Sometimes this function is estimated empirically and sometimes from management experience. An example is shown in Figure 12.3 where managers have been asked to provide

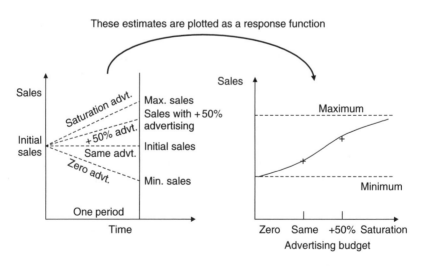

Figure 12.3. Managers' estimates of the effectiveness of advertising

estimates of how changes in advertising spending (as much as possible (saturation), +50 per cent, the current level, and zero advertising) will affect sales.[3] The actual budget amount is then chosen by considering the market share objectives for the brand. For example, if the objective is to maximize the feasible level of sales (given the likely competitive response), then the budget amount would be read off the horizontal axis of the right-hand graph at the point where the response function first reaches its peak.

Because advertising budgeting is such an inexact science, it is always advisable to use more than one method to set an ad budget.

Figure 12.4 shows a general budgeting process. The double-headed arrow between the Marketing and Production budgets links marketing to capital expenditure. One of the current clarion calls of many CEOs is to 'sweat the assets'. By this they mean to get a higher utilization from the current portfolio of assets, and thus 'don't ask for new capital expenditures'. When this happens, marketing managers are often asked to lift their sales targets.

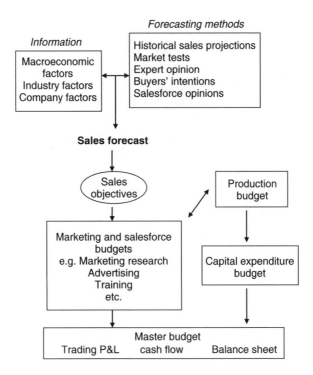

Figure 12.4. A budgeting process

Action Plans

All plans ultimately result in 'work'—tasks, responsibilities, and time-frames. In the marketing plan, this often means setting dates for a new product launch, the trade show, special promotions, the advertising campaign, the annual sales conference, marketing training seminars, etc. It also means assigning people to take responsibility for organizing these tasks. The number and nature of the tasks required by the marketing programmes helps to determine the personnel required and, thus, the people costs of the budget.

Control

While plans and budgets are usually established annually, control periods are much more frequent. For marketing plans, two types of control are needed—strategic and operational. Strategic controls focus on 'doing the right things'. Changes in the business situation such as the merging of two competitors, the start of a price war, or the launch of a breakthrough new product by a competitor may necessitate reassessing some key aspects of the marketing strategy. Strategic controls may be programmed quarterly or half-yearly, or at any time when there is a significant change in the business situation.

Operational controls focus on 'doing things right'. The goal of operational control is to monitor the leading indicators of marketing effectiveness (such as sales, market share, customer attitudes, and satisfaction) and to improve the efficiency of marketing activities (expense-to-sales analysis—for products, territories, customer groups, trade channels, etc.). Two basic accounting questions guide operational control:

- Where are we making money?
- Where are we spending money?

Sometimes it is quite difficult to get timely and accurate answers to both these questions. (When it is, this is a danger signal about the organization's accounting reporting.) The control period for operational aspects of the plan is much shorter than that for strategic control, namely, weekly or monthly.

To illustrate operational controls, McKinsey & Company use a technique called the 'price waterfall' to help their clients manage their transaction prices.[4] Many of their consulting assignments revealed that there is often a

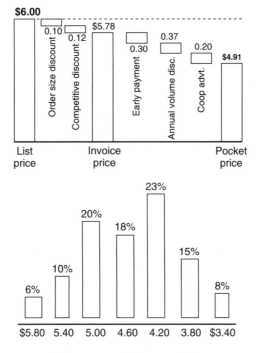

Figure 12.5. Price waterfalls

substantial difference between the 'posted price' of a product on the official price list and the 'pocket price' received by the accounting department. The top portion of Figure 12.5 shows a price waterfall for a company that sells floor coverings to a specific retailer. The official list price is $6.00 per metre. However, this retailer actually pays only $4.91 per metre. A number of different discounts and allowances reduce the list price by 18 per cent. The bottom portion of Figure 12.5 shows the distribution of 'pocket prices' received by the floor covering company from its major retail customers. Understanding why pocket prices vary for each product is a crucial task for marketing managers.

Because operational controls are a critical part of a marketing manager's job (and often their KPIs), it is useful to illustrate another framework that has proven to be useful in many situations. This framework seeks to answer the following question:

Why isn't my brand bought by 100% of target consumers?

Instead of focusing on the traditional issue of how the brand has gained enough consumers to achieve a market share of X per cent, it reverses the issue and focuses on why a brand fails to gain every available target consumer.

The framework starts with the simple flow model of customer acquisition and retention in Figure 12.6. (In a practical situation, this model would be adjusted to reflect the target customer segment's sequence of decision-making.) The logic of the model is that if people are not aware of the brand they cannot consider buying it; if they do not consider it they cannot prefer it; and no preference means no purchase or repeat purchase. The task of the marketer is to gather data for each stage of the model—for his or her brand *and* competitive brands. These data will be:

- the percentage of the total consumers at each stage (? % in Figure 12.6);
- the reasons why target consumers were not aware, did not consider, did not prefer, etc. (The 'No's' in Figure 12.6.)

These data can then be arranged in a table like that shown in Table 12.1.

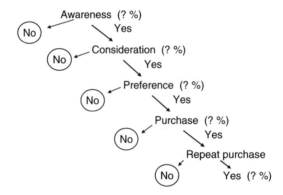

Figure 12.6. Where do we lose our target consumers?

Table 12.1. Where do problems lie?

Brand	Awareness	Consideration (given awareness)	Preference (given consid.)	Purchase First	Repeat
A	30%	70%	60%	60%	80%
B	90	20	40	30	50
C	80	60	20	50	70
D	70	60	50	30	70
E	80	80	70	80	80
Average	70%	58%	48%	50%	70%

Looking across the rows and down the columns of Table 12.1 suggests that Brand A has an awareness problem (relative to its major competitors). It loses 70 per cent of its potential market because target consumers do not know about it. For those that are aware, the brand performs quite well—its consideration, preference, and purchase percentages are all above average.

Brand B has a consideration problem—most target consumers are aware of it, but for some reason they would not consider buying it. Research needs to be done to find out what this reason is. Brands B and C have a preference evaluation problem. Preference is determined by the brand's price, quality, perceived risk, image, etc., relative to competing brands. Brands B and D have a first-purchase problem. Managers need to find out what factors inhibit target consumers who prefer the brands from buying them (e.g. it could be out of stock, the salespeople could be poorly trained, etc.). Brand E is clearly the strongest brand of the group profiled here. All brands (except B) have a similar repeat purchase percentage. (Repeat purchase is determined by satisfaction, continued availability, and no better new brand entering the market.)

The type of data presented in Table 12.1 is also useful for proactive thinking about the competitive market. For example, which brand is most likely to increase its advertising budget and/or change the creative execution of its advertising, and/or change ad agencies? (Brand A.) Which brand might go on promotion (i.e. a temporary price cut)? (Brand B might do this as a way of increasing consideration.) Which brand might permanently lower its price? (Brand C would be a candidate here in order to increase its perceived value relative to competitors.) The market research information that is collected with the data in Table 12.1 would help to answer these and other similar questions.

Good marketing strategy and planning is a big step towards achieving a good marketing outcome. However, without good implementation, as the quotation from James Quinn at the beginning of this chapter suggests, it will have 'no effect on the weather that follows'.

KEY CONCEPTS

- *Marketing plan*—a written statement of the marketing objectives, and the strategy and programmes of action to be taken to achieve those objectives.
- *Marketing objectives*—a statement of the level of performance that the operating unit plans to achieve.
- *Marketing target*—a marketing objective stated in measurable terms.
- *Critical issues*—anything that is currently, or that can, impact on achieving the objectives of the marketing plan.

KEY FRAMEWORKS

- *Marketing planning*—Figure 12.1
- *Critical issues identification*—by convening a critical issues workshop and prioritizing issues in Figure 12.2
- *Advertising budgeting*—using two or more of the following methods to set the advertising budget: objective and task, SOM–SOV, affordable, competitive parity, sales-response-to-advertising
- *Price waterfalls*—Figure 12.5
- *Losing customers*—Figure 12.6 and Table 12.1

KEY QUESTIONS

- Is the planning process more important than the outcome?
- Does the culture of accountability in your organization help or hinder developing a marketing plan?
- Does your marketing plan do an effective job of selling upwards to senior management and downwards to the people who will implement it?
- Does the marketing plan emphasise push and/or pull marketing?

PART B

Making Marketing Work

When Professor Thomas Bonoma was at the Harvard Business School he created a research programme and a course on marketing implementation. What follows in this section draws on the insights of this endeavour.[5]

The poor implementation of a marketing plan can be attributed to either a lack of internal or external 'fit'.[6] *Internal fit* refers to whether or not the organization's marketing strategy and programmes complement each other, and whether the operational systems and controls (such as the process of marketing planning) help or hinder the strategy development and programme implementation. *External fit* refers to the match between the various marketing programmes and the needs of target consumers. The elements of fit are shown in Figure 12.7.

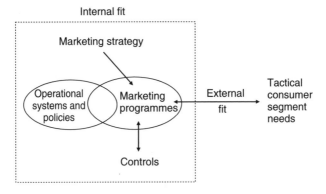

Figure 12.7. Searching for fit

Internal Fit Failures

Many internal fit based implementation problems are caused by developing an inappropriate strategy and sometimes by basing this on a bad business model. A good contemporary example of this misfit occurred when many organizations tried to use the Internet to reconfigure their strategic marketing. For example, Amazon.com is the poster-child of the Internet, yet its business model is yet to yield a profit. In response to Amazon.com's entry into the book-selling market many bricks-and-mortar booksellers spent large sums of money creating a similar Internet marketing programme. What they found was that most people kept buying their books through a traditional bookstore. Also, in the mid-1990s it was thought that the old-fashioned print catalogue industry would be superseded by the e-commerce revolution. 'Who would be bothered leafing through a big, fat catalogue when they could get the same, and often more up-to-date information from the company's website?' It turns out that the answer to this question was quite a large number of people. Research by the New York-based Direct Marketing Association indicates that total US catalogue sales volume (B2C and B2B) rose substantially through the height of the dotcom revolution—from $69.5 billion (in 1996) to $110.2 billion (in 2000).[7] It turned out that bookstores and catalogues are easier to use for most people than a website.

Marketing programmes are the combination of functions that are designed to attain and retain target consumers and to confound competitors. Program-based implementation problems occur when either (*a*) each of these functions do not blend together, or (*b*) the organization does not have the capabilities to deliver the programme. Problems also often occur with changing prices, developing new products, managing the salesforce, and working with members of the distribution channel. Implementation can break down when managers 'take their eyes off the ball'.

Thomas Bonoma suggests that marketers must be good at the basics but they cannot be the best at everything. Also, the best companies concentrate on doing an outstanding job at a few marketing functions. For example, in the 1980s, the personal care division of Gillette was very good at advertising. For decades, McDonald's has excelled at producing food and franchising its outlets. In retailing, the conventional wisdom is that a store will survive if it is good at three of the following Ps, and it will win if it is best at three of these factors:

- Place—location and number of outlets.
- Product—variety, depth, and range of brands.
- Price—lowest or value.
- People—knowledge, presentation, attitude.
- Position—image.

Bonoma calls these the 'showcase' marketing functions of the organization.

Another implementation issue that bedevils every organization is whether the systems employed to allocate resources, change programmes, and make reports foster or inhibit good marketing practice. Systems problems commonly involve ritual ('We have always done it this way!'), politicization ('In this organization, you only tell senior managers what they want to hear!'), and unavailability ('We can never get information about customer profitability!').

One of the most important implementation problems is highlighted by the following quote:

> The folly of rewarding A while hoping for B.
>
> Steven Kerr

This statement comes from a famous paper published in 1975.[8] The paper reviewed a number of situations that clearly demonstrated that 'people do what is inspected, in preference to what is expected'. In the context of marketing, this research suggests that a manager's KPIs (what is inspected) *must* be aligned with the desired actions and outcomes of the marketing plan (what is expected). In many organizations this is not the case. For example,

- In some call centres, the punishment for employees is much more severe for falling short of call targets than the reward is for providing good service to the caller—notwithstanding the customer-focused sentiments in the organization's vision statement.

- In many organizations, senior managers hope that employees will engage in team building, interpersonal relations, mentoring, developing creative new products, making independent decisions, etc., but it formally rewards none of these activities.

- In the 1980s, a computer terminal manufacturer set out to have sales of its new, improved, and higher-margin terminals cannibalize its old product line. However, the sales incentives for the new terminals were set lower than those of the old product line. Also, the new terminals took twice the time to sell and the salesperson required new knowledge to sell them. Sales did not take off.

Thus, aligning people's rewards with the expectations of the marketing plan is arguably the key to its successful implementation.

Operational systems and policy directives—both spoken and unspoken—can often frustrate the implementation of a good marketing plan. One type of policy is the internal culture of marketing throughout the organization. Marketing culture refers to management's shared understanding of the role of marketing in the organization. Despite Peter Drucker's advice, sometimes there is no shared understanding—some managers think that marketing is important while others consider it to be almost irrelevant. Sometimes the shared understanding is quite negative. For example, the partners of many (large) law firms consider that they 'market' their firm (which is true), and that the marketing department is a 'bolt-on' function that is employed primarily to help organize the firm's brochures and promotional events.

Some organizations replace marketing with a culture of 'sales'. Here, the focus is on pushing products and services into the market with as much marketing muscle (often advertising and/or price support) as necessary to reach the planned sales targets. The people who are charged with the responsibility for this are the salesforce and the 'marketers'. In contrast, an organization with a marketing culture is one where everybody in the organization respects customers and the art and science of marketing, and they are interested in finding out how to serve target customers better. I have heard this philosophy expressed as 'If you are not serving a customer, or someone who is, then what are you doing here?'

Another policy factor is directional, in particular the quality of marketing leadership. Key managers must use their personal skills to support and sometimes quietly overthrow poorly functioning systems. For example, to get accurate and timely information about the price waterfall in Figure 12.5 may require some 'informal negotiations' with someone in the accounting department.

External Fit Failures

Marketing failures of external fit usually arise for four main reasons because:

- The products and services offered to target customers do not adequately satisfy their needs. For example, after completing a full-time MBA degree, there has to be multiple job offers from which to choose.
- The communication, pricing, and/or distribution of the product or service fails to attract customers. For example, Sony's betamax video-cassette recorder was a technically better VCR than JVC's VHS recorder—but Sony's marketing strategy undermined the betamax system's potential success.[9]
- Promises made to target customers are not fulfilled by the organization. For example, in the area of CRM there are many examples of organizations that set out to maintain a good relationship with their customers, but that do not invest enough in the IT and customer database that support the CRM system. The result is frustrated customer-contact staff and disappointed customers.
- The products and services bought by consumers turn out to be more difficult to use than expected. For example, many people struggle to use all the functions on some of their technology-based consumer products (such as PCs, video-cassette recorders, mobile phones, etc.). Customer service units and telephone help lines are often needed for post-sale support.

In summary, the marketing literature has much help to offer marketing managers about designing marketing strategy (what to do), but less when it comes to implementing these strategies (how to do it). Bonoma's insights reported in this section are a good start, as is the notion of striving to achieve internal and external fit. The next section of this chapter looks at another major issue that marketers struggle with—how to organize the marketing function.

Organizing the Marketing Function

Many organizations start out their lives with no formal marketing function. The key to survival is production and sales (and a good accountant).

Marketing begins to appear when the salespeople need some marketing research, advertising, and sales promotion. These tasks may initially be outsourced to the advertising agency and marketing research firm. As growth occurs, internal appointments are made in these areas. Soon a more senior manager is appointed to manage the group. What results is a functionally organized marketing group that often has a power struggle with the (original) sales manager.

In 1931, Procter & Gamble formally introduced the Brand Management style of organization as an alternative to having brands managed by a group of functional specialists. 'Each Procter & Gamble brand should have its own brand assistants and managers dedicated to the advertising and other marketing activities of the brand'.[10] Conceptually, the idea was that the brand managers would be mini-general managers—responsible for running their own brand businesses. These managers would compete in the marketplace against competitors, and internally against other brands for the organization's limited resources. Competitor-focused companies encourage this form of organization and culture. Fighting for resources and being benchmarked against other company brands toughens up the brand managers inside the organization so that they are fierce competitors out-side the organization. Companies that adopted the brand management system also liked it because it created a single point of contact with distrib-utors and retailers. More recently, measures of brand equity (discussed in Chapter 7) can be used to monitor the brand's (and brand manager's) performance.

Brand management however has two important downsides. One was mentioned at the beginning of this chapter as the 'brand manager life cycle'. When a new brand manager takes over an existing brand and repack-ages and relaunches it, there is little fundamental change to the brand or its sales. To compensate for this, another activity is to launch a line exten-sion in the hope that a broader product line will attract a wider range of consumers. This strategy soon leads to brand proliferation. For example, in the mid-1990s, Procter & Gamble had thirty-one varieties of Head and Shoulders shampoo and fifty-two versions of Crest toothpaste.[11] This was very effective for keeping competitive brands off the supermarket shelves, but it did not compensate for increasing the cost base of the brand. A sec-ond problem with the brand management system is that it can, and often does, lead to more competition among internal brands than with external brands.[12]

By the early 1970s, the brand management style of organization was the norm for most multi-product companies in the United States (both B2C and B2B). However, it was starting to accumulate some detractors.[13] For example, at Heinz, the branding strategy was organized under the family brand 'Heinz'. Thus, they did not see the relevance of separate brand managers marketing various product lines. Also, at many organizations, the brand managers were young people who were put into the role to learn about marketing. They encountered many problems that were caused by their responsibility for achieving brand targets but their lack of the direct authority to get other managers to comply with their requests. They also contributed to some major marketing mistakes, as when 'American brand managers embarked on a suicidal orgy of trade promotions and coupon offers' in the late 1980s and early 1990s.[14]

A functional brand management, or any other system for organizing marketing, is really at the behest of the bigger decision about how best to structure the organization as a whole. This big-picture issue, together with management fads like re-engineering, downsizing, and outsourcing, all influence how the marketing function is organized. Another influencing force is the current dominant logic of marketing. In Chapter 1, the various approaches were labelled as the: production concept, product concept, selling concept, positioning, and customer value. Currently, marketing's dominant logic is to focus on the customer and to create and capture customer value. Thus, many organizations now use neither a purely functional nor a brand management organizational structure. (As their names suggest, neither of these systems are very consumer focused.)

One organizational form is to modify the brand manager system by superimposing a product category manager above the various brand managers. This form of organization makes dealing with the category management system of powerful retailers more efficient. It is also more customer focused as it better reflects the pattern of buyer behaviour for most supermarket brands outlined in Chapter 4. (Recall that most buyers are polygamously loyal to a number of brands in a product category.)

For the major customers of B2B marketers (including professional services), the marketing function is often organized around industries and/or the business applications of a product or service (such as IT—for airlines, financial services, government, mission-critical applications, etc.), and delivered by specialist cross-functional teams. When customers are big enough, separate teams may service individual key accounts. This is a very customer-focused approach to organizing the marketing function and is generally based on the organization's strategic and tactical segmentation. For the minor customers, marketing may be primarily delivered through salespeople and customer service call centres (staffed by order-takers and technical support personnel). Here, the customer assumes much of the responsibility for knowing what they want.[15] The selling organization provides limited help when asked, and it may offer price incentives to its best customers.

The approach that best fits the thesis of this book is to organize the marketing function around customer segments. For example, the role of senior management at Silicon Graphics is to divide customers into segments determined by their needs and the technology required to satisfy these needs. Each segment is then assigned a NPD team that works with selected lead-user customers to design the next generation of products.[16] In essence, a customer-focused manufacturer like Silicon Graphics hopes to develop four sets of superior capabilities, namely: (*a*) market sensing (viz. learning about customers and competitors), (*b*) product development to meet specific customer needs, (*c*) trade partnering (viz. relationships with suppliers and channel members), and (*d*) customer linking (viz. using the appropriate distribution channels, e-commerce technologies, and types of communication to deliver products and services). Concentrating on these capabilities provides a much better chance of matching the firm's product and service offerings to its evolving customer needs. If managers are rewarded directly on their ability to achieve a balanced set of outcomes for their customer segment, then the chances increase that customers and not brands will be the key focus of the organization.

The roles and responsibilities of a customer segment manager are to facilitate the conversion of organizational resources into customer value. This process was illustrated in Chapter 2 (Figure 2.6 for Caterpillar). For most organizations, to look after a customer segment is a major general management responsibility. Figure 12.8 shows how this responsibility could be organized. A senior marketing manager is responsible for each of the

Figure 12.8. Organizing the marketing function

organization's product-market segments. His or her responsibility is general management in nature. That is, to plan, obtain internal resources, and build a team of marketers to deliver the organization's sales goals for the product-market. The marketing team will be made up of:

- more junior managers to take responsibility for the various tactical segments (TS1, TS2, etc.);
- functional specialists (either internal people or outside professional firms) to work with the segment managers to provide the services necessary to ensure distribution and to attain and retain customers;
- brand managers to work with production to ensure that each brand (B1, B2, etc.) is available and made to specifications, and to monitor the equity of the brand over time.

The organization in Figure 12.8 contains a natural career path for marketers. Junior managers enter the marketing team and learn the art and science of marketing through either the brand manager role or as a functional specialist. They rotate through various roles and when their experience is broad enough they progress to become a tactical segment manager. Here, the focus is more squarely on serving the needs of target consumers and responding to competitors. They also learn about management, strategy, and planning. The best of the tactical segment managers progress to become product-market segment managers who effectively run a small business. From here they move to become senior general managers.

To summarize, there is considerable debate as to how to organize the marketing function inside an organization. Ajay Kohli of the Harvard Business School suggests that it depends on how fast the market is changing and where a firm creates customer value, through product qualities or service.[17] Other advice is easy to find. While this type of contingency approach has merit, if an organization really wants to be customer focused, then it has to be organized by customer segment. These segments can contain a single customer (e.g. a key account) or many customers—it matters little to the fundamental principle. The point is that if customers really are more important than products and services for the growth and prosperity of the organization, then segment managers are needed as the pivots in the organization. They may be supported by a gaggle of brand/product managers, sales and trade-marketing managers, database experts, ad agencies, and researchers, but the final responsibility must seat home to somebody whose performance appraisal is tied directly to delivering a superior end-result benefit to a targeted group of customers.

Retailers also have a new role to play if customers are to receive the portfolio of products and services they desire. Their access to accurate and timely customer information and their relationship with customers provides them with a unique opportunity to work with manufacturers to deliver a better customer experience.

While the best way to organize the marketing function within an organization is an open issue, the design outlined in Figure 12.8 fits the approach to marketing outlined in this book—it is customer focused, and it reflects one of the central organizing frameworks of marketing, namely, market segmentation. Probably the most practical advice one can offer is to find an organizational structure that 'works' and stick with it as the numerous fads of management come and go.

KEY CONCEPTS

- *Internal marketing fit*—the level of congruence among the organization's marketing strategy, programmes, and controls, and the level of support these receive from the organization's operational systems and policies.
- *External marketing fit*—the level of congruence between the organization's offer and its marketing programmes to deliver this, and target customer needs.

KEY FRAMEWORK

- *Organizing the marketing function*—Figure 12.8

KEY QUESTIONS

- Do the KPIs of individual managers align directly with the expectations of the marketing plan?
- When desired outcomes do not meet the objectives in the marketing plan, is the primary reason for this a lack of internal or external fit?
- Does your marketing organization pivot around customer segments, or brands, or marketing functions?

RECAP

The reason to plan is not to produce a wonderful planning document (although this may be a useful outcome), but rather because there is no reliable substitute for disciplined thinking. The process of planning is a good way to capture and organize the knowledge about customers, competitors, and markets that is distributed throughout the organization. Also, the process of planning acts as a form of collective decision-making and starts to get 'buy-in' to the organization's future.

The reasons to develop good control mechanisms are (*a*) to provide early warning of changes in the market and business environment so that adjustments to strategy can be made, and (*b*) to focus on the efficiency and effectiveness of tactical marketing programmes. Data-driven control frameworks (such as the price waterfall) are a good way to identify the key issues that need to be modified.

To conclude this chapter I would like to recount what I think is some sound advice from the CEO of a major successful company. His insight about planning is that:

> Senior managers (especially the CEO) should work *on* the business, not *in* the business.

NOTES

1. L. Taylor, 'Managing in a Crisis: The Jack Welch Formula', *Australian Financial Review Weekend* (13–14 October 2001), 26.
2. One recommendation by J. O. Peckman is to set the brand's SOV at 1.5 times its desired SOM.
3. This is described in G. L. Lilien and A. Rangaswamy, *Marketing Engineering* (Upper Saddle River, NJ: Prentice Hall, 2003), pp. 315–18.
4. M. V. Marn and R. L. Rosiello, 'Managing Price, Gaining Profit', *Harvard Business Review* (September–October 1992), 84–94.
5. T. V. Bonoma, 'Making Your Marketing Work', *Harvard Business Review* (March–April 1984), 2–9.
6. The notion of 'fit' was first introduced by R. Miles and C. Snow, 'Fit, Failure and the Hall of Fame', *California Management Review*, 26, 3 (1984), 10–28, and later expanded in R. Miles and C. Snow, *Fit, Failure and the Hall of Fame* (New York: Free Press, 1994).
7. S. Jarvis, 'A Page-turner', *Marketing News* (8 October 2001), p. 3.
8. S. Kerr, 'On the Folly of Rewarding A, While Hoping for B', *Academy of Management Journal*, 18, 4 (1975), 769–83.
9. M. A. Cusumano, Y. Mylonadis, and R. S. Rosenbloom, 'Strategic Manoeuvring and Mass-Market Dynamics: The Triumph of VHS over Beta', in M. L. Tushman and P. Anderson (eds.), *Managing Strategic Innovation and Change* (New York: Oxford University Press, 1997), pp. 75–98.
10. G. S. Low and R. A. Fullerton, 'Brands, Brand Management, and the Brand Management System: A Critical Historical Evaluation', *Journal of Marketing Research*, 31, 2 (1994), 173–90.
11. *Business Week*, 'Make It Simple. That's P&G's New Marketing Mantra—and It's Spreading', (9 September 1996), pp. 56–61.

12. To help overcome this problem, in 1987 Procter & Gamble introduced category managers to their brand management structure.

13. D. E. Schultz, 'A Better Way to Organize', *Marketing News* (27 March 1995), pp. 12, 15.

14. 'Death of the Brand Manager', *The Economist* (9 April 1994), pp. 67–8.

15. I once met a salesman who was responsible for 60,000 line items. He said that his customers generally knew exactly what they wanted and his responsibility was to find where stocks were available around the world and organize delivery.

16. S. Prokesch, 'Mastering Chaos at the High-Tech Frontier', *Harvard Business Review* (November–December 1993), 135–44.

17. Reported in B. Donath, 'Pick a Role Model: General Motors or Dell', *Marketing News* (12 October 1998), p. 9.

13

Working with External Service Providers

> Good contracts motivate good relationships.
> Bad contracts ultimately lead to bad outcomes.

To implement many of the organization's marketing programmes requires working with outside suppliers of services, such as consultants, distributors, advertising agencies, and market research firms. Good working relationships with service suppliers provide leverage to the marketing team's internal capabilities. This chapter focuses primarily on advertising agencies and market research firms as these are two of the principal outside suppliers of professional services to most marketing managers. The issues that govern the working relationship between the organization and these two agents are similar to those for other service providers.

The previous paragraph referred to the suppliers of marketing services as 'agents'. The reason for this is that there is a considerable body of work in the discipline of economics that looks at many of the issues raised in this last chapter as a 'principal–agent' problem.[1] From this perspective, the key issues for marketing managers are:

- How to write a contract with an external service provider so that they work in the best interests of the organization. As illustrated in the case of advertising agencies, this turns out to be a difficult task.
- How to design a business relationship with the agent that
  —caters for the different interests of the parties;
  —motivates the parties not to 'shirk' (i.e. avoid their responsibilities);
  —caters for their tolerance to absorb risk.

Resolving these issues starts with understanding the nature of the interaction between the organization and its external service suppliers.

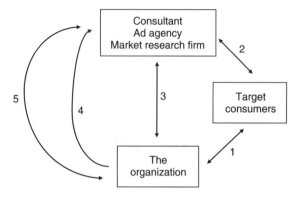

Figure 13.1. Working with external service suppliers

Figure 13.1 shows the five relationships that are of importance:

1. *The exchange between the organization and its target consumers.* This has been discussed in Parts 2 and 3 of this book.
2. *The agent's understanding of target consumers.* One of the things that makes many external service suppliers valuable to an organization is their understanding of various consumer groups. This experience and access to research enables them to enhance the organization's understanding of consumer decision-making, attitudes, purchase motivations, learned experience, etc.
3. *The reasons for engaging the agent.* These focus on helping the organization to (*a*) better understand customers, markets, and competitors (Chapters 3–5), (*b*) create tactical segments (Chapter 6), and (*c*) design, implement, and monitor marketing programmes (Chapters 7–11).
4. *Briefing the Agent.* This sets the scope for the work to be performed, and will also often establish the roles of the parties. For example, some organizations want to use their agents as quasi-marketing consultants while others see little value in this role.
5. *The working relationship between the agent and the organization.* This is governed by the past experience of the parties in dealing with similar suppliers, and the terms and conditions of the engagement contract.

Because much of this book has already dealt with the issues involved with relationships 1–3, this chapter focuses on relationships 4 and 5.

Relationship 4 involves choosing the best (most reputable) supplier available—given the size of the job to be done and the budget available. When a highly reputable organization seeks external help, many service firms will 'bid' for the work. This happens because service firms like to work for good clients (so that they can 'rent' their corporate reputation when seeking new clients), and work on big jobs (so that they acquire industry knowledge that can be used elsewhere). For example, when Westpac, Australia's third largest retail bank, put its $30 million advertising account out to tender, twenty-three agencies were asked to pitch for the account.[2] With multiple potential suppliers, the organization needs a formal buying process to select the supplier.[3]

Relationship 5 involves designing the terms and conditions of the engagement contract. Sometimes this is a very detailed and formal process, in other cases it may involve little more than a verbal agreement finalized by a handshake. Both approaches have their strengths and weaknesses.

Choosing an Ad Agency and a Marketing Research Firm

At one time or another, most organizations will use the services of an advertising agency and one or more freelance marketing research suppliers. Advertising agencies help to strategically plan communications and create and place advertising. Their relationship with large organizations is usually ongoing and may last many years before it is terminated. Many smaller organizations have no ongoing relationship with an ad agency and will only use one for a specific project such as the launch of a new product or service. Table 13.1 lists some of the main criteria why advertising agencies are chosen and why they are terminated.[4]

Table 13.1. Hiring and firing ad agencies

Hiring criteria	Termination criteria
1. Formal presentation	* New senior marketer appointed at the client
	1. Need new creative ideas
2. Liked the agency people	2. Needed a new marketing approach
3. Good proposal	3. Poor account service
4. Past dealings with the agency	4. Senior agency staff no longer involved
5. Agency marketing materials	5. Ads were no longer effective
	6. Agency cost over-runs
	7. Poor media buying

* This is a rare but important event. To let everybody know that the new manager has 'arrived' with some new ideas, he or she may fire the incumbent agency.

For the supply of ongoing research services, long-term arrangements between research firms and organizations are common. For project-based research, the use of marketing research firms is often more of a spot-market nature whereby a contract is written for the supply of services at the current market price. This allows organizations to cherry-pick the best researchers. Outsourcing the gathering of information about markets, competitors, and consumers occurs because most organizations do not have the in-house expertise or resources to conduct this activity, and it often helps to avoid some of the internal politics associated with introducing new information into managerial decision-making.

The difficulty in choosing an ad agency or a research firm is caused because (a) advertising and commercial research rely heavily on the experienced judgement of the practitioners, (b) there are many firms to choose from, (c) all claim experience and expertise, (d) in most countries formal qualifications or certification is not necessary to set up a firm, and (e) most have a good sales pitch. Also, unless you are aware of the techniques and procedures of advertising and marketing research, or you are an experienced user, it is difficult to judge the overall quality of a potential ad campaign or a research proposal (or report).

When experience is lacking, what often happens is the following:

- Establish a list of potential suppliers—from a directory of service firms; the recommendations of other managers, consultants, and academics; and from firms previously used by the organization.
- Brief and seek proposals from three to five firms.
- Ask for the names of clients to contact for a reference.
- Establish a list of criteria to be used to evaluate the firm. This list should include: their understanding of your brief; working to your organization's constraints and budget; the experience of the firm and its key people; staff turnover; the marketing background and formal qualifications of the people; the professionalism of the people; the 'personal chemistry' between the personnel involved and the marketing manager; track record—past clients, the length of relationships with them, and projects completed; relationships with other related suppliers; membership of advertising, marketing, and marketing research associations; and the financial health of the firm.
- Establish a small group to evaluate the proposals—the written document, a formal presentation, and, if possible, a visit to the firm's office. (This group may include at least one outsider—a marketing consultant and/or an academic.)
- From the two or three that seem suitable, bite the bullet and make a choice.

- Learn from the experience and keep a 'paper trail' of the proposals, evaluations, and subsequent satisfaction with the project.

When managers and organizations gain experience with the ad agency and one or more research firms, many will form a closer working relationship with their key people. This is when the broader marketing experience of these firms can add real value to marketing decision-making.

Arguably the two key factors in helping to choose a good professional service firm are (*a*) the knowledge the buyer about the service being acquired, and his or her experience in buying such services—Relationships 3 and 4 in Figure 13.1 (i.e. the more experienced buyers tend to buy better)—and (*b*) the ability to write a sensible contract with the agent providing the service—Relationship 5. The remainder of this chapter discusses these two factors. In Part A the focus is on advertising and ad agencies. Part B focuses on marketing research.

PART A

Working with Ad Agencies

A good working relationship with an ad agency is built on the twin foundations of a good brief and a good contract. However, before a good brief can be written, the manager needs to reflect on his or her personal theory of advertising. Hence, Part A starts with this issue and then proceeds to outline the information necessary to include in a good advertising brief. Following this the focus shifts to contracting issues, namely, how to align the economic incentives of the ad agency with the desire of the client to have less, but more effective advertising. Part A concludes with a discussion of how a manager might assess the work of the agency.

Advertising—How it Works

Before focusing on working with ad agencies, it is necessary to consider the vexing question of how advertising 'works'. This is important because without a mental model of how advertising works, it is very difficult to judge the effectiveness of an agency's work—both their bid proposal and the campaign they will ask you to fund. A good way to understand advertising is to consider four definitions:

- Advertising is the process of getting an idea about a brand into a consumer's head, an idea that will move him or her towards purchase.
- Advertising's job is to communicate to a defined audience information and a frame-of-mind that stimulates action.
- Advertising is an *indirect* form of persuasion, based on information or emotional appeals about product benefits, designed to create favourable mental impressions that turn the mind towards purchase.
- Advertising is a sometimes entertaining and sometimes obnoxious way that consumers use to find out about a product or service.

The first definition came from the internal marketing manual of one of the world's largest consumer goods companies. It reflects what has been called the 'strong theory' of advertising, namely, good ads can persuade people to buy products and services.[5] Many social critics and government agencies subscribe to this theory. We saw this when governments banned the advertising of cigarettes. The assumption was that turning off the flow of advertising would have a significant effect on reducing consumption—new smokers would not be enticed to start (the persuasive effect of advertising), and current smokers would not have their consumption habit supported through the aspirational images in the ads (the reinforcement effect of advertising).[6]

The second definition came from an advertising agency's presentation to a client. Thus, it reflects both the agency's beliefs and its sales pitch. The agency went on to say that the advertising succeeds or fails depending on how well it communicates the desired information and brand position to the right people at the right time. This definition also reflects a 'strong-effects theory' of advertising. However, some ad agencies will concede that advertising is the 'price an organization pays for being in the market'. By this they mean that many organizations have to match their competitors' advertising in order to maintain their SOV in the market. In this respect, advertising has a much weaker persuasive effect.[i]

The third definition comes from one of the world's leading advertising textbooks.[7] It reflects a 'moderate-effects theory' of advertising. That is, the emphasis is on the word indirect. The textbook from which it comes takes 600 pages to describe all the nuances of advertising—some of which will be discussed below.

The fourth definition of advertising came from a consumer. It suggests a 'weak theory' of advertising effectiveness. This theory resonates with

---

[i] This view of advertising lies at the heart of the SOM–SOV budget setting approach discussed in Chapter 12.

most consumers—if we are in the market for a particular product or service, sometimes the advertising leads to a purchase. If we have recently bought the brand, the advertising may act to reinforce our choice. However, in most cases most of the advertising we 'see' is either screened out or ignored.

For a marketer it is important to form an opinion about the likely effects (strong, moderate, or weak) that advertising and other forms of marketing communications will have on target consumers. The best way to do this is to specify (*a*) the marketing task at hand (such as introducing a new product, maintaining or increasing sales for an established product, repositioning a brand, etc.); (*b*) how advertising is expected to work (such as provide information that will change people's beliefs about the product, create emotion, etc.); (*c*) the target consumers' learned experience (a seasoned buyer or a new buyer); and (*d*) their propensity to see and respond to marketing communications. For example, some conclusions from a review of 250 books and papers on the effects of advertising are that:[8]

- The short-term effects of advertising are small, and much smaller than those for promotions. They are also much smaller than the effects of prior use of the product or service. They are significant for approximately one-third of established brands and half of new brands.
- Ninety per cent of advertising's effects dissipate after three-to-fifteen months.
- Returns to advertising are generally diminishing—for most ads the first few exposures are the most powerful.
- Price advertising increases price sensitivity, whereas non-price advertising decreases it.
- Having people like the ad is good, although it is not essential to changing brand evaluation and purchase behaviour.
- Advertising is more effective when it precedes purchase as opposed to reinforcing it.

The problem with the science of advertising is that it offers few concrete findings about how, when, and why (above-the-line) mass media advertising and (below-the-line) promotions work. Most research produces findings that depend on particular circumstances. Hence, in order to avoid putting themselves at the mercy of advertisers (who have a vested interest in spending money on advertising), marketers need to think carefully about how, when, and why they expect advertising to work for their brand or organization. This should be done to help set budgets for advertising relative to other marketing programmes and tactics. It is also useful input into the ad agency's brief, and it will influence the service levels expected from the agency.

Briefing an Ad Agency

A verbal briefing isn't worth the paper it is written on.

The following checklist originated in an ad agency and represents the minimum amount of information the agency account director would like from his or her clients:

- *Background*—key facts about the product market, the brand's objectives, and its target consumers. (Try to build a character study of the target consumer segment and show the role of the brand in this story.)
- *Communication objectives*—what the advertising (promotion, etc.) is *realistically* expected to achieve. Typical objectives include: to stimulate the category need, create brand awareness, develop a brand position, foster purchase intention, assure the consumer about the brand, and increase sales.
- *The brand position statement*—and the thinking behind this as discussed in Chapter 7.
- *Target audience*—demographics, attitudes, beliefs, product usage, etc. That is, the tactical segmentation as described in Chapter 6.
- *Single minded proposition*—this is also called the brand essence, the USP, or the core benefit proposition. Regardless of what it is called, it is important to state clearly what the brand is trying to sell.
- *Supporting features and benefits*—the product onion from Chapter 8.
- *Proof*—research that supports the single-minded proposition.
- *Brand personality*—personal attributes that can be used to describe the brand (as discussed in Chapter 7).
- *Competitive products*—the brands also considered by the target market, and copies of their advertising.
- *Mandatories*—such as published standards of customer service, logos, typeface, etc.
- *Mechanics*—timing, budget, and things that must be done.

For a new campaign with an established agency, the marketing manager and the advertising account director may need to work on a new brief together. In any case, when the Brief is finalized it becomes the plan against which all future advertising is to be judged. The client signs it. So does the agency account director and the creative director. It should not be changed without everybody's agreement—and signature.

No paperwork on earth can automatically produce great advertising. But it does help to maintain costs and stop wandering aimlessly between:

- what the client thinks he or she wants;
- what the creative people would like the client to have;
- what the account director thinks the agency can sell.

Getting the Piper to Play a Better Tune

The Client Lament:

> Half my advertising is wasted, but I don't know which half!
>
> Variously attributed to either

John Wanamaker (founder of a US department store) or Lord Leverhulme of the United Kingdom.

Periodically, the people who work in ad agencies write about the internal workings of their agency. These books often have intriguing titles like *Adland, Confessions of an Advertising Man, Inside the Asylum, Up the Agency,* and *Where the Suckers Moon.*[9] Most of these books are a good read, but inevitably they leave the reader with a feeling of unease about whether or not the agencies are as customer focused as their marketing presentations suggest. The author of *Up the Agency* described the ad agency view of clients in the heady and 'greed is good' 1980s as 'pigs with chequebooks'.

In the 1990s, marketing managers began to take stock of the working relationship they had with their ad agencies. Many ad agency managers also decided that it was time to reconsider their mode of operation (the 'long lunch' really had developed into an art-form), and the value they could add to their client's marketing. One key issue that emerged out of this reappraisal was the role of the standard industry contract between agency and client. This style of contract, which is no longer mandatory, but which is still used by many organizations and their agencies for advertising in the main media (television, radio and print), has the following general form:

- the client pays the agency a service fee based on the amount of money spent on adverting, say 7.5 per cent;
- the client pays for production costs (and sometimes the agency adds its service fee to these);

- the client pays for its advertising in the media;
- the ad agency receives a commission rebate back from the media outlet in which the advertising is placed, say 10–15 per cent.

There is an interesting economic incentive imbedded in this payment scheme. The way for the ad agency to maximize its revenues from a fixed client budget is to maximize the amount of money available for spending in the media. (Whenever the media rebate percentage is greater than the service fee percentage this will occur.) Also, the agency should not be too concerned about negotiating the lowest media rates. If it does get a good deal from the media, it has the economic incentive to simply create and place extra advertisements to capture the 'lost' revenue. Another side-effect of this payment scheme is to place the client's advertising in media that pay their rebates the fastest.

The picture painted here is one of the organization and its ad agency jointly agreeing to a contract that has the economic incentives of the agency not strictly aligning with those of the client—which wants less, but more effective advertising. Beginning in the 1990s, and continuing today, agencies and their clients are struggling to develop (payment) schemes to align both their economic and strategic incentives. Some of the options that are being trailed are:

- share the media rebate between client and agency;
- a simple fee-for-service arrangement where the client gets all the media rebate;
- a simple cost-plus contract;
- a project-based contract;
- a price-cap contract where the client fixes the upper limits for the work of the agency and any savings accrue to the agency;
- a performance-based contract that links the agency's advertising to communication objectives (such as awareness, consideration, brand evaluation) and/or sales, and then pays for achieving target outcomes;
- a strategic partnership between agency and client that is formed based on mutual goals, trust, and information sharing, where rewards are shared according to effort and value created, and risks according to the capacity to absorb them.

The various forms of arrangement above have been shown to be second-best solutions when compared to what is known as a 'self-enforcing contract'.[10] These are contracts where it is in the best interests of both parties to work as effectively as possible for their joint benefit (economic and enhancing both their corporate reputations). This ideal type of contract includes a significant performance component. It also achieves the most important aims of both parties without imposing excessive monitoring costs on either. For example, clients periodically formally review the agency's client service and sanction an independent audit of the media scheduling and buying. These reviews are costly and not necessary with a self-enforcing contract.

In spite of the best efforts of agencies and their clients, it has so far proven to be very difficult to write a good self-enforcing contract. The reason for this is that this style of contract must specify the following:

- a clear set of measurable target outcomes to be achieved that follow from the goals that each party wants to achieve from the business relationship;
- measures of how each of the parties has contributed towards achieving the target outcomes;
- the level of risk that each party is willing to bear;
- a formal profit sharing arrangement that motivates each party to invest in and share management of the relationship;
- a recognition of those actions and arrangements that cannot be effectively monitored and, therefore, are not included in the contract.

Discussions with a number of Australian advertising agencies indicate that many engagement arrangements are designed using a 'mixing-and-matching' rule. The agencies and clients pick various elements from the contracting models outlined above—hoping to gather the appropriate mixture of incentives, trust, and partnership for their circumstances, while minimizing the obvious pitfalls associated with each model. (For example, a cost-plus contract assigns risk mainly to the client, while a performance based contract assigns risk mainly to the agency.) Such mixing and matching, although eclectic and flexible, is not an approach that guarantees a successful outcome for either the ad agency or the organization—especially if one party is small in size relative to the other.

Incentive contracts are part of everyday life in business—senior managers are paid bonuses, salespeople are paid commissions, and production workers are paid piece rates. However, it has only been recently that the advertising marketplace has opened itself to performance-based pay. In the years ahead, marketing managers need to explore how to incorporate pay for performance incentives in their formal arrangements with their ad agencies. A first step in this process is to determine whether or not the organization actually has a formal contract with the ad agency. A recent survey of 109 Australian organizations found that nearly 50 per cent of the marketing managers interviewed did not know if their organization actually had a formal contract with their ad agency. Without knowledge of the supplier arrangement, it is difficult to believe that these managers could fully appreciate how the terms and conditions of the arrangement impacted on the working relationship.

Working with the Ad Agency

The Ad Agency's Response to the Client's Lament:

> Ad agencies say that it is the second half of the client's advertising that is wasted. Media people say that it is the first half of the client's budget that is wasted.

What does the agency's response to the client's lament that 50 per cent of advertising is wasted really mean? Often the developers of advertising say that their creative execution is on target (the first 50 per cent), but the media scheduling (the second 50 per cent) is where the waste occurs. Talk to the media planners and they will respond that it is the creative part of the advertising that is misguided, and if they are in a bad mood, they will say that the agencies charge too much for their service. What these two opinions suggest is that marketing managers need to understand enough about the creative development of their advertising and its placement in the media to be able to ask their advertising agency some informed questions about their recommendations. It is these two components of advertising that deliver what most organizations want from their ad agency—less money spent and more effective advertising.

Assessing Creativity[11]

How can a manager make sensible comments about the creative concepts developed by their ad agency without putting the agency people offside? It is a bit like commenting on modern art with the artist—disagreements are likely to abound! Some managers side-step the problem by agreeing with the agency's preferred option. Others take a more confrontational approach and challenge the agency to 'defend' their options. Either approach is likely to lead to a less than optimal outcome.

The desired outcome from the creative process is to select a 'winning creative idea'. A straight advertisement—stating what the product is, who it is for, and the benefits it offers—sometimes works in direct mail and classified advertising, but it will get lost in the general clutter of advertising in the main media. It is nearly always more effective to use a creative idea to convey the position of the brand. Research has found that a powerful creative idea can increase a brand's sales *many-fold* with the *same* advertising budget. (One minimum estimate is a fivefold increase.) Thus, from a marketer's perspective, investing in finding a winning creative idea is a good commercial (and career enhancing) investment. For the reasons outlined in the next paragraph, it is also a good strategy for the ad agency.

Table 13.1 indicates that one of the key criteria for firing an ad agency is the client's perception of its creativity. Also, as the advertising industry fragments into specialist providers (of direct marketing, sales promotion, public relations, sports marketing, sponsorship, and media planning and buying), many traditional sources of revenue are disappearing from the full-service agency. Another source of lost revenue occurs because marketers are becoming better trained and they are doing more of their own strategic planning for their communication campaigns. Finally, the agencies like winning awards for their creative advertising. Thus, the one unique function that ad agencies offer their clients is creativity.

The dilemma for marketing managers is that the ad agencies are the creative communication specialists but they are the ones paying for the advertising. So how can a marketer increase his or her confidence that an advertisement:

- has a good chance of being a winner; and
- will not be a commercial embarrassment?

Some new research provides the answer to the first question and some old research the answer to the second. Before reviewing this research it is necessary to define a few terms.

For an advertisement, creativity comes in two forms—the creative idea and the executional tactics. These two elements combine with the content of the advertising message to produce an advertisement. The *advertising message* is what to say and is often specified in the brief to the agency. It involves the objectives of the advertising and the brand position. The *creative idea* is the interesting and engaging way to express the brand's position in an advertising format for the chosen media (radio, print, television, etc). The *executional tactics* are how the advertisement gains the target audience's attention and communicates the brand's position.

How to maximize the chance of coming up with a winning creative idea turns out to involve *creating* and *testing* a *large* number of ideas. The exact number depends on the factors described below. Here are two quite different situations. In the first, the advertising task is quite straightforward—tell people about the new product. In the second, the task is much more complex—differentiate the brand in a well-established, competitive marketplace.

- If the ad agency has a good track record of creating breakthrough ads, its testing criteria are accurate, a new product is being advertised, and the manager wants to be 90 per cent sure of obtaining a modest level of sales, then producing and testing about fifteen independent creative ideas will be the most cost-effective way to maximize the chance of finding a winning creative idea.
- If the ad agency has a moderate track record, an average testing method, the product is established in the market, and the manager wants to be 99 per cent sure of creating a real winner campaign, then about ninety-four ideas will be necessary.

These numbers come from a mathematical theory with the delightful name of 'Random Creativity'.[12] They are typically (much) higher than most marketers and many ad agencies would consider. The theory of Random Creativity asks marketers to consider two proposals:

- To allocate more of their total advertising budget to the creative process.
- To refrain from using their own personal preferences to choose the creative ideas presented by their agency for development into the final advertising. (There is no evidence to suggest that client managers or ad agency personnel have a good track record of picking successful advertising ideas. Hence, each idea should be tested with target consumers.)

How to minimize the chance of commissioning an embarrassing advertisement is not a difficult task if the manager has a template against which to compare the executional tactics presented by their ad agency. Professor John Rossiter and Larry Percy have summarized much of the advertising and psychology research literature on learning and persuasion to produce such a template.[13] Before briefly describing this template, it is necessary to state that marketers need to use templates such as this with due consideration to the ad agency's creative process. (Or in more colloquial language, do not ram these ideas down the throat of the agency personnel.)

Figure 13.2 shows the part of the Rossiter–Percy Grid that focuses on creating a brand. The dimensions of the grid were introduced in Chapter 4. Products and services are classified as either high or low involvement and the trigger for purchase is either a positive (e.g. social approval) or negative (e.g. problem removal) motivation (Table 4.1). Each cell of the grid suggests a different set of executional tactics. Examples of these are shown in Table 13.2.

To use the grid, mangers first need to establish in which cell their brand is located—for the target audience (i.e. market segment) of the advertising. This should be based on research evidence, not managerial hunch.

Purchase motivations

	Negative	Positive
Low involvement	Low-risk, 'relief' purchases e.g. • Aspirin • Business magazine	Low-risk, 'reward' purchases e.g. • Premium beer • Business lunch
High involvement	High-risk, 'relief' purchases e.g. • Insurance • Component parts	High-risk, 'reward' purchases e.g. • Fashion clothes • More efficient machine

Figure 13.2. The Rossiter–Percy advertising grid

Table 13.2. Brand advertisement executional tactics

Low-risk, relief purchases

- The presenter in the ad must be perceived as an expert
- Include only one or two benefits
- Benefit claims can be stated extremely
- Use a simple problem–solution format
- People do not have to like the ad

Low-risk, reward purchases

- The presenter must be likeable
- Benefits should be shown or implied, not argued
- Repetition of the ad is important to build up the benefit claim and reinforce it
- Emotional authenticity is the key element and the main benefit
- The emotional execution must be unique to the brand
- The target audience must like the ad

High-risk, relief purchases

- The presenter must be perceived as both an expert and be objective
- For target audiences who have objections to the brand, consider a refutational approach
- Benefit claims must be convincing— do not underclaim or overclaim
- If there is a well-entrenched competitor, and a brand has equivalent benefits, consider comparative ads
- The target audience must accept the ad's main points, but they do not have to like the ad

High-risk, reward purchases

- The presenter must be perceived as similar to the target audience member
- Benefit claims may need support with information
- 'Long copy' is OK if it is well presented
- Tend towards overclaiming rather than underclaiming
- Repetition serves to build up interest, image, and reinforcement
- The target audience must like the ad and identify personally with the product as portrayed in the ad
- Emotional authenticity is paramount

For example, for many people instant coffee is a low-risk, reward purchase. However, some brands are positioned as the coffee to have on special occasions, such as when friends visit. In this case, the brand may well be located in the high-risk, reward cell. In the agency briefing process, the quadrant of the grid can be told to the agency—but not the creative tactics. (This would infuriate the agency creative people.) When the agency's creative team presents rough advertising executions to the marketer, he or she can then use the tactics in Table 13.2 as a guide to evaluate these executions. If the rough advertisements conform to the executional tactics then the chance that the advertisement will fail to achieve its communication objectives is low. If the rough advertisements do not conform, then here is a potentially high-risk/high-reward advertisement. Testing this ad with target consumers prior to further development would be essential.

Media Planning

Media planning comprises making decisions about the media in which to advertise (*media selection*) and how often to advertise (*media scheduling*). Marketers typically know almost nothing about the science of these decisions. Advertising critics argue that many advertising agency people rely too heavily on qualitative heuristics (or rules) and not enough on quantitative models to create their media plans. There are exceptions to this criticism, but it does highlight that media planning is often a 'black art' for many client managers.

There have been three recent developments in this area to help improve the effectiveness and efficiency of media strategy. First, there has been the formation of specialist media buying companies that use their market knowledge and power to get the best deal for their advertising clients. Second, there has been the development of more sophisticated media selection and scheduling computer models.[14] The third development is the (re)emergence of independent companies that conduct audits of an organization's media strategy. The problem here is that many of these firms have no more insight into media strategy than the people they are auditing.

A key concern for many marketers is that some of the key input data into the selection of media is demographics. Demographic matching, as it is called, selects media by matching the demographic profile of the target audience with the demographic profile of the media vehicle audience. The closer the match, the better the media vehicle. As noted in Chapter 6, demographic segmentation of markets is not the preferred method of tactical segmentation—it makes too many assumptions about the latent and expressed needs of target customers. Thus, the process of demographic matching is at best simple and at worst simplistic. (Many media planners, however, disagree—they argue that their many years of experience enables them to overcome the obvious limitations of demographic segmentation.) The best way to overcome the problem of demographic matching is to periodically ask target customers what media they use. A simple solution that is often not included in many marketing research studies.

From a conceptual perspective, the nature of the media planning problem is simple to state. The marketer has one or more communication objectives that he or she wishes to achieve—such as have 80 per cent of the people in the target audience being exposed to the advertisement (this is called 'reach') an average of three times during the advertising period (called 'frequency').[15] However, there are a number of constraints that must be taken into account in the search for the best way to achieve these objectives—such as the size of the advertising budget, the minimum and maximum number of advertisements placed in a particular media vehicle, etc. The discipline of operations research specializes in solving problems of this type. However, many media planners do not subscribe to these techniques, preferring to rely on heuristics they have used for many years. (For example, what has become known as the 'Reach Rule' states that to reach a wide audience buy many competing media vehicles and place one, or a small number of ads, in each vehicle. The 'Frequency Rule' states that to achieve high frequency buy multiple insertions in a few non-competing media vehicles.) Thus, there is a tension between the art and science of media planning.

Without a big investment in learning the scientific side of media planning models, the best a marketer can do is to engage the services of an independent firm to audit the ad agency's recommended media plan. If funds are not available for this, then the marketer can look at the problem from the perspective of an operations researcher. What this means is to ask the two following questions:

> What is the objective we are trying to achieve and under
> what constraints are we operating?

What are the (qualitative) heuristics and the (quantitative) optimization procedures that are guiding the selection of media and the placement of ads in these media?

Asking the ad agency people these questions will generally generate enough information to assess if they seem to be competent.

To summarize, working with advertising agencies poses some interesting management challenges. The two discussed here deal with writing a contract with the agency to get the best alignment of incentives possible, and evaluating the agency's work in a constructive manner. These are difficult issues for both parties to resolve. The first step towards their resolution is to recognize that gains in efficiency and effectiveness can usually be made in both these areas.

KEY CONCEPTS

- *The (advertising) brief*—a formal written document, signed by the client and the agency, that sets out the objectives and deliverables for a service agreement (an advertising campaign).
- *Self-enforcing contract*—a scheme of arrangement that aligns the economic, strategic, and workplace incentives of principal and agent.

KEY FRAMEWORK

- *The Rossiter–Percy grid*—Figure 13.2 and Table 13.2
- *Advertising brief*—the information described in pages 404

KEY QUESTIONS

- Do you subscribe to a strong, moderate, or weak effects theory of advertising for your industry?
- Do you know the terms and conditions of the contract with your ad agency? Is there any performance-based element to the agency's payment?
- How do you evaluate the creative execution and media placement suggested by your ad agency?

PART B

Working with Marketing Research Firms

> Better information leads to better decisions.

Working with marketing research firms differs in some important ways to working with advertising agencies. As noted in Chapter 1 (Figure 1.4), research and the analysis of consumer data plays a pivotal role in the successful development of marketing strategy and programmes. Thus, research is a key activity that should be treated as an investment in the future.

Part B starts by examining two styles of research activity. Big, well-funded organizations employ both approaches in a programmed way. Smaller organizations tend to adopt a more ad hoc approach to doing research. The discussion then moves to pose a question that all organizations should ask before commissioning any new research—how much is it worth? The final two sections look at the key issues of briefing a marketing research firm and evaluating research studies.

Approaches to Commissioning Marketing Research

Many organizations use research on an ongoing basis to track market share, customer buying behaviour and satisfaction, advertising effectiveness, channel performance, brand equity, brand loyalty, etc. Here, the basic philosophy is one of sequential learning—learn new information, integrate the new information with existing knowledge, make necessary changes, learn more, digest the learning, make changes, etc. In organizations that adopt this style of data gathering, managers are often heavily involved in the design of the research and they may become quite astute observers of consumer behaviour. Also, research gets shared throughout the organization. It is used as an integral mechanism for creating a learning organization.

Other organizations adopt a project mentality where research is undertaken to answer specific questions. For example, as described in Chapter 6, one big project is to conduct research to create a tactical segmentation of the market. Other issues that may trigger a research project include:

- a sudden fall in sales;
- the impending launch of a new product;
- a recommendation from the advertising agency;
- the launch of a CRM programme;
- the start of a price war;
- a new competitor enters the market;
- the organization enters a new market;
- to use up money in the research budget;
- when some new information is needed to justify a decision already made or to fine-tune such a decision.

The last two reasons for doing a research study are quite common. Many organizations have a policy that research funds not spent in a budget period will result in less new funds being allocated in the next period. Also, some research studies are done to justify a decision that has already been made. For example, as we saw in Chapter 7 (Figure 7.4), the Buick division of General Motors decided to launch a new luxury, two-seater sports sedan called the Reatta to compete with cars like Nissan's 300ZX and Toyota's Supra. The idea was to help reposition Buick as a more innovative car company. They then embarked on the most extensive, state-of-the-art series of research studies ever conducted at that time by a US auto company. Management needed to find out the image and competitive position of such a new car from Buick, characteristics of potential buyers, and demand for the new car. In effect, the decision process was: (*a*) let us make a new, stylish two-passenger car that looks nothing like the rest of the product line, and then (*b*) we will use research to find out who will buy this new car. (It turned out to be a market failure.)[16] Finally, there are occasions when a research study will be commissioned by one manager as a weapon with which to win an argument with another manager. Many astute marketing researchers will not get involved in such projects.

To draw a contrast between the ongoing and project styles of research, the following is a characterization of project research:

- A marketing problem or issue triggers the need for some research.
- The search commences for spare money to fund the research.
- A brand or marketing manager takes responsibility.
- A research brief is prepared.
- Research suppliers (often three to five) are consulted and asked to bid for the work.
- During the selection process, the research brief is refined to fit the budget and the research supplier's preferred approach.
- The study is done and presented to selected managers—overheads and a short report (and sometimes a data file if an astute manager requests it).
- During the presentation, the research supplier is asked a few questions about any findings that do not correspond with the audience's expectations. They are then politely thanked and asked to leave, at which point the real discussion takes place.
- Within six to twelve months the study is lost within the organization.
- Eighteen months later, someone else in the organization suggests that a similar study is needed.

To many marketers and market researchers this description is too close to the truth for comfort. It relegates the research firm to an outsource supplier with little chance to add any further insight than that contained in (or constrained by) the research report. This is often a short-sighted strategy because experienced researchers can provide valuable information to an organization that is outside a specific research brief.

Many big companies like Gillette conduct both types of research as described in Exhibit 13.1. Procter & Gamble probably conducts more market research than most other companies—interviewing more than one million people in connection with over 1000 products each year. Procter & Gamble manage the research function through two separate research groups, one that focuses on advertising and the other on market testing. Each group is staffed by internal marketing research specialists, and researchers are assigned to each product operating division. In contrast, at Hewlett-Packard research is controlled by a headquarters group—the Market Research and Information Centre. This group is a shared resource across all divisions and provides background information on industries, markets, and competitors. Decision Support Teams provide customized research consulting services.[12] When research is conducted on the scale of Gillette, Hewlett-Packard, and Procter & Gamble, the philosophy is that research will be used for a variety of purposes, and because each research technique has a different array of technical strengths and weaknesses, a pot-pourri of research is needed. When an organization does not have the internal expertise and/or the resources of a big company, it must be careful to spend its research budget wisely.

Exhibit 13.1. Marketing research at Gillette

1. *Annual national consumer studies*—to determine what brands of razors and blades are used, and to collect demographic and consumer attitude data.
2. *National brand tracking studies*—to track the use of razors and blades and to monitor brand loyalty over time.
3. *Annual brand awareness studies*—to determine the share of mind that Gillette products have.
4. *Bi-monthly consumer use tests*—ask consumers to use a single variation of a product for an extended period of time and to provide their evaluation of it.
5. *Monthly retail audits*—to provide market share data along with information regarding distribution, out-of-stock, and inventory levels for the various Gillette products.
6. *Laboratory research studies*—to test the performance of existing products and to help in the design of new products. They also test competitors' products.
7. *Various research studies*—to answer specific questions of concern and interest.

From G. Churchill, *Marketing Research* (Fort Worth, TX: Dryden Press, 1999), p. 63.

How Much is Research Worth?

> Managers often under-invest in gathering new information.

An interesting research study to conduct is to ask a number of research suppliers to quote for, say, five focus groups, 100 face-to-face interviews, and 200 completed telephone interviews. What is often found is that the quotes (or posted prices) for each type of data collection are quite similar. There are a number of reasons for this:

- the (fieldwork) costs to the research firms are similar;
- they know each other's prices;
- they know that buyers shop around;
- they each offer a similar service;
- many buyers have trouble judging the quality of a focus group or a completed interview.

There is a marketing paradox revealed whenever professional service suppliers offer their services to different organizations at the same price. The paradox arises because while the price paid for the service is the same, the value derived from it is seldom the same. To illustrate this, consider two organizations that commission 200 customer interviews. Assume that one wants the information to review if there has been any change in brand evaluation from a recent advertising campaign, while the other wants to pre-test a new product concept that, if launched, will require a substantial commitment of funds. Clearly, the information is more valuable in the second case because it will influence the pending Go or No-Go new product decision. (In the first case the investment has already been made.)

It is interesting to contrast the price spread among local research suppliers with that of other professional service providers. For example, the top guru consultants have been known to charge (and get) $100,000 for a day of talking to a group of businesspeople. Lesser-known (or one-book) consultants may get up to $50,000. The top academics will charge $20,000 per day while the cheapest will charge out at a couple of thousand per day. This price spread for a day full of ideas is far greater than typically found among market research firms. Why the difference?

One reason is supply and demand—there are many suppliers of research services but only a handful of speakers who can entertain and inform an audience of businesspeople.[18] A second reason is that few professional service providers sit down and calculate what the value of their information is before posting a price for their services. (Most have a daily rate.) Most professionals and managers have never considered the question of whether it is possible to calculate how much market research information is actually worth. It is possible, and it depends on the following factors:

- the importance of the decision to be made (e.g. the investment required, the impact on the company, etc.);
- the uncertainty surrounding the decision (i.e. how much is currently known);
- the risk tolerance of the decision-maker (both the organization and the managers);
- how accurate the market research information will be.

Thus, before commissioning research a marketing manager, and his or her research supplier, should always ask:

What is the maximum amount that should be paid for the required information?

In Chapter 9, this was called the VIU or EVC price. In the context of buying research, the calculations to establish this price proceed in a different fashion. They are based on what is known as Bayesian Decision Theory, the original postulates of which were first published by the Reverend Thomas Bayes in 1763.

To illustrate the approach to calculating the value of a market research study consider the two cases (A and B) of a potential new product launch shown in Exhibit 13.2. The purpose of this simple example is to (*a*) introduce the idea of decision theory in the context of valuing market research information, and (*b*) to try to convince you that this type of calculation is a worthwhile exercise. While a full-blown example is beyond the scope of this book, this example illustrates that we often underestimate the potential value of new information.

Exhibit 13.2. Valuing research

Figure 13.3 shows two situations facing a marketing manager. (These diagrams are called decision trees and the probability figures on the right-hand branches would be the manager's best current estimate of the market conditions.) The questions to be answered by the marketing manager are:

- What is the value of a perfectly reliable market research study (i.e. 'perfect information')?
- What is the value of a typical less than perfect research study?
- Should the new product be launched?

In Case A, because there is no chance of making a loss, the product should be introduced—it will make either $4 million if the market demand is strong

cont.

Exhibit 13.2. *cont.*

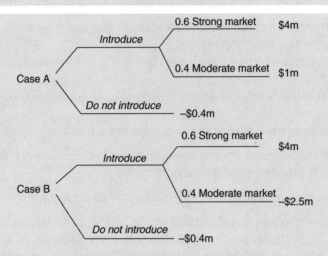

Figure 13.3. The value of market research

or $1 million if the market demand is moderate. If the new product is not introduced, the company will incur costs of $400,000.

The decision theory approach to evaluating the problem in Figure 13.3 uses the concept of Expected Value (EV). The EV calculations that are necessary to answer the questions posed above for Case A are the EV (*a*) of introducing the new product, (*b*) of not introducing the new product, (*c*) of the overall decision tree (i.e. both the 'introduce' and 'do not introduce' decisions), (*d*) if the decision is made under certainty, and (*e*) of perfect information:

$$EV_{Introduce} = (0.6 \times \$4m) + (0.4 \times \$1m)$$
$$= \$2.8m$$
$$EV_{Not\ introduce} = (1.0 \times -\$0.4)$$
$$= -\$0.4$$
$$EV_{Overall} = (\$2.8m - \$0.4m)$$
$$= \$2.4m$$
$$EV_{Certainty} = (0.6 \times \$4m) + (0.4 \times \$0)$$
$$= \$2.4m$$
$$EV_{Perfect\ information} = EV_{Certainty} - EV_{Overall}$$
$$= \$2.4\ m - \$2.4m$$
$$= \$0$$

In Case A, the value of perfect information is zero and, therefore, the value of a less reliable market research study is zero. In this case, the manager does not need to do any research to tell him or her to launch the new product because market demand will be either strong or moderate and the overall EV is greater than that for not introducing the new product.

In Case B, the situation is not as clear-cut. Here, the company will make a loss of $2.5 million if market demand is only moderate. (Let us assume that they have made some commitments to retailers, such as a payment for putting the product in the supermarket that will not be fully recovered if demand is only moderate.) Now, using the formulas above and the numbers in the bottom decision tree, the EVs are: Introduce = $1.4 million, Not Introduce = −$0.4m, Overall = $1.0 million, under Certainty = $2.24m, and Perfect Information = $1.24m. The decision to introduce the new product would be made because $EV_{Overall} > EV_{Not\ introduce}$. What these calculations suggest is that a perfectly reliable market research study would be worth a maximum of $1.24 million—a lot more money than most people would expect given the small amounts involved in Case B.

Given this situation, the manager would then need to calculate the EV of a less than perfect market research study. Accuracy is determined by a host of factors that are outlined in any good marketing research book.[19] Using an estimate of accuracy, calculating $EV_{Research}$ is done using Bayes' rule, a rather formidable equation and one not described here. The prudent course of action is to obtain the assistance of an operations researcher or a statistician to help work through the calculations. (There are also personal computer programs available to help structure the problem and to do the calculations.[20]) At this point if $EV_{Research} >$ Posted Price of the research supplier, then the study should be commissioned.

The key issue in this section is that managers (and their research suppliers) often under-value new information. With a little help from someone trained in decision theory, it is possible to quantify the potential contribution of market research and, thus, overcome one of the key limitations of modern marketing noted in Chapter 1, namely, the reluctance to calculate the financial contribution of marketing programs.

Briefing a Marketing Research Firm

A problem well formulated, is a problem half solved.

If you talk to the managers of marketing research firms, one of their key criticisms of marketers is that they do not spend enough time preparing the brief they give to research firms. The root cause of this problem is often that managers have trouble articulating the decision problems that they face. For example, a common reason that research is initiated is because the manager lacks information that he or she thinks is necessary to make a decision. ('If I know more about customer needs, then I can figure out a plan of action.') Research that seeks more general information about an issue often turns out to be interesting, but it often does not suggest cost-effective actions.

Research can only be well designed when the business issues and the alternative courses of action being considered are specified. For example, a brand manager might be interested in his or her brand's advertising effectiveness. The bigger business issue that may also be relevant here is how much should be spent on advertising, and the impact of this on the spending of other marketing programmes.

Thus, a research brief needs to state the marketer's concerns together with alternative courses of action, and the circumstances from which they were generated. Astute researchers will probe for this background information if it is not stated in the brief. (For example: who will use the information; what is their tolerance for risk and thus what level of accuracy is required for the findings; who else will be influenced by decisions flowing from the research; what is the culture of the organization to research (advocate or sceptical); what opinions are currently held about the issues being researched; what research has been done previously on this topic; who are the competitors and what are they doing; etc.)

The courses of action being considered frame the manager's decision problem. That is, what needs to be done. This decision problem then needs to be translated into a research problem before the researcher can construct the appropriate research design, data collection, and analysis procedures. This translation is generally achieved through discussions between the manager and the researcher. In many cases, this dialogue is one of the most important facets of the research project because it helps to refine the problem and to establish limits on what the new information can legitimately tell the manager. Table 13.3 provides some examples of decision problems and their associated research problems.

Other issues that researchers would like to know, and that sometimes managers are reluctant to divulge, are:

- the research budget;
- the timeframe for decision-making;
- whether other research firms are being asked to bid for the work;
- the marketplace situation that prompted the research request;
- what other information is available (such as previous studies) about the decision and research problems;
- relevant constraints that managers or the organization are under;
- any hypotheses held by key managers;
- the scope of the study, that is, which customer segments to focus on;
- importance of the project (the new information is 'nice to know' versus 'need to know');

Table 13.3. Decision problems and their associated research problems

Decision problem	Research problem
Develop a new brand name	Test various names for how they are pronounced, their positive associations, the link to key product features, etc.
Increase market penetration	Evaluate new distribution outlets, current brand awareness, etc.
Launch a new product	Design a test-market to estimate first purchase and repeat purchase
Launch a CRM programme	Evaluate how attributes of the programme—incentives, rules, etc.—affect application, use, and customer loyalty
Increase leads from a trade show	Measure the evaluation of the company and its exhibit, salesperson response to attendees, etc.

- how this research should feed into the organization's customer database and knowledge management system.

Once the purpose and scope of the research have been established, a formal research brief should be prepared. These documents take many forms; however, they should contain the following information:

- Project Title.
- Statement of the General Marketing Problem.
- Statement of the Purpose of the Research including the decision and research problems, and the scope and limitations of the research.
- Research Methodology and Data Sources.
- Project Stages and Time Estimates.
- Roles and Responsibilities of the Parties (marketing manager, researcher, fieldwork suppliers, etc.).
- Costs.
- Research Project Deliverables.

This document should be signed by the marketing manager and the researcher—because signatures have a powerful effect on gaining agreement and commitment.

Evaluating Research

At various times throughout the year managers get the opportunity to attend research presentations and to read research reports and scientific articles. Chapter 1 suggested that much of this research will be of limited scope and/or practical value. In fact, it suggested that all research come with the warning—*caveat emptor*—let the buyer beware. Given that research should be evaluated with care, how can this be done?

People who are experienced with research have a mental checklist that they instinctively go through when reading a research report. The type of research being presented will determine the appropriate research designs and, thus, the precise set of evaluative criteria. For example, if the research is

- *exploratory* (where it seeks to understand the nature of the problem and gain insights and ideas), then research designs are quite flexible, and the evaluative criteria are less stringent than if the research is
- *descriptive* (where it seeks to describe the characteristics of consumers or estimate the proportion of people or organizations in a specified population), or
- *predictive* (where specific predictions such as next year's sales are sought), or
- *causal* (where cause and effect statements are required). Here, there are many subtleties and pitfalls—especially when data are gathered in a field setting as opposed to a controlled laboratory setting.[21]

With a detailed knowledge of the scientific method and some experience, evaluating the four types of research is relatively straightforward. However, without this knowledge base managers are forced to rely on broader principles to judge the quality of research. One such set of principles is 'Is the research ...'

- *Relevant*—to the decision problem.
- *Rigorous*—in that the research is built on good theoretical foundations and employs a sound methodology.
- *Revealing*—because the results provide new insight, or they establish a new relationship, or confirm a previous finding that was not well established.

Marketing managers should be confident in their ability to judge the relevance and revelation of a piece of research. However, where they may flounder is with the theoretical and methodological aspects of a study.

In these circumstances, academic marketers can be asked to help evaluate these aspects of a study.

KEY CONCEPTS

- *Decision tree*—a decision flow diagram showing the structure of a problem.
- *Expected value*—the value of a course of action obtained by multiplying its possible outcome by the probability of that outcome occurring.

KEY FRAMEWORKS

- *Bayesian decision theory*—Exhibit 13.2
- *Market research brief*—the information described on page 423

KEY QUESTIONS

- Is marketing research an ad hoc (project-based) activity and/or a programmed investment in your organization?
- Do you routinely calculate the expected value of (new) marketing research activities?
- Are your research briefs too brief? (Or do they contain all the information desired by your research firms?)
- How do you evaluate the quality of research? Do you need help here?

RECAP

Consultants, ad agencies, and market research firms provide specialist services to marketing managers. Being outside the organization enables them to look at the marketing issues with more detachment than most insiders. They can also become a valuable source of advice to the marketing team. Their experience with a range of organizations in different industries gives them a broader perspective than most marketers. However, to gain the most benefit from these professional service firms requires the development of a commercial arrangement that is based on sound economic foundations. Many of the contracts of engagement that are currently used do not motivate both the organization and the agent to maximize their effort to achieve a common goal. Just as a manager's KPIs drive his or her behaviour, so too do the explicit and implied terms and conditions of the contracts written between the organization and its suppliers.

NOTES

1. For an introduction to principal–agent theory see P. Milgrom and J. Roberts, *Economics, Organisation and Management* (Englewood Cliffs, NJ: Prentice Hall, 1992).

2. N. Shoebridge, 'Saatchi Wins Westpac Work', *Australian Financial Review* (15 May 2003), p. 26.

3. See, for example, D. H. Maister, *Managing the Professional Service Firm* (New York: Free Press, 1993), chapter 10.

4. This table is based on P. C. N. Mitchell, H. Cataquet, and S. Hague, 'Establishing the Causes of Dissatisfaction in Agency–Client Relations', *Journal of Advertising Research*, 32, 2 (1992), 41–8; and G. R. Dowling, 'Searching for a New Ad Agency: A Client Perspective', *International Journal of Advertising*, 13, 3 (1994), 229–42.

5. J. P. Jones, 'Advertising: Strong Force or Weak Force? Two Views an Ocean Apart', *International Journal of Advertising*, 9 (July–September 1990), 233–46.

6. There is little empirical evidence to suggest that these advertising bans, by themselves, have had any dramatic effect on reducing consumption. The reasons for smoking are far more complex than can be attributed to advertising.

7. J. R. Rossiter and L. Percy, *Advertising Communications and Promotion Management* (New York: McGraw-Hill, 1997), p. 3.

8. D. Vakratsas and T. Ambler, 'How Advertising Works: What Do We Really Know?' *Journal of Marketing*, 63, 1 (1999), 26–43.

9. T. Bull, *Inside the Asylum* (Sydney: Australian Print Group, 2000); A. Coombs, *Adland* (Sydney: Willian Heinemann Australia, 1990); P. Mayle, *Up the Agency* (London: Pan Books, 1990); D. Ogilvy, *Confessions of an Advertising Man* (New York: Atheneum, 1964); R. Rothenberg, *Where the Suckers Moon: An Advertising Story* (New York: Alfred A. Knopf, 1996).

10. T. M. Devinney and G. R. Dowling, 'Getting the Piper to Play a Better Tune: Understanding and Resolving Advertiser–Agency Conflicts', *Journal of Business-to-Business Marketing*, 6, 1 (1999), 19–58.

11. This section draws heavily from Rossiter and Percy (1997), chapter 7.

12. See Rossiter and Percy (1997), chapter 7—Appendix, pp. 202–7.

13. Rossiter and Percy (1997), chapters 8–10.

14. J. R. Rossiter and P. J. Danaher, *Advanced Media Planning* (Boston: Kluwer Academic, 1998).

15. Often alternative media plans are summarized in terms of their combined reach and frequency. This is called gross rating points, and is calculated as Reach × Frequency.

16. G. Urban and S. Star, *Advanced Marketing Strategy* (Englewood Cliffs, NJ: Prentice Hall, 1991), chapter 13.

17. P. Kotler, *Marketing Management* (Upper Saddle River, NJ: Prentice Hall, 1997), p. 114.

18. Each year the American Marketing Association publishes lists of US and international research firms in its publication *Marketing News* (www.ama.org).

19. See, for example, G. A. Churchill, *Marketing Research* (Fort Worth, TX: Dryden Press, 1999).

20. For an example of this PC software see G. L. Lilien and A. Rangaswamy, *Marketing Engineering* (Upper Saddle River, NJ: Prentice Hall, 2003). For commercial versions of this type of software see www.palisade.com.

21. See T. D. Cook and D. T. Campbell, *Quasi-Experimentation: Design and Analysis Issues for Field Settings* (Chicago: Rand McNally, 1979).

EPILOGUE

THE LEARNING ORGANIZATION

> The more things change, the more they stay the same.

I was once asked to talk to the marketing team of a big Australian television station—about 100 people. Not knowing very much about the marketing of television stations and programmes, I went to the library and did some research. Here, I found an old book that detailed the viewing habits of UK television viewers. From this research, I abstracted three overhead slides worth of findings that I used to introduce my talk. At this point I paused and asked the audience if my research reflected their current situation. Their resounding response was yes. I then made a tactical error—I showed them the source of the research. The two senior managers who hired me thought this was terrific. The others were not so sure. It directly challenged their mantra that the pace of change in their industry was accelerating, rather than standing still.

In this book, I have tried to apply the lesson from the television station talk, namely, to identify and describe those basic ideas that have driven good marketing practice over the years. The selection of these ideas has been done from the perspective of a marketing team. It has also been done with a touch of scepticism as reflected in the saying at the top of the page. Also, hopefully my selection of ideas reflects what I call the marketing manager's lament, namely:

> How do I balance creating and delivering value to the customer, with my KPIs that require me to capture value from the customer.

While I was rewriting the manuscript for the last time, I was 'shadowing' a marketing manager in a mid-size organization. Both of us got the chance to practice many of the ideas in the book—so far with encouraging results.

Some of the lessons I relearned during this process were:

- Do not get captured by every marketing fad. Most of them have appeared before using a different (brand) name.
- Do the planning, simply because its value lies in the discipline of the process.
- Develop an organizational culture that understands and respects the role of marketing.
- Create a supportive organizational infrastructure.
- Strive to quantify the impact of marketing programmes, but be careful how
  —things are measured;
  —how measures can take on a life of their own.
- Understanding customers is good marketing practice. Tactical segmentation is the key to unlocking this insight.

INDEX